ETHICAL CROSSROADS IN LITERARY MODERNISM

ETHICAL CROSSROADS IN LITERARY MODERNISM

edited by **Katherine Ebury, Bridget English, and Matthew Fogarty**

CLEMSON UNIVERSITY PRESS

© 2023 Clemson University
All rights reserved

First Edition, 2023

ISBN: 978-1-63804-075-0 (print)
eISBN: 978-1-63804-076-7 (e-book)

Published by Clemson University Press
in association with Liverpool University Press

Clemson University Press is located in Clemson, SC.
For more information, please visit our website at www.clemson.edu/press.

Library of Congress Cataloging-in-Publication Data
CIP Data available on request

Typeset in Minion Pro by Carnegie Book Production.

Contents

Acknowledgments   vii

Contributors   ix

Introduction   1
    Katherine Ebury, Bridget English, and Matthew Fogarty

I The Ethics of Mind and Body

1. *An Béal Bocht* and the Ethics of the Modernist Laughing Apocalypse   31
    Paul Fagan

2. "Grey Figures Bent Like Hooks": The Ethics of Representing Older Age in Djuna Barnes's Early Journalism and Late Interviews   51
    Jade French

3. The Solar Plexus and Animalistic Power in D. H. Lawrence and Isadora Duncan   67
    Carrie Rohman

II Planetary Ethics

4 Reparative Ethics, or the Case of Anna D. Whyte 87
    Marian Eide

5 Interrogating the Ethics of Cosmopolitanism in Stella Benson's Travel Writing 105
    Shinjini Chattopadhyay

6 Wittgenstein's Modernism: Apocalypse and Ethics 125
    Ben Ware

III Legal Ethics

7 Charles Reznikoff's *Testimony*: Ethics and the Reader 145
    Kieran Dolin

8 What's Love Got To Do With It? Law and Literature in 1920s British Somaliland 161
    Katherine Isobel Baxter

9 Modern Tort Law and Anthony Powell's *A Dance to the Music of Time* 177
    Mimi Lu

IV Intersectional Ethics

10 "Criteria of Negro Art": Ethical Negotiations in the Harlem Renaissance 197
    Laura Ryan

11 "And This Is How 'The Feminists' Are Made": Ethical Collaboration Between Eleonora Duse and Gabriele D'Annunzio 217
    Zsuzsanna Balázs

12 Reading James Joyce in the Wake of the #MeToo Movement 235
    Julie McCormick Weng

Notes 253

Index 299

Acknowledgments

This project was conceived in 2020, during one of the worst moments of the COVID-19 pandemic, and we appreciate the determination and patience of everyone involved. The pandemic illuminated many of the racial, economic, and political tensions underlying contemporary society, demanding a re-evaluation of the ethical dynamics that connect us to each other, to our non-human cohabitants, and to the planet we all share. We are first and foremost grateful to our contributors for trusting us with their learned and inspirational responses to this ethical challenge. Sincere thanks are also due to Clemson University Press, especially Alison Mero, who has been an immense help while seeing the volume through to publication. We are also grateful to John Morgenstern for his early editorial guidance. Thanks are due to our anonymous peer reviewers who helped improve the project from its initial plan; these reviewers were prompt, insightful, and supportive. We are grateful to the editors of the Modernist Constellations book series, Lauren Arrington and Emilie Morin, and we are very happy to contribute to this exciting new stream of research in modernist scholarship. The artist John Himmelfarb was very kind in allowing us to use his image *Inland Romance: Architectural Science* for the volume's cover design, and we deeply appreciate his generosity. Finally, we are pleased that the Brooklyn Library gave permission for the use of archival images from the *Brooklyn Citizen* in Chapter 2.

Contributors

Zsuzsanna Balázs is Assistant Professor at Óbuda University in Budapest, Hungary. She obtained her PhD in Drama at the University of Galway in 2021. She has written extensively on W. B. Yeats, modern Irish drama, and modern Italian theatre through a queer and gender studies lens. Her first monograph, *Queering W. B. Yeats and Gabriele D'Annunzio: Modernist Playwrights*, is set to be published by Palgrave Macmillan in November 2023.

Katherine Isobel Baxter is Professor of English Literature at Northumbria University. A scholar of colonial and postcolonial literatures, she has published in journals such as *Arts, The Conradian, Journal of Postcolonial Writing, Journal of Commonwealth Literature, Literary Geographies, OLH,* and *Textual Practice*, as well as in a range of edited collections. She is the author of *Imagined States: Law and Literature in Nigeria 1900–1966* (2019) and *Joseph Conrad and the Swan Song of Romance* (2010). Her current research investigates desert mobilities, ecologies, and borders with a focus on colonial and postcolonial Somaliland.

Shinjini Chattopadhyay is Assistant Professor of Global Anglophone Literatures at Berry College in Mount Berry, GA. She completed her PhD in English Literature at the University of Notre Dame. She received her MPhil and MA in English Literature from Jadavpur University in

Jadavpur, Kolkata, West Bengal, India. She researches British and Irish modernisms and global Anglophone literatures. Her monograph-in-progress, *Plurabilities of the City*, investigates the construction of metropolitan cosmopolitanism in modernist and contemporary novels. She is the author of several book chapters and journal articles, which have been published in *James Joyce Quarterly*, *European Joyce Studies*, and *Modernism/modernity Print Plus*.

Kieran Dolin is Senior Honorary Research Fellow in English and Literary Studies at the University of Western Australia. He is the author of *Fiction and the Law: Legal Discourse in Victorian and Modernist Literature* (1999) and *A Critical Introduction to Law and Literature* (2007), and the editor of *Law and Literature* in the Cambridge Critical Concepts series (2018). He contributed a chapter to *The Social Work of Narrative: Human Rights and the Cultural Imaginary* (2018). He is currently researching literary engagements with the recognition of native title and the rejection of *terra nullius* in Australian law.

Katherine Ebury is Senior Lecturer in Modern Literature at the University of Sheffield. She is the author of *Modernism and Cosmology: Absurd Lights* (2014) and of *Modern Literature and the Death Penalty, 1890–1950* (2021), and is the co-editor of the edited collection *Joyce's Nonfiction Writing: Outside His Jurisfiction* (with James Fraser, 2018) and the *James Joyce Quarterly* special issue "Joyce and the Nonhuman" (with Michelle Witen, 2021). She has written articles and chapters on topics including modernism, science and technology, representations of law and justice, and animal studies.

Marian Eide is Professor of English and Women's and Gender Studies at Texas A&M University. She is the author of *Ethical Joyce* (Cambridge, 2002), *After Combat: True War Stories from Iraq and Afghanistan* (Potomac, 2018—with Michael Gibler, col. ret. U.S. Army-Infantry), and the *Terrible Beauty: The Violent Aesthetic and Twentieth-Century Literature* (UVA Press, 2019), as well as more than a dozen articles on twentieth-century literature and culture. She has been a fellow at the Tanner Humanities Center at the University of Utah and at the Glasscock

Center for Humanities Research. Her research concerns ethics, aesthetics, and violence.

Bridget English is Senior Lecturer in the English Department at the University of Illinois at Chicago. She is the author of *Laying Out the Bones: Death and Dying in the Modern Irish Novel* (Syracuse U.P. 2017) and has published articles and chapters on illness narratives and institutions of care, crime fiction, death, and trauma studies. Currently, she co-convenes the Irish studies scholarly seminar at the Newberry library, is co-editing *The Corpse in Modern Irish Literature: Materiality, Textuality, Economics*, and is working on a monograph titled *Self-Destructive Modernisms: Suicide, Medicine, and Failure in the Modernist Novel*.

Paul Fagan is an Irish Research Council Fellow at Maynooth University, a co-founder of the International Flann O'Brien Society, a founding general editor of the *Journal of Flann O'Brien Studies*, and an elected member of the International James Joyce Foundation Board of Trustees. Paul is the co-editor of *Irish Modernisms: Gaps, Conjectures, Possibilities* (2021) and *Stage Irish: Performance, Identity, Cultural Circulation* (2021), as well as four edited volumes on Flann O'Brien. He is currently finalizing two monographs, *Irish Literary Hoaxes* and *Celibacy in Irish Women's Writing, 1860s–1950s*, and two edited collections on the nonhuman in Flann O'Brien and *Finnegans Wake*.

Matthew Fogarty is the author of *Subjectivity and Nationhood in Yeats, Joyce, and Beckett: Nietzschean Constellations* (Liverpool, 2023). He has published articles in the *Irish Gothic Journal, International Yeats Studies, Modern Drama*, and the *Journal of Academic Writing*. His latest article is forthcoming in the *James Joyce Quarterly*. His current book project, provisionally titled *Identity Politics and the Jazz Aesthetic: Ethnicity, Gender, and Class in Modern Transatlantic Literature*, explores how white writers from Britain and Ireland have used and abused the jazz aesthetic to address formative sociopolitical developments and complex ethical concerns.

Jade Elizabeth French works on ageing, care, and intergenerationality. She is currently a Doctoral Prize Fellow at Loughborough University. Previously, she was a research fellow as part of the ESRC-funded project "Reimagining the Future in Older Age." She has written on modernism and ageing in articles for *Feminist Modernist Studies*, *Women: A Cultural Review*, and M*odernism/modernity Print Plus*.

Mimi Lu holds a DPhil in English Literature from the University of Oxford and a first-class BA and LLB from the University of Sydney. She is currently reworking her doctoral thesis into a monograph, *The Idea of a University in Modern English Literature*. The book critically examines how literary works since the turn of the twentieth century have engaged with the politics of higher education discourses and problematized ideals and narratives about the university as an experience, a mediator of culture, and an engine of social mobility. She is also working on an interdisciplinary research project, *Twentieth-Century English Literature and Tort Law*.

Julie McCormick Weng is Assistant Professor of English at Texas State University. She has co-edited two volumes: *Science, Technology, and Irish Modernism* (Syracuse, 2019) with Kathryn Conrad and Cóilín Parsons, and *Race in Irish Literature and Culture* (Cambridge, 2024) with Malcolm Sen. Currently, she serves as Secretary of the American Conference for Irish Studies.

Carrie Rohman is Professor of English at Lafayette College. She has published widely in animal studies, modernism, posthumanism, and performance. She is author of *Choreographies of the Living: Bioaesthetics in Literature, Art, and Performance* (Oxford, 2018) and *Stalking the Subject: Modernism and the Animal* (Columbia, 2009) and is co-editor with Kristin Czarnecki of *Virginia Woolf and the Natural World* (Clemson, 2011). Rohman is currently co-editing a volume of essays titled, *Broken Record: Narratives of Gendered Abuse in Academia*, with Mary K. Holland and Carlyn Ferrari.

Laura Ryan is an Irish Research Council Government of Ireland Postdoctoral Fellow at the University of Galway, pursuing a project titled "Writing Homelessness: Down and Out in Modernist Literature." Her work has been published in *English Language Notes, Literature Compass, Études Lawrenciennes, Resources for American Literary Study*, and *The Modernist Review*, and she has contributed chapters to *Connections and Influence in the Russian and American Short Story* (2021) and *The Bloomsbury Handbook to D. H. Lawrence* (2024). She is currently completing a monograph on D. H. Lawrence and the Harlem Renaissance.

Ben Ware is the Co-Director of the Centre for Philosophy and Art at King's College, London. He is the author of *Dialectic of the Ladder: Wittgenstein, the "Tractatus" and Modernism* (Bloomsbury, 2015) and *Living Wrong Life Rightly: Modernism, Ethics and the Political Imagination* (Palgrave, 2017), and the editor of *Francis Bacon: Painting, Philosophy, Psychoanalysis* (Thames & Hudson, 2019). His next book, *On Extinction: Beginning Again at the End*, will appear with Verso in 2024.

Introduction

Katherine Ebury, Bridget English, and Matthew Fogarty

Discontent with the prevailing culture, modernist artists sought to break the world apart in order to remake it, calling into question long-held assumptions about ethics and consciousness, identity, religion, responsibility, and accountability. Further, the scientific discoveries and technological innovations that took place during this period resulted in a culture that was in need of near constant redefinition. *Ethical Crossroads in Literary Modernism* seeks to re-examine these ethical questions in light of the present moment by engaging with recent scholarship and the extended canon of the new modernist studies. The COVID-19 outbreak and its similarities with the Pandemic of 1918 have brought these issues to the fore once again, exposing the tensions between our ethical responsibilities and the deep-seated racial/class divisions and political schisms ingrained in modern societies. Our age is one in which social media offers new avenues for ethical judgments, community building, and public shaming; for example, we note the extreme popularity of the "Am I the Asshole?" (AITA) Reddit forum, with over four million subscribers, which describes itself as "A catharsis for the frustrated moral philosopher in all of us, and a place to finally find out if you were wrong in an argument that's been bothering you." Thousands of people per day respond to ethical dilemmas posted here, including real, semi-fictional, and entirely fictional narratives, voting whether or not someone is justified in their words and actions. O tempora, o mores! And yet, in their letters and diaries, as well as their central creative achievements, we should remember that we often see modernist artists coming to sharply formed judgments on the life and work of their fellow beings, as well as drawing for us more blurred or ambiguous portraits of ethical dilemmas. Many AITA-style stories have come down to us in various modernist autobiographies and biographies, including Wyndham Lewis's extended account of James Joyce's embarrassment on publicly receiving a pair of Ezra Pound's hand-me-down shoes in front of himself and T. S. Eliot, as well as the younger Joyce's own rude judgment that Yeats was "too old" to receive Joyce's help.[1] This is true of the work as well as the life. Elsa Högberg has recently explored how in essays like "Character in Fiction" (1924) and *A Room of One's Own* (1929), Virginia Woolf, in dissecting the failings of characterization and narration in certain forms of realist fiction, is also critiquing "the complicity of this 'I' with a patriarchal, militaristic and imperial civilisation."[2] In short, Woolf's sharp critical judgments argue for the replacing of such non-modernist/anti-modernist writing by something ethically and aesthetically much hazier: "Against such assertions of the hyper-masculine 'I,' whose aggression is political as well as ethical, Woolf posits the hesitancy compelling the modernist writer and artist."[3] In acid prose, Woolf advocates for hesitancy, for a messier, melting approach to life, the mind, and ethical dilemmas.

In our teaching of modernist literature, our students are often most drawn to ethical debates, whether those be the classic ones, about marriage and fidelity, crime and punishment, class conflict, or updated frameworks of colonialism, the environment, implicit bias in medicine and law, or sexual consent. This volume seeks to address some of those concerns and to bring to light other ethical questions underlying modernist literature. Our volume is divided into four thematic subsections, "The Ethics of Mind and Body," "Planetary Ethics," "Legal Ethics," and "Intersectional Ethics," thus expanding the scope of discussion beyond the realm of interpersonal and intercultural relationships. Our students may also find modernist works conservative or reactionary, even where authors intended their work to advance a progressive ethical stance for their day; in addressing connections between modernism and Fascist art and politics, we must acknowledge that not all modernist authors will have intended even this much. This volume offers our authors a space for both interventions which hold modernism to account for its ethical and political failings and blind spots (particularly in relation to race and gender), as well as those that reflect on its radical and positive influence.

Our primary objective in this volume is to draw attention to these new frameworks. Our concern here is primarily with ethics (Greek: *ethos, ethikos*, meaning character and customs) rather than morality (Latin: *mores, moralis*, meaning manners and customs), with ethics essentially conceived by our authors in relation to concepts of responsibility to the other and fair representation of their claims. Although there is a growing field of excellent scholarship on modernism and theology/religion which critiques previous critical assumptions that modernism was entirely secular, the modernist authors and texts under discussion in this volume have substantially chosen to create ethical frameworks beyond organized religion, instead foregrounding the many and varied ethical crossroads and dilemmas that are a feature of modern life.[4] Very few of these works of criticism on modernism and theology/religion (with the exception of Susan Stanford Friedman) use their religious framework to address questions of ethics including personal actions, aesthetic choices, and political activism as they are more generally concerned with the intertextuality between modernist and religious texts. Although we acknowledge that in previous scholarship, ethics and morals, as well as ethics and religion, have been treated interchangeably, the distinction we make here is in keeping with a modernist emphasis on the individual and the subjective, as well as the responsibility of the artist.[5] Necessarily, all these considerations are entangled with aesthetics. As Lee Oser influentially argues, "Individual consciousness is the privileged medium of the modernist view of things. In Yeats, Eliot, Joyce, Woolf, and Beckett, ethics is itself a form of aesthetics." Oser locates the grounds of being for modernist ethics and aesthetics in an Aristotelian mode of thought, adding greater flexibility to modernist ethics through the use of concepts such as dramatization and the mask, as well as an emphasis on the body.[6]

Relatedly, in his early commonplace book, the young James Joyce records a set of aesthetic (and ethical) questions, likely dating from 1903–4, which are derived from his Jesuit education and, especially, from Aristotle's *Rhetoric*. For Aristotle, a questioning approach fits an understanding of rhetoric as the counterpart of philosophical dialectic. Aristotle's art of linguistic persuasion also fits neatly into the study of human character and psychology; indeed, much of the *Rhetoric* is devoted to a study of the mind and emotion and ethics as to rhetorical techniques. As Maksymilian Del Mar explores, through approaches to ethical, political, and legal judgment that kept Aristotle's attitude to rhetoric alive, "emotion comes to be recognized as important […] as a mode of experiencing style when reading and listening, and one that is of ethical significance."[7] This mode of thought ultimately led to the contemporary critical methods developed by James Boyd White and the law and literature movement. In his commonplace book, Joyce notes eight questions that concern relationships between artworks and emotions and the body:

1. I desire to see the Mona Lisa. Is it therefore beautiful or is it good?

2. Spicer-Simpson has made a bust of his wife. Is it lyrical, epical or dramatic?

3. Is a chair finely made tragic or comic?

4. Why are statues made white for the most part?

5. Why are not excrements, children and lice works of art?

6. If a man hacking in fury at a block of wood makes there the image of a cow (say) has he made a work of art?

7. Can a photograph be a work of art?

8. Are houses, clothes, furniture etc. works of art?[8]

These questions offer deep insight into Joyce's ethics and aesthetics simultaneously. By questioning whether the Mona Lisa is beautiful, or good, or both, Joyce is interrogating to what extent the artist's normal human interactions with their environment (social, domestic, and natural) produce good and beautiful actions and artworks. Several of these questions stay with Joyce and are eventually expressed in published form in *A Portrait of the Artist as a Young Man* many years later, as part of his protagonist Stephen Dedalus's aesthetic theory. As Joyce senses here, like many modernist artists, it is probable that the most meaningful and lasting ethical actions he made in his lifetime (good and bad) were made within artworks. W. H. Auden would later ironize the period of high modernism, from a religious and World War II perspective, as part of a time and place, "Where conscience worshiped an aesthetic order/And what was unsuccessful was condemned" ("Kairos and Logos," 1941). This was the same period in which Auden also asserted that "poetry makes nothing happen" ("In Memory of W. B. Yeats," 1939).[9] While Auden's judgments are hostile, they are nevertheless provocative; we do find ethics and aesthetics to be so intertwined within modernism that these works could appear to be a Paterian/Wildean expression of the value of "art for art's sake." But this volume, by contrast, explores how we find these works "making things happen" all the time, without being didactic; readers of modernism find aesthetics and ethics tag teaming each other within an individual work, sometimes within an individual sentence, with immensely variable meanings. Indeed, recent criticism has focused on unearthing how even New Criticism, a methodology arising from modernism, offers an ethics of reading far richer than narrow formalism. As Robert Archambeau argues, particularly in relation to a rereading of the work of I. A. Richards, within New Critical praxis ethics and aesthetics, utility and pleasure, are balanced and experienced more powerfully by the disinterested mind. He asserts that

> Contrary to what I was told, though, it turns out that the New Criticism is in fact part of a long tradition of ethical thinking, a tradition that, in an apparent paradox, is ethical not despite, but because of, its insistence on aestheticism.[10]

While our authors reach beyond New Criticism to include historicist and theoretical approaches, they also situate these literary texts in global contexts, seeking to rediscover lost or forgotten texts and authors, and many of their arguments about ethics in these works depend on sensitive, nuanced textual readings which aim to balance utility and pleasure.

Ethical Crossroads in Literary Modernism is the first book-length study to use such an expansive and cutting-edge definition of modernist ethics—previous work has been restricted to one narrower issue such as modernist animal ethics, human nature, the political imagination, colonialism and transnational modernism, and modernist transgressions; others have been restricted to one canonical modernist author such as James Joyce, Virginia Woolf, or Samuel Beckett. This book thus acts as both the definitive introduction to the topic of ethics in modernism and offers a series of original essays which are likely to reshape their own subfields. In their influential 2008 survey of developments in modernist studies, Douglas Mao and Rebecca Walkowitz comment on the transnational turn in modernist studies, noting three categories that best exemplify existing scholarship on transnational modernism: expansion of the archive to include alternative traditions; transnational circulation and production of art; and modernist responses to imperialism and anti-colonialism.[11] This volume as a whole addresses several of these areas and, while including chapters on major canonical authors such as James Joyce, Djuna Barnes, and W. E. B. Du Bois, expands the spatial and vertical boundaries of modernism by including several interventions on lesser-known modernist writers who represent a wide geography and a variety of literary forms such as travel writing and journalism. These include the writing of New Zealand modernist novelist Anna D. Whyte; British travel writer Stella Benson; Margery Perham's writing on African affairs and decolonization; Djuna Barnes's journalism; and Isadora Duncan's life writing. Analyzing these non-fictional works alongside and in dialogue with fictional texts like novels, poetry, and drama offers a more nuanced view of how the experience of modernity—including colonial expansion, war, laws, technologies, and emerging views of the environment—shaped modernist ethical discourses. The expansion of modernist geographies to include Somaliland, New Zealand, Japan, China, India, Cambodia, and Vietnam (among others) decenters the Eurocentric focus of modernist studies and destabilizes the center-periphery model that has long dominated much scholarship on modernist literature.

In order to understand how these texts engage and grapple with some of these ethical questions, it is necessary to comprehend the historical context and world literary systems which shaped and altered modernist ethics and which were in turn recast by the ethical dimensions of these literary works. As Joe Cleary's recent book *Modernism, Empire, World*

Literature indicates, the modernist period (extending roughly from 1890 to the Cold War) was itself characterized by instability and rupture and "represents a moment when the Western European literary system, as it had hitherto been regulated by France and England, was decisively restructured" by a "series of literary 'revolutions' both in its metropolitan core and in its peripheries."[12] Whereas Cleary's book is concerned with the wider political and economic systems which determine the market value of literary works and establish the power structures that make up the world literary system, *Ethical Crossroads* registers these shifting power structures on a micro level, through the internalized ethics that inform individual conceptions of self and place in the world. In its capacious understanding of modernist writing and sweeping geographical range, *Ethical Crossroads* interrogates the ethical questions surrounding consciousness, identity, responsibility, and accountability in a world literary context. Thus, the contributors to this collection examine the complex ethical dynamic of observer/observee and how written observations of the behaviors, actions, and movements of another person or culture place new ethical demands on the author of that text, whose vision is clouded by their own prejudices and beliefs. As Marian Eide's chapter in this collection suggests, literary texts that contain problematic racialized descriptions should not simply be passed over, but should instead be read suspiciously and reparatively, to best address the ethical dimensions they pose. This kind of a reading of literary texts offers more than insight into a cultural moment or into the functioning of a world literary system; it serves instead to bring these texts into the present moment and to put them in dialogue with the ethical questions and dilemmas that continue to animate contemporary discussions of race and gender.

In this regard, Kwame Anthony Appiah's thinking on cosmopolitanism and the collective identities of race, ethnicity, gender, and sexuality is central to this collection. In *The Ethics of Identity* (2005), Appiah discusses the interconnectedness of individual and collective identities and the moral demands of social categories and culture. For Appiah, social selfhood is predicated on economic, social, geographical, and political circumstances which in turn contribute to our concept of ourselves as individuals.[13] A sense of rooted cosmopolitanism and a self grounded in multiple global communities is necessary to the foundation of an ethical identity. This grounding in the local as a foundation for any kind of universal ethical obligations, while somewhat idealistic, provides a model framework for understanding how identities become narratable in relation to larger social and cultural categories. Appiah gives us a way of managing the ethical demands between ourselves as individuals, and those we assume through cultural and social alliances, suggesting that these conflicting commitments can be reconciled, but he ultimately leaves out those identities that defy neat categorization. As Eide explores in her chapter, Appiah is also an "Ethicist Columnist" for the *New York Times* and his advice on everyday ethical questions is a key way that the influence of his thought reaches ordinary Americans, as well as *New York Times* readers worldwide. In turn, these tensions between individual, national, communal and the identities that defy these categories can be said to form the basis for modernists' exploration of ethics.

Recent scholarship on ethics and modernism has either been inspired by or has looked to push beyond the "ethical turn" away from poststructuralism inspired by Emmanuel Levinas's philosophy in the late 1990s. In the case of *Ethical Joyce* (2002), for example, Eide sees in Joyce's multi-perspectivism a sustained elaboration of his belief that "the ethical subject is responsible for [the] other no matter how incommensurable the differences between them."[14] For Levinas, the term "other" describes that which is "like me" but "not me," thus denoting that which remains incomprehensible and therefore cannot be consumed or re-appropriated by the "self." Where G. W. F. Hegel could see only a "life-and-death struggle" to attain superiority in this face-to-face encounter, Levinas identifies an ontological foundation for his ethical alterity.[15] In *Joyce's Nietzschean Ethics* (2013), Sam Slote identifies echoes of Friedrich Nietzsche's anethical perspectivism in Joyce's modernist experimentations, insofar as their "stylistic variety projects an ethical stance in that it conveys a manner of living."[16] He traces this philosophical strand from the free indirect discourse used in *Dubliners*, through the stream of consciousness deployed in *A Portrait of the Artist as a Young Man* and *Ulysses*, and to the radical mode of experimentation that characterizes *Finnegans Wake*. For anyone even passingly familiar with Nietzsche's philosophy, it will come as little surprise to learn that the focus here is primarily placed on one's capacity to create one's own values and consequently oneself.

In *Modernist Commitments: Ethics, Politics, and Transnational Modernism* (2011), Jessica Berman also turns to Joyce's multi-perspectivism to highlight the apolitical limitations in Levinas's philosophy. Rather than beginning at Levinas's ontological and therefore politically neutral vantage point, Berman reads *Ulysses* as a prime example of what Hannah Arendt calls "enlarged thinking," that is, "a political mentality cognizant of the perspectives and voices of others and derived from within the web of stories in which we are situated."[17] For Berman, this further exemplifies how modernist literature is equipped to address the knotty ethical issues around race, ethnicity, gender, and sexuality. This idea that modernist experimentations can move beyond the somewhat static confines of philosophical writing by foregrounding a multiplicity of diverse experiences, while simultaneously immersing the reader within the ethical complexities that suffuse these experiences, is central to Berman's argument. Indeed, this principle largely informs her wide-ranging analysis of literary works produced outside the metropolitan epicenters most closely associated with aesthetic modernism. In Mulk Raj Anand's *Untouchable* (1935) and *Coolie* (1936), for instance, Berman identifies a cosmopolitan mode of Indian modernism that extends Joyce's critique of traditional *Bildung* and the colonial modernity that it typically bolsters. Likewise, in her analysis of the gender politics evident in Virginia Woolf's experimental 1920s writing, Berman observes an ethical commitment to moving beyond the personal that is further expanded by the movements between metropolitan center and colonial periphery that largely characterize Jean Rhys's writing in the 1920s and 1930s.

Berman's comparative chapters establish a conceptual framework for the more radical expansions of modernist boundaries that comprise the book's remaining chapters. These include an assessment of several under-discussed Indian women writers, such as Cornelia Sorabji, Iqbalunnisia Hussain, G. Ishvani, and Kamala Sathianadhan. In addition to expanding the geographical parameters of modernism by exploring how these writers rejected the distinctions between public and private spheres, as well the roles assigned to women within them, Berman shows how Sorabji's ethically conscious writing exploits a liminal space between aesthetic modernism and autobiographical and report writing. These vertical boundaries are further expanded by Berman's re-evaluation of the synergies between war writing and modernist experimentation. As well as highlighting how modernist multi-perspectivism can emerge from first-person experience in the context of Max Aub's six-novel Spanish Civil War cycle, *El laberinto mágico* (*The Magic Labyrinth*), published between 1943 and 1967, Berman explores how the converse of this might be achieved with specific reference to multimedia war propaganda. In aesthetic modernism, it seems, *e pluribus unum* is a two-way street. Finally, in the fragmented working-class voices that capture the essence of political disenfranchisement in Jack Conroy's *The Disinherited* (1933) and the abuses and subjugations foisted upon women in Meridel Le Sueur's *The Girl* (1939), Berman identifies the traces of a communal orality that transcends the conventions of realist literature and those of a modernism that prioritizes narrative interiority. Whether it be in relation to the gender, class, or race politics explored in these very different texts, each of these chapters demonstrate how the experimental hallmarks of literary modernism provide a suitable vehicle to engage with the ethical complexities that Appiah prioritizes and Levinas neglects.

Beckett scholarship has been similarly energized by Levinas's ethical alterity in the early twenty-first century, even though the critical debate concerning Beckett's literary ethics has taken entirely different turns. These critical developments were largely inspired by Alain Badiou's rejection of Levinas's ethical alterity on the grounds that it depends on religious assumptions that are simply camouflaged and cast to perform as ontological principles. Rather than defining what it means to be in terms of the singular "I," as have philosophers from Aristotle to Levinas, Badiou proposes that subjectivity is better characterized in pluralistic terms, i.e., as a mathematical set of human subjects. The Badiouian "event" describes a seismic and potentially transformative societal rupture that exposes the variables that inevitably exist within these mathematical sets but are typically obfuscated by cultural and political hegemonies.[18] For Badiou, Beckett's late writing constitutes an ethical movement away "from a programme of the One [...] to the pregnant theme of the Two, which opens out onto infinity."[19] Since the publication of Badiou's *On Beckett* (2003), scholars have tried to extricate Beckett's writing from the ethical readings of his work inspired by both Badiou and Levinas. In *Badiou and Beckett* (2006), for instance, Andrew Gibson forges something of a middle ground between the ethico-political ramifications that Badiou associates with the event and the strain of aporetic uncertainty that permeates Beckett's *oeuvre*. While acknowledging that Beckett constructs realities in which the event is "always theoretically possible" insofar as his characters appear to invoke, recall, or mimic it at times, Gibson concludes that these Beckettian realities are ultimately worlds "in which the event can scarcely be said to take place at all."[20] In *Beckett, Literature, and the Ethics of Alterity* (2006), Shane Weller argues likewise on the grounds that Beckett's aporetic uncertainty is fundamentally "anethical" because it refuses to distinguish between what is ethical and what is unethical.[21] Similarly, in *Beckett and Ethics* (2008), Russell Smith points out that, "in Beckett's world, if the Levinasian face-of-the-Other ever succeeds in commanding the subject's attention [...] the outcome is rarely the 'primordial phenomenon of gentleness' that Levinas anticipates."[22] But this is something of an oversimplification.[23] Although Levinas does associate this primordial obligation with "gentleness," in *Totality and Infinity* and elsewhere, the idea that one inevitably feels "accused" and "persecuted" by these ethical demands also recurs throughout Levinas's writing. In *Otherwise than Being or Beyond Essence*, for example, Levinas describes the subject as "the persecuted one, [...] accused beyond his fault before freedom."[24] Indeed, he later explains this self-other relationship in terms of subjectivity being held as a "hostage."[25]

In her recent work on intimacy in Virginia Woolf, using theory by Levinas, Butler, Irigaray, and Kristeva, Elsa Högberg finds that "Woolf's aesthetic configuration of interiority was a way of expressing ethical and political commitments" and that her work "inspires recognition of each individual's opacity and inviolable irreducibility."[26] Citing Berman on the challenges of using Levinas to consider intimacy in a modernist framework, Högberg suggests that Butler and Kristeva, and in fact Woolf herself, "go beyond Levinas in their respective approaches to intimacy as a precondition for any non-violent resistance to nationalism and conformist thinking."[27] Högberg herself goes beyond previous scholarship in considering the ethics and the explicit politics of intimacy beyond the erotic, which comes into its own most fully in her final chapter on *The Waves* "as a pacifist text whose politics proceeds as a Kristevan act of intimate revolt: the momentary surrender of individual autonomy through the self-reflective communication of interiority, an introspective process vital to the subject's capacity to question the nationalist and proto-fascist ideals shaping its formation."[28] As made clear by the subsections that comprise *Ethical Crossroads*, titled "The Ethics of Body and Mind," "Planetary Ethics," "Legal Ethics," and "Intersectional Ethics," this volume further extends the boundaries of how we conceptualize and define literary ethics.

The Ethics of Mind and Body

The opening section of essays begins by addressing the established trope of the representation of mind and body in modernism; a first wave of modernist scholarship, led by modernist authors' nonfictional writing, centered the uniqueness of the representation of consciousness, which was followed by subsequent critical attention to embodiment, often led by an engagement with feminist, queer theory, and/or medical humanities approaches. We place this topic firmly in relation to our theme of ethical conflicts and crossroads, using new and neglected authors, as well as new theoretical frameworks and contexts. Our authors consider the ethics of a primarily anthropological perspective, with the writers under discussion taking on the role of observer and mediator of other lives, and in general of human behavior. Recent scholarship in this area more often concentrates on the body, but we do see influential works addressing the mind, such as Eric Rundquist's *Free Indirect Style in Modernism: Representations of Consciousness* (2017), Andrew Gaedtke's *Modernism and the Machinery of Madness: Psychosis, Technology, and Narrative Worlds* (2017), and Thalia Trigoni's *The Intelligent Unconscious in Modernist Literature and Science* (2021). Critical work on the body has tended to draw on a disability studies approach, whether explicitly framed as such, like Maren Tova Linnett's *Bodies of Modernism: Physical Disability in Transatlantic Modernist Literature* (2017), Michael Davidson's *Invalid Modernism: Disability and the Missing Body of the Aesthetic* (2019), and Jeremy Colangelo's *Diaphanous Bodies: Ability, Disability, and Modernist Irish Literature* (2021), or combining this approach with medical humanities and biopolitical approaches as in Elizabeth Outka's *Viral Modernism: The Influenza Pandemic and Interwar Literature* (2019) and Peter Fifield's *Modernism and Physical Illness: Sick Books* (2020). A prominent concern of this section will be the modernist author's involvement in and detachment from the ethical claims sourced in the unique minds and bodies of others and thus offers a biopolitical focus: O'Nolan creates a charged landscape of suffering bodies (Fagan), Barnes develops a perspective on her native New York linked to the experience of older inhabitants (French), and Isadora Duncan and D. H. Lawrence turn their focus inwards, on the solar plexus and its associations with knowledge and movement (Rohman).

Beyond the global and local frameworks that inform modernist ethics, these chapters are centrally occupied with the divisions between body and mind that emerged as distinct medical categories during the modernist period. In addition to movements across geographical borders, Barnes, O'Nolan, Lawrence, and Duncan are also concerned with movements of the body and its connection with psychic and physical forms of knowledge. The question of who has the right to exert control over the bodies or minds of another, whether through racialized frames of seeing or through the medical gaze, is one that underlies modernists' depictions of the ethical demands of observing and of being observed.[29] In her performative journalism article, "How it Feels to Be Forcibly Fed" (1914), Djuna Barnes voluntarily subjects herself to being forcibly fed by a doctor, who inserts a feeding tube into her nose, throat, and stomach, in order to empathize with the hunger-striking British suffragettes. Barnes's experiment reverses the roles of observer and observee: as a journalist who has put herself in the place of a suffragette forcibly undergoing this medical procedure Barnes is both subject to the male doctor's examinations but is also, in her role as a journalist, recording her own observations of herself undergoing the procedure. She writes,

> I saw in my hysteria a vision of a hundred women in grim prison hospitals, bound and shrouded on tables just like this, held in the rough grip of callous warders while white-robed doctors thrust rubber tubing into the delicate interstices of their nostrils and forced into their helpless bodies the crude fuel to sustain the life they longed to sacrifice.[30]

Barnes's "hysteric vision" thus links her own experiences to the suffragettes, binding the injustices and bodily violations of the individual to the feminist collective and linking their concerns to those of other victims such as prisoners. In her depictions of violations of bodily autonomy, Barnes brings to the fore larger ethical concerns over how to repair the damages inflicted on individuals by medical and social institutions.

Our volume opens with Paul Fagan's chapter, which interrogates the topos of "apocalyptic time" in literary modernism as the locus of both a radical liberation from the dictates of history and a profound ethical danger, as witnessed in the draw of fascist and eugenicist projects of destructive regeneration for many of modernism's key figures. Reframing the debate through a new reading of Brian O'Nolan's (also known as Flann O'Brien) 1941 Irish-language novel *An Béal Bocht*, Fagan argues that a changed relation to the material body—as a locus not only of suffering but also of a transformed relationship to the limit—has been under-theorized as a necessary coordinate for understanding the ethics and evaluating the ethicality of the modernist literary apocalypse. This chapter addresses this gap, and interrogates its ethical stakes, by placing O'Nolan's writing into conversation both with Frank Kermode's pioneering work on distinct modes of modernist apocalyptic temporality and Julia Kristeva's theory of the carnivalesque laughing apocalypse. The relevance of Kristeva's thought for unpacking the ethical thrust of O'Nolan's carnivalesque of the modernist apocalypse in *An Béal Bocht* is located in O'Nolan's stylistic rendering of impoverished, suffering bodies through a comic tone which evokes not disgust or pity at the finitude of human existence, but rather a laughter that is ethically oriented.

Jade French's second chapter in this section analyzes why, as a young woman reporting on New York City in the early twentieth century, Djuna Barnes chose to highlight experience and ageing as integral to the "new." This chapter explores how and if Barnes's observations raise questions of how to ethically represent and acknowledge older people's experiences of modernity: how might a modernist writer experiment with relaying the experience of active participation in society as well as difficult marginalization? The first half of this chapter examines how Barnes writes different experiences of ageing in light of an emerging youth culture, exemplified by Greenwich Village's bohemian scene. French close reads her interviews "Veterans in Harness" (1913) and travel piece "Hem of Manhattan" (1917) to debate the moral implications of celebrating older age. In the second half of the chapter, French turns to Barnes's own experiences of being reported on in older age in mid-century New York. In doing so, she reflects on how literary criticism must also remain alert to the nuances of late-life creativity. The question of ethics is thus dealt with through two strands: the first explores how Barnes attempts to bring older subjects back into view as integrated participants of the new, and the second explores Barnes's own defiance in the face of decline, as she witnessed New York's next wave of avant-gardism.

Closing this section on mind and body, and beginning to explore a focus on the planetary, Carrie Rohman discusses the importance of the solar plexus as a source of "knowing" in modernist work and how it has yet to be fully acknowledged or theorized. This plexus functions as a modernist organ, a privileged site of corporeal awareness, for modernist artists. Both D. H. Lawrence and Isadora Duncan champion the solar plexus for its connection to innovative, intuitive psychic formations and artistic developments. Moreover, both thinkers' centering of the sun—their solar imaginaries—bespeak a broader environmental or ecological situating of the human within its cosmic and earthly webs that is often gendered as distinctly feminine. These eco-ethical modernist attunements to the solar plexus value forms of bodily knowing that exceed "human" boundaries and privilege other-than-rational forms of creativity and relationality. Lawrence's theorizing of creatural, womb-like energetic knowing resonates with Duncan's often gendered and more-than-human artistic innovations. This chapter examines the solar plexus as the "great nerve-center" of "dynamic consciousness" in the texts and paintings of Lawrence and the practices or theories of Duncan, with a particular interest in connections between the solar plexus and dynamisms, movement, and gendered "knowing." Rohman further situates their bioaesthetic emphases on the solar plexus in relation to current ideas about affect and neo-materiality in contemporary art and performance.

Planetary Ethics

Strongly growing areas within modernist studies are planetary and animal studies approaches that have an inbuilt sense of ethics and which deserve a full consideration that compares and relates these concerns to a wider debate about ethics and aesthetics in modernism. Susan Stanford Friedman's *Planetary Modernisms: Provocations on Modernity Across Time* (2015) was influenced by the work of Gayatri Chakravorty Spivak's *Death of a Discipline* (2003) which used readings of modernist authors including Woolf and Conrad in coining the term "planetarity."[31] Friedman's application and development of this concept for a global modernist studies was a landmark and transformative volume for the field; as Friedman reflects, "*Planetary Modernism* does emerge from a strongly ethical standpoint" in aiming to reconfigure our approach to global modernism in ways that might "examine the intersection of the earth's human modernities with the earth's nonhuman species, diversities and cosmic rhythms."[32] As this shows, Friedman's definition of the planetary encompasses an expanded global modernist canon, including a wider geography of representation of peoples and cultures (see Eide and Chattopadhyay in this section), with ecological concerns including deep time and concepts of apocalypse and crisis linked to climate change (see Ware). Earlier in our introduction we reflected on how this volume aims to hold modernism accountable for its ethical failings, as well as to offer a new perspective on its radical influence and potential. This section very much addresses that aspect of the volume, as our authors use different reading models to weigh up and respond to the ethics of modernist writing, in both a global and a local framework—with Whyte considering the European traveler in Florence in fiction, Benson producing cosmopolitan travel writing, and Wittgenstein responding ethically to the political challenges of international politics, Fascism, and the Cold War.

Friedman's influence is therefore visible in two strands of recent modernist scholarship: postcolonial modernism, often dealing with travel, and modernist ecocriticism. Scoping work on Friedman's concept of the planetary had an immediate influence, for example, on Anna Snaith's *Modernist Voyages: Colonial Women Writers in London, 1890–1945* (2014), while it has also subsequently inspired scholarship by Thomas S. Davis and Nathan K. Hensley in the form of their *Modernism/modernity* essay cluster, "Scale and Form; or, What Was Global Modernism?" (2018), Richard Begam and Michael Valdez Moses, *Modernism, Postcolonialism, and Globalism: Anglophone Literature, 1950 to the Present* (2019), and Kevin Riordan, *Modernist Circumnavigations: Around the World in Jules*

Verne's Wake (2022). Recent works published in the area of ecocriticism often take a planetary approach, including Peter Adkins's monograph *The Modernist Anthropocene: Nonhuman Life and Planetary Change in James Joyce, Virginia Woolf and Djuna Barnes* (2022), as well as edited collections by John McIntyre and Jon Hegglund, *Modernism and the Anthropocene: Material Ecologies of Twentieth-Century Literature* (2021) and Alex Goody and Saskia McCracken's *Beastly Modernisms: The Figure of the Animal in Modernist Literature and Culture* (2023). This section takes us beyond a Levinasian approach to ethics because the ethical responsibility is imagined not to a singular or representative other, but rather to a whole planet. Similarly, Clarissa Dalloway, picturing her death, imagines a radical intimacy between self and world that goes a little beyond a Levinasian sense of self and other and which is both quite precise and very blurry: she would be "laid out like a mist between the people she knew best, who lifted her on their branches as she had seen the trees lift the mist, but it spread ever so far, her life, herself."[33] By late in Woolf's career, in response to conflict, her sense of planetary enmeshment and deep time (merely implied here in *Mrs. Dalloway*) has become stronger, as in *Between the Acts* (1941), her character, Mrs. Swithin, sister of a retired Indian army officer, muses on

> rhododendron forests in Piccadilly; when the entire continent, not then, she understood, divided by a channel, was all one; populated, she understood, by elephant-bodied, seal-necked, heaving, surging, slowly writhing, and, she supposed, barking monsters; the iguanodon, the mammoth, and the mastodon; from whom presumably, she thought, jerking the window open, we descend.[34]

Sheltered within a traditional English country house, supported by imperial capital, Mrs. Swithin imagines a planet that pre-dates the meanings of her life and its ethical and political context; this perspective, other characters believe, constitutes her oddity.

This section opens with an important methodological intervention, in the form of Eide's contribution to this volume, on "Reparative Ethics," which considers Levinas's engagement with literary texts to suggest a potential method for formulating reparative responses to aesthetic practices that both reflect and perpetuate inequities. In engaging with repair as a model, the essay considers the repercussions of restoring to the aesthetic tradition itself voices that have been forgotten or excluded. Using the chosen case study of Anna D. Whyte's forgotten Bloomsbury novel, *Change Your Sky* (1935), which considers the ethics and politics of travel and tourism, Eide argues it offers both a meaningful addition to the modernist literary movement and another, historically characteristic, instance of the racial harms casually inflicted in literary representation. Joining the provocative methodological interventions proposed by Paul Ricœur and Eve Kosofsky Sedgwick with the ongoing movement for political reparations, Eide's essay proposes that suspicious and reparative reading work in tandem when the ethical impetus is driven by the mitigation of harm. Eide's model of combining suspicious and reparative reading techniques to create appropriate responsiveness both to the text and its ethical dilemmas is something which implicitly animates many essays in this volume, as our authors seek to generate new nuanced readings of ethical issues which are also rich and useful aesthetic responses.

In the second chapter of this section, following on from Eide's concern with travel and sharing with her an interest in applying Appiah's work to modernism, Shinjini Chattopadhyay explores an understanding of the planetary which relates it to the ethics of modernist cosmopolitanism. Chattopadhyay uses the work of Appiah, who cautions against regarding cultural communities as static, closed, and internally homogeneous—and different from all others. Appiah explains that it is the ethical responsibility of the modern individual to explore the internal diversity of both domestic and foreign cultures and initiate dialogues between them. Chattopadhyay shows how modernist cosmopolitanism anticipates Appiah's model and creates a dialogue between the local and the global where the global does not obscure the particularities of the local and the local does not remain circumscribed within parochial boundaries. The cosmopolitan synergy between the local and the global which is traditionally perceived as endemic to modernism is also discernible in feminine middlebrow writing, especially travelogues. Chattopadhyay analyzes British author Stella Benson's (1892–1933) travelogue, *The Little World* (1925), through Appiah's framework of cosmopolitanism and demonstrates that Benson's travels in Japan, China, India, and other parts of the world depart from the tradition of nineteenth-century travel writing where the colonies are primitivized and exoticized. Benson's cosmopolitan travel writing is a case study which expands the purview of modernism by replicating the ethic of fostering multiple and flexible affiliations uncircumscribed by national and cultural boundaries and envisaging a decolonial worldview.

Closing out this section, Ben Ware considers a different understanding of Friedman's concept of the planetary, by proposing that modernism can provide us with a new way of seeing our catastrophic present—a present marked by a series of intersecting ecological, biological, and geo-political crises. Turning to the work of the philosopher Ludwig Wittgenstein, the chapter moves through three stages. Building on his work in *Modernism, Ethics and the Political Imagination* (2017), Ware first makes the case for grasping not only the literary and aesthetic qualities of Wittgenstein's work, but also, and more specifically, for seeing him as an exponent of what he terms "philosophical modernism." Second, the essay turns to a number of Wittgenstein's remarks on the atomic bomb and what he calls the "apocalyptic view of the world," and brings these remarks into dialogue with the work of a number of other literary and philosophical figures, including Gertrude Stein, Günther Anders, and Theodor Adorno. Third, Wittgenstein's remarks on apocalypse provide us with a crucial link to his later philosophy, specifically the *Philosophical Investigations*. He demonstrates that in the *Investigations*, it is not simply the language of the book that we might describe as apocalyptic, but also the fundamental conception of philosophy that we find therein. This conception of philosophy is also avowedly ethical: it involves seeing language, self, and the world otherwise; a practice, he argues, which becomes inseparable from the imaginative activity of seeing the future otherwise.

Legal Ethics

This section addresses ethics within the framework of law and literature methodology. The law and literature movement has had, in many ways, a parallel development to new modernist studies, with its key journal, *Law & Literature*, founded in 1988, compared to *Modernism/modernity*, which began in 1994. As with planetary approaches, legal humanities work has an inherent concern with ethics, but the intersection between modernist studies and law and literature has not yet taken off in a big way, despite some landmark studies. Key books include Ravit Reichman's widely influential, *The Affective Life of Law: Legal Modernism and the Literary Imagination* (2009), Paul K. Saint-Amour's *Modernism and Copyright* (2011), Rex Ferguson's *Criminal Law and the Modernist Novel* (2013), Robert Spoo's *Modernism and the Law* (2018), Matthew Levay's *Violent Minds: Modernism and the Criminal* (2019), and Katherine Ebury's *Modern Literature and the Death Penalty, 1890–1950* (2021). Despite this range of books, there have been fewer conferences and article publications on the topic of law and modernist literature. This may be due to a methodological challenge for modernist scholars who wish to do law and literature work, in that (as Greta Olson has argued in her survey of the field) the nineteenth-century novel is often "the model for the literary in Law and Literature" and that we have thus seen an overemphasis on realism, on flatter narratives and characters, and on simpler moral and ethical lessons.[35] Olson goes on to "caution against idealizing the realist novel" within law and literature because of "the representational techniques and political agendas that the realist novel tends to render invisible," meaning that this is a good time for applying law and literature methods to richer and more difficult texts produced by modernist authors. Therefore, applying these methods to modernist texts to look at ethics enables the methodology itself to grow and change. In this section, our authors are thus expanding definitions both of modernism and of law and literature in readings which address the ethical response of the reader to legal questions. This is especially appropriate as recent law and literature scholarship has been grappling with the ramifications of affect theory for the field.[36]

At the very start of Anthony Powell's *A Dance to the Music of Time*, from the novel *A Question of Upbringing* (1951), a perspective opens that considers the relativity of law, society, and ethics when they are placed in aesthetic patterns which reflect deep time. Watching workmen who have been mending a road in winter standing around a brazier, the narrator observes:

> The men at work had made a kind of camp for themselves, where, marked out by tripods hung with red hurricane-lamps, an abyss in the road led down to a network of subterranean drainpipes. […] For some reason, the sight of snow descending on fire always

makes me think of the ancient world—legionaries in sheepskin warming themselves at a brazier: mountain altars where offerings glow between wintry pillars; centaurs with torches cantering beside a frozen sea. [...] The image of Time brought thoughts of mortality: of human beings, facing outward like the Seasons, moving hand in hand in intricate measure [...] unable to control the melody, unable, perhaps, to control the steps of the dance.[37]

These abstract and yet affecting reflections about the music of time arise from seeing the workers laboring and at risk in systems of modernity, protected incompletely by the law and by the personal and social ethics of those who view and represent them (as Mimi Lu is very much attuned to in her chapter).[38] Powell is also concerned in the passage about their free will to make ethical decisions, as the people the passage aestheticizes, as well as all people in deep time, are twice described as "unable" to exert control of their lives. The essays in this section are thus about intersections of law and affect within modernist texts.

In the first essay in this section, Kieran Dolin considers how Charles Reznikoff's poetic sequence *Testimony* distills hundreds of legal cases into an Objectivist form that privileges the neutral representation of facts. The emotional reticence of the poems has been read as an artistic and ethical limitation, and more recently as highlighting the suffering of lost voices. This essay argues that despite stripping normative and affective discourses from his poetic cases, Reznikoff participates in the ethical project of modernism. His Objectivist poetics exhibits the "inchoate" ethical searching that Jil Larson discerns in the modernist novel. For Melba Cuddy-Keane, "Modernist ethics meets the question of how to live ethically in a questionable world with a paradoxical conjunction of metaphysical uncertainty and individual answerability."[39] Dolin argues that this emphasis on responsiveness rather than rules is central to Reznikoff's poetic witnessing. Commenting on his poetic method in 1969, Reznikoff proposed that readers of the poems perform an interpretative function similar to the adjudicatory work of a jury hearing evidence. The form of *Testimony* therefore gives rise to a hermeneutic ethical activity on the part of its readers. The chapter focuses on the suffering bodies of animals and humans, especially children, as a result of cruelty or industrial accident, motifs announced in the opening poems of the work. Building on scholarship by John Michael, Dolin explores how such starkly violent Objectivist images consequently function as a *punctum* for the reader, opening the historical frame to the present moment.

The next essay, by Katherine Baxter, unpacks the place of love and literature in shaping British perceptions of the colonies in the interwar years, interrogating the affective entanglements of law, ethics, and emotion in the literary and colonial discourses of the period. To do so, the essay focuses on a little-known novel by Margery Perham, *Major Dane's Garden*. In the mid-twentieth century, Margery Perham was one of the most influential voices in Britain on matters of African colonial administration. Her first attempt to explore how Britain should govern its colonies, however, is *Major Dane's Garden*, a romantic novel set in British Somaliland. In this novel, Perham pitches two modes of colonial rule against each other: the first represented by the character of a thrusting military careerist, Cavell; the second represented by Major Dane, a maverick administrator, loved by those over whom he rules. The novel is focalized through Cavell's wife Rhona, who embarks on a chaste yet erotically charged affair with Dane. Baxter shows that by contextualizing the novel's affective entanglements, we can see how the centering of love in colonial ethics obscures other kinds of ethical attention—to race, politics, economics, religion, and other forms of social being. The essay thus demonstrates how Perham's experimentation with popular and middle-brow genres of the modernist period is deployed to shape an affective relationship to the colonies grounded in a troublingly eroticized ethics.

The last essay in this section, by Mimi Lu, continuing and concluding Dolin's and Baxter's approach to law and affect, considers how developments in modern tort law were critically processed and refracted through the literary imagination. It uses Anthony Powell's *roman-fleuve*, *A Dance to the Music of Time* (1951–75), to explore some of the key intersections—as well as frictions and divergences—between literary, cultural, and legal history, between the emerging legal principles of negligence and literary narrativizations of accidental harms, between juridical and poetic justice, so to speak. Powell's fictions, Lu argues, exemplify how literature in this period not only scrutinized the fraught dynamics and moralities of interpersonal relations and obligations but also the adequacy of tort law itself as a form of protection against the careless behaviors that seemed endemic to modern society. Lu's close readings aim to reveal how emplotments of tortious actions in twentieth-century literature constituted an important part of a collective cultural project to interrogate the law's ethics and its normative parameters, judicial and policy-driven delimitations of liability, and the types of narratives, interests, and individuals that the law has tended to privilege and protect over others.

Intersectional Ethics

The final section of the volume is animated by an intersectional approach, as originally developed by Kimberlé Crenshaw in 1989,[40] shortly before the new modernist studies movement began (which some scholars date to 1994 and some to 1999).[41] In a connection with the previous section, Crenshaw is a legal scholar. Intersectionality has been increasingly discussed in modernist studies by Sonita Sarker and others, especially as the result of an important conference on queer modernism and intersectionality held in Britain in 2018, which had a big impact on a new generation of scholars.[42] As Ann Mattis has recently argued, "The concept of intersectionality is indispensable to contemporary feminist analysis because it underscores the overlapping nature of race, sexuality, gender and other identity markers," and adopting this approach "makes modernist-feminist studies more accessible to students."[43] This approach is thus very suitable to inform accessible and nuanced readings of competing ethical claims and responsibilities in modernist texts. Our authors in this section have digested and synthesized an intersectional approach in both modernist studies and in twenty-first-century culture to offer new ethical readings and perspectives, addressing a diverse range of issues including a nuanced understanding of racial passing, racial uplift, and individualism in the Harlem Renaissance (Ryan), a queer and feminist reading of the Duse–D'Annunzio collaboration (Balázs), and an intersectional, historicist, and timely reading of how modernist portrayals of sexual consent look different after the #MeToo movement (Weng). Here an understanding of intersectionality informs the subtlety of the analysis of competing values and demands, as well as a sophisticated sense of the challenges of authorship, balancing, as Eide argued for earlier in the volume, suspicious and reparative readings.

Zora Neale Hurston's *Their Eyes Were Watching God* (1937) opens with a gnomic statement which reflects on gendered differences within the Black community in relation to a life of ethical action:

> Ships at a distance have every man's wish on board. For some they come in with the tide. For others they sail forever on the horizon, never out of sight, never landing until the Watcher turns his eyes away in resignation, his dreams mocked to death by Time. That is the life of men.
>
> Now, women forget all those things they don't want to remember, and remember everything they don't want to forget. The dream is the truth. Then they act and do things accordingly.
>
> So the beginning of this was a woman and she had come back from burying the dead. [...] The people all saw her come because it was sundown. The sun was gone, but he had left his footprints in the sky. It was the time for sitting on porches beside the road. It was the time to hear things and talk. These sitters had been tongueless, earless, eyeless conveniences all day long. Mules and other brutes had occupied their skins. But now, the sun and the bossman were gone, so the skins felt powerful and human. They became lords of sounds and lesser things. They passed nations through their mouths. They sat in judgment.[44]

For the Black community of Eatonville that Hurston's protagonist Janie has been part of and is returning to, ethical judgment is a luxury that cannot be part of the day's work, but which waits for evening. Ethical judgment at the end of the passage is a collective exercise too, which Hurston looks somewhat askance at; in the sentence about women, which reflects on her protagonist, she is keen to leave space for individual action and for dreams that are sourced in everyday reality, "Then they act and do things accordingly." But Hurston depicts how these ethical actions will be harshly judged, even though they stem from Janie's free sexuality and do not cause harm to others. The previous section of this volume concerned the limitations of the legal understanding of ethics, but in Hurston's passage we see the pleasures and dangers of collective moralizing, beyond law, and perhaps more powerful than law, of tradition and custom. As we will learn by the end of the novel, Janie has faced a legal trial about the circumstances of her lover's death before she returns to Eatonville and has been vindicated by a white jury; Hurston hints that her battle with her community will be more challenging. This passage reveals an ethics and a politics of intimacy similar to that explored by Högberg in Woolf, but it is necessary to use an intersectional lens to see how these ethical aspects are different for Janie as a Black woman, as the ethics of creativity was for Hurston as an African American modernist writer. In this section, we explore how intersectional approaches can reveal aesthetic and ethical challenges in modernist representation, whether they concern the individual and autonomy (Ryan), the collaborative (Balázs), or the partnered (Weng).

In the first essay in this section, Laura Ryan explores the ethical conflicts at the crossroads of racial representation and aesthetic autonomy. The artists associated with the New Negro movement—the phenomenon now best known as the Harlem Renaissance—were intent upon countering the harmful racial stereotypes long propounded by white America; they looked to create and celebrate a new and specific Black identity and aesthetic. Like their white modernist counterparts, then, Harlem Renaissance writers sought to break from the values and forms of the past to establish new ways of thinking and living. Yet young Black modernists were not always afforded the same artistic autonomy or freedom from constraint that many white modernists enjoyed; they were often beholden to the standards of an older generation, held up as a "Talented Tenth" responsible for "uplifting" the race, and accountable to the wider community. In short, matters of aesthetics and ethics were thoroughly intertwined. Ryan interrogates some of the ethical quandaries and pressures faced by Harlem Renaissance writers, how they negotiated them, and how these negotiations shaped their work and responses to it. Referencing key figures, including W. E. B. Du Bois, Alain Locke, Jean Toomer, Langston Hughes, and Zora Neale Hurston, this essay deals with the ethics of responsibility to one's race, and particularly the ethical implications of racial passing, the involvement of white patrons, and individualism. It argues that the Harlem Renaissance must be understood as a phenomenon arising from a myriad of ethical binds, competing ideologies, and moral compromises; such an understanding highlights the extent to which Black art and Black artists today continue to bear the weight of communal responsibility.

Continuing the intersectional focus of this section, Zsuzsanna Balázs offers a queer reading of Gabriele D'Annunzio's drama, enabled by an exploration of how he was embedded in queer modernist, feminist networks throughout his dramatic career. The view of D'Annunzio as a nationalist writer, womanizer, and fascist ideologue has overshadowed crucial facets of his life and works, which would challenge and nuance the established approaches to D'Annunzio. His drama was shaped by the most influential and forward-thinking New Women of the time, including Sarah Bernhardt, Eleonora Duse, Irma Gramatica, Emma Gramatica, and Ida Rubinstein. These women experimented with *travesti* roles, and their acting was an ethical action aimed to draw attention to the predicament of marginalized, stigmatized individuals in society. The aim of this chapter is to reinterrogate the ethics of collaboration and Eleonora Duse's influence on D'Annunzio. Balázs argues that the Duse–D'Annunzio collaboration worked to question the deeply entrenched, regressive moral principles of early twentieth-century Italy regarding women's place in society, same-sex intimacies, and sexuality. Balázs's chapter is in two parts. The first section looks at the context, exploring Duse's social activism in the regressive atmosphere of early twentieth-century Italy. The second part offers a detailed queer and dramaturgical reading of D'Annunzio's first play, *The Dead City* (*La città morta*, 1896), focusing on repressed same-sex desires and ephemeral queer moments in the script. This chapter underscores Duse's role as a feminist and queer icon who shaped D'Annunzio's ideas of gender and sexuality.

Part of a new wave of scholarship on sexual ethics heralded by Robin E. Field and Jerrica Jordan's *#Metoo and Modernism* (2023), Julie McCormick Weng's chapter closes the volume by exploring ways of reading representations of consent in the work of James Joyce in the wake of the #MeToo movement from 2017 onwards. She shows that across his writings, Joyce depicts instances of sexual abuse, assault, and harassment in turn-of-the-twentieth-century Ireland. As Weng argues, however, Joyce also "offers pathways for imagining nonviolent, uncoercive sexual intimacy. He presents an ethic of sexual intimacy that is bound up with an ethic of empathy," represented during Stephen Dedalus's adolescent sexual development in *A Portrait of the Artist as a Young Man* (1916) and in Leopold and Molly Bloom's courtship and marriage in *Ulysses* (1922).

Weng's overall approach argues that Joyce's study of sexual ethics can contribute to the ongoing goals of the #MeToo movement—"to cultivate new discourses of sexual assault and consent in order to effect change and prevent sexual violence." While feminist scholarship has always been crucial to the new modernist studies, this timely piece implicitly reflects a sense that our field is currently at a particular ethical crossroads, both in our critical practice and in our professional behavior, making it a fitting conclusion to our collection.

I

The Ethics of Mind and Body

CHAPTER ONE

An *Béal Bocht* and the Ethics of the Modernist Laughing Apocalypse

Paul Fagan

Modernism is apocalyptic. Whether representing astronomical, technological, cultural, or posthuman change, the horror of war or the threat of nuclear crisis, the modernist invests their theme with a Millenarian end-of-the-world flavor.[1] Frank Kermode insists that "the sense of an ending" is "endemic to what we call modernism," while Roger Griffin identifies "apocalyptic time as a central topos of the modernist imagination."[2] An apocalyptic outlook is not only a thematic and tonal staple of modernist expression, but also a driver of its formal innovations; as Erik Tonning observes, "the modernist impulse to 'make it new' in art, in thought, in society and politics is itself an incipiently apocalyptic one, poised between imaginative representations of an Old Era or civilization and the experimental promise of the New."[3] Thus, an "enduring fascination with catastrophe underlies the last century's foremost literary and philosophical expressions but also," Ruben Borg reflects, "perhaps more paradoxically, its key ethical debates."[4]

The present volume's focus on the ethics and ethicality of the modernist project requires a confrontation with this creative emphasis on rebirth through a violent break with and within time. Whether triggered by the end of certain ways of living, modes of "the human," structures of power, or orders of reality, the modernist apocalypse offers the reader, potentially, both

1. a radical liberation from the dictates of tradition and teleological history; and

2. a break from the unified perspective and objective clock time of realist expression which allows for a multi-perspectival ethics of alterity.

Yet Elana Gomel reminds us that "the narrative chronotope of the end time" serves also "as the locus of political and ethical danger,"[5] as witnessed in the draw of fascist and eugenicist projects of destructive regeneration for many of modernism's key figures.[6]

To date, discussions of the ethics of the modernist eschaton have focused on the radical temporality of an event that forges a new relationship between the testament of tradition, the crisis of the present, and the possibility of the future. In my intervention into this conversation, I do not take issue with this critical commonplace; indeed, the changed relationship between time and timelessness in twentieth-century writing will be central to the argument that I advance here. However, I propose that a changed relation to the material body—as a locus not only of suffering but also of a transformed relationship to the limit—has been under-theorized as a complementary and necessary coordinate for understanding the ethics and evaluating the ethicality of the modernist literary apocalypse. I suggest that new light can be shed on the topic by placing Kermode's pioneering work on distinct modes of modernist apocalyptic temporality into conversation with Julia Kristeva's theory of the carnivalesque Laughing Apocalypse, via Borg's writing on the ethics of finitude in modernist writing. To reframe these debates, I place particular significance on the provocative distinction Kristeva develops between moralistic (revelatory) and ethical (laughing) apocalypses through their distinct approaches to the body as a site, respectively, of an abjection that must be purged, or of a carnivalesque reversal that produces not horror at the collapse of meaning, but amoral, complicit laughter.

To narrow my focus in relation to this expansive theme, I spotlight the apocalyptic imagination of Irish late modernist Brian O'Nolan. His writing foregrounds abject representations of bodies that trouble the limits of "the human," while at the same time interrogating these images through a carnivalesque ethics of excess that defies moral codes.[7] Apocalypse is a core thematic focus of his English-language novels *At Swim-Two-Birds* (1939) and *The Third Policeman* (written 1940, published 1967) and the narrative focus of his late-career work *The Dalkey Archive* (1964), each published under the pseudonym "Flann O'Brien." Yet I suggest it is in the Irish-language novel *An Béal Bocht*—published in 1941 under the editorial persona "Myles na gCopaleen"—that we find O'Nolan's most ambivalent encounter between the moral, propositional apocalypse and the Kristevan Laughing Apocalypse. If the former is manifested more straightforwardly in the book's satire of Irish cultural politics, the latter is to be found in its more complex stylistic rendering of impoverished, suffering bodies through a tone which evokes not disgust or pity "at the finitude of human existence,"[8] but rather a laughter that is amoral, yet ethically oriented. O'Nolan renders apocalyptic abjection *comic* not as a means of ironic distancing or amelioration, I propose, but to advance a Kristeva-like ethics which (1) *rejects* the apocalypse's rhetoric of a regenerative violence that reimposes order, morality, and purity, and (2) *identifies with* the abject that troubles the conventional limits of the embodied self.

My wager is that O'Nolan serves as an ideal candidate for my interrogation of the ethics of twentieth-century avant-garde eschatology as his writing both embodies and critiques modernism's apocalyptic mindset. In other words, O'Nolan attempts to have his cake and eat it too with regard to modernist apocalyptic schemes, writing within the paradigm of an apocalyptic break with tradition that he submits, at the same time, to comic ridicule. Accounting for the peculiarities of the temporal and corporeal dimensions of his apocalyptic vision requires both Kermode's and Kristeva's perspectives on twentieth-century end-time narratives. As such, I will first outline each of these theories and their relationship to O'Nolan's apocalyptic style in turn, before turning to my close reading of *An Béal Bocht*'s specific response to the ethics of modernist apocalypse.

End Times

Kermode identifies apocalyptic narratives as enacting a changed relationship to time—through them, "[w]e project ourselves […] past the End, so as to see the structure whole, a thing we cannot do from our spot of time in the middle."[9] The temporal ethics of such apocalypse narratives informs the distinction that Kermode draws between:

1. a "naïve" apocalypticism, which decries the decadent decline of the present age and predicts, or wills, a literal, and imminent, destructive revitalization which will initiate a mythical New Era;[10] and

2. the "clerkly skepticism" of the "theologian, poet, or novelist," who knows that "it is not merely upon the people of a certain moment but upon all men that the ends of the world have come," and thus understands apocalypse as a mode of crisis, revelation, and transformation that is "immanent rather than imminent."[11]

For Kermode, any naïve apocalyptic imaginary opens itself to an "irrationalism" whose "ideological expression is fascism" and whose "practical consequence" is the Final Solution.[12] A profound ethical danger of a certain strand of modernism is its flirtation with "naïve" apocalypticism and its consequent "fascination with the rhetorical and aesthetic manifestations of fascism."[13] Indeed, Griffin insists that fascism must be understood as "an *alternative modernism*," rather than as an outright rejection of modernist thought and cultural politics.[14] Building on Griffin's work, Tonning perceives that "a revolt against Western modernity construed as disintegrative and moribund, in the name of a future regeneration" characterizes *both* "epiphanic" (or aesthetic) modernism *and* the "'programmatic' (or socio-political) modernism" inscribed in palingenetic programs of national cleansing.[15]

In opposition to the delirious, but morally certain, genocidal political violence of the naïve, imminent apocalypse, Kermode poses the ethical imperative of a clerkly skepticism that foregrounds "the conflict between the deterministic pattern any plot suggests, and the *freedom* of persons within that plot to *choose* and so to alter the structure, the relations of beginning, middle, and end."[16] It is the task of the clerkly writer to de-mythologize apocalypse by thinking the radical change that eschatological writing both fears and desires in terms "of crisis rather than temporal ends"—even as this crisis entails a specific "relation to the future and to the past."[17] And it is only by rejecting the End's imminence and acknowledging its immanence that those who would theorize or write the crisis of their moment "avoid the regress into myth which has deceived poet, historian, and critic."[18] It is thus by its specific "imagery of past and present and future," and not its "confidence in the uniqueness of [the twentieth-century] crisis,"[19] that the traumas and desires, moral imperatives and ethical impasses of the modernist apocalypse can be known.

Kermode maps onto the distinction between naïve and clerkly apocalypses "a pattern of anxiety" that recurs, "with interesting differences, in different stages of modernism."[20] Modernism's first phase, which Kermode identifies with Pound, Yeats, Lewis, Eliot, and Joyce, is, in his estimation, "clerkly enough, skeptical in many ways; and yet we can without difficulty convict most of these authors of dangerous lapses into mythical thinking":

> All were men of critical temper, haters of the decadence of the times [...]. All, in different ways, venerated tradition and had programs which were at once modern and anti-schismatic. This critical temper was [...] consistent with a strong feeling for renovation [...], but skepticism and a refined traditionalism held in check what threatened to be a bad case of literary primitivism.[21]

Kermode singles out Yeats and Eliot as exemplary of modernism's distinguishing capacity to inhabit and blur the boundaries between naïve and clerical modes, as two apocalyptic poets who did not take their predictions of the End "literally," yet *nevertheless* "believed them in some fashion."[22]

Kermode contrasts this "traditionalist modernism," which was "emphatic about its living relation to the past" with what he calls "anti-traditionalist modernism"—the surrealist, avant-garde, schismatic modernism of Dada, for example.[23] This anti-traditionalist modernism is "more interested in the possibilities of a break with the past; of considering the present in relation to the end without calculations based on history."[24] For Kermode, "what distinguishes the new from the older modernism most sharply [...] is not that one is more apocalyptic than the other but that they have such different attitudes to the past. To the older, it is a source of order; to the newer it is that which ought to be ignored."[25] When evaluating the ethicality of a specific instance or trend of modernist apocalyptic writing, then, Kermode compels us to ask whether tradition is revived to reinforce a moral framework onto the chaos of the twentieth century (even as this framework is secularized), or the relation to the past is sundered to insist upon an ethical openness to the future and the freedom to avoid, negotiate, or radically reimagine a deterministic teleology and the dictates of history.

Borg refines the specific ethical coordinates of this debate when he observes that the modernist eschaton is distinguished from both Millenarian narratives and "the postmodern desire to destroy time" by virtue of its "desire to revive time, to reaffirm its reality and its power" towards an ethics of finitude.[26] Modernist avant-garde writing, Borg perceives, "transform[s] the apocalyptic experience" by "bringing about a shift in perspective that complicates the relation of time to its limit."[27] Thus, the modernist apocalypse "forces us to rethink the concept of the limit" itself and "highlights a gap within the historical subject."[28] This gap, Borg writes:

> spells *both* finitude *and* freedom for the individual: on the one hand, it guarantees subjective agency through the openness of a future that is not-yet-given; on the other, it puts identity in crisis, marking the self with an originary self-difference [...]. In this sense, the gap is also an inherent limit or constitutive boundary. There can be no ethics without an acknowledgement of this limit, [...] without an awareness of the partiality of one's own perspective.[29]

Rather than solely a function of a renewed, but abstractly intellectualized relationship to tradition (a key aspect of modernist writing for sure, but, ultimately, a perennial theme of apocalypse), the modernist apocalypse advances an "understanding of ethical freedom predicated upon a certain experience of the reality of time, and of its finitude."[30] Under such terms, the understanding of "a modern ethics of temporality, most of all one that is charged with an apocalyptic tone," requires careful attention to whether the concept of the limit is understood in a particular work "as a limitation, a prohibition, a paternal 'no'" or "as an extremity, a frontier, the natural habitat of the *avant-garde*."[31]

O'Nolan's writing interrogates modernist temporal ethics by echoing its apocalyptic register, yet in a tone and style that voids it of moral certainty and in an attitude skeptical of *both* traditional *and* modernist claims to revelation. The ethical scheme of *At Swim-Two-Birds* turns on the Pooka MacPhellimey's inquiry whether "the last number" will be odd (thus entailing the revelation of "truth") or even (thus marking the victory of "evil").[32] Yet this teleological scheme of sequence and termination is both advanced and undercut across O'Nolan's novel, which proffers "three openings" and "one hundred times as many endings."[33] As Maebh Long shows, the text's ahistorical fragmentation of Irish literary materials suggests that a cultural "apocalypse is already at hand," yet the narrator's constructed fictional world is finally consigned to flames and "dies, not with a bang but a whimper."[34] Elsewhere, the protagonist of *The Third Policeman* suddenly finds himself living posthumously in an eternity characterized by the absurd simultaneous functioning of change and stasis. As Borg reflects, even as the novel's hellish setting suggests a framework of moral punishment, the narrator's apocalyptic rebirth into a form of living death constitutes "a violent event, occurring outside any margin of expectation," which calls for "a complete reorganization of the order of reality" and the undoing of an "entire system of values."[35] In O'Nolan's final novel, *The Dalkey Archive*, the scientist De Selby creates an anaerobic environment that re-aligns human perception to time's simultaneity. The "comic debauch"[36] of this temporal scheme facilitates a carnivalesque travesty of both tradition and modernism, in the novel's humiliating resurrections of Augustine and Joyce. By these means, De Selby intends to enact a "prescribed doom, terrible but ineluctable" upon the world;[37] yet the prophesied apocalypse never comes to pass, as the contradictions of an imminent, teleological apocalypse and the insistence on the simultaneity of time—a figure of the End's immanence and perpetual deferral—cannot be reconciled.

Each of these themes is relevant for understanding the ethical thrust of O'Nolan's apocalypses: a parodic image of modernism's conflation of naïve and skeptical modes; a skewed relation to the authority of both biblical and modernist sources; a foregrounding of tone and literary style (the encounter between innovation and cliché, horror and gallows humor) in scription of the End. Thus, O'Nolan labors to void the modernist apocalypse of moral certainty and authority by playing up its pretenses and contradictions: namely, its *having-its-cake-and-eating-it-too* approach to naïve and skeptical apocalyptic modes, which claims a subjective freedom from the dictates of history while leaving the door open to a profound ethical danger for the abjected Other and for bodies marked as less-than-human.

The Laughing Apocalypse

In his essay "Of an Apocalyptic Tone Recently Adopted in Philosophy," Jacques Derrida writes that "nothing is less conservative than the apocalyptic genre," which, "[b]y its very tone, the mixing of voices, genres and codes, [...] can also, in dislocating destinations, dismantle the dominant contract."[38] Yet, for Kristeva, such an outcome is not a given. In her thinking, by contrast, apocalyptic discourse is inherently moralizing, reactionary, authoritarian, and produces genres in which a "sacred horror for the feminine, the diabolical, and the sexual [is] expounded."[39] Kristeva insists that such a formulation of apocalyptic thought can only be moral, not ethical; an attempt to reimpose a strict, delimiting categorization and moral order in response to an abject disgust at the body's transgressed limits (we need only recall that the first Nazi book burning was of transsexual research at Hirschfeld's Institut für Sexualwissenschaft, where gender-affirmation surgeries were performed). The logic of biblical eschatology—and its diverse manifestations across literary genres and cultural-political movements, including certain strands of modernism—endeavors to mark, repress, destroy the horror of bodily materiality and difference. Despite its claim to the revelation of a profound truth, "[i]n no case," Kristeva writes, "is there philosophical unveiling or reasoning demonstration of the hidden" in "the rigid [...] moral position of apocalyptic inspiration."[40] She insists that the apocalypse's moral rigidity needs to be transgressed before it can reveal ethical (rather than didactic, moral, ideological) truth and become a proper subject of philosophical inquiry.

In *Powers of Horror*, Kristeva theorizes abjection as a revulsive reaction to that which defies categorization, or any limit transgression where meaning breaks down, where the distinction between self and other collapses. Such moments of abjection constitute "the ultimate coding of our crises, of our most intimate and most serious apocalypses."[41] In her later work, such as *Strangers to Ourselves* and *Nations without Nationalism*, Kristeva develops more fully the ethical imperative that her understanding of abjection demands: "We have to recognize *ourselves* as strange in order better to appreciate the foreigners outside us, instead of striving to bend them to the norms of our own repression."[42] For Kristeva, confronting apocalypse's revulsive response to the body's transgressive materiality is a central ethical imperative for twentieth-century writers. Yet, she insists, such an ethical position cannot be achieved through moralizing condemnation or an ethics of alterity, in which the self/Other binary is upheld and even fetishized. Rather, Kristevan ethics turn upon a thoroughgoing identification with the abject that undoes the strict limits of the unitary, stable, humanistic self upon which the Western revelatory apocalypse's moral position and ideological certainty depends, by allowing us to see the self as Other, to encounter the stranger within.

Kristeva counters the moralizing revelation with the carnivalesque spirit of what she terms the Laughing Apocalypse, or "an apocalypse without god [...] without morality, without judgment," without "ideology, thesis, interpretation, mania, collectivity, threat, [or] hope."[43] This is an apocalypse that maps onto the topsy-turvy world of inverted hierarchies, grotesque bodily functions, and suspended moral orders captured in Bakhtin's work on the medieval carnival. As Kristeva writes, carnival "does not keep to the rigid, that is, moral position of apocalyptic inspiration; it transgresses it, sets its repressed against it—the lower things, sexual matters, what is blasphemous and to which it holds while mocking the law."[44] Integral here is Bakhtin's insistence on the "deep philosophical" meaning and political-ethical force of a form of folk laughter that enables "a peculiar point of view" in which "the world is seen anew" and allows for the revelation of an "unofficial truth."[45]

Kristeva distinguishes the twentieth-century Laughing Apocalypse from medieval carnival in two crucial ways. The first is the disappearance of God from the apocalyptic scene—a distance or absence "which cause[s] horror to exist and at the same time take[s] us away from it, grip[s] us with fear and by that very fright change[s] language into a quill, a fleeting and piercing one, a work of lace, a show of acrobatics, a burst of laughter and a mark of death."[46] The second is its apocalyptic tone, which pairs "abjection and piercing laughter" to emphasize not "the Death of God but a reassumption, *through style*, of what lies hidden by God."[47] This "double stance between disgust and laughter, apocalypse and carnival," expresses, simultaneously, both "a strange rent" and an "endless synthesis" between "an ego and an other—between nothing and all."[48] Crucially, for Kristeva, such a carnivalesque vision of an immanent, godless apocalypse entails the "obverse of a radical nihilism."[49] Its laughter, instead of disgust, at the material body constitutes a queer event in which the grotesque Other, the taboo desire, the collapsed limit are not abjected as objects of horror but embraced as sites of uncanny recognition and of radical ethical potentiality.

As we have seen, aspects of modernism's millenarian spirit of *making it new* betray a moralizing apprehension of modernity along class, gender, race, and sexual lines that is coded in a rhetoric of tradition and disclosure. Without overturning this ethical problematic for modernism and its critics, I suggest we can trace a countering impulse in certain strands of modernist Laughing Apocalypse which explore a radical ethical register that turns upon a comic or carnivalesque—rather than tragic or pathological—tone in representing the abject body: Céline (for Kristeva, the twentieth-century author of the Laughing Apocalypse *par excellence*), Kafka, Artaud, Barnes's *The Book of Repulsive Women* and *Nightwood*, Joyce's "Circe" and *Finnegans Wake*, Beckett's *Endgame* and *Trilogy* (indeed, all of Beckett's mature writing), and, crucially for my purposes here, O'Nolan.[50]

Any direct parallel between Céline and O'Nolan is complicated by Céline's anti-Semitism, which O'Nolan's work does not share (even as it bears aspects of Céline's misogyny).[51] There are other meaningful discrepancies between the authors: O'Nolan's laughter is more varied, including laughs (silly, absurd, punning, satirically civic-minded), which are alien to Céline's world.[52] Yet I am intrigued by how well Kristeva's identification of a "double stance between disgust and laughter"[53] in Céline's work serves also to explicate a specific, and integral, relationship between apocalypse and carnival in O'Nolan's comic rendering of the abject body. The key to the comparison in my thinking is "the importance of tone in modulating different moral and political attitudes to the body, or to death-on-display" in O'Nolan's oeuvre, but also "the inability of any single theory of humor to explain the irresistible coincidence of death and laughter" in his poetics.[54] The recurrent focus in O'Nolan's writing on the abject body, and on "queer" revelations of the stranger within, is distinguished by its comic inspiration, the *comedy* of its own abjection.

Imminent and Immanent Ends

An Béal Bocht presents itself as the memoir of Bónapárt Ó Cúnasa, who documents the life of dehumanized poverty, famine, and perpetual rain that is the fate of the people of the small Gaeltacht Island of Corca Dorcha. The memoir doubles as a confession, in which Bónapárt details the circumstances in which he discovers Maoldún Ó Pónasa's treasure in the carnivalesque utopia of Cruach an Ocrais (Hunger Hill), buys a pair of boots from town that he conceals from the community and comes to be tried in a language he cannot speak and imprisoned for a murder he may or may not have committed.

A naïve apocalyptic tone rings out from the opening line: "I am noting down the matters which are in this document" to provide a "testimony of our times [...] because our types will never be there again nor any other life in Ireland comparable to ours who exists no longer."[55] Indeed, the islanders feel themselves in every moment to be on the edge of the infinite: Bónapárt's mother "set[s] her face towards eternity"; the Sean Duine Liath (the Old-Grey-Fellow, Bónapárt's grandfather and ersatz father figure) is observed "meditating on eternity itself"; Sitric Ó Sánasa, a figure of grotesque poverty, is in every living moment "not far from eternity."[56] Everywhere, the islanders read the signs of their end. On the eve of his birth, Bónapárt tells us, his estranged father pointed towards "the bad sign that the ducks are in the nettles" and prophesied: "Horror and misfortune will come on the world tonight."[57] This augury is the novel's first hint at Bónapárt's potential role as antichrist (elsewhere he describes himself as speaking "like a false prophet").[58] When Bónapárt notices, in a subsequent chapter, that the floor of their home is red from the blood spouting from the Old-Grey-Fellow's feet, he inquires: "is [...] [t]he end of the world and the termination of the universe [...] with us,"[59] and his mother likewise asks: "is it the way [...] that the Gaelic misery is at an end and that the paupers are waiting for the final explosion of the great earth?"[60] Towards the end of the novel, the islanders read Bónapárt's bootprints as signs that the dreaded Cat Mara (literally, "cat of the sea"), a portent of doom among the people of Corca Dorcha, has arrived on the island: "The wonder lasted for two days, everyone expecting that the heavens would collapse or that the ground crack and the people would be swept away to some lower region."[61] As Gregory Darwin notes, "the humor here derives from the unexpected transformation of 'Cat Mara' from a figure of colloquial Gaeltacht speech, meaning 'calamity,' into a literal feline monster."[62] Yet, as the illustration provided in the text reveals, this apocalyptic beast is in fact the island of Ireland itself.

In Chapter 4, the Old-Grey-Fellow enters the house "terrified" and "trembling," before warning Bónapárt that "the end of the world will arrive before that very night. The signs are there in plenty through the firmament."[63] The omens are comical at first and harmless in their reiteration of the novel's core imagery: the "frightening things" witnessed by the Old-Grey-Fellow include a ray of sunshine, a breeze going and returning across a field, a crow screeching with a pig's voice.[64] But what truly frightens the Old-Grey-Fellow is his sighting of an "elegant, well-dressed gentleman" speaking Gaelic. The unbelievable testimony leads Bónapárt to assume the Old-Grey-Fellow is "raving in a drunken delirium"—"If it is true," Bónapárt concedes, "the end of the world is here today."[65] The apocalypse is thus marked by the arrival of the *Gaeilgeoirí*—the "self-serving cultural asset-stripping visitors to the Gaeltacht"[66] who come to the island to document that Irish is still spoken and has not died out completely.

The apocalyptic import of the vision of Ireland as the Cat Mara and the appearance of the *Gaeilgeoirí* marks the satirical, moral, drive of the text's imagery, with its propositional content that the inhabitants' misery and poverty is caused by an abusive Irish cultural politics that romanticizes the island natives as noble savages (one ethnographer records the sound of a pig grunting as a perfect instance of the language). But their arrival does not bring the prophesied end of their world—indeed, they are the ones who, in carrying over the apparatuses and reinforcing the catastrophic effects of the colonial British state, maintain the islanders' perpetual suffering to bolster their own cultural politics and uphold their narrative of national authenticity.

Yet this propositional, moral dimension of the novel's satire is undercut by the amorality of the islanders themselves—as much as such actions are conditioned by their circumstances—they are recurrently given to thieving, lying, and manipulating their situation to their own ends. The islanders "never seek to rise above their station, but submit themselves fully, and oftentimes for the benefit of the ethnographer's fascinated gaze, to the stereotypes that fix their condition" so that their misery is "both *lived* and *staged*."[67] If their suffering is apocalyptic, it is presented in a style that implies that "even absolute hopelessness can be reworked into a mannerism, or an amusing refrain."[68] This parodic tone—which pulls the rug out from under even the novel's own ostensibly moral satirical critique—is manifested most fully in Bónapárt's refrain that *"ní bheidh ár leithéidí arís ann"* (our likes will not be there again), which rehearses the ironically romanticized apocalyptic theme of the people of Corca Dorcha living on the edge of cultural, linguistic, and material extinction. Yet this naïve apocalyptic rhetoric is both deflated through its secondary status as an intertextual echo taken over from Tomás Ó Criomhthain's *An t-Oileánach* and burlesqued through its excessive repetition—a habit or rhetorical tic, rather than a revelation of truth.

The apocalyptic tone is established already in the novel's paratexts. Two different forewords were penned under O'Nolan's pseudonym "Myles na gCopaleen," who feigns to present himself solely as the editor of Bónapárt's memoirs. The foreword used in the first and second editions is dated *"The Day of Want*, 1941" and a new foreword for the third edition is dated *"The Day of Doom*, 1964." The Irish original of the first foreword is *"Lá an Ghátair*, 1941," and is taken from the Irish translation of the Book of Tobit 4:9, in which Tobit advises his son not to be overly generous with his possessions, *"eidh stór maith á chur i dtaisce agat do lá an ghátair"* (for you will store up a good treasure for yourself against the day of necessity). This image of the impending day of want is subtly echoed across *An Béal Bocht*, for instance in the image of Bónapárt's mother constantly boiling "a houseful of potatoes to stave off the day of famine."[69] Amy-Jill Levine describes the Book of Tobit (apocryphal in non-Catholic traditions) as "[c]ombining ethical exhortation and prayers with broad humor" to give "theologians a view of God who tests the faithful, responds to prayers, and redeems the covenant community."[70] While certain aspects of the plot map onto *An Béal Bocht*—the role of family in relation to community and tradition, the focus on money, the acquisition of a wife for the son to continue the community's traditions—they are grotesquely travestied. In O'Nolan's text, the father is absent, as is the God or moral arbiter who would reward and redeem the oppressed community; the acquisition of money leads to Bónapárt's incarceration; his wife, Nábla, is made to marry him against her will and soon dies in the putrid stench of Corca Dorcha, along with their only son, and with him any lineage connecting the past through the present to the future.

The Irish original of the second foreword's date, "*Lá an Luain*, 1964" literally means Doomsday, but plays on the homophony with the Irish for Monday "*dé Luain*," implying that—despite all their prophecies of an imminent end—the islanders' apocalypse is a routine, regular occurrence. While the novel's apocalypse was framed as imminent in the first two editions (signaling the day of want that is *to come*), in its third iteration Doomsday is already here. The 1964 foreword situates the novel's republication in a period of decay ("The sweet Gaelic dialect [...] is not developing but rather declining like rust")[71] and places the text into a parodic relation with tradition, as na gCopaleen recommends that *An Béal Bocht* "be in every habitation and mansion where love for our country's traditions lives at this hour when, as Standish Hayes O'Grady says, 'the day is drawing to a close and the sweet wee maternal tongue has almost ebbed.'"[72] Yet everywhere the implication in the novel is that a staged or performed adherence to tradition—to the ideology and clichés of "*na dea-leabhair*" (the good books)—is exactly what determines the poverty-stricken conditions of Corca Dorcha.[73] It is what keeps them stuck in the violent time of Tribulations by promising them a mythical New Era that never arrives. This aspect of the text entails both a political critique and an aesthetic-philosophical critique of the traditionalist modernism in which tradition is revived supposedly to reinforce a moral framework onto the chaos of the twentieth century (here we must keep in mind that the novel is composed amid the unfolding horror and crisis of World War II). Yet, in *An Béal Bocht*, there is also no possibility for a schismatic break with the deterministic dictates of tradition owing to the material constraints of the body subjected to real economic and cultural power—if such a scheme is conceivable to the bourgeois Dadaists of the continent, it is closed to people of Corca Dorcha.

In Bónapárt's memoir itself, the standard apocalyptic arc is given an ironic twist, as there was no golden age: "it was always thus."[74] In fact, the Gaels always imagine things were *worse* in the past: when there was "the time of the Deluge" in the Old-Grey-Fellow's youth, he "heard [his] father praising the good weather and saying it was fine and there was nothing wrong with it compared with the sky-crucifying that people got when he was a young fellow."[75] The comment plays into the cultural satire of perpetual self-pitying martyrdom signaled in the novel's title—to "put on the poor mouth" (*an béal bocht a chur ort*) is to exaggerate the direness of one's situation to evoke sympathy or gain charity. Yet it also establishes a new relation to eschatological time, as the apocalypse is *both* behind us *and* to come (again). Not only is there no romanticized point of origin for the Gaels, there is no imagined future utopia. Bónapárt's mother declares that there will never "be any good settlement for the Gaels but only hardship for them always,"[76] a point on which the Old-Grey-Fellow agrees: "I don't think there'll ever be good conditions for the Gaels."[77] Little wonder, given this influence, that Bónapárt reflects that "eternity" may be "bad" but the future in Corca Dorcha will be "infernally insufferable"[78] and that many of the island's inhabitants "set out for eternity gladly"[79]—even as their desired end proves unobtainable. In his murder trial, Bónapárt is condemned to serve a sentence of twenty-nine years, just like his "father"[80]: the apocalyptic rhetoric of "our likes will not be there again" ultimately is revealed as a rhetorical sleight of hand to conceal that the Gaels are stuck in this circular hell forever.

We note, then, the novel's strange apocalyptic temporality. Here, the End, despite the narrator's surface rhetoric, is not a fixed, imminent teleological point (the end of history, the end of time, the end of the human, the end of a certain way of life) but immanent, inherent to every moment. *And yet*, despite the text's gestures towards the immanence of a perpetual apocalyptic crisis, the inhabitants of the Gaeltacht are condemned to a fate determined, apparently, by history and tradition itself: the Gaels "can't escape from fate."[81] Even the modernist reintroduction of time into this eternal cycle proves hopeless: "the old-grey-fellow possessed a golden watch since the day of the *feis* but I never understood the utility of that small machine or what point on earth there was to it."[82] In this space that collapses the distinction between pre- and post-apocalypse, time is defeated yet trickles on pointlessly, and the timeless duration of the afterlife is one in which putrid, abject horror and carnivalesque, delusional, excessive, amoral laughter are folded into each other in this scription of the apocalypse.

Moral and Laughing Apocalypses

In Kristevan terms, this eternal cycle of bodily suffering "is the horror of hell without God: if no means of salvation, no optimism, not even a humanistic one, looms on the horizon, then the verdict is in, with no hope of pardon—the sportful verdict of scription."[83] Throughout the novel, the catastrophic destruction that both never arrives and is already here is marked by a focus on the abject body. The putrid stench of Ambrós the pig is "Reminiscent of a corpse"; Bónapárt's encounter with the Cat Mara fills him with "terror, […] fear and melancholy and disgust" as the air becomes "putrid with an ancient smell of putridity"; the speaking corpse of Maoldún seizes the narrator with "a flood-tide of sickness or terror or disgust."[84] Everywhere, the scenery suggests "a life so stark, so far removed from social norms that it becomes indistinguishable from death" and "a world putrefied at its core," marked by "the sense of pervasive rot."[85] It is a world of stark, brutally rendered violence, from the "destructive blow on the skull" that the teacher administers to all the schoolchildren of Corca Dorcha[86] to the injuries Bónapárt suffers during his fall from Cruach an Ocrais. Thus, the novel blends the naïve and the clerical, the immanent and the imminent apocalypse. Yet it is its comic focus on the body and death that invites a Kristevan analysis of its apocalyptic ethics.

The catastrophe of the Long Dance in Chapter 4 "intensifies the satirical tone established earlier in the novel, targeting the provincialism of revivalist attitudes and the identification of authentic Gaelicness with exaggerated misery"; yet the scene's mechanics deny "the reader any clear ideological or rhetorical purchase on that theme."[87] Bónapárt relates:

> The dance continued until the dancers drove their lives out through the soles of their feet and eight died during the course of the *feis*. Due to both the fatigue caused by the revels and the truly Gaelic famine that was ours always, they could not be succoured

when they fell on the rocky dancing floor and, upon my soul, short was their tarrying on this particular area because they wended their way to eternity without more ado. Even though death snatched many fine people from us, the events of the *feis* went on sturdily and steadily.[88]

The image calls to mind the persecution of the Jewish population of Warsaw after the 1939 German invasion, when the innocent were "compelled to dance atop tables for hours on end."[89] Yet, as Borg and I have written elsewhere, the episode also captures the specific quality of the encounter of death and laughter in O'Nolan's gallows humor:

> The body is often posed as a strange spectacle in O'Nolan's work, and its representation in this manner is typically bound up with acts of moral judgement, as in the resolution of *The Third Policeman*. But here the picture plainly exceeds the moral framework. The obscenity of turning poverty and death into a folksy public event—the body an exhibition of famine and fatigue, a broken thing that won't stop dancing—flouts any expected correspondence between art and proper measure or poetic justice. Nor can the scene be played for a cheap laugh. Yet the strain it puts on decorum is already profoundly comic, and immediately political.[90]

Here, I would add that this is a variation of the paradigmatic scene of the Laughing Apocalypse, which Kristeva describes as "Music, rhythm, rigadoon, without end, for no reason."[91] As in Céline's Laughing Apocalypse, there is "no glory in this suffering; it is not an ode: it opens up only onto idiocy"—it is a scene of "violence, blood, and death," of "[h]uman beings caught flush with their animality, [...] beyond all 'fancies,'" a site of "suffering, which only humor and style cause to tilt out of the accounts of the Freudian neuropath."[92]

It is in this identification with the abject, in a scene of "[h]uman beings caught flush with their animality," that the novel's ethical vision emerges. Corca Dorcha is a liminal space of John the Revelator style scenes of transformed and transgressed human–nonhuman limits (pigs that speak Gaelic, men confused for seals) that recall and travesty the Book of Revelation. For most critics, the inability to distinguish between inhabitants of the Gaeltacht and pigs or other animals speaks to an unwillingness on the part of the bourgeois intellectual to see subaltern groups on their own terms or even as human beings.[93] The view that such cohabitation—even familial solidarity—with the nonhuman animal represents a form of degradation is given voice by the school inspector, who asks: "Isn't it a shameful, improper and very bad thing for ye to be stretched out with the brute beasts, all of ye stuck together in the one bed?"[94] However, an alternative reading is available here, which departs from the inspector's (and the critic's) association of the Corkadorghans with animals as degrading, dehumanizing, and abject. These two impulses compete throughout the novel, as a meaningful, if comically rendered, companionship between the human and the nonhuman—in which, beyond satirical or fabular readings of nonhuman life, the pigs and humans of *An Béal Bocht* share equally the horror, difficulty, and joys of life—is paired with a sense of Kristevan abjection. Yet they come together, significantly, when Sitric Ó Sánasa decides to leave the island and live with the seals, where he finds "freedom from [...] the famine and the abuse of the world."[95] Accepting his abjection, identifying with his own abjected animality, Sitric *becomes* a human-seal, "wild and hirsute [...], vigorously providing fish with the community with whom he lodged."[96] The comic, carnivalesque scene gains its ethical purchase through a different form of apocalyptic transformation, through an identification with the abject in which Sitric moves beyond binaries—island and mainland, time and eternity, human and animal—to a third, liminal space, where he achieves a different, carnivalesque form of living death, "buried alive and [...] satisfied, safe from hunger and rain."[97]

An Béal Bocht critiques the modernist location of ethics in apocalyptic temporality—in its reimagined relation to tradition that, O'Nolan implies, both abstracts and is powerless against the reality of a violence backed up by real power. The novel's blurring of apocalyptic temporal modes—imminent and immanent, traditional and avant-garde—is part of a strategic attempt to expose a disjunction between apocalyptic morality and ethical thought. Yet it is its focus on the body as a locus not only of suffering but also of a transformed relationship to the limit that adds "the merciless crashing of the apocalypse" to carnival's pairing of "the high and the low, the sublime and the abject."[98]

Conclusion

Across his work, O'Nolan writes about the end of the world writ large, but also other diverse and refracted endings: of tradition, of time itself, of the human, of the self. Sean Pryor pursues the ethics of his writing in the "conflict between freedom and determinism," but concludes that O'Nolan's novels "are obsessed by sin yet seem to laugh at genuine ethical reflection."[99] My reading is exactly the inverse of this: O'Nolan seeks a genuine ethical reflection by laughing at a rhetoric of moral certainty that hinges upon a movement of sin to salvation, violence to rebirth. By the same token, I agree with Rónán McDonald's contention that O'Nolan's "satire seems leached of normative value and detached from a moral target," but depart from his conclusion that as a consequence his "satire shifts into the more ethically evacuated, ludic parody that we associate with postmodernism."[100] In my understanding, O'Nolan's modernist apocalypses distinguish themselves by virtue of the fact that they stage an ambiguously carnivalesque double of the modernist apocalypse that is shot through with a comic spirit which both ridicules an early modernist obsession with tradition and reflects on the impossibility of a break with tradition in an Ireland wrestling with the ghosts of its past and a Europe plunged into fascism and war. His rendering of this crisis recalls Kristeva's Céline in this one aspect: his "apocalyptic laughter" emerges from an "affective ambivalence" that rejects "treatise, commentary, or judgment," and from which no "party," "side," or "class comes out unscathed, that is, identical to itself."[101] As such, O'Nolan's art allows us to more clearly distinguish and problematize the moral and ethical dimensions of the modernist apocalyptic imaginary—just as this apocalyptic framework can help us to situate and characterize O'Nolan's art more precisely—by allowing us to think an apocalypse voided of moral certainty, yet which nevertheless provokes a laughter in its readers that insists upon their complicity.

CHAPTER TWO

"Grey Figures Bent Like Hooks"

The Ethics of Representing Older Age in Djuna Barnes's Early Journalism and Late Interviews

Jade French

Djuna Barnes began working as a journalist in 1913, taking work so as to support herself living alone in New York. The periodicals she worked for positioned her as their "modern woman" on the ground, as Barnes was tasked with reporting on the fads and fashions of Greenwich Village's new artistic communities. An emphasis on the new is often equated to "youth," leading Cynthia Port to note that "ageing is a topic that was excluded from modernism's definition of itself."[1] It is therefore notable that Barnes's reports of New York—which often hinged on presenting new experiences of bohemian art—included many older subjects who informed her observations of the expanding city. Modernization narratives often sideline older people in urban areas by presenting them as irrelevant to an industrialized workforce and outpaced by change.[2] Haim Hazan notes that there is a prevailing sense that as we age adults retreat from the modern world, representing older adults as "unchanging inhabitants" in the cities they live in and offering "no mechanism allowing for their development" once aged past youth.[3] Although Barnes was tasked with reporting on the contemporary moment by the nature of her trade, she defies the equation that "new" equals "youthful" by reporting on New York's experienced actresses, older trendsetters, and working veterans.

Barnes's observations raise questions of how to ethically represent and acknowledge older people's experiences of modernity: how might a modernist writer experiment with relaying the experience of active participation in society as well as the potential marginalization experienced in light of fast-paced change? First, in this chapter, I explore how Barnes approaches different life stages—from *dilettante* young women to middle-aged mothers and older shopkeepers—as a way of satirizing her audience's expectations of the new. Her early work reports on a New York that is populated with, shaped by, and indebted to older people's stories. Amelia DeFalco suggests, in questions of ageing and ethics, it is often the case that older people are "seen as objects of ethical dilemmas and policy rather than [...] the *subjects* or *agents* of ethical discourse."[4] That Barnes places her older subjects into a journalistic frame is noteworthy, but just how far do they gain agency? At times, there remains a tension between the positive focusing on stories of older age in a modernizing world and the erasure of the voices she seeks to highlight. By close reading her series of interviews "Veterans in Harness" (1913) and travel piece "Hem of Manhattan" (1917), I explore the moral implications of only celebrating older age to suggest Barnes overlooks more difficult aspects of representing age and autonomy.

In the final part of the chapter, I examine Barnes's own experience of being reported on in newspaper interviews in her later life. What ethical questions arise as Barnes moved from being the reporter, to being reported on? I turn to philosophers of ageing, Hanne Laceulle and Jan Baars, and their work on counter narratives and self-realization, which advocates for new stories, told by older people, that can offer alternatives to dominant decline narratives.[5] They argue it "requires moral agents with virtues like endurance, steadfastness, courage, creativity and resilience to take the lead in challenging damaging stereotypes."[6] I suggest that Barnes rejects a narrative of decline, which frames older age as a time of biological and creative loss, through correspondence and archival notes. Furthermore, I explore if Barnes acts as a moral agent in creating such counter-narratives, reframing her reclusivity as a creative and courageous mode. Overall, this chapter grapples with what it means to be represented as an autonomous, older person in Barnes's work and life—from the early journalism to her late interviews—as she engages in a tricky balance between representing agency and passivity to varying degrees.

I The Scene of the New: Ageing Represented in Barnes's Early Journalism

In the early twentieth century, Barnes wrote for a variety of periodicals including the *Brooklyn Daily Eagle*, *New York Morning Telegraph*, and *Vanity Fair*. As a freelance reporter, Barnes's commissions hinged on conveying stories that were contemporary, vital, and first-hand. Barnes was not above yielding to what she viewed as the public's vicarious desire to experience the new changes occurring in the city. Within this desire, Barnes was interested in representing the relationship between the observed and the observer. Diane Warren examines the tension between looking and being looked at in Barnes's interviews, which are at their most potent when they "turn their gaze towards the spectator" and the "act of looking."[7] The journalistic gaze is one usually couched by a code of ethics and an attempt to remain unbiased and objective, producing work that can be held accountable and independently judged. Barnes's journalism does not always operate under such constraints. Alex Goody suggests Barnes does not "differentiate between factual journalism and fictional writing," instead combining the two "to foreground the intractability of the 'real' that evades authentic portrayal."[8] Barnes acted as an observer of the city to pull apart the ironies of modern life. In this ironic space, however, there was often little room for journalistic principles. Barnes delighted in language, epigrams, and aphorism, which Nancy Levine notes often led to those being interviewed by Barnes finding the "witty, alternately racy and orotund" words that were placed in their mouths were "unmistakably Barnes's own."[9] Furthermore, using the pseudonym Lydia Steptoe, Barnes was able to create even more distance between herself and her enigmatic reportage style, to anonymously parody the fashionable scenes of New York and Paris from close quarters. As such, in Barnes's interviews it is difficult to disentangle the speaker and subject, as she sets herself up as a *subjective* reporter of modern life, one who is interested in revealing deep, human truths about her subjects through fictional and creative ends.

As a subjective reporter, Barnes often used her audience's desire for instant access to satirize youth culture. Cheryl Plumb outlines how Barnes satirized the association between "newness" and youth culture, often embodied by what she perceived as the cult of the naïve young woman.[10]

Her insider status gives Barnes's coverage authority and a knowing tone. In the article "Against Nature: In Which Everything that is Young, Inadequate and Tiresome is Included in the Term Natural" (1922) Barnes, in the voice of Lydia Steptoe, declares: "I hate the *jeune fille*. There isn't that much youth."[11] Barnes was against displaying the scene of the new as only the purview of the young but was also wary of wealthy middle-aged or older women who sought to insert themselves into the new to position themselves as youthful. In "Becoming Intimate with the Bohemians" (1916), Barnes critiques a middle-aged woman she dubs Madame Bronx, a stuffy mother "heavily laden with jewels" who walks with her "two lanky daughters."[12] Whilst in Greenwich Village, Madame Bronx and her daughters seek out the modern woman, characterized by their bobbed hair and artistic smocks. Elsewhere, Barnes skewers "white-haired ladies with necks encased in flaring Flemish collars" who gathered in women-run, avant-garde tea-rooms to soak up a youthful, European atmosphere.[13] Barnes lampooned all these younger, middle-aged, and older people who might think pursuing the new would lead to social rejuvenation or acceptance. In Barnes's view, one cannot access the vibrance of modernity by mere association to youth culture: it has to be lived.

Rather than the trends of youth culture, Barnes values accumulated life experience, gained through ageing. In *The Confessions of Helen Westley* (1917), the actress archly suggests that youth has been a burden, saying, "to be young, to be beautiful—how mournful, how sad, how ironical."[14] Westley proposes instead that growing older enhances beauty and values the experience of age, bemoaning that a theatrical audience cannot see her face up close, where "every line, every muscle of my countenance is worthy of study."[15] In another interview with actress Yvette Guilbert, Barnes reports that the fifty-two-year-old film performer and former model for Toulouse-Lautrec wears her age "more like a decoration than a calamity, more like a friendship between her and life."[16] Throughout these celebrity interviews, Barnes draws attention to the ways in which ageing and experience are an asset. Lillian Russell is at pains to portray her life experience: "What, after all, is there great in being beautiful? To be a great woman, a great person, one must have suffered."[17] In contrast to a youth-obsessed culture, Russell thanks Barnes "For not having asked [her] a single question about the way I preserve my good looks."[18] In cultural gerontology,

Jan Baars suggests we must have "some deepening of life experience," to understand "that much of what is presented as 'new' amounts to 'more of the same.'"[19] Barnes uses Madame Bronx and the *jeune fille* as ironic devices as they pursue the new on the surface, never realizing they are seeking merely "more of the same" as they attempt to gain access to modernity in the city by following trends. Barnes reserved her admiration for subjects who could embrace both their experience and age.

It is in Barnes's profile of a mysterious "bead-seller," Peter Bender, that we see a sustained exploration of the contrast between new trends aimed at youth culture and the experience of an older, more authentic, foil. Bender is a bead-seller described in a magically "battered and time worn" shop filled with "shining bead tapestries," "mute dim crucifixes," and "the ancient mellowness of the sunlight."[20] Barnes undercuts the urgent presentism associated with fashion with this ancient and timeless scene. The article is accompanied by a photograph of Bender, who stares into the camera in seemingly stiff garb, a high Victorian-style collar at his throat. For Goody, Barnes's illustrations frame her subjects "as art" that Barnes deploys "as a deliberate strategy to deconstruct the difference between the actual and the illusory."[21] The photograph of Bender, who faces the camera, staring into the lens out at the viewer, seems anchored in the past. With closely cropped hair and a gray beard, his eyes collect a few wrinkles, and his mouth is pulled into a knowing smile. Yet the top button is undone, the tie loosened, perhaps indicating something is askew in this old-fashioned portrait. The illusory enters into the way Barnes intervenes and destabilizes some of the signifying meaning of this older man by framing him with strings of beads. Readers at the time would have associated beading with the fringed figure of the flapper, often depicted as the epitome of an alluring and freeing youth culture. Barnes drapes beads around his face like a curtain pulled back, suggesting that, rather than an austere figure, Bender is as trendy as a flapper. Barnes plays with the gaps between reality and illusion, using visual stereotypes of older age to enhance the ironies of Bender and a pedlar of style, beauty, and trends.

Barnes twice establishes in words what the photograph depicts, that Bender is "a small white-haired old man" and an "eccentric old man" even as she playfully juxtaposes this fact with his wise knowledge that extends to bohemian beads, beaded handbags, and handmade girdles, "because

Figure 2.1 "There are Beads and Beads, But Peter Bender Knows Them All," *Brooklyn Citizen*, July 4, 1920.

there are beads and beads, but Bender knows them all."[22] Roland Barthes speaks of text and image as entering into a "parasitic" relationship where the viewer is led to certain conclusions by which the "text loads the image, burdening it with a culture, a moral, an imagination."[23] Juxtaposition is also important for Goody, who suggests the placement of Barnes's articles, short stories, and illustrations are key to her "examination of the moral possibilities" of such a communication with the reading public, one that she approached with an "ambivalent eye" to develop her own subjective stance.[24] When Barnes's reports are placed back into their newspaper context, different readings emerge as her work is put in dialogue with the crowded columns. In the case of Bender, we see the ways in which other news pieces interact with his role as the purveyor of new trends: the older man turned decorative. The article and image aim to destabilize the viewer's expectations of how a wise, older man might function in society, peering out at them from between politics and society news draped in decadent beads. Barnes's journalism offers an intervention into the new scene of the modern city by sharing the stories of older people, using photography and illustration to encourage her audience to witness—and question—the placement of her subjects in both image and text.

II "Veterans in Harness" and "Grey Figures Bent Like Hooks": Case Studies in Observing Older Subjects

In 1913, Barnes worked on an interview series for the *Brooklyn Daily Eagle* titled "Veterans in Harness" which sought to share very specific experiences, interviewing mainly older Irish immigrants to show how their jobs (waiter, conductor, postman, engineer, and physical educationalist) are integral to the operations of city life. Opening each profile with a "scene," Barnes places the reader directly in the present world of the older men being interviewed over their working day: the opening setting brings us into the present moment, the "evening is advancing," the "water is rolling," the "lights are low."[25] This present moment is key to one ethical way of representing these older New Yorkers: as active agents of change and autonomous over their place within the city. As Baars suggests, one central stereotype that older people face is being perceived as unable to live *presently* in their contemporary moment.[26] Barnes's interviews imply otherwise. Rather than focusing on reminiscence, Barnes is instead interested in how older people continue to be crucial contributors to the fabric of the working city. The veterans we meet are of a specific *present* place and time as the series observes these older men in their daily lives to demonstrate how they not only populate the landscape of the early twentieth century but are crucial to its functionality as a modern city.

One way to read Barnes's interviews with the veterans is as an engaged observer who seeks to demonstrate the value and autonomy of these older men. As Christopher Wareham suggests, an ethics of ageing "should place the ageing person at the centre. They should be moral agents or subjects rather than problematic objects in the discourse."[27] The veterans in Barnes's pieces are not only central to the narrative, but in charge of the action. In her interview with tram conductor, "Kid" Connors, they go "on the run," as he is described in dynamic detail amplified by the moving train, "swaying, swinging, six-wheel cars, the jumping, rolling, rock-a-bye four-wheeled cars."[28] As a conductor, Connors's daily life is embedded in the movement of the city, and he is committed to servicing New York's growing population. Barnes revels in connecting the older man with the speed of the city. The haste of the modern city does not overwhelm Connors: rather, he and his colleague, the wise old "motor-man" John Kelley, navigate the tracks as the "din of heavily laden trucks and the sounds of a noisy city from streets full of color" pass them by.[29] Barnes's profile suggests that Connors and Kelley are just as future-orientated and speed-obsessed as any Futurist. The conductor's long life is contrasted to his role in the city, the frantically mobile older person is again firmly placed in present: "year, 1913; time, 3:30," and the future might be "any day."[30] Connors and Kelley operate in the modern city as they continue to contribute as active participants in their work. In the depiction of speed and urgency, Barnes acknowledges the older workers as having newsworthy stories.

Another way to read Barnes's valorization of the veterans' work, though, is from a more ambiguous position. Although Barnes's interviews seek to give the veterans autonomy, her subjective perspective sometimes blurs the lines between the celebratory and the metaphorical. Wareham continues that an ethics of ageing "should reflect the idea that ageing occurs, if not throughout the whole course of life, then at least through most of it."[31] For Barnes, the veterans are fixed as old men and their longevity is mined for metaphorical value. Metaphor underpins the profile of "Uncle Tom" Baird, who is the oldest interviewee at eighty-nine years of age. Barnes focuses on his sixty-five-year-long career as a Union Ferry Company engineer, highlighting his labor as a feat of old age.[32] Baird's "endless gripping" of the rope mirrors his "long grip on life," the years stretching behind him reflecting and glorifying his hard work.[33] It was not only Barnes who foregrounded Baird's continued activity and dedication to work. His obituary appeared in the *Brooklyn Daily Eagle* in 1917, four years after Barnes interviewed him. Here, again, Baird's commitment to work is placed as his most important attribute as the paper reports he passed away at ninety-two years of age. As "the oldest marine engineer and Freemason and Oddfellow in this State," it is newsworthy that he was still "very active" and known to socialize with his "old cronies" from the ferry company, "retirin[g] upon a pension at the age of 90 years."[34] Work and activity are foregrounded in both Barnes's interview and the *Brooklyn Daily Eagle*'s obituary in ways that glorify and fix him in an active, older age and yet which obscure political questions of pensions, retirement, and class that see these veterans work so long.

There is perhaps, then, an *unethical* power dynamic between the interviewer (Barnes) and interview subjects (the veterans). Catherine Degnen suggests that when interviewing older subjects, the autonomous "self [is] created in its telling, in its performance, and in its reception by others."[35] The ideal interview would center the speaker and be used as a tool for an individual to express their identity. In the veteran interviews, each man's experience is mediated through Barnes's fascination with contrasting their advanced years with their active, social participation. By aligning the men so closely with their work, the interviews risk reducing the veterans' lived experience to nothing but labor and longevity, even as Barnes purports to witness their individual contributions to the city. On the other hand, Barnes's interviews present the veterans as the backbone of the modern city, as immigrant laborers who have spent their whole lives in service to New York. Barnes challenges the youthful purview of the new by representing these older men as contributing to the social fabric of the growing city. The question of autonomy lies at the very heart of Barnes's interviews with the veterans: how much can we take what they say at face value, and how far is Barnes foregrounding their lived experience? As Goody suggests, the veterans are editorialized by Barnes, as each opening scene implies their economic and political status, often waking in the dead of night to begin their work, their labor often unseen.[36] The reality of their work is couched by class and identity, whereby autonomy is privileged over reckoning with the lived difficulties that might underpin their experiences. For Jennifer

Parks, Martha Holstein, and Mark Waymack, the neoliberal focus on individual agency and healthy ageing "obscures the fact that we ultimately lack control over aging, illness, disability, suffering, and death." And as we grow older, it becomes difficult to "admit this lack of autonomy."[37] Barnes's profiles of the veterans privilege positive images of autonomy and wisdom over a more realistic portrayal of her subjects' inner lives and any difficult realities of ageing.

In contrast to the celebratory tone of the veterans' profiles, we find in another feature an example of Barnes actively ignoring more difficult lived experiences of ageing. In an article titled "Hem of Manhattan" (1917) for the *New York Morning Telegraph*, Barnes takes a yacht trip around the island, which is advertised as a pleasure cruise.[38] Barnes notes the other participants are conventional tourists, more naïve young women dressed in childish "gingham and dimity gowns" who wish to witness the "educational" parts of New York but, as Barnes sardonically intones, "they didn't see it."[39] Barnes instead ironically describes the pleasure cruise as "three hours and a half [of] misery, poverty, death, old age, and insanity."[40] The cruise passes by a series of islands housing prisons, asylums, and care homes. Barnes describes how they pass an "Old Man's home," where the older men appear as "[g]ray figures bent like hooks" moving around verdant gardens.[41] The older men are contrasted to the blooming garden as "futile pollen […] whose scattering will bring no profit of the world."[42] Unlike the veterans, who continue to contribute to the city through their labor, these men are characterized as an economic drain. Entering the last stage of life, they exist on the periphery of the modern city. Barnes imagines her reader saying "[e]nough, enough, this was a pleasure trip! Pass on and describe its beauties."[43] As a rhetorical device, this statement is aimed at the other participants on the boat tour and her readers, but it also allows Barnes to "pass on" from a difficult subject. Barnes is invested in reporting on only one type of older person in the modern city.

By taking a subjective stance as a reporter, Barnes's observations become compromised by what DeFalco calls the image of the "disdained double."[44] Disdain arises on seeing the image of the older self reflected back in another subject and the perceived dependency of "old age" impacts what once seemed like an autonomous, unwavering selfhood.[45] In her observations of Manhattan's forgotten, institutionalized population,

Barnes regards the older men on the margins of New York as not only worthy of forgetting but figures to be feared as a symbol of what the future holds. Although the men are only introduced for a moment, the act of looking away indicates a type of uncanny representation best forgotten. Chris Gilleard and Paul Higgs note how modern media offer conflicting representations of ageing and older age, alternating between "super-hero seniors" such as rock stars and models and "pitiable old people placed in care homes."[46] In Barnes's journalism we see this same dichotomy replicated. How best to acknowledge and represent older people's autonomy is a difficult topic within the ethics of ageing. Images of the "third age" or "young old" dominate, representing the experience of older people who remain active, solvent consumers, and workers in society.[47] Barnes's early journalism provides a much-needed perspective against the dominant discourse of youth cultures that often accompanies early twentieth-century representations of the "new," as she favored accumulated wisdom and experience. Yet, in doing so, perhaps these pieces overemphasized positives and agency.

III On Being Represented: Barnes's Counter-Narratives Against Decline

On her return to Greenwich Village in 1940, Barnes saw her position evolve from being a public reporter *of* the city's action to someone now worthy of being reported *on*. Even as she returned to the site of her earlier journalistic escapades—her residence at Patchin Place was a mere three blocks over from Washington Square—she no longer had a platform to report on the new Village inhabitants. Barnes stayed at Patchin Place for the next forty years, until her death in 1982. Her longevity produced a lasting anecdote, reported on by Phyllis Rose in the *New York Times*: fellow Patchin Place resident, E. E. Cummings, would often throw stones at Barnes's windows to enquire "are you still alive, Djuna?"[48] As something of an apocryphal account, this comment encapsulates the way Barnes has been presented in her later years: as reticent and reclusive. To complicate matters, Barnes somewhat cultivated the image of herself as a recluse, writing to Natalie Barney, "I live the life of a Trappist."[49] In this version of events, Barnes was left behind by new modernization taking place in a rapidly changing New York, just like the older people she had once reported on. Indeed, many critical volumes on Barnes have been tempted, as Caselli notes, to "set up the opposition between bohemian Djuna and elderly Trappist," which is, in essence, a story of decline.[50]

"Decline narratives" can be reductive narratives. Margaret Gullette defines decline narratives as normative cultural scripts that frame old age only as a period of loss and decreasing capability.[51] When decline is framed as a biological inevitability, Gullette argues, this, in turn, "constrains narrative options in our culture."[52] Ageism results when there is a lack of opportunity to tell a variety of stories about ageing. Therefore, Laceulle and Baars argue that "counter-narratives" to the dominant discourse of decline are ethical interventions, mobilizing "self-realization as a moral concept."[53] Laceulle and Baars define an effective and ethical counter-narrative as one that enhances "the capabilities people possess to create, cultivate and further develop their moral identity, expressing who they are and who they want to become, instead of seeing them merely as representatives of a marginalized social category."[54] As such, within this narrative approach, all manner of stories of older age must be heard, making room for issues of frailty and finitude without being defined by them, or only offering a limiting version of superhero ageing in their place.

One example of Barnes's counter-narrative to reports of decline can be seen in her responses to a German newspaper article. In 1970, an article in the *Frankfurter Zeitung* reported that Barnes was in dire straits, making a comparison between her once glamorous reputation to what they now saw as her reduced status. The article described Barnes as living in "complete seclusion" and "impoverished and lonely," occupying a room that "consists almost entirely of books, a table crowded with papers, a bed; a small side room, a kitchenette, in which one cannot turn around," as well as suggesting Barnes only lived off ice cream and suffered from a variety of illnesses.[55] Now, as the older subject being observed, Barnes is reported on as an older woman living without autonomy, lonely in an overcrowded home and subsisting, childishly, on ice cream. To accept this version of events at face value, however, is to also give power to a one-sided decline narrative. When one fan, a woman named Helga Mulhauser, sent Barnes money and a bunch of lavender after reading the article, Barnes wrote back to say she could not accept the gifts and to reassure her that "I am not moping in a dusty corner, I am not living alone from being neglected."[56] In these declarative statements, Barnes takes what Cruikshank might call "the ultimate countercultural stance" as she seeks to establish her worthiness and value in the face of the dominant script.[57] Importantly, too, Barnes here hints at living alone through choice not from neglect or loneliness, reframing the reclusiveness as a decision rather than an inevitable determinant of older age.

We find, in other private correspondence, that Barnes again sought to reclaim her autonomy after this article was published. Samuel Beckett read the same article as Mulhauser and found the report so bleak that he was inspired to send Barnes a sum of $3,375. Barnes accepted this donation whilst also disputing its necessity. After reading a translation of the article, she wrote to Beckett again to emphasize that she "must disclaim any likeness to me."[58] Barnes refuted the idea that her living situation represented a narrative of dependency by instead reporting to Beckett on her newly painted rooms as a site "where I write and take my savage pleasure."[59] Indeed, she writes that living on is a must, and she explains to Beckett that "[i]t's dying that has now become prohibitive. At this moment I am working again."[60] From one writer to another, Barnes stresses the importance of her ongoing, creative inner life, stressing, "I am not 'bitter' because I am not 'better' appreciated [...] I am (occasionally) savage about the condition of the world. That's all."[61] Barnes's responses to this article suggest that to lose any independence would signal an end to the identity she had spent a lifetime cultivating and she is at pains to explain her own perspective. Indeed, in this letter, Barnes's counter-narrative creates and cultivates the self-realization of an author flourishing at work, expressing something about who she is and who she wants to become. Barnes's living conditions are reclaimed in her letter to Beckett as an active, working environment of a productive writer, affording her the agency she imbued many of her older subjects with in her own early reportage.

When it came to other reports on her late life, Barnes also privately asserted her autonomy as she made notes on articles and kept them in her archive. In 1971, aged seventy-nine, Barnes was interviewed for the *New York Times* by Henry Raymont under the headline, "Djuna Barnes, Writer, Emerges from Solitude." Raymont reports how Barnes "light-heartedly controlled" occasional slips into the biographic reminiscences she had vowed to ban from the interview."[62] Again, Barnes was characterized as a reclusive subject. For her own record, Barnes wrote different comments and marked passages on the four copies she kept of the piece. The comments on each individual copy are in different colored pens, suggesting that she revisited these articles at different times to convey different feelings about this public positioning of herself. The interview, Barnes writes, is "mostly bosh," the description of *Nightwood* that opens the article is "nonsense," "rot," and "silly," and she queries the idea that she only has a couple of friends left in E. E. Cummings and Henry Miller by writing: "Don't know Miller, not particularly fond of Cummings."[63] That Barnes insisted on correcting the record intimates that she sought to retrieve a voice often lost in the gaps of being represented by someone else in the future, rewriting her archive to make sure her version of events could be found.

In Barnes's archive, we find counter-narratives to the dominant perspective of decline that offer more nuance than her early reportage. On the one hand, that her modernist reportage so centrally includes older men and women demonstrates an ethical refusal to associate the modern world only with youth culture. Instead, Barnes presented New York in the early twentieth century as a city indebted to older citizens who had built and continued to maintain its key signifiers of modernity: be that Peter Bender's bead shop, the veterans who kept the new elevated trains moving, or the labor activists who continued campaigning. But, for all that older people are central in Barnes's narratives, they are not always fully rounded subjects. Barnes oscillates between lauding the positive attributes of active ageing to ignoring the lived difficulties of New York's institutionalized population. In her later years, Barnes found herself the subject of the ethical quagmire of how to represent, witness, and truly relate an older person's experience. As mid-century New York once again changed around her, Barnes began to be written about as a fading light. Her own continuing writing practice was ignored in favor of a narrative depicting her as the bohemian, modern woman turned reclusive eccentric. To reflect on our own ethical position as literary critics, we must remain aware that depicting Barnes as retreating, silent, or inflexible might preclude us from paying attention to her active, creative agency in later life. As per Laceulle and Baars, we must not overemphasize this activity as the whole story as she also embraced and performed the idea of being reclusive, living monastically, and finding difficulty in daily life. In Barnes's "savage pleasure" there remains something vicious or unrestrained, even painful. As Daniela Caselli reminds us, instead of looking for conclusive answers, the "real" Barnes "cannot simply be discovered, but needs to be read, and such readings are never definitive."[64] In later years, Barnes conveyed a deep understanding of both the pleasure and pain being represented as an older artist. As such, Barnes's supposed retreat from modernist networks is not a story of decline but an attempt to take back control of her story, albeit to more private ends than her early, more public, journalism.

CHAPTER THREE

The Solar Plexus and Animalistic Power in D. H. Lawrence and Isadora Duncan

Carrie Rohman

The importance of the solar plexus as a source of "knowing" in modernist work has yet to be fully acknowledged or theorized.[1] This physical energetic center, typically described within the chakra systems as the third "navel chakra," is generally understood to reside in the lower abdomen, but it has also been imagined in areas higher up in the torso. Due to the increased global prominence of yoga practice in recent decades, many will be familiar with this chakra, associated with the color yellow and with ideas about personal power. In the period associated with high modernism (1890–1945), the solar plexus emerges as a kind of modernist organ, privileged by writers and artists of the period as a site of corporeal awareness and inspiration. D. H. Lawrence and Isadora Duncan in particular champion the solar plexus for its connection to intuitive psychic formations and innovative artistic developments. Moreover, both thinkers' centering of the sun—their solar imaginaries—bespeak a broader environmental ethic or ecological situating of the human within its cosmic and earthly webs. These modernist attunements to the solar plexus highlight an awareness of interbeing, and assert that the living in general are organically connected. They further enact various forms of attractive vitalism, a drawing together of human and/or nonhuman forces and powers, which we can connect to recent work on new materialisms that emphasize how matter itself has power and life and agency.[2] Moreover, Duncan's and Lawrence's attachments to a solar, embodied consciousness resonate with current questions about the importance of decentering overly cognitive assessments of art and aesthetics, and thus reverberate with a number of contemporary ethical frameworks that restructure human relations and values as creatural and entangled in the more-than-human world. For instance, Taney Roniger has recently discussed an arising ethical position in the art world "in which the individualistic, oppositional, ego-oriented worldview of the dying order gives way to one marked by integration, interdependence, and a passionate mutualism."[3]

Both Duncan and Lawrence place immense emphasis on the solar plexus as an embodied source or center that is "outside" of traditional cognition in their respective work. The intensity or level of the privileging of this bodily constellation in their philosophies can hardly be overstated. Here I focus on Duncan's claims about her choreographic practice in her life writing, but also in her detailed theoretical essays about dance. I also draw from the current practices of third-generation Duncan dancers who work within a direct line of her teachings and practices, as they have been handed down in the last century. Lawrence's somewhat genre-defying and infrequently studied works, *Psychoanalysis and the Unconscious* (1921) and *Fantasia of the Unconscious* (1922), include his more philosophical reflections on the solar plexus, and his short story, "Sun," provides a fictional example that is indicative of his solar ethics, an ethics which is partially marked by a maternal discourse of somatic exchange. Both Lawrence and Duncan develop new ethical frameworks that de-center human and rationalistic conventions in favor of ecological and creatural energetic commitments and experiments, wherein human being and acting are relational, embodied, vitalistic forms of "knowing." Their craft varies, as Lawrence depicts these ethical commitments through his characters and their bodily experiences and modes of consciousness, while Duncan primarily enacts and performs her solar ethics through performance and choreography (and also theorizes these views in her essays about dance). But there are striking correlations between their artistic and philosophical ethics, including the overcoming of conventional and normative social and aesthetic forms and the need for humans to be receptive toward cosmic and inhuman forces. And, again, a strikingly maternal set of values subtends Lawrence's ideas about humans' "first" knowing, so that umbilical and womb-centered concepts take on a powerful primacy in his ethical systems. Duncan also frequently places the child, woman, and creature at the center of her thinking and her artistic innovations. She was famously known for dancing while pregnant, a truly bold act in that era, and for her post-performance commentaries that at times highlighted feminist views.[4] Thus a bodily and at times gendered eco-ethics often coheres around solar imaginaries, for both of these modernists.

One of Duncan's most often-cited claims, which comes from her autobiography, circulates around the idea that she cultivated her most significant insights for dance innovations by attuning to her own solar plexus. Duncan insists that her advances in overcoming tired, historically normative dance movement—by harnessing a "natural" and authentic creatural way of dancing—flowed from the innate wisdom of her solar plexus. The relevant passage comes from Duncan's autobiography, *My Life* (1927):

> I spent long days and nights in the studio seeking that dance which might be the divine expression of the human spirit through the medium of the body's movement. For hours I would stand quite still, my two hands folded between my breasts, covering the solar plexus. [...] I was seeking, and finally discovered, the central spring of all movement, the crater of motor power, the unity from which all diversions of movements are born.[5]

Duncan imagines the solar plexus as above the abdomen and between the breasts, therefore "higher up in the torso" than some other thinkers, as I mentioned earlier. Carrie Preston has recently reiterated that Duncan cites this area as the central source of human movement. Preston focuses on the solar plexus as the soul's organ and "the motor propelling dance."[6] She rightly points out how thinkers at the time often associated the solar plexus with torsion and certain industrial actions.[7] But a few lines beyond the mention of a motor in Duncan's autobiography, we find the following elaboration of this movement source, as Duncan juxtaposes ballet's axis, the lower spine, with the solar plexus for modern dance: "I on the contrary sought the source of the spiritual expression to flow into the channels of the body filling it with vibrating light [...] when I listened to music the rays and vibrations of the music streamed to this one fount of light within me."[8] While the motor image is compelling for various reasons, I tend to read the "motor" as a contemporary technological development that Duncan uses for troping or translating a more trans-historical and "natural" vibratory force, which is here associated with rays and eruptions of light in the body's "sun."

As I have discussed in earlier work, Duncan's ideas about rhythm and the vibratory connect human creativity to supple and innovative biological and cosmological forces.[9] The concept of vibration or cosmic rhythm is central to her theorizing in *The Art of the Dance*. Duncan's ideas about the foundational teaching of movement to children, for instance, are deeply bioaesthetic; vibration, in Duncan's writings, can be understood as the harnessing and displaying—the participatory intensifying—of cosmic forces or possibilities. These participations inevitably link the artist, the dancer, and the child to the forces of the earth, to matter, to "natural" rhythms and animals. In this connection, Duncan's "universal gesture," as taught by Lori Belilove of the Isadora Duncan Dance Foundation, involves an acknowledgment of the earth and sky, and the greeting of other beings, including "animal friends."[10]

Moreover, as Jeanne Bresciani, Artistic Director and Director of Education for the Isadora Duncan International Institute, notes, the "Duncan Vibrato" is a fundamental concept in Duncan technique.[11] Bresciani describes this vibration as the aftermath of energy that emerges from the solar plexus and runs through and beyond fingers, toes, and eyelashes, and then through the head, which tilts back.[12] In this sense, the solar plexus is understood to be a kind of ubiquitous power source that animates the entire dancing body, that energizes its experience of movement, performance, and dance-being for the modernist (and modern) dancer. That Bresciani describes the vibrato of the solar plexus as energetically running all the way through the dancer's eyelashes emphasizes its powerful and pervasive potency in Duncan's conception and performance of the dancing body. This creative dynamism of the solar plexus within the Duncan legacy connects to neo-vitalisms that have recently developed, with emphases on the ideas of Bergson and Deleuze, in particular. For instance, Elizabeth Grosz notes that

> Each [Bergson and Deleuze] distinguishes life as a kind of *contained dynamism*, a dynamism within a porous boundary, that

feeds from and returns to the chaos which surrounds it something immanent within the chaotic whole: life as a complex fold of the chemical and the physical that reveals something not given within them, something new, an emergence, the ordered force of invention.[13]

The vibratory animation of the solar plexus that radiates outward even through the eyelashes recalls a number of Deleuzian concepts such as impersonal life, immanence, and various more-than-human becomings. In my later discussion of Lawrence here, I will specifically return to Deleuze's ideas about the aesthetic tendency in general as an animal capacity which precedes the human, a concept that has been central to my own theorizing of bioaesthetic forces in literature, art, and performance.

Like Duncan's, Lawrence's centering of the sun—his solar imaginary—is similarly pivotal in his broad taxonomies of human ontology in the modernist age. Lawrence is repeatedly keen to emphasize that the living in general are all organically connected. In *Apocalypse* (1931), he writes:

> That I am part of the earth my feet know perfectly, and my blood is part of the sea. My soul knows that I am part of the human race, my soul is an organic part of the great human soul, as my spirit is part of my nation. In my own very self, I am part of my family. There is nothing of me that is alone and absolute except my mind, and we shall find that the mind has no existence by itself, it is only the glitter of the sun on the surface of the waters.
>
> So that my individualism is really an illusion. I am part of the great whole, and I can never escape ...
>
> What we want is to destroy our false, inorganic connections, especially those related to money, and re-establish the living organic connections, with the cosmos, the sun and earth, with mankind and nation and family. Start with the sun, and the rest will slowly, slowly happen.[14]

This primacy—"start" with the sun—is clearly echoed in the absolute centrality that Lawrence gives to the physical/metaphorical power of the solar plexus (and even the cardiac plexus) in his extensive attempts to theorize a kind of human unconscious or preconscious in *Psychoanalysis and the Unconscious* and *Fantasia of the Unconscious*. Largely motivated by Lawrence's rebuffing of Freudian principles, these works center bodily organs or regions in an attempt to map out the psychic and living foundations of human beings. He insists that the most basic and primal "knowing" for human beings is linked to the solar plexus, a physical center located in the stomach, or behind the navel (physiognomy charts often place it slightly higher than the navel, deep inside the abdominal cavity). Early in *Psychoanalysis and the Unconscious*, Lawrence describes his view of the unconscious as "that essential unique nature of every individual creature, which is, by its very nature, unanalyzable, undefinable, inconceivable," and for which he laments "*soul* would be a better word" if that term were not so distorting.[15] He goes on to ask,

> If, however, the unconscious is inconceivable, how do we know it at all? We know it by direct experience. All the best part of knowledge is inconceivable. We know the sun. [...] It is necessary for us to know the unconscious, or we cannot live, just as it is necessary for us to know the sun.[16]

While Duncan does not theorize the role of the solar plexus as intensively as Lawrence does, her claim of discovering her greatest source of spontaneous creatural dancing in this same bodily location illustrates a decisive modernist praxis that overlaps to some degree with Lawrence's notion of knowing by "direct experience." Duncan's emphasis might be said to dwell in her refusal of conventional and normative forms of dance practice, throughout her quest for and development of spontaneous movement; Lawrence's own characters, in "Sun," and also in novels like *Women in Love*, also struggle with fixed normative roles, and they work to break free from social and embodied expectations through spontaneity. To some degree, there is a passivity for the human actor that both thinkers require: we must wait for the energies of nature to inspire our dance movement (Duncan), and we must wait for the sun to revivify our "first" center of knowing, if we have lost our way by becoming too rationalist (Lawrence).

Lawrence continues to theorize the importance of the solar plexus in *Fantasia of the Unconscious*. Here, he includes a chapter called "Plexuses, Planes and So On," in which he argues that the solar plexus is the source of an other-than-rational knowledge in humans, just as it is in animals:

> The primal consciousness in man is pre-mental, and has nothing to do with cognition. It is the same as in the animals. [...] The first seat of our primal consciousness is the solar plexus, the great nerve-centre situated in the middle-front of the abdomen. From this centre we are first dynamically conscious. For the primal consciousness is always dynamic, and never, like mental consciousness, static. Thought, let us say what we will about its magic powers, is instrumental only, the soul's finest instrument for the business of living. Thought is just a means to action and living. But life and action rise actually at the great centres of dynamic consciousness.
>
> The solar plexus, the greatest and most important centre of our dynamic consciousness, is a sympathetic centre. At this main centre of our first-mind we know as we can never mentally know. Primarily we know, each man, each living creature knows, profoundly and satisfactorily and without question, that *I am I*.[17]

Like Duncan, Lawrence associates the solar plexus with a specific kind of knowledge. But it is a knowledge more in the blood—to use Lawrence's own terminology—than in the head.[18] Craig Gordon discusses Lawrence's "dynamic consciousness" and "embodied consciousness" in the context of tubercular discourses and epidemics at the time, which long affected Lawrence's personal health. Gordon frames the powerful, healthy solar plexus in Lawrence's writing as opposing the weak-chested and stooped figure of the tubercular, and notes that Lawrence was "spectacularly reticent" about the disease that would ultimately take his life.[19] This dynamic corporeal knowledge-force of the solar plexus is the same as in the animals, Lawrence insists. The creatural way of being in the world that

Lawrence's characters seek throughout his oeuvre might well be linked to the becoming-animal and becoming-wave that Duncan seeks in her artistic practice. Like Lawrence, Duncan rejects a flatly cognitive notion of aesthetic power, writing in her section on the iconic solar plexus experience referenced earlier:

> After many months, when I had learned to concentrate all my force to this one Centre I found that thereafter when I listened to music the rays and vibrations of the music streamed to this one fount of light within me—there they reflected themselves [sic] in Spiritual Vision *not the brain's mirror*, but the soul's, and from this vision I could express them in Dance—.[20]

As mentioned earlier, Lawrence associates the soul with a preconscious or unconscious essence that he locates in the solar plexus, rather than in the "head" or brain. His account of the brain in *Psychoanalysis and the Unconscious* makes plain his contempt for the overly mental:

> The brain is, if we may use the word, the terminal instrument of the dynamic consciousness. It transmutes what is a creative flux into a certain fixed cypher. [...] [The idea] is thrown off from life, as leaves are shed from a tree, or as feathers from a bird. Ideas are the dry, unliving, insentient plumage which intervenes between us and the circumambient universe. The mind is the instrument of instruments; it is not a creative reality.[21]

Moreover, Lawrence describes the "primal" consciousness that radiates from the solar plexus as always "dynamic" and never "static." He essentially makes the claim that primal knowledge is knowledge that *moves*. Pairing Duncan's and Lawrence's attentions to the solar plexus reveals how this physical center was understood by modernist thinkers as a seat of creatural consciousness. We might note that neither of them ever possessed what might be called a "complete" philosophy. Lawrence's ideas especially were always changing and evolving, and as they both died at relatively young ages, we lack a very mature set of theories from each artist. Yet the provisional and moving knowledges they do provide might be said to uncannily mirror a solar image that continues to radiate outward, seeking its living manifestations in ever new concepts and artistic forms. And thus, their ethical platforming of difference, the new, change, and more-than-human movement also has fascinating overlaps with the "minor" figures of woman and child.

Lawrence's ideas about the centrality of the solar plexus are further refined in connection to the mother–child dyad, the umbilical cord, certain pulse-rhythms, and "wireless" maternal communications in his treatises on the unconscious. Movement itself continues to be a crucial element of these dynamics. As Layla Salter explains of Lawrence, "Oedipus was a term that forced him into dialogue with Freud and inspired key beliefs regarding the mother and son connection that he would revisit throughout his career."[22] Of course, his novel *Sons and Lovers* (1913) takes the mother–child dyad as one of its principal themes, and Lawrence insists in *Fantasia* on the primacy of the parental connection. There Lawrence claims that:

> A child in the womb can have no *idea* of the mother. I think orthodox psychology will allow us so much. And yet the child in the womb must be dynamically conscious of the mother. Otherwise how could it maintain a definite and progressively developing relation to her. This consciousness, however is utterly non-ideal, non-mental, purely dynamic, a matter of dynamic polarized intercourse of vital vibrations, as an exchange of wireless messages which are never translated from the pulse-rhythm into speech, because they have no need to be.[23]

Lawrence's emphasis on wordless, dynamic pulse-rhythms brings to mind Jane Bennett's work on vibrant matter, and thus the associations between Lawrence and Duncan link fruitfully with recent work in new materialisms. When Bennett describes a vital materialism as articulating "the elusive idea of a materiality that is *itself* heterogeneous, itself a differential of intensities" where "there is no point of pure stillness, no indivisible atom that is not itself aquiver with virtual force," we ought to think of Lawrence and Duncan, and their theories of pulsating, non-ideal and non-mental moving forces that are fundamental to creatural being and artmaking.[24]

Returning to the question of the child as one of the keystones in Duncan's theories, her essay "Youth and the Dance" helps situate the role of the child and of the childlike in her theoretical taxonomy. She opens this essay by claiming the following: "The child is gloriously full of life. He leaps endlessly, filled with the intoxication of movement. He is a young animal, growing in the midst of a joyous exaltation, drawing in with the intensity of all his being the forces for his future life" (the use of the male pronoun seems mostly conventional; Duncan trained a few boys, but mostly girls).[25] We can imagine that she meant these statements to describe all children in an untrained state. Duncan's description of the child resonates with her broader vibratory bioaesthetics, that I have discussed earlier in this chapter. The child is more animal than human, a creature exalting in intensities and forces that are harnessed for the future or the new.

Salter is once again helpful in emphasizing that the dynamic consciousness the child has of the mother particularly is due, in Lawrence's view, to the direct connection with the "maternal blood-stream" that is facilitated by the numinous solar plexus center, which exists "under the navel."[26] Thus the child's "blood-consciousness," a concept so central to Lawrence's creatural cosmology, is fundamentally linked to this plexus, and to the "current" that flows between mother and child:

> the great centre, where, in the womb, your life first sparkled in individuality. This is the centre that drew the gestating maternal bloodstream upon you, in the nine-months lurking, drew it on you for your increase. This is the centre whence the navel-string broke, but where the invisible string of dynamic consciousness, like a dark electric current connecting you with the rest of life, will never break until you die and depart from corporate individuality.[27]

Salter reinforces the point that Lawrence views the solar plexus as, in a very real sense, the fountain of life itself, and Salter elaborates the connections between Lawrence's mysterious life force and Bergson's *élan vital*, which Lawrence directly references on page 96 of *Fantasia*.[28] While Salter makes various points about Lawrence describing blood-consciousness as a human capacity, with Bergson's ideas exceeding the human, my own work and that of other ecocritics has repeatedly framed Lawrence's blood-consciousness as a posthumanist, creatural force that ought to be understood as transspecies.

Lawrence's short story "Sun" is naturally an important text for thinking through his solar theories.[29] "Sun" opens on a diagnostic note, since Juliet's doctors order up a solar encounter: "'Take her away, into the sun,' the doctors said."[30] Many critics have noted the way this line echoes the instructions of Lawrence's own doctor to have him convalesce at the ranch in New Mexico in 1925.[31] Despite her very civilized skepticism—"She herself was sceptical of the sun"—Juliet permits herself "to be carried away, with her child, and a nurse, and her mother, over the sea," to Sicily, where she is to convalesce.[32] It is worth noting that the maternal connection is amplified here with the child, the nurse, and the mother comprising Juliet's companions. Motherhood is, importantly, a source of frustration for Juliet at the story's outset: "The child irritated her, and preyed on her peace of mind. She felt so horribly, ghastly responsible for him: as if she must be responsible for every breath he drew. And that was torture to her, to the child, and to everybody else concerned."[33]

Once Juliet really begins to surrender to the sun, her transformation gets underway. The sun's power is registered first in her breasts, the organs that Lawrence theorizes as "seeing": "The breasts themselves are as two eyes."[34] In the short story, Lawrence writes, "Soon, however, she felt the sun inside them [her breasts], warmer than ever love had been, warmer than milk or the hands of her baby."[35] The sun takes Juliet beyond her "merely" human forms of affection and serves as a spur to larger environmental forms of embodied knowledge. The emphasis on breasts and drinking milk echo Lawrence's claims about the solar plexus being the "first great fountain and issue of infantile consciousness."[36] He continues, "At the solar plexus the new psyche acts in a mode of attractive vitalism, drawing its objective unto itself as by vital magnetism. Here it drinks in, as it were, the contiguous universe, as during the womb-period it drank from the living continuum of the mother."[37] It is notable that the solar plexus in Lawrence's framework has this over-arching connection to maternal powers and energies. Lawrence is often reasonably called to account for his "phallic" ideologies, and yet, what can be identified as his feminist predilections are often just as compelling, in terms of his philosophical views. This particular kind of intersubjective, vitalistic knowing is a cardinal value in Lawrence's intellectual and artistic systems, and its prime exemplar is the knowing between mother and child.

Juliet's initial encounters with the sun also produce a kind of catholic physical engulfing. The sun does not privilege mind over body, nor does it privilege bodily sectors: the sun "faced down to her with his look of blue fire, and enveloped her breasts and her face, her throat, her tired belly, her knees, her thighs and her feet."[38] This image clearly implies that *all* of Juliet connects with the sun; she is transformed in part because the sun does not make distinctions. The "shape" of the solar is worth considering, in finer detail. Its complete radial and outward energetic orientation, a quality almost always represented in human images with outward-reaching flames, lines up with many of Lawrence's philosophical values. We might see the form of this image-energy as particularly suited to Lawrence's interests in creating new ethical concepts and metaphors for living and being, rather than remaining caught in outmoded models or languages. The outward limbic reaching of the solar also resonates with a kind of teleo-searching that Whitehead indicates is central to the most basic organismic kind of creativity and change that characterizes life and matter at its most foundational. In fact, solar flames mirror human or creatural extensions of self into the unknown ecological surround and could be viewed as limbic or tentacle-like.

The seemingly idiosyncratic question of limbs appears in recent discussions of process philosophy and the interweaving of human and nonhuman forces and dynamics. William Connolly, for instance, during his discussion of Whitehead's concept of the eternal object and "real creativity in human and nonhuman processes" mentions the "repetition with variation of certain patterns in leaves, wings, and mammal limbs" as patterns that persist in the current cosmic epoch.[39] In this discussion, he is exploring the ways that different thinkers understand the emergence of the genuinely new amidst systems of relative stability. Connolly considers how Whitehead construes forms or tendencies that resist entropy or tend to cohere in a given epoch of "chronotime," and comments: "[t]o what extent does the march of real creativity in human and nonhuman processes require eternal objects to sustain them? It seems to me, now at least, that a universe of real creativity could be marked by flexible *tendencies* toward patterns that persist and evolve as the world changes."[40] Connolly then turns to the idea of "preadaptations" in evolved systems, which set preconditions for the creative development of new functions or abilities (but do not "pre-ordain" those changes). His prime example comes from Brian Goodwin, who suggests that "the wings of primitive birds set preadaptations from which the limbs of animals and humans eventually evolved."[41]

Also compelling here is the way in which the limbs or appendages of the living in general can be seen as both actually performing—but also marking in a more "representational" mode—the "teleodynamic searching" that Connolly and others have identified as central to the basic organismic creativity of all living beings. Connolly picks up the term teleodynamic from Terrence Deacon, who describes living organisms as self-maintaining, correcting, and reproducing.[42] Connolly goes on to conjecture about how organisms affect creative self-transformations in light of work by such figures as Whitehead and Nietzsche. In relation to Lawrence, these analogies tend to give the sun an organismic quality, and further attest to his broad animism, in which he sees all things as having an internal energy-force. The process of teleodynamic searching, by which beings "test" the unfolding of their own emergent newness or otherness within the world of becoming, seems especially suited to the kinds of experiments in being that Lawrence's characters often undertake, and to the overcomings that Duncan sought in her artistic endeavors. The living organism's reaching outward through extremities or limbs both is and represents its morpho-dynamic, creative becoming-other in the world. This, we can say, is a most fundamental creative property of life itself, and Lawrence and Duncan seem especially biotic in their creative commitments. In fact, Lawrence uses additional images in *Psychoanalysis* and *Fantasia* that reprise these energetic qualities of outward "shoots," rays, or limbs. In *Psychoanalysis*, Lawrence tries to provoke the reader by arguing that "We are forced to attribute to a star-fish, or to a nettle, its own particular and integral consciousness," and a few lines later he writes of primal consciousness as "spinning the nerves and brain as a web for its own motion, like some subtle spider. [...] [the] spinning spider of the first human consciousness."[43] While his analogies are seemingly tossed off for the larger purpose of querying "the birth of consciousness," there is clearly a kind of somatic specificity to star-fish and spiders, with their radial limbs, that suggests a similar energetic and outward movement or orientation, like the solar plexus.

Returning to Lawrence's story, the "de-civilizing" effects of sunning are immediately registered in Juliet's reaction to her child, and so the story serves to emphasize the primal mother–child dynamic that Lawrence insists is fundamental to the workings of the solar plexus. Again, Lawrence is partly motivated in his work on the solar plexus by a frustration with Freudian and Jungian ideas, but his own theories sometimes resemble them.[44] Juliet's boy is needy and clinging during their initial time in the Mediterranean, but rather than return this "love anguish" to her son, she removes his clothing and orders him to play out of doors. Because he still embodies the self-consciousness of the socialized, the child is frightened and resists this freedom. Juliet, however, is indifferent to his "trepidation" and vows that the boy will not learn to be like his father, "[l]ike a worm that the sun has never seen."[45] Once Juliet decides to strip her son of the trappings of civilization, Lawrence immediately informs us that she is "no longer vitally interested in the child," and, more importantly, that he "thrived all the more for it."[46]

As I have noted in earlier work, the familial returns through the back door in this story, since Juliet's relationship with the sun is figured as a heterosexual, and thus potentially reproductive one; she thinks "of the sun in his splendour, and her *mating* with him."[47] The gender dynamics of the story have received widespread attention, as have the worship thematics of Lawrence's work.[48] I have previously emphasized the interplay between ecological elements in the text and Lawrence's ideological explorations, and returning to the story with a deepened interest in the solar plexus reinforces my sense that we need to stay with an eco-ethical lens, in order to read this story in our contemporary moment.

Lawrence uses animal images to describe how Juliet's initial feelings of burden about her child are transformed into a more dynamic and moving kind of relationship. At first she "had had the child so much *on her mind*, in a torment of responsibility, as if, having borne him, she had to answer for his whole existence."[49] Soon the source of her obligation shifts out of the head—or nerves if we want to use Lawrence's own terminology—and into the body, or blood. Later in the narrative, the nature of her obligation shifts as well. When her naked child stumbles near some prickly thorns, Juliet is "quick as a serpent, leaping to him."[50] She is even "surprised" by this display of spontaneous protective behavior and remarks to herself, "What a wild cat I am, really!"[51] These moments resonate with Lawrence's claim that the solar plexus allows us to know "as we can never mentally know. Primarily we know, each man, each living creature knows, profoundly and satisfactorily and without question, that *I am I*."[52]

This moment of embodied, solar knowing is also importantly relational, maternal, and animal. Lawrence suggests that there is a kind of primal, parental responsibility not dictated by social expectations but located in our inhuman, creaturely instincts or affects. The affective in Lawrence resonates with contemporary interests in affect theory.[53] While we should acknowledge problematic links to a naturalized maternal "instinct" here, we also have to consider the way in which Lawrence's depictions can be connected to a Darwinian and biocentric force that binds mammals to the evolutionary success of their offspring. Moreover, the awakened creatural posture in Juliet coincides with Lawrence's insistence that the "primal consciousness in man is pre-mental, and has nothing to do with cognition. It is the same as in the animals."[54] The child's own behavior shifts to a solar, more-than-human quality: "The child, too, was *another creature*, with a peculiar, quiet, sun-darkened absorption."[55] Thus the child also seems to shift away from a "clinging" social anxiety and toward what we might view as a parallel mode of being and ethical orientation to Juliet, one that is more present and ecological.

The radial, outward movement of the solar also reinforces some of Lawrence's recurring motifs—those of movement, change, and even dance—motifs that clearly echo Duncan's modernist experiments with the moving body. While Juliet does not properly dance in this text, the "flow" between her body and the sun is a vital element of her therapeutic self-overcoming:

> By some mysterious power inside her, deeper than her known consciousness and will, she was put into connection with the sun, and the stream flowed of itself, from her womb. She herself, her conscious self, was secondary, a secondary person, almost an

onlooker. The true Juliet was this dark flow from her deep body to the sun.[56]

The "real" Juliet is a flow, a sympathetic sharing of energy and dynamism, we might say, with the sun. The story's images of Juliet's womb also reinforce the foundational role of maternal ties in Lawrence's ideologies.

In this connection, Lawrence's watercolor that was produced for the Black Sun Press edition of "Sun," is of particular visual interest. He describes his image in its margins as "The greater Sun, with the daily sun as his breast-gem."[57] Lawrence's Mayan god figure is inverted and extremely beetle-like, appearing with the back exposed, as if suspended by the "feet"—although no human-like feet appear—and looking forward toward the viewer.[58] The figure has multiple yellow-red flames radiating from its hybrid body, and several of the blue strokes also mimic the lick of a flame, around the head and beetle-like exoskeleton. The breast plate is indeed the most solar-plexus like sun image that we know of, in Lawrence's visual oeuvre.[59] The positioning of the figure seems quite circus-like, a kind of acrobatic depiction as if this deity is mid-swing or somersault. And thus, the dancerly and moving qualities at play in this painting emphasize my arguments here well. Moreover, the flames can be read as limbic and teleo-searching, the outward licks of creative self-othering.

It is important to note that Lawrence appears to use only the three primary colors in this painting: red, blue, and yellow. The darker outlines on and around the head, arms and "upper" torso-carapace appear to be blue overlaid on the red paint. Since the Mayan Sun God is sometimes associated with Eagle in traditional depictions, the acrobatic or aerial posture further implies a creatural bird-like flight, movement, or dance. The lettering in the word "SUN" at the bottom of the image is also highly sinuous. The "S" appears serpent or swan-like, and the "U" rather uncannily mimics a uterine shape—all in keeping with bioaesthetic thematics, and Lawrence's emphasis on the "womb" in the story, an organ that seems at times to be analogous to the solar plexus.

I want to conclude this discussion with a consideration of how Lawrence's and Duncan's ideas about bodily sources of consciousness in the solar plexus reverberate with very current discussions of contemporary art, embodiment, bioaesthetics, and new materialisms. My own recent work on a bioaesthetic force that humans borrow, share, or co-inhabit with other creatures suggests that all human artistic tendencies have some fundamental connection to animality that is based in strategies of excess, display, intensification, and elaboration or iteration. In earlier work, I have linked this idea that the aesthetic *itself* is animal, rather than "human," to the aesthetic expression of crucial modernist and contemporary artists. The theories of Gilles Deleuze and Elizabeth Grosz, in particular, have helped to make my claims about the bioaesthetic possible. Deleuze insists that the territorial, the affective, and the rhythmic structures of the expressive and aesthetic are clearly locatable in animal practices. Indeed, Deleuze grounds the aesthetic itself in the animal and inhuman, rejecting the notion that art is primarily representational and maintaining that art is linked to affects and intensities that exceed human boundaries. Thus, Deleuze and Guattari claim, "Not only does art not wait for human beings to begin, but we may ask if art ever appears among human beings, except under artificial and belated conditions."[60] Similarly, Deleuze and Guattari ask whether "art is continually haunted by the animal."[61]

Deleuze conjectures, "Perhaps art begins with the animal, at least with the animal that carves out a territory and constructs a house."[62] He also suggests that the territory (which will get translated into the frame) "implies the emergence of pure sensory qualities, of sensibilia that cease to be merely functional and become expressive features."[63] These claims ought to be linked more regularly with Lawrence's and Duncan's similar ideas, particularly their fixations on the solar plexus. Deleuze is keenly interested in Lawrence, of course, but this overlap in their work could use further elaboration. It is an interesting point that even in very recent discussions of Lawrence, scholars and writers often marginalize or take a dismissive attitude toward *Psychanalysis of the Unconscious* and *Fantasia of the Unconscious*, as though these works are too speculative and amateur, too "weird" and naïve to warrant "real" intellectual consideration.[64] But the rising importance of the affective in our contemporary views of human functioning, including in artmaking, should prompt us to return to Lawrence's full range of ideas about consciousness not in the head, but in the bodily apparatus. Indeed, given that Timothy Morton so consistently encourages our attentions to the "weird," and queered, in general, we might return to these strange texts of Lawrence with a particular renewed interest.

A recent online symposium, organized by the contemporary artist and art critic Taney Roniger, called "Thingly Affinities" (December 2020), took as its spur the fact that, as Roniger frames it, many current artists are interested in a return to valuing embodied form in visual art, after a long emphasis on the conceptual in visual (and performance) art. This shift emphasizes artistic form as "a conduit to the larger world, a means by which we experience our fleshly connections to the rest of nature" and seeks to rethink artistic form as being linked directly to the frameworks of "ethical posthumanism."[65] The symposium brought together a wide range of thinkers and artists, but the live presentation by David Abram, for instance, demonstrates how Lawrence's and Duncan's ideas about embodiment are resurfacing in these contemporary discussions.[66]

Abram repeatedly notes in his work that the body is our source for metamorphosis. He elaborates the ways that perception is sensual, sensuous, and embodied. For Abram, "reason" is just another form of embodied "magic" that ought to be understood in the wider context of an extremely catholic animism, an animism that clearly resonates with the materialisms of other contemporary thinkers like Jane Bennett and Bruno Latour. Abram's ideas undoubtedly echo Lawrence's own notions, quoted above: "For the primal consciousness is always dynamic, and never, like mental consciousness, static. Thought, let us say what we will about its magic powers, is instrumental only, the soul's finest instrument for the business of living. Thought is just a means to action and living. But life and action rise actually at the great centres of dynamic consciousness."[67] Lawrence's and Duncan's versions of modernist "knowing" thus seem newly, potentially transformative as ethical frameworks, in an age where our embodied, creatural engagement with the world has become ever more urgent. Their ethical commitments refocus our attention to forms of bodily knowing that exceed "human" boundaries in ways that affirm weird, ecological, other-than-rational forms of creativity and relationality.

II

Planetary Ethics

CHAPTER FOUR

Reparative Ethics, or the Case of Anna D. Whyte

Marian Eide

In his 2021 *New York Times* column, "The Ethicist," Kwame Anthony Appiah cautioned a reader against destroying her grandfather's Orientalist paintings, observing "I'm not an enthusiast for destroying art, even when, in some sense, it expresses morally disturbing attitudes. Art is, among other things, a reflection of the ethos of its time. If we are to understand our past, it's unhelpful to destroy the evidence." Considering the long history of purging art in conformance with current religious, social, and political principles, Appiah cautioned: "Moral criticism of this sort often conflates questions about the character of the artist with questions about the character of the art, or confuses the question of what attitudes the art expresses with the issue of what attitudes it will produce in the viewer."[1] Appiah's point about destroying evidence of the historical past is a trenchant one and much debated as monuments to white supremacy are reconsidered globally. I am less certain than he that we actually need visible evidence of "morally disturbing attitudes" in private collections or on public display. Yet he identifies an ethical crux that haunts literary studies: to what extent one might conflate the attitudes of art with those of the artist or their effects on the audience has been actively debated for at least sixty years. Pretending that "morally disturbing attitudes" are not embedded in the structures we live within today, is also, to use Appiah's word, "unhelpful." We must take seriously the ethical impact of racist inclinations represented across aesthetic forms. Our interpretive practices, I believe, must be oriented to repairing the unjust conditions represented in aestheticized racialism.

Reparation was precisely the impetus for a reader who posed her own ethical dilemma to Appiah a few months later as she pondered how to handle a family portrait of a slave-holding ancestor and whether to sell the painting and donate the money in the service of "an organization focused on reparations." Appiah responded first by quoting the famous opening lines of L. P. Hartley's novel, *The Go-Between*: "The past is a foreign country: They do things differently there."[2] For Appiah, the issue "is not that we shouldn't make moral judgments of other times or other places," but we must, in his view, take into account the "different norms" of the past as if we were accounting for differing cultural norms in another country. Appiah recognizes the unjust legacies of previous norms, but cautions:

> We can't just put it behind us. Nor must we remove from our homes or our albums every picture of someone implicated in evil. We are not responsible for what they did and do not have an individual responsibility to atone for it. We can't undo these injustices; their victims aren't here to receive recompense. But as a society, we can acknowledge our difficult history—with both its vices and its virtues—and aim to address the persisting wrongs that derive from past moral error. In doing so, articles from that history like your family portrait can provide tools for reflection.[3]

Taking individual responsibility, however problematic and flimsy it may be, is the precise aim of the slave-holder's descendant as she considers the portrait in the context of a twenty-first-century reparation opportunity. The letter writer hopes that a painting can contribute to reparative politics if only through a philanthropic gesture. This chapter is motivated by a similar question: how can aesthetic engagement have reparative potential? If the aesthetic is a "tool for reflection," it may also be an instrument for repair even when its biases threaten social harm.

Appiah's response, however articulate in aesthetic terms, does not seem to address his readers' moral investments. The first wishes to account for the harm done by orientalist images in her position as the inheritor of several. Her project is to consider how her ownership or destruction of these paintings addresses and even repairs damages of the past. The second writer considers her own good fortune won through this ancestor's racist exploitation of enslaved people; she wishes to take some action to acknowledge and even mitigate past harms in a way that contributes to a more equitable future. In thinking this way, I would argue, the letter writers evince an ethical disposition to the paintings in keeping with the philosophical claims of Emmanuel Levinas. They hold themselves responsible for the artifacts and their history, their ancestors and their racial privilege, and at the same they time consider both those conditions of responsibility in the face of a third entity, those persons harmed by this representational tradition in the past and in the present. They ask how aesthetics might be entangled in their ethical responsibilities.

Where Appiah limits the potential impact of the aesthetic, Emmanuel Levinas several decades earlier understood the relation between text and reader as more powerful. Quoting one of the poets he most admired, Levinas remembered: "I cannot see any basic difference," Paul Celan wrote to Hans Bender, "between a handshake and a poem."[4] Levinas understands this metaphor in ethical terms as a touch that recognizes the other, that reaches across unknowability to take responsibility for that other. Writing about the Nobel-laureate, Hebrew-language novelist, Shmuel Yosef Agnon, Levinas claims that his literary language "like an intricate lace, stands the minute script of commentaries on commentaries."[5] His metaphor applies more broadly to literary texts, their language is knotted into an intricate lace, and their structures of signification work through the patterns of commentaries on commentaries, interpretation on interpretation. Levinas's lace metaphor presents literature as a complex surface through which other surfaces can be seen as framed and re-presented by the intricacy of knotted patterns.[6] The literary work, then, extends as a handshake that anticipates our reception, and also as lace work in which hermeneutic paratexts, a concept I will return to below, are viewed in conjunction with the work itself. Our hermeneutic engagements can mark the depredations of the past in accord with present ethical commitments. The lace work of the literary text and the paratexts a scholar joins to hermeneutic effort can anticipate and offer at least provisional repair for the harms done in an encounter, for example, with Orientalist imagery or with the portrait of a man who enslaved other people.

To understand more fully what these metaphorical claims for the written form would mean to Levinas, one might consider first his philosophical and theological thought. To condense a corpus like his to a few sentences is to distort. However, literary scholars have been drawing on his work for several decades, so this précis will serve only as a reminder or cue.[7] Levinas argued that the human condition is to be born always already in a condition of responsibility to others.[8] That condition entails not only that one bears an obligation to the other, but also that one responds to others in such a way as to further their responsibility as well. For Levinas this ethical condition is neither inert nor permanent but evolving and developing. The ethical is not "Said," to use his terminology, but "Saying." The ethical implications of the literary were complicated by this dynamic tension between the Saying and the Said. Levinas oscillated in his views of literature over the course of his career, moving between a Socratic understanding of literature as mimesis and therefore an inert form (Said) and literature as a living interaction (Saying). Where text is merely representational in the sense that Levinas explores in "Reality and its Shadow," it is fixed and passive, imposing a copy of the real in the place of contact with that reality and distorting it by transfer into another form. When literature is fixed on the page as Said, it draws readers away from the real world and our responsibilities in and to it. When Levinas wrote *Otherwise than Being* it was literature's disruptive quality that drew him. When literature is Saying, when it is a handshake that reaches toward the reader, touches, and obliges the reader, it invites us back to our responsibilities. In reading, one is oriented through the work of art toward the Other.

However, that encounter with the other, that handshake with the stranger, is not necessarily companionable. Levinas made his point of departure the potentially hostile dimensions of such encounters, assuming that the Other might wish to take the self as its object, might even be willing to obliterate the self. Levinas reflected: "I have not done anything and I have always been under accusation—persecuted."[9] Even before we become selves and certainly before we attain the freedom assumed by his existentialist peers, we may be persecuted, we may be accused of faults for which we do not necessarily see ourselves as responsible.[10] Faults such as a descending from a person who owned others as slaves. We are held hostage by the claims of an Other who confronts us even as they shake hands.[11]

The paintings' owners have not themselves committed ethical breaches but, like Levinas and unlike Appiah, they hold themselves responsible for repairing the harms of the past. They see themselves in responsible relation to those third entities, who bear witness to the encounter with the aesthetic object as it represents past harms and those who committed them.

Following Levinas, then, the jarring elements of a racist past and its repercussions in the present are not inert evidence to be judged and then passed over. The image reaches out to its reader as if extending a hand, but that gesture fails where the ethical responsibility of the artist freezes the subject as its racial Other. The racial Other is fixed on the page, as if Said, in violation of the subject's socially constructed and connected place in the world. One of Levinas's contributions to the study of literature as an ethical enterprise is to remind readers that when we approach literature as either representational or thematizing in its main function, we miss the actual work the text does in extending itself to the reader, accusing as much as inviting, opening as much as representing, altering as much as thematizing.[12]

I had a qualm similar to Appiah's interlocutors when, as a scholar pursuing archival work in sympathy with both reparative politics and reparative modes of interpretation, I first encountered the work of New Zealand modernist Anna D. Whyte, who published two novels with Virginia and Leonard Woolf's Hogarth Press, and then virtually disappeared from the literary world. Only thirty copies of the two novels she wrote, *Change Your Sky* (1935) and *Lights Are Bright* (1936), remain in the holdings of libraries listed by WorldCat. A member of the colonial class within the British Empire, daughter of a sea captain, and widely traveled herself, Whyte's two novels share a global vision marked by the kinds of historical limitations Appiah recognized, limitations and biases that make her work of interest in addressing questions of reparative reading both as an endeavor of canon expansion based on historical and archival research and as an ethical question about how the harms of the past might be mitigated. Anna D. Whyte's *Change Your Sky*, on which I will focus here, invites the kind of engagement favored by modernist scholars because it is so insistently allusive that it already appears on first reading with a cultural commentary weaving itself into a literary texture that extends from Medici Florence to the contemporaneous Bloomsbury movement. The novel is built on a narrative foundation and thematic structure provided by E. M. Forster's *A Room With a View* (1908) in which a disparate set of British characters meet in a Florence pensione, wander the city, and find their lives altered by their encounters with the city, its people, and with each other. *Change Your Sky* interacts fully with its Florentine setting, drawing on one character's knowledge of Dante and another's obsession with the quattrocento Medici family.

My aesthetic pleasure in Whyte's novel came to a crossroads when I looked up an unfamiliar word she uses to describe one of the guests at the pensione; an unidentified ageing woman is described thus: "Her hair stood up in curls all round her head, like a golliwog that was turning a little grey." The simile here is both mystifying and racially charged. The golliwog, I learned, was a racist icon akin in popular culture to "Aunt Jemima," "Sambo," or "Stepin Fetchit."[13] It drew on white racist stereotypes of Africans mediated through American minstrel culture. The image—often reproduced as a doll—has black skin recalling the burnt-cork painted faces of minstrels, the doll's eyes are wide and rimmed in white, their lips exaggerated in size. The caricature was introduced into Anglophone culture in the modernist period first by Florence K. Upton, who invented the golliwog for a series of children's books published between 1895 and 1909.[14] "Soon after the publication of the first book in 1895 it became a commercially used symbol to sell a large array of products."[15] Perhaps the most familiar appearance of the golliwog is in Enid Blyton's "Noddy Series" of children's books from the 1940s.

These racist dolls inhabited nurseries around the Anglophone world in the nineteenth and early twentieth centuries. The rag dolls are thought to imitate the toys of Black, enslaved children, dolls cobbled together from scraps lying around in the brutal plantation economy.[16] One may imagine the affectionate labor of creating dolls for the comfort and play of children afforded no manufactured toys. Additionally, in these homemade dolls, enslaved children might find approximations of themselves, their dark skin and natural curls. Yet these simple objects of love were picked up in a minstrel tradition in which African American culture was appropriated by white performers and manufacturers not in recognition or appreciation but in a cruel parody performed to enforce the structures of racism that uphold white privilege. Those parodies were prevalent at the time that Anna D. Whyte was composing her vision of tourist Florence.

It is difficult to understand, however, why one ageing woman would have hair that needed to be described through this popular racist image, "a golliwog turned gray." The casual introduction of this simile does not open itself to an ironic reading such as James Joyce's reference to the doll in *Ulysses*, when he presents Cissy Caffrey, through the ironic distance of Gerty McDowell's interior monologue as "Madcap Ciss with her golliwog curls."[17] It is Gerty's racism Joyce captures here through free indirect discourse; the description does not necessarily reflect Joyce's own racial attitudes.[18] But this figure from *Change Your Sky* is described by a third-person, omniscient narrator, potentially creating a stronger link between the racism of the image and the possible racist presumptions of the author. Whyte's casual reference testifies to the bigotries of the past and forces the contemporary reader to reckon with earlier forms of racism and their visible legacies in the present. Her metaphor triggers an exhausting history in which Black readers had to prepare themselves regularly to encounter such assaults on their subjectivity. While I agree with Appiah that we cannot merely dismiss the racist past made evident in Whyte's allusion, I follow Levinas in suggesting that we *are* responsible for the harms of that past and might take "individual responsibility to atone for it."

The question Whyte's work raises for me is both a canonical question and a reparative one. Why recover and adapt a text to the canon if our only response to it is critique? I am not suggesting that the established, classical canon of one hundred years ago remains intact. Rather, I am suggesting that our critical enterprises are canon forming. When I recover a text from the archive or a forgotten shelf in the library and deem it worthy of scholarly commentary, I suggest also that it may be of pedagogical interest, joining then the contingent and ever-expanding canon of texts deemed appropriate for reprint, discussion, and even student examination. Suspicious readers may wish to identify Whyte's errors, both moral and political, so as to reflect critically on the racialist thought of her times, yes, but we already know about the worst depredations of the modernist period, and while the critique bears repeating, and the racial attitudes continue to echo loudly into the twenty-first century globally, nonetheless this approach to reading modernism does quite a bit to confirm a reader in her desire for moral purity but it does little to address the ethical challenges that literature could, perhaps, prepare us for. The reparative ethic I propose here recognizes that the potentially hostile encounter between reader and text presents an ethical challenge and suggests a contemporary need for repair.

In rereading the golliwog moment reparatively, the reader finds an ally in Homi Bhabha's theory of mimicry. Bhabha's understanding of these iterative imitations as mimicry opens up a space where one can see that the adaptation of Black racial markers in racist white inventions makes visible the arbitrariness of those racial markers.[19] The natural hair parodied in the golliwog doll, diminished and alienated in this tradition, appears in the novel on a white woman's head, indicating the arbitrary cultural constructions that manufacture racial difference in order to instill generational power imbalances. In the world of the novel, whether intended by the author or repaired by the reader, these curls cross racial lines and are marked by a mimicry that undermines the differential structures the dolls and their narrative counterparts and commercial equivalents were designed to uphold. That mimicry is not endemic to the representation itself, rather an ethical disposition necessitates such critical intervention motivated by repair.

If we address literary works previously neglected by a more settled canon, we might be inclined to recover only those admirable texts that pass the scrutiny of our hermeneutics of suspicion, to use Paul Ricœur's term, those that are compatible with the moral impulses of the current moment.[20] As we consider the ethical ambiguities found in the imaginative worlds of the past, we may, however, as Appiah suggests, wish to preserve a history of assumed inequity, while marking the places where the inequity is reinforced or resisted in the imagination.

In the wake of the poststructuralist turn and the deep textual attentions it demanded, and also following the Foucauldian approach that found in literature the edifices of the discursive disciplinary and institutional structures that produce an inequitable world, over the last several decades, scholars have gone back to the basics and asked: now how do we want to read the works that matter to us? Can we let go of the hermeneutics of suspicion?[21] Is archival recovery morally compatible with this reparative impulse when texts express repressive or alienating views?

I would like to propose here a model of reparative reading, an ethical practice of textual engagement that calls on our responsibility in the Levinasian sense, a responsibility borne in the nuances of interpretive work as itself a mechanism for ethical practice.

Eve Kosofsky Sedgwick's influential chapter in *Touching Feeling*, "Paranoid Reading and Reparative Reading, or, You're So Paranoid, You Probably Think This Essay Is About You," invited readers to approach literary texts with what she called reparative reading, which she defined as "additive and accretive." "It wants," she writes, "to assemble and confer plenitude on an object that will then have resources to offer to an inchoate self."[22] For Sedgwick, the reparative impulse meets text with erudition in which knowledge is neither measured nor targeted but generative and generous. The reparative appreciates waste and leftovers, the fragmentary and liminal. Its approach to literature is affective, enjoying unexpected connections, noticing beauty and stylistic flourishes. Reparative reading is kind to readers in their "project of survival" and especially generous in so far as the reader is often threatened by the assumptions of the traditional literary canon but may find places of repair and self-recognition within that canon from which to extract sustenance, "even of a culture whose avowed desire has often been not to sustain them."[23] I read in Sedgwick's interpretating writers like Proust the impulse to see healing in texts that recognize the reader in her subjugated place. I would like to open her term to the obligations of the reader to meet others whose needs are not anticipated by the text. The hermeneutic of suspicion was developed precisely to address the threatening assumptions embedded throughout the history of literature in texts whose "avowed desire" has been to diminish those deemed "other." A reparative practice must account for that "project of survival" both where the aesthetic has "resources to offer an inchoate self" and where it mirrors that self back to the reader in distorted, damaging rhetorics.

Sedgwick's approach is particularly apt when the text offers the reader solace or retreat, a place to repair. Here I am offering a Levinasian alternative because, as I will outline below, Levinas assumes the ethical encounter may be a hostile meeting in which one is responsible to and for an Other who may be harmful to the self. I propose the possibility of an ethical engagement which intends to repair social connections where trust has been broken. Ta-Nehisi Coates made a social and political "Case for Reparations" by calling for the recognition of historical harm and its present consequences as "the price we must pay to see ourselves squarely." For Coates, reparation is not merely a compensation for previous wrongs. Rather, he suggests a "reckoning that would lead to spiritual renewal" and "a revolution of the American consciousness, a reconciling of our self-image as the great democratizer with the facts of our history." Coates believes that "wrestling publicly with these questions matters as much as—if not more than—the specific answers that might be produced." With reparation, there is a collective understanding of shared debt to the most vulnerable among us, not just for past violations but for a future with improved social connections. "More important than any single check cut to any African American," Coates contends, "reparations would represent America's maturation out of the childhood myth of its innocence into a wisdom worthy of its founders."[24] Appiah's approach accords in some ways with that of Coates in that he believes that eradicating the traces of historical wrongs bolsters a myth of past innocence. But he does not acknowledge that preserving the evidence of wrongs done produces additional emotional harms in the present and serves to normalize racial fantasies of the past. Preservation may be less effective than repairing those wrongs through our aesthetic practices. Ethical repair, I am arguing in the wake of Coates's writings, is not an end goal but an interpretive process.

Interpretive practices will be reparative when we anticipate and address the way the attitudes inscribed in the literatures of the past act on the sensibilities of both past and present readers. Returning to the image of *poesis* as a handshake, I understand Levinas to evoke Celan in order to propose writing as an aspect of the ethical condition in that it reaches across the divide between a self and an Other to acknowledge, to greet, and to form an agreement; the varying functions of the handshake in social circumstances map onto the varying functions of *poesis*. As such, *poesis* is not an inert representation or utterance "Said" by the writer and consumed by the reader, but an active engagement between the writer and reader who, in making meaning together, form a responsive, responsible engagement. The poem anticipates the reader as an Other, distinct and unknown, while the reader approaches the poem acknowledging the artist's possible intention and at the same time unable precisely to comprehend that intention but only to respond to its effects within the work.

Levinas recognizes the ethical engagements of literary writing in so far as it follows what I will call a paratextual principle, in partial accord with Gérard Genette's conception of paratextual commentary by someone other than the author (allographic) whose function is to enhance and guide the reading of a literary or sacred text.[25] For Levinas, the paratextual principle (as opposed to the representative principle of which he was suspicious) enlivens text as Saying, rather than Said. When poetry—a word he uses as synonymous with *poesis* or the act of creation, and applicable in his thinking to aesthetic productions more generally—opens itself to multiple interpretations and invites debate over time, then writing functions much like scripture in that commentators may find in *poesis* principles for right living and spiritual understanding, but principles that may vary and diverge greatly even when derived from the same passage. To comprehend Levinas's approach, one might picture the Talmud's page—both Mishnah and Gemara—as Levinas himself often did; there sacred text is presented on the same plane with its multiple Rabbinic interventions.[26] Rather than representing life as it once was in the times of Abraham or Rebecca, perhaps, the text creates a world of the mind in which contemplating multiple possibilities at once produces interpretation as an ethical relation. The reader is not alone with the text contemplating an interior world or producing a sense of the moral good only from individual experience or stable textual truth. One faces sacred text always already in responsible relation to God and his Word but also to other readers and their understanding, interpretation, and experience. Similarly, in literature, the reader finds herself in conversation with commentary that surrounds the text as an imagined paratext, presenting writing as dialogue, forming a community of dissent, albeit with a unified purpose of finding the good and true in study and dialogue. This dynamic is why Levinas appreciates—both admires and extends or amplifies—Celan's image of poetry as a handshake.

Levinas's heuristic of the poem as handshake suggests a hermeneutics of intention that proceeds in an asymptotic relation to the much more prevalent hermeneutics of suspicion that the modernist canon has long invited. Both approaches invest in the intentions of the text, one defensively, the other appreciatively. Both acknowledge the rocky path that extends between reader and author. But with Levinas's paratextual paradigm in mind, the challenge for the reader of secular literature is that the text's intention does not derive from God, as many believe to be the case with sacred text, but from the minds of mere humans. When readers extend their hands to the poetic encounter, they may be engaging with a text that seeks to harm by way of domination, neglect, or distortion. What stands between the reader and shaking hands with the devil are the paratexts, the multiple interpretations that mediate an encounter with, for example, "golliwog curls." Levinas was interested not only in literature with the kind of lengthy and layered interpretive tradition that appreciates traditionally canonical works but also with recent writing. Many of his short essays in *Proper Names*, for example, are addressed to his contemporaries, works that may only carry the initial mediation of journalistic book reviews that are as evaluative as they are interpretive. Here one shakes hands with a stranger who has not first been introduced by a friend. In this sense, his essays on literature provide modernism's scholars with reparative principles for encountering texts that have been neglected by the canon.

In the wake of Levinas's ethical intervention, I reach toward my concern for the text's responsibility in the face of a third who witnesses this relation, and I am, as a result, acutely aware of the triggering effects of such racist images. Interacting with the text in a paratextual vein, I mark the allusion in the marginal commentary that implicitly resides alongside the text, such that both the allusion and its triggering racial assumptions are enlaced on the same surface of meaning making. While this interaction might be understood methodologically as an instance of the hermeneutics of suspicion, it might equally be understood as reparative in the sense that the text is both enjoyed for its beauty and recognized as a part of the racist legacy. Rather than casting the text back into the obscurity of WorldCat, reparative reading recognizes the extent to which such racist ideas permeated Anglophone culture not just in the works of Upton and Blyton, but pervasively, such that Black readers of Whyte's period could expect regularly to be confronted with hateful mimicry. To repair, one must first acknowledge and then pay this debt to the text's responsibility for its harms.

Whyte in this low moment of racial parody is also one of the Others to whom I am responsive and thus responsible, though she may, like the Other in much of Levinas's thought, threaten me or other readers with harm. It is not an issue of confusing intention with effect or of confusing the perceived effect of the work with the view of its maker, as Appiah claims; rather, it is necessary in the ethical encounter to grapple with this complex matrix of responsibility, threat, and repair. Both the reparative and the suspicious or paranoid reading, if we are to follow Levinas, must be responsive and responsible, thus operating with an eye to repair that is cognizant of the artwork's situation in the world and of its effect.

Paratextual principles and the repairs they offer, however, are markedly different from Levinas's actual encounters with *poesis*. While Talmudic in his approach to philosophy, he was haphazard in his treatment of literature. He would refer to a scene within a literary text with no reference to its context, the events that surrounded the lines he extracted, the narrative point of view, rhetorical play, or translational vagaries. His most famous repeated invocation is a line from Fyodor Dostoevsky's *The Brothers Karamazov*. In translation, the passage reads: "For know, dear ones, that every one of us is undoubtedly responsible for all men and everything on earth, not merely through the general sinfulness of creation, but each one personally for all mankind and every individual man." Levinas quoted this passage from Dostoevsky often. In an interview, later published as "Ethics and Infinity," he said: "We are all responsible for all men before all, and I more than all the others."[27] Elsewhere he paraphrased: "Each of us is guilty before everyone and for everyone, and I more than the others."[28] It seemed of little interest to Levinas when referencing Dostoevsky that the line was from a work of fiction rather than in the author's unmediated perspective, that the passage is not exactly as he quoted it, that it refers first to monks in secluded life, that it is said by a priest, and finally that it is remembered later by Alyosha, who is not sure he is quoting Father Zossima exactly correctly. One might shudder at Levinas's lack of precision in reference. And while Levinas describes literature as lace in that we can read between the lines, as we see through the knot work (which is a kind of obvious point for those of us who engage seriously with literature), his own practice was to surf the wave of the line as if it were not supported by an entire ocean. I might object to this approach, which bears none of the gravity of his more systematic treatment of sacred or philosophical text, except for this: there is something very honest and potentially methodologically promising in his habit of messy citation. For readers carry in their minds singular events or lines separated from their context, devoid of their narratological instantiation, and sometimes oblivious to their rhetorical complexities. Those lines and scenes greet us like a handshake, as if acknowledging our specificity and even exalting it.[29] Rather than demanding of Levinas that he show the narrative sophistication of Gerald Prince or the rhetorical finesse of Kenneth Burke, I would like to instead name Levinas's habit the scenic method and make the case for its ethical potency.

Levinas's method, then, might be fruitfully adapted. The passage from Dostoevsky that he cited so often drove his philosophy and made richer and more immediate the ideas he was exploring. As Arthur Cools explains, focusing on a singular scene, Levinas transformed narrative by a reduction, in the philosophical sense, "to a single event which reveals the breakdown of all given meanings of a common world."[30] Cools goes on to argue: "Through reduction, the scene transforms the narrative into something spectacular—a visibility without context." Similar to Alain Badiou's later ethical emphasis on singularity, Levinas's "reduction of narrative meanings that is expressed through one single, recurrent image" allows the "singular meaning of the event" to emerge powerfully.[31]

The golliwog reference is particularly available to this mode of interpretation but might on its own lead one to dismiss the novel entirely. To illustrate the reparative potential of both the paratextual and scenic methodological principles, I would like to consider another scene from *Change Your Sky*, in which Ms. Elspeth Stirling, who comes to Florence to trace the lives of the Medici family from their roots in the fourteenth century to the collapse of their power in the sixteenth century, is trapped in the Chapel of Princes, which was commissioned by these quattrocento art patrons. She is equipped in her Medici project with an outdated guidebook, *Saunterings*, which informs her ordinary decisions, from packing her own tea and navigating public transportation, to visiting buildings, murals, and paintings commissioned by the Medici.

Stirling's obsession is to know the Medici, prying into their lives and their legacies. In spite of her enthusiasm for the Medici clan, Stirling is initially indifferent to or even repulsed by a chapel they commissioned.

For the first time during her stay in Florence Miss Stirling disliked something that was connected with the family of the Medici. The room had a venomous appearance and she was quite glad to walk out of it along the passage leading to the new sacristy, where the statues of Michelangelo lounged in front of the Grand Dukes Julian and Lorenzo. These statues expressed a brutal assurance, an animal strength that was also a little distasteful to Miss Stirling.[32]

Having already perused Elvira Grifi's guide to the Cappella in preparation for her own visit, Stirling's perception may be formed by the earlier visitor's words: "This building imposing only from its size and for the display of gorgeous magnificence, is of poor taste and little artistic merit."[33]

Michelangelo carefully designed the space to catch changing patterns of light on the statuary, which allegorically refers to time (Day and Night, Dawn and Dusk); however, paradoxically, Stirling's primary experience of the space occurs overnight as she is locked into the chapel by a careless docent and a lackadaisical guard. Ironically, Michelangelo was also locked into the area. In his case, he was hiding from imperial troops in 1530. A republican sympathizer, he took refuge in a small room off the "*stanza segreta*" adjacent to the chapel, where he spent two weeks distracting himself by sketching figures and faces on the walls. Although he was pardoned and called back to Rome to continue work on the basilica, he did return to this sacristy project, although it remained incomplete during his lifetime.

Stirling's plot line thus carries with it a number of potential paratextual connections: This spinster's story revises the narratives of several single women who populate *A Room With a View*. The lives and political legacies of the Medici intertwine with Stirling's experiences of the rising Fascist movement portrayed in the novel's present. There is much to consider about Stirling's sequestration in relation to its paratextual allusions. Having traversed that method in considering the golliwog allusion, here one might instead follow Levinas's scenic approach.

Trapped in a venomous space that reminds her of the Medici propensity to poison their foes, by ten in the evening she gives up on any chance that her traveling companion or the other guests at the pensione have noticed her absence, that anyone will seek to release her. She pulls together the wooden chairs made available to visitors and worshippers and forms an uncomfortable bed where she sleeps fitfully for a few hours. Her dreams are populated by the figures and events she has been studying and particularly by the murder of two Medici that took place in the building:

> The awful scene of the Pazzi conspiracy in the Cathedral was now acted before her. Giuliano and Lorenzo were kneeling before the altar, the Pazzi stabbed Giuliano, and Lorenzo escaped into the sacristy. Then followed the revenge. Miss Stirling had often enjoyed this story, but now the heads of the conspirators all yawned, tortured and bloated, before her, as they hung from the windows of the Palazzo Vecchio. They seemed to come nearer and nearer until they were almost on top of Miss Stirling, until they were inside Miss Stirling, until they *were* Miss Stirling, she was them, they were her. She woke screaming from this dreadful vision, and lay trembling in the darkness.[34]

The objects of her inquiry become one with Stirling in this passage. Allowed into her consciousness by study and contemplation they become a part of her consciousness, her way of understanding the world. Not only is Stirling haunted by the Medici, experiencing their travails as if they were her own, she also feels for the first time the dreadful repercussions of the Pazzi's conspiracy. Instead of feeling narrative pleasure in a gruesome story she experiences the horror of brutal executions as if she were herself in attendance and as if the bodies of the dead were an animated threat. Instead of inhabiting the Medici world she loves, she is herself overcome and invaded by their enemies. The relation between self and other, until this point abstract, becomes in her dream pressing and real. No longer separate from the past, she is inhabited by it, as Whyte emphasizes with the italicized "*were.*"

Stirling had been unique among the travelers at the pensione in keeping almost entirely to herself. Although accompanied by a resentful niece, she pursued only her own historical interests. In this moment of relation to others, which threaten her if only in dream, she becomes aware of her subjectivity as interconnected not by choice but in essence. Finally released by the opening of the chapel for tourists the next morning, she flees back to the pensione, fragile and upset, and seeks out the company of another visitor with whom she shares her carefully packed tea. Stirling emerges from her isolated night with a basic reassessment of her fundamental preference for independence and self-sufficiency, appreciating instead a sense of communal interdependence. Her terrifying experience is transformative. Once independent to the point of callous disregard, she comes to appreciate the importance of community.

This scene remains in my memory as an emblem both of Levinas's insight into the fundamental ethical relation that precedes being, but also of his anarchic scenic method of reading literature. While the complex paratextual allusions can inform my reading, the scene resides in my memory in a naïve illustration of the Levinasian principle, in which one is responsible to the other who threatens one with harm, and in that responsibility one is also connected to those who would repair the harms done. The Medici chapel scene testifies to our vulnerability, to the harms we inflict on one another, and the reparation made possible by the resonant images of literature that accompany us on the "project of survival." Even where the text threatens the reader with harm, it returns the reader to the resources of communities of interpretation that would act to repair that harm. The hermeneutic of suspicion need not necessarily supplant or be supplanted by the reparative mode. The two approaches might most effectively be joined together in the ethical project.

CHAPTER FIVE

Interrogating the Ethics of Cosmopolitanism in Stella Benson's Travel Writing

Shinjini Chattopadhyay

Introduction

The relationship between literary modernism and the middlebrow has been historically contentious. Middlebrow literary productions are accused of lacking refinement and substance when contrasted with the highbrow. They are also found guilty by some of propagating inferior aesthetic ideals in the interest of catering to popular taste and stimulating sales.[1] Virginia Woolf famously expressed her disdain for the middlebrow in an unsent letter to the *New Statesman*, where she accuses the middlebrow of "nastily" combining life and art with "money, fame, power, or prestige."[2] She angrily notes that the middlebrow "goes to the lowbrows and tells them that while he is not quite one of them, he is almost their friend. Next moment he rings up the highbrows and asks them with equal geniality whether he may not come to tea."[3] While Woolf accuses the middlebrow of indulging in unrefined aesthetic ideals, she also draws attention to the in-between status of the middlebrow, situated between highbrow modernist art and lowbrow popular culture. She notes that the middlebrow is "neither one thing nor the other" and resides "betwixt and between" the highbrow and the lowbrow.[4] Although Woolf finds that the transitional status of the middlebrow contaminates the purity of highbrow aesthetics, it is this very in-between location that makes the middlebrow aesthetically unique. Faye Hammill writes that "[t]he middlebrow provided a vantage point from which high culture, popular culture, and middlebrow culture itself could be critically observed."[5] Hammill disproves the idea that the mingling of the brows within the middlebrow inevitably leads to artistic miscegenation and inferior aesthetic productions. According to her, the middlebrow, despite commanding "unexpected depths and subtleties," has been deprived of adequate scholarly attention for several decades due to the misconception of it being aesthetically simple and not requiring close analyses.[6] However, recent scholarship has blurred the boundaries between high, middle, and lowbrow literature. Melissa Sullivan and Sophie Blanch refer to Douglas Mao and Rebecca Walkowitz's call for modernism's "vertical" expansion in "The New Modernist Studies" and argue that the middlebrow is "one of the obvious starting points" for such expansions. They claim that the study of the middlebrow is ideal "for researching the impact of reading publics and reading practices upon modernism, and for incorporating neglected or obscured authors or texts into modernist studies."[7] The vertical expansion of modernist studies towards the middlebrow can be facilitated especially by tracing the overlaps of ethical values between the two. Early to mid-twentieth century modernism is particularly marked by a cosmopolitan ethic—James Joyce's cosmopolitan Dublin, Virginia Woolf's multicultural London, and Jean Rhys's polycultural Paris stand as examples—which is also shared by contemporary middlebrow literature. Middlebrow author Stella Benson's (1892–1933) travelogue, *The Little World* (1925), shares the values of modernist cosmopolitanism and challenges the traditional distinction between modernist and middlebrow literatures.

Modernist cosmopolitanism is founded upon the Stoic etymology of the term "cosmopolitan"—"citizen of the world." Bruce Robbins and Paulo Lemos Horta note that cosmopolitanism, since its inception, has the dual meaning of "*detachment* from one's place of origin or residence" and *attachment* to cultures other than one's own which enables one to participate in "some larger, stronger, or more compelling collective."[8] Cosmopolitanism thus motivates one to transcend geographical and cultural boundaries and contributes to the development of an antiparochialism.[9] The ideas of antiparochialism, transnationalism, and multiculturalism resonate with modernism and lead to the emergence of modernist cosmopolitanism.

However, modernist cosmopolitanism does not always recognize that for certain minority communities (for instance, refugees and immigrants) transnationalism and multiculturalism are achieved at the cost of displacement and dispossession and amount to an "unhappy and painful experience."[10] Modernist cosmopolitanism, despite such shortcomings, formulates an emphatic critique of imperialism. Jessica Berman writes that modernist cosmopolitanism arises in the context of widespread imperialism and burgeoning ethnocentric nationalism in the early to mid-twentieth century. Modernist cosmopolitanism offers "an antidote to rank parochialism or the kind of cultural imperialism enforced by the spread of empire and the travels of late capitalism."[11] Berman opposes Eurocentrism in her theorization and situates modernist cosmopolitanism in a global context. She considers the varying colonial conditions in which authors from across the world, such as Henry James, Jean Rhys, Rabindranath Tagore, and Mulk Raj Anand, shape their modernist cosmopolitanism. She writes that whereas James moves to London "as heir to the European tradition, ready to demonstrate the best of what the upstart American nation has to offer," Rhys is a "penniless escapee from the white creole society of Antigua" and Tagore and Anand develop their modernist cosmopolitanism "under conditions of Indian coloniality."[12] Although Berman locates modernist cosmopolitanism in a geographically expansive context by bringing together authors from the global north and the global south, she limits her analysis to authors who are unarguably situated within the highbrow—James, Woolf, Rhys, Tagore, and Anand. But in this chapter I show that the ethical concerns of modernist cosmopolitanism are not exclusively circumscribed within highbrow modernist literature but also reproduced in middlebrow literature. Benson's *The Little World* shares the values of modernist cosmopolitanism because it opposes imperialism and forges transcultural and transnational connections across the world.

Modernist cosmopolitanism is significantly motivated by the relentless global movements of modernist authors. Alexandra Peat in her monograph, where she examines the relationship between modernist travel writing and spirituality, notes that various technological developments of early to mid-twentieth century—the construction of railway networks, the reign of ocean liners, and the emergence of commercial aviation—allowed modernist writers to travel widely.[13] The relentless global mobility of modernist authors contributed to a substantive body of modernist travel literature. Paul Fussell, in one of the first critical works on modernist travel literature, examines how various modernists, such as Graham Greene, Evelyn Waugh, and D. H. Lawrence, translate their travel experiences into works of modernist literature. In recent criticism Tim Youngs builds upon Fussell's critical framework of modernist travel literature. He notes that, "[m]any prominent modernists produced travel texts" and compiles a list (which he confesses is "far from complete") of modernist authors who are inspired by their travels, such as W. H. Auden, E. E. Cummings, D. H. Lawrence, Wyndham Lewis, Katherine Mansfield, John Dos Passos, John Steinbeck, Evelyn Waugh, Rebecca West, and Edith Wharton.[14] Travel writing by modernist authors often imbibes modernist aesthetic experimentations. David Farley notes that various modernist literary practices, such as broken syntax, non-linear narrative, and the juxtaposition of prose, poetry, and photography, emphasize the modernist aspect of E. E. Cummings's *Eimi* (1933), W. H. Auden and Louis MacNeice's *Letters from Iceland* (1937), and Rebecca West's *Black Lamb and Grey Falcon* (1941).[15] However, travel writing is not only circumscribed to high modernist literature. Middlebrow literature, similar to high modernist literature, is also impacted by the expansion of travel in the early to mid-twentieth century, which leads to the emergence of travel writing within the middlebrow. Hamill writes that middlebrow magazines "constructed travel as an opportunity to acquire knowledge and prestige as well as to experience pleasure and luxury."[16] The extensive travel experiences enabled high modernist and middlebrow authors to develop a shared sense of modernist cosmopolitanism. Modernist cosmopolitanism shapes the ethical concerns of middlebrow travel writing. The sense of cosmopolitanism enables middlebrow travel writing to develop an ethic of transnational solidarity and also a critique of imperialism.

We can notice prominent instances of a modernist cosmopolitan ethic in Benson's travel writing. Benson was born in England in 1892. She was a prolific writer who commanded a wide readership in her time. She wrote several novels, such as *I Pose* (1915), *This is the End* (1917), *Living Alone* (1919), *The Poor Man* (1922), and others. She received enthusiastic reviews for her works. When the *Spectator* and the *Westminster Gazette* reviewed *The Poor Man*, she commented about the reviews that they were not "a review at all but a thundering burst of praise."[17] Benson's *The Little World* is a product of her extensive travels. As a child, Benson traveled widely with her mother for health reasons. Later as an independent traveler she visited the United States and Asia. She married a customs officer in 1921 and lived in China after her marriage until her death in 1933. Her prolonged stay in China was intermittently punctuated by visits to England and other parts of the world.[18] In *The Little World*, Benson collects sketches and articles she had written about her trips for various newspapers and magazines, such as the *Nation and Athenaeum*, *Country Life*, *Woman's Leader*, *South China Morning Post*, the New York *Bookman*, and other venues. The short articles in the book recount her visits in the late 1910s and early 1920s to the United States, Japan, Hong Kong, China, India, Cambodia, Laos, Myanmar, Thailand, and Vietnam. The articles analyze the cultural particularities of these countries and indicate Benson's modernist cosmopolitanism. Although the cosmopolitan impulse of *The Little World* is evident, it has not been read through the lens of cosmopolitan theory. Benson's work, Katrina Gulliver notes, was forgotten after World War II.[19] Benson has received scant attention from contemporary scholarship. Debra Rae Cohen has examined how Benson's fusion of fantasy and realism in her wartime novels "illuminate the workings of conflicting ideologies on the home front" through a unique hybrid genre.[20] Klaudia Hiu Yen Lee has shown that the transnational mobility of female characters in Benson's *I Pose* and *The Poor Man* symbolize how women subvert "the constraints imposed by social restrictions and expectations."[21] Cohen's and Lee's works are important for understanding Benson's relationship with modernity. But Walter Mignolo has famously stated that modernity is always accompanied by its darker side—coloniality.[22] The cosmopolitan ethic of Benson's travel writings, which have received scant scholarly attention, reveals how the idea of modernity is intertwined with coloniality. My examination of Benson's travelogues illuminates Benson's critique of imperialism and colonialism. My analysis reveals that the cosmopolitan ethic of Benson's travel writings enables them to create connections with foreign cultures without resorting to imperialist tropes of exoticization or primitivism. Benson depicts the cultural particularities of various colonial locations she visits and objectively assesses colonial and cultural differences. However, Benson's cosmopolitan ethic is marked by the tensions that it does not altogether condemn British colonialism and sometimes reverts to passing cultural stereotypes. But it does succeed in echoing the ethical priorities of high modernism in its critique of imperialism and investigation of cultural heterogeneity in most parts. Thus, Benson's travel writings formulate a cosmopolitan ethic that anticipates ideas of transnational solidarity.

Kwame Anthony Appiah has identified cosmopolitanism as an essential ethical concern for modern life in *Cosmopolitanism: Ethics in a World of Strangers*. In this chapter I follow Appiah's theorization of cosmopolitanism to analyze Benson's modernist cosmopolitanism, which significantly overlaps with Appiah's theorization. Appiah identifies the crux of cosmopolitanism as valuing differences and not discriminating on the basis of otherness. He writes,

> So there are two strands that intertwine in the notion of cosmopolitanism. One is the idea that we have obligations to others, obligations that stretch beyond those to whom we are related by the ties of kith and kind, or even the more formal ties of a shared citizenship. The other is that we take seriously the value not just of human life but of particular human lives, which means taking an interest in the practices and beliefs that lend them significance. People are different, the cosmopolitan knows, and there is much to learn from our differences.[23]

Appiah identifies that cosmopolitanism has two principal characteristics. First, cosmopolitanism enables one to develop active interests about communities to which one is not directly connected through kinship or citizenship relationships. Second, when one engages with different communities, cosmopolitanism encourages one to distinguish among the particular beliefs and practices of these communities and observe both overlaps and differences between various cultures. Thus, Appiah's conceptualization of cosmopolitanism highlights transcending all ties of commonality—racial, national, familial, etc.—and exploring cultures in all their differences and specificities.

However, early to mid-twentieth-century middlebrow literature is well known for being rooted in the home and domesticity. In this regard, the transnational ethics of cosmopolitanism might appear to contradict the ethics of the middlebrow. However, a close inspection of the middlebrow reveals that transnational concerns are not extrinsic to it. Nicola Humble, in her pioneering study of middlebrow novels, has shown that although middlebrow novels center around middle-class domesticity, they also address larger concerns of class politics, gender identity, and international relations. Humble identifies the middlebrow as the site where the new middle-class identity is formed, and the middlebrow empowers the middle class to challenge the hegemony of gender and class normativity instead of reinforcing it.[24] Thus, crossing the borders of gender and class norms is essential for the ethics of the middlebrow. Transcending the borders of class and gender anticipates the cosmopolitan ethic of the middlebrow which enables the middlebrow to cross the borders of nations and communities. Benson's travel writing enacts the ethic of cosmopolitanism by frequently crossing national and communal borders. Particularly, Benson's writing echoes Appiah's framework of cosmopolitanism because it is not only inspired by the desire of transcending borders, but also motivated by the impulse to investigate cultural differences. For instance, when Benson visits Hong Kong, she carefully studies the local culture. She insists on exploring the local cuisine and the local theatre, even though some of the local students warn her, "Oh, no, marm, you didn't could like such thing. Chinese theatre too much superstitions… ."[25] Although Benson mistakenly uses "all the wrong little condiment-saucers," she thoroughly enjoys her encounter with the local cuisine in Hong Kong.[26] Thus, Benson does not engage with the unknown as exotic others. She is interested in exploring the specificities of foreign cultures which Appiah identifies as one of the central concerns of cosmopolitanism. I demonstrate that Benson's modernist cosmopolitanism critiques imperialism and colonialism and advocates for transnational connections without racial or cultural prejudice.

The Female Traveler and Cosmopolitanism

Benson's modernist cosmopolitanism heavily relies on the way in which she engages with gender norms. Her cosmopolitanism not only reaches across ethnic and cultural borders, but also transcends gender boundaries.

Martha Nussbaum, one of the foremost thinkers of cosmopolitan theory, explains that cosmopolitanism is not only concerned with cultural and national borders; it also addresses other aspects of identity, such as gender identity, linguistic background, or kinship ties. She puts forward a model of cosmopolitanism in which the individual is surrounded by a series of concentric circles. She envisions the concentric circles in the following way,

> the first one is drawn around the self; the next takes in one's immediate family; then follows the extended family; then, in order, one's neighbors or local groups, one's fellow city-dwellers, one's fellow country-men—and we can easily add to this list groupings based on ethnic, linguistic, historical, professional, gender and sexual identities.[27]

In this intersectional model of cosmopolitanism, the individual is surrounded by multiple circles representing various ethnic, racial, cultural, gender, linguistic, and kinship communities. The individual uninterruptedly moves from one sphere of belonging to the next and develops a shared sense of belonging with multiple gender, ethnic, or linguistic communities. Benson echoes Nussbaum's model of cosmopolitanism by extending her cosmopolitanism to crossing gender boundaries. She challenges the gendered norms of travel writing and reinvents the figure of the female traveler. Susan Bassnett notes that from the sixteenth century until the twentieth, male travelers dominated the sphere of travel writing and they were portrayed as "heroic risk-taking traveller[s]."[28] Many British women travel-writers from the late nineteenth and early twentieth centuries, such as Mary Kingsley (1862–1900), Gertrude Bell (1868–1926), and Dame Freya Stark (1893–1993), also replicated the rhetoric of heroism. Robert Aldrich writes that much of the reputation of these writers rested on "the idea that they had gone where no white women had gone or written about before, to places deemed inhospitable if not fatally dangerous to the 'fair sex.'"[29] Benson does not portray herself as a heroic pioneer exploring unknown depths of the world. Rather, she occasionally reveals the vulnerabilities of travelers. She recounts a moment when a group of Chinese soldiers attacks a boat of tourists. She describes the helplessness of the tourists in the face of imminent danger and sarcastically writes that the soldiers turned their guns on "a little gentle herd of inquisitive globe-trotters, armed only with cameras, field-glasses and Mosquitol."[30] Her description deliberately portrays the tourists in an unheroic light. She implies that the unarmed little gentle herd of tourists are incapable of heroic feats and unable to protect themselves against armed soldiers. She also indicates the lack of heroism in the figure of the solo female traveler. She writes how in Japan she navigates her way with a broken arm in a sling and struggles with two suitcases and a typewriter while being "swept into gutters by jinrickshas and at the same time be[ing] bitten by a horse with a straw petticoat."[31] These challenges are handled by Benson without any heroic grace. Benson extends her rhetoric of un-heroism to her male co-travelers as well. For example, Benson's husband, who accompanies her on a few of her trips in the United States and China, is far from a heroic figure. During moments of distress, Benson's husband does not assume the role of the heroic savior and she does not depict herself as the damsel in distress. On the contrary, the husband sometimes unwittingly creates challenges on their trips. For instance, when traveling in the United States, he gets both Benson and himself in a tricky situation when he misplaces the money that comprises almost all of their travel funds. Benson, instead of relying on her husband to come up with a solution, wades barefoot in slimy mud in a desperate attempt to recover the money.[32] Avoiding the grandeur of heroism in her sketches allows Benson to focus on the everyday details of her trips. The focus on everyday specificities helps Benson usurp the predominant figure of the heroic male traveler. Revealing the everyday complexities of world travel as experienced by a female traveler enriches Benson's modernist cosmopolitanism.

Benson continues revising the figure of the female traveler by not locating her travels in the binary between domestic and public spaces. Bassnett notes that studies of travel writing by women often situate women travelers in a duality between private and public spaces. She writes that women travelers are often portrayed as dissatisfied with domesticity and as seeking an escape in their travels, "[w]omen travellers are often presented as having been somehow able to break free of the constraints of contemporary society, realizing their potential once outside the boundaries of a restrictive social order."[33] Benson circumnavigates such binaries and does not present travel as a more suitable alternative to domesticity. She travels for the love of travel and not out of spite for domesticity. She combines her travel and domestic life and includes several sketches from her honeymoon in the United States and from the time she accompanied her husband in China. Her marriage or domestic duties do not limit her agency and mobility in her travels. She practices flexible movements between domestic and public spheres and nullifies the gendered distinction between the two. Her flexible movement between domestic and public spheres allows her to be at home anywhere in the world and fortifies her modernist cosmopolitanism.

While Benson revises the above-mentioned gender conventions of travel writing, she also carefully records the gender conventions of the communities she visits. Benson was a suffragist and an ardent champion of women's rights.[34] She unhesitatingly expresses her discontent at the moments of women's disempowerment that she frequently encounters on her travels. She sarcastically recounts how women are patronized and infantilized by men in California. She writes, "[i]n California a woman becomes almost tired of being supported in and out of public vehicles as though she were fainting, of having kerbstones and puddles pointed out to her as though she were blind."[35] Her criticism of the patriarchal society in Tonkin (a historical region now forming most of northern Vietnam) is more scathing. She notes that Tonkinese men seldom work and only supervise their wives, mothers, aunts, and daughters who contribute all the labor. The women do all the farming and even carry heavy loads of water across fields. Benson concludes her criticism regretfully noting, "[e]ven the buffalo finds it undignified to be influenced by a mere woman in Indo-China."[36] Benson not only criticizes the condition of foreign women but also that of British women in colonies. She is astonished to find that British men and women in India still conform to Victorian values. She writes that the British men in India are disconcerted by the idea of "Women-in-Men's-Professions" and the "Labor Party" (known for advocating for women's rights among other things). She notices that while British men in India are actively involved with empire building, British women are side-lined in the imperial process and have to keep themselves occupied with "a houseful of servants and a kiddie to look after."[37] Benson thus expresses her disappointment at the varying levels of women disempowerment in the countries she visits. Her frank criticism of the gender norms of various countries aligns her cosmopolitanism with the framework of modernist cosmopolitanism because she not only expresses her appreciation for multicultural local details but also articulates her criticism where necessary.

Although Benson empowers the previously marginalized figure of the female traveler, her race and class identity situate her in a position of power and privilege. Her cosmopolitanism is largely informed by her privilege to travel around the world which is bestowed on her because of her race and class position. Her privilege of traveling and global mobility could make her cosmopolitanism appear elitist and therefore incongruous with the model of modernist cosmopolitanism. Berman, in her theorization of modernist cosmopolitanism, emphasizes that one of the principal ways in which modernism reinvents cosmopolitanism is by distancing the idea of cosmopolitanism from that of elite world travel. She states that, "modernist writers place cosmopolitanism under a kind of pressure that yields a revised model, one that does not necessarily rest on privileged world traveling."[38] In Berman's framework, Benson's cosmopolitanism may not qualify as a modernist cosmopolitanism since it is largely informed by "privileged world traveling." But Benson's cosmopolitanism does indeed qualify as modernist because she does not portray herself as an elite globetrotter; instead she explores the challenges of global mobility for the non-elite. She democratizes her cosmopolitanism by revealing how she travels under financial constraints and takes up odd jobs to pay for her travel expenses. Unlike the elites, traveling is not entirely a leisure activity for Benson. She recounts the various jobs she takes up in California, such as "a University coach, a lady's maid, a collector of overdue bills for an irascible firm, a salesman of boys' books—and, last of all, an editorial reader."[39] Similarly, she finances her travels in Japan through her writings. She writes, "While my money lasted and on the proceeds of a couple of newspaper articles and an 'Interview with Stella Benson,' I managed to go to Kyoto and back."[40] In China she works as an X-Ray operator and in India she writes "desperately sprightly articles for newspapers."[41] Such accounts make visible the logistics and challenges of traveling. That Benson does not gloss over the fact that she needs to take up jobs to finance her own travels prevents her from appearing as an elite globetrotter who funds their travel with ancestral wealth. Benson reinvents the figure of the traveler as someone who is not solely preoccupied with the cultural multiplicity of travel destinations, but as someone who also addresses their own financial conditions.

Benson, in terms of her class position, does not lay claim to the privileges usually enjoyed by elite travelers. But she is aware of the privileges that are inevitably bestowed on her because of her race and national identity. She acknowledges that despite her financial instability as a traveler, she enjoys a more secure position than the citizens of many other countries on certain occasions. When she finds herself in the middle of a war in Sichuan, China, she witnesses how the civilians are taken captive by the army: "I saw the peaceful men of those villages standing with blank dead faces, roped one to the other in long strings, waiting for their burdens."[42] She notes her own relatively secured position compared to the Chinese civilians. She writes,

> Wherever we went groups of Chinese civilians watched and followed, hoping that wherever British arrogance might lead the way, they might follow with safety. But they were disappointed. We were rather ignominiously rescued by an Englishman in a motor boat. And as I looked back at the less fortunate refugees left without friends upon that filthy shore, I was sorry to look so insolently safe.[43]

Benson acknowledges that her Anglo-Saxon racial identity and British nationality protect her within the turmoil. She notes that although the Chinese civilians were in a more vulnerable position and needed to be rescued as much as her, their national and racial identity contributed to their precarity instead of protecting them. Benson reveals how inequalities created by differences in racial and national identities impact multicultural contact. She indicates that the different participants in intercultural interactions often have varying levels of privileges and precarities. In so doing, Benson reveals the complexities of multicultural communications and echoes the modernist impulse of putting pressure on the mechanics of cosmopolitanism.

Although Benson is aware of how national and ethnic identities can put certain communities at a disadvantage, in certain cases she ignores ethnic and cultural specificities. For example, in her sketches of her extensive travels in the south of the United States, she does not mention the racial tensions which are an inseparable part of the country's past and present. Furthermore, some of her comments about foreign communities occasionally appear as dismissive of the internal heterogeneity of said communities. Her observations, such as "Filipinos remain extremely Filipino,"[44] "the Chinese are a painstaking race,"[45] "The Annamites, an obsequious people,"[46] seem to obliterate to some extent the diversity of the communities in question. These instances show that Benson occasionally falls short of recognizing the cultural particularities of various communities and resorts to broad generalizations. The impulse to dismiss cultural heterogeneity creates limitations in Benson's modernist cosmopolitanism. However, Benson's critique of imperialism and her commitment to dismantle the colonizer/colonized hierarchy reinforces her modernist cosmopolitanism.

Modernity/Coloniality

Benson's modernist cosmopolitanism is motivated by an acute desire to transcend national borders and engage with communities, places, and cultures beyond England. She describes in minute details her visits to the United States and various countries in Asia. When she describes the foreign places and cultures, she does not resort to exoticism. Appiah notes that cross-cultural communications are difficult, but they are also manageable with the right intent. He writes,

> The problem of cross-cultural communication can seem immensely difficult in theory, when we are trying to imagine making sense of a stranger in the abstract. But the great lesson of anthropology is that when the stranger is no longer imaginary, but real and present, sharing a human social life, you may like or dislike him, you may agree or disagree; but, if it is what you both want, you can make sense of each other in the end.[47]

Appiah notes that intercultural communications become challenging when one is operating on imaginary assumptions about foreign cultures instead of knowledge gleaned from direct contact. He emphasizes first-hand contact with cultural alterities which make intercultural exchanges productive. His framework of engaging with the stranger is identifiable in Benson's work: in *The Little World* Benson does not describe strangers as imaginary others. Instead, she reverses the imperial practice of exoticizing the Oriental other and presents the possibility that even the imperial English subject can be potentially placed in the position of the unfamiliar other. She describes the occasion when she goes to see a Geisha show in Yokohama, Japan, and at the end of the show the Japanese dancers express interest in her foreignness.

> Later they [the Japanese dancers] took a certain interest in me as though in a curious animal. They pulled my hair gently to see how it worked; they cooed with surprise while experimenting on it with Japanese pins—an experiment to which bobbed hair does not conveniently lend itself. They felt the materials of my clothes with industrious impersonal hands, untied my sling, opened my handbag and, finding a tobacco pouch and cigarette papers in its unladylike depths, demanded patronizingly to be showed how to roll.[48]

In this instance, Benson reverses the Orientalist gaze which is conventionally directed from the Occident toward the Orient. She describes the dance performance but does not stop with that because that would have positioned the Japanese performers as powerless objects of Benson's imperial gaze. She continues recounting how the performers interact with her after the performance. She illustrates that the performers treat her almost like a fascinating foreign object when they touch the material of her clothes with "industrious impersonal hands." The dancers even subject Benson to their gendered gaze. Benson indirectly notes that the dancers consider smoking cigarettes an "unladylike" habit and they "demanded patronizingly" that Benson show them how to roll cigarettes. Thus, the dancers not only perceive Benson as an exotic foreigner but also as someone who does not fit with their gender expectations.

Portraying the gaze of the dancers from their point of view helps Benson turn the Occidental subject into an object of exoticization by the Orient. Through this reversal of gaze, she acknowledges the challenges of intercultural encounters. Her ironical reverse exoticization contrasts many of her predecessors and contemporaries. Bassnett notes that many nineteenth-century travel writers, both male and female, "moved secure in the knowledge of their own superiority, quick to patronize or mock" the culture and mannerisms of the often non-Western other. She gives the example of travel-writer May French-Sheldon, who in the foreword of one of her travelogues refers to the people of Africa as "natural primitives."[49] Many of Benson's contemporary travel writers, such as Isabelle Massieu and Alexandra David-Néel, continue the practice of representing their travel destinations as exotic locations.[50] Massieu, in the introduction to her 1914 travelogue on Nepal and India, paints these countries with the rhetoric of exoticization—"les vieilles terres d'histoire et de civilisation [...] de mystérieux et de profond qui nous enveloppe et nous captive."[51] In contrast, Benson departs from the rhetoric of framing her destinations as unknowable exotic places. She echoes Appiah and indicates that challenges in knowing foreign cultures can be surmounted by directly engaging with multiple cultures and by not reducing them to imaginary others. When the Japanese women touch Benson's clothes and explore her handbag, they get exposed to new cultural materialities. Thus, although the encounter begins with a stance of exoticization, the direct contact with cultural alterity ultimately leads to a cosmopolitan moment of intercultural exchange.

Benson further avoids exoticizing foreign cultures in her own encounters with cultural multiplicity. She observes foreign cultures from close proximity and does not subscribe to imaginary assumptions of cultural otherness. She recognizes the particularity of each culture and community and produces varied descriptions of places. Benson writes:

> We reached the port of Chefoo [present Yantai] late on our sixth night. All next day, while coolies, dyed bright blue with indigo, piled into lighters the oozing sacks of our cargo, the skipper and I explored the sun-stricken sordid city of Chefoo. It seemed to me—after Hongkong [sic]—a city baked and caked in squalor.[52]

> On the Brahmapootra River the crescent fishing boats lay like new moons on the water and between them and the sand-dunes the dwelling boats floated, square and matronly, with a prosaic noise of clucking hens and whooping babies, under square-shouldered sails drawn together at the foot like great honey-colored fans.[53]

> Los Angeles is a sophisticated city; it has no eccentricities and no heart. It is approached through oil fields that tower in skeleton groups like thin enormous dead forests.[54]

Benson produces distinct descriptions of varied locations from across the world, such as the city of Chefoo [present Yantai] in the People's Republic of China, the Brahmapootra River in north-east India, and Los Angeles in the United States. She pays close attention to the local details like the dwelling boats on the Brahmapootra or the oil fields in Los Angeles. When she draws attention to the unique local details of the different locations, it prevents her from exoticizing the cities as unknowable. The attention to details emphasizes Benson's first-hand engagement with these locations. She also does not create any false equivalence among the locations and highlights their distinctiveness. For example, she emphasizes that Chefoo presents a contrast to Hong Kong. She does not create any unwarranted equivalence between Oriental cities. Her description of the tranquil Brahmapootra also presents a contrast to the squalor of Chefoo. Thus, she draws attention to the internal heterogeneity of Oriental cities. She establishes that each Oriental location has its own distinct cultural identity which is different from other Oriental locations. In this way Benson preserves the cultural specificity of particular locations and prevents them from being co-opted into a global homogeneity.

Appiah notes that the detractors of cosmopolitanism warn that it erases local particularities and imposes global homogeneity in a process he calls "cosmopolitan contamination." He disproves the possibility of cosmopolitan contamination by arguing that the idea of preserving cultural purity is unreasonable because every cultural community is always already heterogeneous and therefore not susceptible to contamination. He writes that, "Cultural purity is an oxymoron. The odds are that, culturally speaking, you already live a cosmopolitan life, enriched by literature, art, and film that come from many places, and that contains influences from many more."[55] For Appiah, heterogeneity is endemic to all cultures. Benson proves the inevitable heterogeneity of the Orient by producing distinct descriptions of various locations in the continent. She does not subsume the individual locations under the broad and vague category of Asian culture. The minute attention to local details helps Benson produce a cosmopolitan account of the continent that is premised on cultural heterogeneity and avoids cosmopolitan contamination.

Benson's attention to local details allows her to observe how multiple layers of cultural traditions and multiple histories accumulate in various locations. For instance, she observes the palimpsestic cultural multiplicity of early twentieth-century Manila,

> The traveler toils across acres of imported America towards the hotel which rears itself, indecently opulent, above a waste of junk and lumber yards and gray hot grass—and suddenly, like the first pioneers in California, he meets the challenge of the old world again across the desert—here is Spain again, Manila, girdled with her golden wall and crowned with a romantic sun.[56]

Here Benson dissects the cultural cross-currents in Manila. She observes how the "imported" new world of America merges with the old world of Spain on the soil of Manila. Her description draws attention to the multi-layered cultural fabric of Manila and reveals the inherent cosmopolitanism of the location. Benson, in addition to examining the multiculturalism of a location horizontally across spaces, also observes the cultural pluralism of a location vertically across time. In the case of Macao, she describes how the cultural plurality of the location has evolved across time:

> The city of Macao is old, but it seems older than its years. Here, I think, you have China victorious. Portugal lies drugged and asleep in the arms of China. The empty shell of Portuguese taste is there, the colored plaster walls, the low corrugated red tile roofs, the quiet gardened convents, the churches full of a vulgar and ardent daylight ... Yet the city seemed to me almost wholly Chinese at heart.[57]

Benson reveals that the colonial history of Macao has multiple layers. By noting the Chinese and Portuguese cultural forces in the city, she conveys the complex colonial heritage of the location. For a long time, Macao was under dual Chinese and Portuguese jurisdictions. After the Opium Wars, the Portuguese moved to end the dual rule and establish an exclusively Portuguese government. The period from 1849 to 1976 is recognized as the colonial period of Macao.[58] Benson indicates how the Chinese and Portuguese cultural forces interact with each other in Macao's urban fabric. She observes that the Portuguese influence noted in "the colored plaster walls, the low corrugated red tile roofs, the quiet gardened convents" of the city is only an "empty shell of Portuguese taste." She believes that, despite Portugal's colonial rule, only vestiges of Portuguese culture remain in Macao. She thinks that the dominant cultural tradition in Macao is Chinese culture which is why the city is "Chinese at heart." Her observation suggests that the Portuguese imperialist hegemony has not been able to efface or appropriate local Chinese culture in Macao. Instead, the dominant presence of Chinese culture and the residual presence of Portuguese culture create a cultural hybridity in the city.

When Benson examines the local particularities and internal cultural heterogeneity of various global locations, she does not create hierarchies between the Orient and the Occident or between colonies and the imperial center. She does not resort to the rhetoric of declaring the imperial West as superior to and more progressive than all other cultures. She observes the uniqueness of the communities she comes in contact with and avoids the binaries of superior/inferior and primitive/progressive when she approaches foreign cultures. Her refusal to consider the imperial West as the inevitably superior culture is motivated by her criticism of imperialism. She disapproves of how colonialism intervenes with local cultures in Laos:

> We came into Laos by the new front door, the new French trail that has succeeded in humping itself proudly over the mountains between Vinh and Thakhek; we must leave Laos by the old back door, the dubious tremulous old jungle track that does not interest engineers or the enterprising owners of motor buses.[59]

Here Benson expresses her suspicion for the imperial civilizing mission. She calls the French trail "proud" to induce irony. Benson, by showing colonial processes in the light of irony, refuses to glorify imperial intervention as progress towards modernity. Instead, she reveals the opportunism of imperialism. Noting that the old jungle track is of no interest to engineers, she draws attention to the insincerity of the imperial intent of working towards the welfare of the colonies. She implies that imperial "progress" will be limited to those parts of the colony which yield profit and will not be extended to parts which do not immediately benefit the imperial mission. Benson's critique of imperialism is the most prominent in her condemnation of war. She witnesses wars in various countries she visits and depicts the ruination caused by wars. She witnesses a war on one of her visits to Beijing and expresses her horror at the plight of the soldiers,

> They were like ghosts passing through the flushed twilight of the X-Ray room, they seemed to have no past and no future. They were the ruins of a lost army, their leader had forgotten them [...] Collectively, experience seems to teach them nothing, and though these have fallen and been forsaken, others fight on, for no ideal, for no cause, for no reward, for no reason.[60]

She laments the fate of the soldiers and the futility of war, criticizing how the soldiers are dehumanized by imperialism, which robs them of their past and future, and any sense of purpose. The soldiers are reduced to pawns in the grand scheme of imperialism and they go on wars for reasons unknown to them. Benson, writing soon after World War I, thus expresses her disdain for war and rising fascism. Instead, she champions international solidarity which reinforces her modernist cosmopolitanism.

Benson's critique of imperialism is also self-reflexive in that she turns a critical eye towards her own Englishness. At the end of *The Little World*, she writes that, "in the end we are broken reeds for British prestige."[61] In this statement, she expresses that English pride and prestige are often unfounded. She does not suffer from any aggressive nationalist sentiment and does not believe in the superiority of colonial English culture. However, the critique remains incomplete. Even though Benson does not believe in the superiority of imperial British culture or her own

Englishness, she does not produce any overt critique of British colonialism in the way she criticizes French colonialism in Laos. Thomas Bender identifies self-reflexivity as an essential characteristic of cosmopolitanism and writes that, "[t]he experience that makes a cosmopolitan is at once a partial understanding of the other and an enriching partial re-understanding of one's self."[62] Whereas Benson is always interested in exploring the particularities of other cultures, the "re-understanding of one's self" remains incomplete in her case. Her self-reflexivity does not entirely extend to critiquing the negative impacts of British imperialism on the colonies. The lack of critique of British colonialism weakens Benson's self-reflexivity and constitutes a limitation in her cosmopolitan ethic.

Conclusion

Benson's cosmopolitanism strongly echoes Appiah's model of cosmopolitanism and international solidarity. The merit of Benson's cosmopolitanism, despite its above-mentioned limitations, resides in how from within the middlebrow she replicates the principal ethical concerns of modernist cosmopolitanism. Benson, in her description of foreign places, cultures, and peoples, avoids Orientalist tropes, critiques Western imperialism and Englishness, and explores the particularities of diverse foreign cultures without essentializing them or placing them in an inferior position compared to imperial Western cultures. She also departs from long-standing traditions of travel writing and displays the modernist impulse of revising a genre. She opposes the figure of the elite traveler and addresses the everyday challenges of a middle-class female traveler, rejects the heroic overtones of travel writing and emphasizes the mundanity of world travel, and reinvents the figure of the female traveler as someone who wants to travel for the excitement of knowing new cultures rather than as an excuse to escape domestic duties. Benson's modernist cosmopolitanism thus facilitates the vertical expansion of modernist studies into the middlebrow. In so doing, she transcends her immediate borders of race, class, gender, and nation and engages with cultural diversity all across the world.

CHAPTER SIX

Wittgenstein's Modernism
Apocalypse and Ethics

Ben Ware

Immanuel Kant's eighteenth-century invitation to imagine an "end of all things" no longer feels like just a thought experiment.[1] In a new age of intersecting crises—ecological, biological, geo-political—the very survival of the human species is, once again, in question. We live in an apocalyptic age, where the catastrophe has, in one sense, *already happened*. While the situation clearly calls for urgent political action (the activation of what Walter Benjamin once termed "the emergency brake" on capitalism's runaway train), it also demands new forms of ethical and theoretical thought.

In this spirit, the current chapter turns to an unlikely source: the Viennese modernist philosopher Ludwig Wittgenstein. Wittgenstein's first work, the *Tractatus Logico-Philosophicus*, was itself born out of apocalyptic times. When World War I broke out in 1914, Wittgenstein, then a student in Cambridge under the tutelage of Bertrand Russell, was adamant that he must go to the front line and fight, believing that the proximity to death would make him a better thinker. As absurdly heroic as this now sounds, Wittgenstein, as it turns out, wasn't wrong: as the bullets flew overhead during the Brusilov offensive of June to September 1916, the young philosopher scribbled down in his notebooks some of the most important lines of the work that would later become the *Tractatus*. This short book (first published in German in 1921) invites its reader to recognize as "nonsense" what they had previously taken for "sense" (i.e., the book's propositions);

to "throw away the ladder" (of nonsensical sentences); and to come to "[see] the world rightly."[2] Simply put, what the book aims to effectuate is a transformation of the reader's philosophical desire; something which the author himself described as "ethical."

Wittgenstein's posthumously published second work, the *Philosophical Investigations* (1953), also emerged out a period of historical catastrophe: the rise of Nazism, World War II, and, later, the emergence of the Cold War. Like its forerunner, the *Investigations* is an ethical work: its intention is to bring its reader to a clearer picture of their "philosophical disquietude." While a standard philosophical narrative argues for a clear-cut distinction between the "early" and "later" Wittgenstein, it is in fact much more useful to emphasize the dialectical connection between the *Tractatus* and the *Investigations*: both texts share an avowedly "therapeutic" aim, but under the pressure of different social, historical, and intellectual forces they come to adopt different methods, forms, and styles. In a significant passage in the Preface to the *Investigations*, Wittgenstein writes that having had occasion to re-read his early work it now appears to him that the *Tractatus* and the *Investigations* could be published together in a single volume. He also writes that "the latter could be seen in the right light only [...] against the background of my old way of thinking." The two works, we might say, present us with *two faces of modernism*.

The argument that follows in this chapter moves through three stages. First, it makes the case for grasping not only the literary and aesthetic qualities of Wittgenstein's work, but also, and more specifically, for seeing him as an exponent of what I will here call *philosophical modernism*. Second, the essay turns to a number of Wittgenstein's controversial remarks on the atomic bomb and what he calls the "apocalyptic view of the world"; and it brings these remarks into dialogue with the work of a number of other literary and philosophical figures, including Gertrude Stein, Günther Anders, and Theodor Adorno. Third and finally, although Wittgenstein's remarks on apocalypse appear in his private, post-War notebooks, they nevertheless provide us with a crucial link to his later philosophy, specifically the *Philosophical Investigations*. In the *Investigations*, it is not simply the language of the book that we might describe as apocalyptic, but also, and more importantly, the fundamental conception of philosophy that we find therein. This returns us not only to the view of philosophical modernism previously outlined, but also to a new way of thinking the ethical in our own era of converging catastrophes.

I

How are we to conceive of Wittgenstein's relation to modernism? Is modernism an *internal* component of Wittgenstein's philosophical practice, or is it an *external* tradition to which his philosophy in some way relates? What exactly is it that we mean when we speak of Wittgenstein as a modernist figure?

According to Terry Eagleton, in a now famous series of remarks: "Frege is a philosopher's philosopher, Bertrand Russell every shopkeeper's image of the sage, and Sartre the media's idea of an intellectual. But Wittgenstein is the philosopher of poets, playwrights, novelists and composers."[3] For Eagleton, the *Tractatus* belongs to the great wave of early twentieth-century European modernism; and therefore the true coordinates of the text are not Frege or Russell, but rather Joyce, Schoenberg, and Picasso—what Eagleton calls "all those self-ironizing modernists who sought in their own fashion to represent and point to their representing at a stroke."[4]

This view of Wittgenstein's modernism—one which conceives of the relation in essentially *aesthetic* terms—is now very much what I want to call *the standard view*. To the extent that Wittgenstein is thought of as a modernist at all, then it is, as Marjorie Perloff puts it, because his "way of tackling philosophical problems is best called *aesthetic*": aesthetic in its creative use of "exempla, apposite images, parataxis, and sudden leaps of faith."[5] To adapt a remark from Stanley Cavell's 1971 study *The World Viewed*, we might thus say that what makes Wittgenstein a modernist is that his "philosophy exists in the condition of art."[6]

And of course all of this, in one respect, is true—absolutely and vitally true. No understanding of either the *Tractatus* or the *Philosophical Investigations* can proceed without taking seriously the literary and aesthetic dimensions of the works. As early as his wartime *Notebooks*, Wittgenstein describes his problem as one of finding the right form of expression for his thoughts. "My difficulty," he remarks in 1915, is only "an enormous difficulty of expression." In a later letter to the publisher Ludwig von Ficker, Wittgenstein writes (about his "Logisch-Philosophische Abhandlung") that "the work is strictly philosophical and at the same time literary: but there's no gassing in it."[7] The literary dimensions of the *Tractatus* are also recognized by the logician Gottlob Frege:

> The pleasure of reading your book can [...] in no way arise through the [...] content, but [...] only through the form, in which is revealed something of the individuality of the author. [The book] thereby becomes an artistic rather than a scientific achievement; that which is said [...] takes a back seat to how it is said.[8]

It will be useful here to briefly pause and compare Frege's insightful, although ultimately unsympathetic, remarks on the literary elements of the *Tractatus*, with those of a number of more recent European philosophers and theoreticians—figures who one might expect to be much more open and sympathetic to the aesthetic and literary dimensions of Wittgenstein's work.

II

In a series of interviews conducted in 1989, the French philosopher Gilles Deleuze is asked for his thoughts on Wittgenstein. Initially reluctant to engage the topic, Deleuze finally opens up to his interlocutor Claire Parnet:

> For me [Wittgenstein] is a philosophical catastrophe [...] [His work marks] a regression of all philosophy, a massive regression. The Wittgenstein matter is very, very sad. They [the Wittgensteinians] impose a system of terror [...] under the pretext of doing something new. It is poverty instituted as grandeur. [...]
>
> There isn't a word to describe this danger. It seems, especially since all Wittgensteinians are mean and destructive, if they win there could be an assassination of philosophy. They are philosophical assassins.[9]

What is perhaps most striking about Deleuze's remarks, is not simply their dismissive (even contemptuous) tone, but the fact that they come from a philosopher who is elsewhere utterly committed to the "mobile relations" between philosophy and literature; to what he calls "the smooth space" which allows for philosophy-becoming-literature and literature- and art-becoming-philosophy.[10] In their 1991 text, *What is Philosophy?*, Deleuze and his collaborator Félix Guattari refer to figures such as Kierkegaard and Nietzsche as "hybrid geniuses" who "use all the resources of their 'athleticism' to install themselves within [a space of] difference, like acrobats torn apart in a perpetual show of strength."[11] Wittgenstein, however, surely *the* great inheritor of Kierkegaardian and Nietzschean philosophical acrobatics in the twentieth century, is completely absent from the Deleuze–Guattari picture.

In many respects, Deleuze's interview comments reprise a view of Wittgenstein's philosophy put forward, several decades earlier, by members of the Frankfurt School. Theodor Adorno, for example, in his *Hegel: Three Studies*, cites the final proposition of the *Tractatus*—"Whereof one cannot speak thereof one must be silent"[12]—and takes it, reductively, as an example of "extreme positivism," which, in his words, "spills over" into a "gesture of reverent authoritarian authenticity."[13] Herbert Marcuse's 1964 study, *One Dimensional Man*, moves in a similar direction. According to Marcuse, Wittgenstein's later work "militates against intellectual non-conformity"; "reaffirms the prevailing universe of discourse and behaviour"; and in its demand for absolute clarity functions like the philosophical equivalent of a Stalinist politburo:

> The intellectual is called on the carpet. What do you mean when you say …? Don't you conceal something? You talk a language which is suspect. You don't talk like the rest of us, like the man in the street, but rather like a foreigner who does not belong here. We have to cut you down to size, expose your tricks, purge you.[14]

There is of course no mention here of Wittgenstein's own émigré ("foreigner") status and a life spent not "belonging"; no mention of the fact that his philosophy issues no decrees, but, much like Marcuse's own, is thoroughly committed to a liberatory battle against the bewitchment of the intellect; no mention of the fact that rather than a bureaucratic levelling of language and discourse, what Wittgenstein *actually* calls for—explicitly at one point, and elsewhere implicitly—is for philosophy to be written *only* as a kind of poetic or creative composition: "I think I summed up my attitude to philosophy when I said: philosophy ought to be written only as a poetic composition."[15] It would thus seem that Wittgenstein is not entirely misguided in his pessimistic prediction that his work would not be understood. Writing in the Preface to the *Philosophical Investigations* he remarks that although his work *might* "bring light" into one brain or another, this is not very likely. "My type of thinking is not wanted in this present age," he comments to his friend Maurice O'Conner Drury: "I have to swim so strongly against the tide. Perhaps in a hundred years people will really want what I am writing."[16]

The only recent continental philosopher to pay any real attention to the literary and aesthetic dimensions of Wittgenstein's writing has been Alain Badiou. Taking his cue from the French psychoanalyst Jacques Lacan, Badiou reads Wittgenstein as a prototypical "anti-philosopher": a figure who, in the tradition of Kierkegaard, Nietzsche, and Lacan himself, exposes the "dishonesty" of conventional modes of philosophizing, acting, in Badiou's words, as an "awakener" of his audience.[17] Badiou highlights the early Wittgenstein's "art of writing," his "abstract literary audacity"; and he suggests that the text to which the *Tractatus* should be compared is Mallarmé's *A Throw of the Dice Will Never Abolish Chance*. According to Badiou:

> The affirmative and hierarchical unfolding of propositions, the metaphorical tension combined with a mathematising rigour, the latent irony of the figures, the absolute self-sufficiency and yet the reference to an "overcoming" of the Book: all these features bring together the two projects.[18]

While Badiou is certainly correct to highlight what we might call the "Mallarméan side" of Wittgenstein—the side of him concerned with syntax, precision, and structure—there are nevertheless two key problems with his overall account. First, like Eagleton and Perloff, Badiou conceives of Wittgenstein's modernism primarily in aesthetic terms:

his anti-philosophical *act* is, Badiou says, "*archi-aesthetic*" (or "chiefly aesthetic"). In this respect, his approach to Wittgenstein's modernism is very much in line with what I'm calling the standard approach. Second, there is a problem with Badiou's notion of anti-philosophy: a concept which does not simply refer to philosophy which is divested of its theoretical pretensions, but one which, in the context of his account of Wittgenstein, crucially entails an ineffabilist dimension:

> The antiphilosophical act consists in letting what there is show itself, insofar as "what there is" is precisely that which no proposition can say. If Wittgenstein's antiphilosophical act can legitimately be declared archi-aesthetic, it is because this "letting be" has the non-propositional form of pure showing. [...] It is thus a question of firmly establishing the laws of the sayable (of the thinkable), in order for the unsayable (the unthinkable, which is ultimately given only in art) to be *situated* as the "upper limit" of the sayable itself.[19]

The problem here, then, is that while Badiou praises Wittgenstein's break with traditional, theory-producing modes of philosophy, the aspect of his work that he deems *most significant* is his so-called *theory of saying and showing*. "Anti-philosophy," as Badiou puts it, paraphrasing *Tractatus* 4.14, "must set limits to what can be thought; and, in so doing, to what cannot be thought."[20] On its own terms, then, Badiou's notion of anti-philosophy, when applied to the early Wittgenstein, would appear to be at best contradictory: it rehearses the standard, doctrinal reading of the *Tractatus*, while simultaneously claiming that the book does not advance doctrines and theories and is instead committed solely to the idea of philosophy *as an act*.

Where might we therefore turn for an understanding of Wittgenstein's relation to modernism—one which avoids conceiving of the matter in exclusively aesthetic terms (what I'm calling the standard approach); and one which, at the same time, sidesteps the pitfalls of Badiou's notion of modernist anti-philosophy? Here I'd like to suggest that understanding Wittgenstein as a modernist figure requires us, first of all, to begin with a different understanding of modernism itself: one which treats it not (or not chiefly) as an aesthetic category, nor indeed as a chronological one, but rather—first and foremost—as a *philosophical concept*. What will it mean then to think of modernism as a philosophical concept? We might argue that philosophical modernism comprises three closely connected strands: (i) the temporal, (ii) the methodological, and (iii) the formal. In relation to Wittgenstein's work, these three strands can be elucidated as follows:

(i) The temporal strand

Philosophical modernism is characterized by an affirmation of the *new* and a *conscious awareness* of one's own philosophical enterprise *as new*. It makes its claim on the present through a rejection of the old—understood as past forms, past ideas, past ways of seeing—in the name of a commitment to a philosophically, aesthetically, ethically, or politically transformed future. This emphasis upon the new is, however, far from unproblematic: (i) it seems to preserve a secret tie to the past, being dependent upon that which it seeks to overturn; and (ii) to the extent that the new is *endlessly* announced, it cannot avoid succumbing to the logic of *the same*. Nevertheless, it is still the new upon which philosophical modernism insists.

Example (i)

> I myself still find my way of philosophizing new, & it keeps striking me so afresh, & that is why I have to repeat myself so often. It will have become part of the flesh & blood of a new generation.[21]

(ii) The methodological strand

Philosophical modernism advances by way of *negation*. While negation can take numerous and diverse forms, drawing on the work of Walter Benjamin we might say that negation is first and foremost an activity of "clearing away. [...] Not always by brute force; sometimes by the most refined means. [...] What exists is reduced to rubble—not for the sake of the rubble, but for that of the way leading through it."[22] Here, then, negation is not to be equated with *unqualified destructiveness*; rather, the activity of negation is always invested with a positive force, one which aims at establishing a new foundation.

Example (ii)

> Where does this investigation get its importance from, given that it seems only to destroy everything interesting: that is, all that is great and important? (As it were, all the buildings, leaving behind only bits of stone and rubble.) But what we are destroying are only houses of cards, and we are clearing up the ground of language on which they stood.[23]

(iii) The formal strand

Philosophical modernism strives to find new *forms* for the expression of philosophical thought—an activity which requires opening up a space *outside* the discursive universe of traditional philosophy. In this respect, philosophical modernism places particular emphasis not just on what is said, but on *how* it is said and the *impact* of what is said on the reader. The reader's emotional and affective engagement with the text is thus, we might say, already anticipated by the text itself. Moreover, if one wishes to locate the ethical point of works of philosophical modernism, then this consists less in looking at what any specific author has to *say* about ethics, and more in examining the kinds of formal or rhetorical work that individual texts actively perform.

Example (iii):

> My propositions are elucidatory in this way: he who understands me finally recognizes them as [nonsense], when he has climbed out through them, on them, over them. (He must so to speak throw away the ladder, after he has climbed up on it.)
>
> He must surmount these propositions; then he sees the world rightly.[24]

In what follows, then, I want to suggest one way in which Wittgenstein can be grasped as a *philosophical modernist* in the way just outlined. Focusing specifically on the second, methodological strand—which I associate with negation and Benjamin's "destructive character"—I will argue that Wittgenstein's later work can be understood as *apocalyptic*, not simply in tone, but also, and more importantly, in terms of its *philosophical method*. This method can be viewed under a changed aspect once it is considered in light of a number of cultural and political remarks which Wittgenstein makes during the 1930s and 1940s.

III

Throughout his notebooks of the 1930s and 1940s, Wittgenstein makes numerous remarks, which, in different ways, evoke the sense of an ending. In 1931, for example, when thinking about his work in philosophy, he says to himself: "I destroy, I destroy, I destroy."[25] In the same year, he comments that "[i]f my name lives on then only as the *Terminus ad quem* of great occidental philosophy. Somewhat like the name of the one who burnt down the library of Alexandria."[26] In the "Big Typescript," he comments that "*all* that philosophy can do is to *destroy idols* [...] [a]nd that means not creating a new one"; and, moreover, that philosophy itself, at least in part, consists in destroying "certain prejudices that are based on our particular way of looking at things."[27]

In 1946, however, whilst sketching out what would become his *Philosophical Investigations*, Wittgenstein makes an altogether more startling claim: one that is, at least on the surface, less a comment on his own philosophical enterprise and more a piece of social, political, and cultural critique:

> The hysterical fear of the atom bomb the public now has, or at least expresses, is almost a sign that here for once a really salutary discovery has been made. At least the fear gives the impression of being fear in the face of a really effective bitter medicine. I cannot rid myself of the thought: if there were not something good here, the philistines would not be making an outcry. But perhaps this too is a childish idea. For all I can mean really is that the bomb

creates the prospect of the end, the destruction of a ghastly evil, of disgusting soapy water science and certainly that is not an unpleasant thought; but who is to say what would come after such a destruction? The people now making speeches against the production of the bomb are undoubtedly the dregs of the intelligentsia, but even that does not prove beyond question that what they abominate is to be welcomed.[28]

What then, ethically and philosophically speaking, should we make of these remarks, written almost exactly one year after the bombings of the Japanese cities of Hiroshima and Nagasaki—events which left almost a quarter of a million people dead, many of them civilians? We might begin by placing Wittgenstein's comments alongside other modernist responses to the bomb, notably Gertrude Stein's fragment "Reflection on the Atomic Bomb," also written in 1946:

> I never could take any interest in the atomic bomb [...]. That it has to be secret makes it dull and meaningless. Sure it will destroy a lot and kill a lot, but it's the living that are interesting not the way of killing them, because if there were not a lot left living how could there be any interest in destruction. Alright, that is the way I feel about it. They think they are interested about the atomic bomb but they really are not not any more than I am. Really not. They may be a little scared, I am not so scared, there is so much to be scared of so what is the use of bothering to be scared, and if you are not scared the atomic bomb is not interesting.[29]

If Stein is radically *disinterested* in the bomb (a striking example, perhaps, of modernist boredom and subjective withdrawal), then Wittgenstein appears deeply *invested* in it; and for what would seem to be two connected reasons. First, the bomb offers the prospect of an "end," the destruction of a "ghastly evil," and, specifically, the termination of what he calls "soapy water" scientism. Second, the bomb might be thought of as a welcome invention precisely because those opposing it (including the likes of Russell and Einstein) are, in Wittgenstein's words, "philistines," the "dregs of the intelligentsia." While Wittgenstein is quick to acknowledge that the latter is perhaps a "childish idea" (he is simply welcoming what his intellectual opponents are against), his general remarks about the bomb need to be understood in relation to a number of other statements which he makes during the same period. The following remark from 1947 is here especially important:

> *The truly apocalyptic view* of the world is that things do *not* repeat themselves. It is not e.g. absurd to believe that the scientific & technological age is the beginning of the end for humanity, that the idea of Great Progress is a bedazzlement, along with the idea that the truth will ultimately be known; that there is nothing good or desirable about scientific knowledge & that humanity, in seeking it, is falling into a trap. It is by no means clear that this is not how things are.[30]

According to Wittgenstein, then, the truly apocalyptic view is one that sees humanity marching directly towards its end (without the chance to repeat, to learn from past mistakes); but this end emerges as a real possibility only with the arrival of the so-called scientific–technological age. In the epoch of "great progress," in which science becomes the only accepted form of knowledge, humankind sinks into a world of "infinite misery," into a new "darkness," in which "peace is the last thing that will find a home."[31] On this point, Wittgenstein comes strikingly close to the view put forward by Theodor Adorno and Max Horkheimer in the opening pages of their *Dialectic of Enlightenment*: "the fully enlightened earth radiates disaster triumphant."[32]

Taken together, Wittgenstein's two remarks thus present a distinctly apocalyptic outlook: (i) we are faced with the prospect of a final end ("the bomb"); but (ii) this end also reveals or unveils (*apo*, "away" + *kalupto*, "cover") an important truth about capitalist modernity: what appears at first blush as human "progress" (technological–scientific advancement) turns out in fact to be the very motor of world annihilation. Consequently, it may be necessary, as Wittgenstein suggests, for the end of *a* world—the frenzied world of technoscience—in order to prevent an even more catastrophic end—the total destruction of our existing forms of (ecological, human, and non-human) life.[33]

IV

It will be useful here, ethically speaking, to bring Wittgenstein's remarks on the bomb, modernity, and apocalypse, into dialogue with the work of Günther Anders, the German Jewish thinker given the epithet "*Atomphilosph*" (the "nuclear philosopher"). A contemporary of Herbert Marcuse, Bertolt Brecht, and Hannah Arendt (to whom he was married from 1929 to 1937), Anders devoted much of his work in the 1950s and early 1960s to exploring the relationship between technology and catastrophe, especially the threat of nuclear extermination. According to Anders, we have become "inverted Utopians": "while ordinary Utopians are unable to actually produce what they are able to visualize, we are unable to visualize what we are actually producing."[34] This *Promethean gap*—"our capacity to produce as opposed to our power to imagine"—"defines the moral situation [facing us] today."[35] Our society is, Anders argues, a society of machines and technological devices; and it is through these that the great "dream of omnipotence has at long last come true."[36] This dream, however, turns out to be the very nightmare from which we cannot awake, precisely because "we are [now] in a position to inflict *absolute destruction* on each other."[37] With these new "apocalyptic powers," we enter what Anders calls "The Last Age":

> On August 6, 1945, the day of Hiroshima, a New Age began: the age in which at any given moment we have the power to transform any given place on our planet, and even our planet itself, into a Hiroshima. On that day we became, at least "modo negative," omnipotent; but since, on the other hand, we can be wiped out at any given moment, we also became totally impotent. However long this age may last, even if it should last forever, it is "The Last Age": for there is no possibility that it's "differentia specifica," the possibility of our self-extinction, can ever end—but by the end itself. [...]
>
> Thus the basic moral question of former times must be radically reformulated: instead of asking "*How* should we live?", we now must ask "*Will* we live?"[38]

Surviving the threat of extinction will entail, at least in part, expanding our capacity for fear and anxiety and cultivating a *renewed sense of the apocalyptic*. As Anders puts it:

> Our imperative: "Expand the capacity of your imagination," means, in concreto: "Increase your capacity of fear." Therefore: don't fear fear, have the courage to be frightened, and to frighten others, too. Frighten thy neighbor as thyself. This fear, of course, must be of a special kind: 1) a fearless fear, since it excludes fearing those who might deride us as cowards, 2) a stirring fear, since it should drive us into the streets instead of under cover, 3) a loving fear, not fear *of* the danger ahead but *for* the generations to come.[39]

We need, then, to become *enlightened doomsayers*.[40] Anders distils this doomsaying metaphysics into a short parable which creatively retells the Old Testament story of Noah:

> One day, he [Noah] clothed himself in sackcloth and covered his head with ashes. [...] [He was] asked if someone had died, and who the dead person was. Noah replied to them that many had died, and then, to the great amusement of his listeners, said that they themselves were the dead of whom he spoke. When he was asked when this catastrophe had taken place, he replied to them: "Tomorrow." Profiting from their attention and confusion, Noah drew himself up to his full height and said these words: "The day after tomorrow, the flood will be something that will have been. And when the flood will have been, *everything that is will never have existed*. When the flood will have carried off everything that is, everything that will have been, it will be too late to remember, for there will no longer be anyone alive. And so there will no longer be any difference between the dead and those who mourn them. *If I have come before you, it is in order to reverse time*, to mourn tomorrow's dead today. The day after tomorrow it will be too late." With this he went back whence he had come, took off the sackcloth [that he wore], cleaned his face of the ashes that covered it, and went to his workshop. That evening a carpenter

knocked on his door and said to him: "Let me help you build an ark, *so that it may become false.*"[41]

For Anders's Noah, the catastrophe is therefore both *necessary*, fated to occur, and a *contingent accident*—one that need not happen. The way out of this paradox, based on a new understanding of the relation between future and past, requires us to act *as if* the catastrophe has already happened—or is fated to happen—in order to prevent it from becoming true. By acting *as if* the catastrophe has already taken place, we are able to project ourselves into the post-apocalyptic situation and ask ourselves what we could and should have done otherwise.

There is an important distinction to be drawn here between Anders and Wittgenstein, as well as a crucial point of connection. In Anders's case, the prophecy of catastrophe is made in order to prevent it from becoming true. Whilst we are living in the "Time of the End," we must, as he puts it, "do everything in our power to make The End Time *endless*," to prevent it from becoming "The End *of* Time." His position is thus, simultaneously, apocalyptic (since it believes in the possibility of The End of Time), and *anti-apocalyptic* (in the sense that it fights against human-made apocalypse).[42] Wittgenstein, by contrast, would seem (at least in his notebooks) to believe that it is only "the *prospect* of the end" which allows us to imagine a future beyond the "infinite misery" of capitalist "progress."[43] It is therefore the threat of extinction itself which promises to re-connect us with our basic humanity. And it is here, precisely, that the key connection with Anders becomes clear: both philosophers are conscious of themselves writing in *a moment of danger*; and both, in different ways, encourage "an alteration in the mode of life of human beings."[44] While their work is directed towards the realization of a more *humane world*—a world that fully accords with human needs and potentials—it would nevertheless be correct to say that both are *pessimists*, albeit of a distinctly dialectical type. As Anders writes: "if some, paralyzed by the gloomy likelihood of the catastrophe, have already lost courage, they still have a chance to prove their love of man by heeding the cynical maxim: 'Let's go on working as though we had the right to hope. Our despair is none of our business.'"[45] Wittgenstein, similarly, appears to endorse tragic hope in the face of pseudo-scientific optimism. As his close friend Rush Rhees recalls:

Walking home [...] Wittgenstein remarked that when someone said he was optimistic *because* the law of historical development showed that things were bound to get better, this was nothing he could admire. "On the other hand, if someone says: 'By the look of them, things are getting worse, and I can find no evidence to suggest that they will improve. And yet in *spite* of this, I believe things will get better!'—I can admire that."[46]

V

While Wittgenstein's remarks on apocalypse appear in his private notebooks, they nevertheless provide us with a crucial link to his later philosophy. The epigraph of the *Philosophical Investigations*, drawn from the playwright Johann Nestroy, warns readers that "progress [...] always looks much greater than it really is," while the book's Preface speaks of "the darkness of this time": a reference no doubt to the catastrophic period, 1936–45, during which the book was composed. In the body of the *Investigations*, we hear of machines "bending, breaking off [and] melting"; exploding boilers; and people who see "the cross piece of a window as a swastika."[47] But it is not simply the language of the book that we might describe as apocalyptic, but also, and more importantly, the fundamental conception of philosophy that we find therein. This is expressed very clearly in the meta-philosophical remarks at §§89–133. Here Wittgenstein carries out a kind of apocalyptic–anti-apocalyptic move: he strives to bring to an end not philosophy as such, but rather philosophy as *a discourse of the end*—that is, philosophy which takes as its goal "crystalline purity," "perfect order," "complete exactness"; philosophy which serves to prescribe and insist that *this is how things must be*.[48]

Where then does this striving after the ideal of perfect order and crystalline purity come from? As Wittgenstein suggests in the *Blue Book*, it has its roots not in philosophy itself, but in certain social and cultural tendencies, and specifically the way that science-as-ideology structures and conditions philosophical thought: "Philosophers constantly see the method of science before their eyes, and are irresistibly tempted to ask and answer questions in the way science does. This tendency is the real source of metaphysics, and leads the philosopher into complete darkness."[49] Being held captive by a picture of "the ideal" is, Wittgenstein says, akin to having "a pair of glasses on our nose through which we see whatever we look at. It never occurs to us to take them off."[50] But perhaps the answer is not the *removal* of the glasses absolutely (there can, after all, be no pure and unmediated act of seeing); rather, what is required is a radical *perspectival shift*. Here, once again, we encounter the end of one world (or, in this case, the end of one particular regime of seeing)[51] and the opening up of a new one: a world of unknown familiarity. This brings us to the second sense of apocalyptic in the later Wittgenstein: the revelatory and indeed *the ethical* moment signposted at §129, where we are alerted to the "aspects of things that are most important for us," which are *right in front of our eyes*, but which are "hidden because of their simplicity and familiarity." Here philosophy is being presented as an activity which involves re-learning how to "look" at the world. Its aim, according to Wittgenstein, is to loosen the grip of fixed ways of seeing; to destabilize routinized habits of thought and perception, bringing us to the point from which it is possible to view the everyday through a dialectical optic.

The fact that philosophical problems are always expressions or symptoms of the social and political world in which they are entangled means that the injunction to change how we see can also have a number of far-reaching consequences. For instance, by striving to see things otherwise, we also, in the words of the critic Fredric Jameson, initiate a "reawakening of the imagination of possible and alternate futures, a reawakening of that historicity which our current system—offering itself as the end of history—necessarily represses and paralyses."[52] Understood in this way, seeing language, self, and the world otherwise becomes inseparable from the imaginative activity of seeing the future otherwise. In our own apocalyptic moment—a period of accelerating climate change, ecological breakdown, and new inter-imperialist conflicts—nothing, we might argue, could be more urgent.

III

Legal Ethics

CHAPTER SEVEN

Charles Reznikoff's *Testimony*
Ethics and the Reader

Kieran Dolin

Charles Reznikoff's poetic sequence, *Testimony*, distills hundreds of legal cases into an Objectivist form that privileges the neutral representation of facts.[1] Early reviewers and critics found the emotional reticence of the poems troubling, as David Perkins noted: "Reznikoff's factuality or mere objectivity has seemed to many readers a moral limitation."[2] In the 1990s, Geneviève Cohen-Cheminet argued for the "ethical intransitivity" of Reznikoff's poetics, concluding that because Reznikoff's poetry "holds back interpretation and foregrounds facts," there is an "instability of reader-relative meanings."[3] Despite this "obscure literality," other critics have discerned an ethical dimension to Reznikoff's work. Benjamin Watson argues that the aim of *Testimony* is to allow the suffering of millions of voices buried in legal archives to be heard.[4] In a similar vein, Ranen Omer-Sherman believes that Reznikoff "exercised a profound influence on the ethical as well as the ethnic expansiveness of American poetry" in both his poems drawn from cases and his urban Imagism, innovating "a poetics of witness, a respect for the reader's moral imagination."[5] This paper locates Reznikoff's stripping of normative and affective discourses from his poetic cases within the practice of Objectivism, which contributes to a broader cultural phenomenon, a "complex ethical framework" that Ravit Reichman has called "legal modernism."[6] Linking the development of novelistic representations of subjectivity in the interwar period to the emergence of the tort of negligence, Reichman argues that "legal modernism" represented an avowedly normative response to the proliferation of traumatic injuries in modernity, centered not just on the perception of injustice but on "how the affective experiences produced by these wrongs could be harnessed to do something right."[7] As a qualified lawyer who abandoned that career for poetry, but was drawn to legal texts as sources for a consciously modernist poetic project, Reznikoff would seem a likely contributor to this ethical formation, except for the apparent absence of affect and ethical discourse in his verse amidst its foregrounding of injury. The present paper addresses this conjunction by examining Reznikoff's staging of the encounter between humans and machines, which emphasizes the ethical value of the individual person in the emergent industrial society. In the late 1920s, working for the American legal encyclopedia *Corpus Juris*, Reznikoff was reading voluminous quantities of law reports, searching for precedents. In his own account:

> Once in a while I could see in the facts of a case details of the time and place, and it seemed to me that out of such material, the century and a half during which the United States has been a nation could be written up, not from the standpoint of an individual, as in diaries, nor merely from the angle of the unusual, as in newspapers, but from every standpoint—as many standpoints as were provided by the witnesses themselves.[8]

Occasional factual details, that is, stood out as synecdoches of social history, an experience that inspired the idea of a poetic collage of instances of injustice, a catalogue of American mores. The following example is typical of the terse narrative style and form that Reznikoff developed:

> It was early in the morning,
> drizzling,
> and because of the fog
> still dark.
> The old woman began to cross the railroad tracks
> slowly.
> No sound of whistle or bell

or glow of headlight—
and the speeding engine struck her.[9]

Introducing the prose *Testimony* that Reznikoff published in 1934, Kenneth Burke observed that the voices of the individual "bearers of testimony" were filtered by the law's criteria of relevance, its "principle of selectivity."[10] This is certainly true of law reports and may have been true of the prose text that Burke was discussing, but Reznikoff's poetic texts are, I would argue, less determined by legal concepts. Notwithstanding this, Burke acknowledged the documentary value of the text, and discerned an underlying "vein of sympathy" in Reznikoff's "testimony."[11]

Reznikoff continued over many years to pursue the poetic adaptation of the law reports. He set out his "method of revision" in a handwritten note preserved among his papers:

1. Write all seemingly good lines

2. Examine every word to remove all possible latinisms and unnecessary words

3. Examine the meaning of the sentences in their order

4. Examine the rhythm of the lines

5. Examine the rhythm of the whole

6. Then revision by contemplation.[12]

There are echoes of the Imagist manifestoes in these practical, although much more succinct and fragmentary, directions ("Use no superfluous word," the emphasis on rhythm). The origin of the poems in written texts about actions and events, however, allows for a palimpsestic reflection on discourses rather than a primary commitment to visual impressions. The intriguing phrase, "rhythm of the whole," gestures to a dynamic pattern of segmentation and recurrence that has come to be known as serial form.[13] Each of the five parts of *Testimony* is divided into regional sections, the North, the South, and the West. Although these reflect the different law report series from which the cases emerged, they also represent three regions with conspicuous cultural and social connotations, namely the industrial northern states, the agrarian south, and the frontier west. Each of these sections is further divided into topics taken from the American legal reference book *Corpus Juris*, on which Reznikoff worked in the 1920s: descriptive headings such as Social Life, Domestic Scenes, Boys and Girls, Machine Age, Property, Negroes, Railroads, and Chinese contain clusters of poems of distilled factual accounts. Rhythm is achieved through the reappearance of these topics which function as themes explored through seemingly endless variations of circumstance. Reznikoff also introduces, less frequently, variations in the type of action: stories of deliberate or accidental harm; stories that include ethical actions amidst a plethora of others marked by ethical indifference. Together, the poems constitute a portrait of how abuse of others ramified throughout American society in the period 1885 to 1915. Benjamin Watson demonstrates through a comparison of Reznikoff's renditions and their source texts that the poet "both appropriated and altered the wording without scruples," showing that the word "revision" understates the creativity involved in the perception, selection, and arrangement of facts and phrases into an artistic object.[14] In the words of Cohen-Cheminet, he was "less a recorder than a construer of the world."[15] The first volume of completed poems was published in 1965, the second three years later.[16] Watson's use of the word "appropriation" raises the question of whether Reznikoff turned his mind to the ethical implications of this poetic practice. According to Watson, the poet recognized a paramount obligation to be faithful to the "emotions he had discovered" in his sources.[17] In a 1976 interview with Janet Sternburg and Alan Ziegler, Reznikoff stressed the public nature of his documentary sources: "One reason for using the case books is that a case is in the public domain. No one has a right to it, but everyone can use it."[18] Although his general ethical understanding of the matter was determined by the law, he did safeguard the privacy of the litigants, as the following note placed at the commencement of *Testimony* indicates: "All that follows is based on law reports of the several states. The names of all persons are fictitious and those of villages and towns have been changed."[19] While such disclaimers are routinely included in novels and films as protection against libel claims, the long gestation of the text and the historical nature of the sources, at least fifty years earlier than the time of publication, suggest that Reznikoff had carefully considered the ethics of his chosen form. It is likely that in doing so he also considered the ethical significance of the stories he was telling.[20]

Michael Eskin points out that current discussions concerning the relationship between literature and ethics were paralleled in the earlier twentieth century, citing Kurt Pinthus's 1920 observation that there was "a momentous turn toward the ethical" among writers responding to the upheavals of World War I.[21] Reznikoff therefore is not unique: aesthetic experimentation was frequently motivated by "ethical fire," as G. Matthew Jenkins puts it. Jenkins regards all the Objectivist poets as crucial to the inauguration of a "new reconsideration of ethics from one that is essentially rule-based or self-directed [...] to one that is oriented through formal experimentation towards what is other, towards *the* Other."[22] Despite its Levinasian terminology, Jenkins's argument is consistent with what critics such as Jil Larson and Melba Cuddy-Keane have established for the history of the novel in the early modernist period, that with the breakdown of the strong deontological morality of the nineteenth century, a more "inchoate" ethical searching became visible.[23] As Cuddy-Keane argues, "Modernist ethics meets the question of how to live ethically in a questionable world with a paradoxical conjunction of metaphysical uncertainty and individual answerability."[24] Despite the "pluralism and ambiguity" of ethical ideas, the "obligation to respond" applies to readers as well as to characters in fictional worlds.[25] Although the latter readings of modernist ethics are grounded on novels, rather than poetry, the strongly narrative element in *Testimony* which derives its origin from legal cases suggests their usefulness for this study.

Reznikoff's association with the Objectivist poets was cemented by his inclusion in the 1931 issue of *Poetry* magazine that outlined their aims and principles. As a nexus rather than a movement, Objectivism was variously described by its different affiliates.[26] George Oppen called Objectivism "a realist art in that the poem is concerned with a fact which it did not create."[27] William Carlos Williams focused on the poetic product as the salient characteristic: "the poem, like every other form of art, is an object that in itself presents its case and its meaning by the very form that it assumes."[28] Rachel Blau DuPlessis and Peter Quartermain argue that these two aspects—"attention to the materiality of both the world and the word"—are integrated in Objectivist poetics.[29] DuPlessis argues that the Objectivist label

> usefully designates a general aesthetic position in modern and contemporary poetry in work based, generally, on "the real," on history not myth, on empiricism not projection, on the discrete not the unified, on vernacular prosodies not traditional rhetoric, on "imagism" not "symbolism" or "surrealism" and on particulars with a dynamic relation to universals."[30]

In a 1969 interview, Reznikoff used an analogy while invoking Oppen's realist dimension:

> By the term "Objectivist" I suppose a writer may be meant who does not write directly about his feelings but about what he sees and hears; who is restricted almost to the testimony of a witness in a court of law [...] Now suppose in a court of law you are testifying in a negligence case. You cannot get up on the stand and say, "The man was negligent." That's a conclusion of fact. What you'd be compelled to say is how the man acted [...] The judges of whether he was negligent or not are the jury and the judges of what you say as a poet are the readers.[31]

At the time of this interview, the two volumes of *Testimony* had not long been published, and so the comparison has deep roots in his own artistic practice. Earlier in the same interview, Reznikoff emphasized that such Objectivism was a goal, appealing to a poetic principle from the late T'ang period: "Poetry presents the thing in order to convey the feeling. It should be precise about the thing and reticent about the feeling."[32] The surface absence of affective diction from Reznikoff's poems does not therefore imply a lack of ethical concern. Rather, both the content and the form of *Testimony* give rise to a hermeneutic ethical activity on the part of its readers.

This activity is mobilized through an intense focus on the suffering bodies of animals and humans, especially children, harmed through the operation of machinery, violence, or chance. These motifs are signaled in the opening poems of the work. The first presents the story of a man gratuitously strangling his donkey using the plow lines with which he normally worked the animal. The first verse describes the process he followed; the second focuses on the fate of the animal: "His dead body was found next morning,/fifteen or twenty feet from the stable door;/the neck, just back of the head,/badly bruised."[33] The second poem, which describes the case of a sick man removed from a streetcar and laid on the ground, his legs ending up across the tracks along which the tramcars were running, is discussed below. In both these texts there are inexplicable elements, but a sense of the vulnerability of organic life in the industrialized world, and of diminished responsibility for the safety or welfare of others, can be inferred as readers are led to reflect on the images. Reznikoff frequently foregrounds such stark scenes of injury or death, shaping his poetic form to increase the shock to the reader. The great variety of incidents covered in *Testimony* makes a comprehensive analysis of its ethical interests impossible. This chapter focuses therefore on the human–machine encounter, especially involving children, and on exclusion from motorized public transport.

To explore his technique and its effects, I shall discuss a representative example: "Two streetcars coupled together." In this poem, a young newsboy boards the front car while it is in motion, aiming to sell papers to the commuters. Reznikoff does not report how well he succeeded, cutting straight to the child's realization of the danger of his action:

> Then he stood on the bottom step of the first moving car,
> afraid to jump off,
> for fear the wagon coming alongside
> would run him over.
> People at the crossing at the corner
> were waiting to get on,
> and the conductor shoved him off the step—
> and he fell
> under the wheels of the second car.[34]

The critical actions are delayed till the last three lines of the text, expressed paratactically through the use of line breaks and the repetition of "and."[35]

Separating the subject and predicate of the last clause across two lines intensifies the image of the child falling and the shock of the outcome. The alternation of long and short lines creates a rhythm in which the stream of events is punctuated with momentary reflection or opposition, but all are told in an unemphatic voice which flattens even the conductor's action. Yet alongside this objective effect, Reznikoff endows the story with figurative resonances, through which its ethical and political aspects become readable. The child was treated like an autonomous economic agent and incorporated in the complex mobile networks of modern urban society, "shoved" off the system that he had "jump[ed]" aboard by an adult official who apparently only acknowledged responsibility to the company and its passengers. The incident was a singular one, but Reznikoff's poetic re-presentation of it opens up some of the capitalist imperatives which led to the boy's impulsive and opportunistic act and to the conductor's officious and disdainful response.

The absence of any direct reference to norms of moral commentary or affective discourse in this poem and across *Testimony* more broadly does not portend an indifference to ethical inquiry. Rather, it recalls the "inchoate" ethical sensitivity that Larson observed in late Victorian novels, and which she distinguished from the more explicit moral discourses of earlier fiction. In this context, a distinction between "ethics" and "morality" is often drawn. Derek Attridge, for example, suggests the importance of distinguishing between "the most fundamental ethical demands, which always involve unpredictability and risk, and specific obligations governing concrete situations in a given social context, which require the greatest possible control of outcomes."[36] Paul Ricœur, similarly, reserves "the term 'ethics' for the aim of an accomplished life and the term 'morality' for the articulation of this aim in norms characterized at once by their claim to universality and by an effect of constraint."[37] In connection with this poem, the reader is led by the structure of the text to visualize the cutting short of the newsboy's life and to reflect on the role of the conductor in a context dominated by fast-moving vehicles, violently and peremptorily enforcing the rule that only paying passengers had a right to be on board, without reference to any consideration of the boy's well-being. Although Reznikoff's *Testimony* pre-dates the distinction proposed by Ricœur, Attridge and others, his representation of the treatment of the newsboy by the conductor implies the limitations of deontological notions of "morality" and the need for a more responsive, situational "ethics."

In withholding any overt attribution of responsibility from the poem, Reznikoff perhaps recognizes the difficulty of perception and decision in such circumstances. As a narrative the text acknowledges the shifting perception of events, at first recording the boy's belief that the two streetcars were coupled together as a fact, and later registering his realization that they were simply in a line. This inconsistency is allowed to stand, reflecting the text's privileging of images above narrative coherence, which in turn suggests Reznikoff's emphasis on the complexity and speed of modern mechanized reality. Readers, however, are implicitly invited to reflect on the details of that representation and can form their own judgments on the actions represented.[38]

Reznikoff's childhood in New York, as the son of Jewish immigrant milliners who often moved house, sensitized him to the hardships faced by workers. The America into which he was born, and from which he drew his cases was marked by what John Fabian Witt has called "an industrial accident crisis of world-historical proportions."[39] Deaths and injuries involving machinery multiplied on the roads and railways, in factories and mines. The speed and complexity of such machinery and its enormous power in correlation with the inadequate attention to safety of those operating it, as well as the dominant ideology of free market economics, produced a "cascade of injuries" that attracted the scrutiny of unions, charities, journalists, and eventually policymakers.[40] Campaigns for legal and social reform were mounted in the decades between when the cases came to court and when Reznikoff began the *Testimony* project. Out of this period emerged major legal responses to this crisis, notably the modern law of negligence, and no-fault workers' compensation, as well as a movement to end child labor. Witt cites the photographs of Lewis Hine as a significant source of documentary evidence of the personal injury crisis and of child labor practices in particular.[41] Reznikoff's contribution to this major normative shift was to preserve a memory of the many whose suffering gave rise to these campaigns. Monique Claire Vescia identifies strong parallels between Objectivist poetics and the ethical and political aims of documentary photography in the 1930s, arguing that both movements had an overriding commitment to "capturing the actual."[42] For Vescia, Reznikoff's sharply visual imagery and "deceptively simple diction" invite comparisons with the medium and practice of documentary photography in this period.[43] The testimonial poetics that Reznikoff created and refined in the 1930s and subsequent decades shared this impulse, and its seemingly detached representation of the facts of earlier legal cases can be seen as an ethical and political critique of the *laissez-faire* liberal roots of this crisis.

However, while Hine's photographs of child workers were interventions in specifically reformist campaigns to outlaw child labor or to introduce improved protection for workers and their families, Reznikoff's poems highlight ongoing but unregarded aspects of social reality, such as racism, men's abuse of women, violence against children, greed, and the inherent danger of modern machinery. In his wide-ranging essay on Reznikoff, Charles Bernstein argues that "Reznikoff's poetry reminds [us] of very general facts that we already knew—[that] are in plain view—but which we have difficulty accounting for." More specifically, he suggests that "Neglect [or] disregard—the socially obscure, the forgotten and repressed, the overlooked—[...] was his subject." Bernstein connects Reznikoff's capacity to acknowledge the suffering of these others to the self-effacing quality of his poetic voice and stance, which allows "the event itself to speak, as if without interference, without teller."[44] Far from signifying a modernist aesthetic detachment or "the indifference of the juridical gaze," therefore, Bernstein contends that Reznikoff worked to create a "poetics of adjacency" grounded on ethical witnessing to the lives of forgotten people.[45] Geneviève Cohen-Cheminet believes that the form of *Testimony* undermines any linguistic "adjacency" to the original witness statements, but concludes that Reznikoff is a "second-degree witness," that is, a witness to the testimonies of witnesses who have disappeared.[46] It is arguable, then, that what has been read as emotional reticence in the poetry can be better understood as ethical receptivity. Bernstein further cites Wittgenstein's dictum that "A poet's words can pierce us," a metaphor that is especially applicable to the images of violent injury or death with which Reznikoff concludes many poems, including the poem just discussed.[47] Given Vescia's analogy between Objectivist poetry and photography, it is impossible in this context not to think of Roland Barthes's distinction in *Camera Lucida* between the *studium* and the *punctum*, between the conscious historically or culturally coded meaning of a photograph and the effect of a detail within that *studium* that punctures it and seizes the viewer's attention. The *punctum*'s potential to expand in the reader's consciousness leads Barthes to liken it to a haiku.[48] John Michael has argued that the *punctum* provides a way of theorizing the ethical potential of poetry and photography: "It is by its unpredictable and uncoded elements, its punctual and idiosyncratic being in the reader's experience, that the lyric or the photograph actually enters lived time and living history."[49] It is the stark and surprising details in Reznikoff's images that "prick" the attention of readers and prompt ethical reflection.

Thus far, I have tended to discuss individual poems, but as both Bernstein and Vescia note, Reznikoff's use of serial form necessitates "attending to the relation of the part to the whole (and the whole to the part) [...] along lines that also suggest the relation of the shot to the sequence (in film and photography)."[50] In devising the form of *Testimony*, Reznikoff wished to transcend the limits of methodological individualism, to represent "as many standpoints" as possible by accumulating incidents and grouping similar cases together in a series of temporal waves.[51] Bernstein argues persuasively that the "most typical relation between sections is one of simultaneity of occurrences, as if each poem were preceded by an implied 'meanwhile.'"[52] To read Reznikoff's text serially is to be confronted with a dispiriting catalogue of violence, misconduct, or accidental damage, in which occasional but ineffectual glimmers of ethical awareness are seen. The second poem in Reznikoff's collection, "On a Sunday—a bleak drizzling day," concerns a man who suddenly falls ill on a streetcar, vomiting. When asked to leave, he tries to do so but faints. When carried off and laid on the ground beside the tracks by the driver and another passenger, a convulsion shifts his position "so that his legs were across a rail of the tracks."[53] A woman and another man notice this and move him to the sidewalk, and the poem ends: "Here he remained/in the drizzle." This concluding image circles back to that of the opening line, "a bleak drizzling day," intensifying the sense of the man's abjection. Reznikoff's narrative of the incident on the streetcar stresses the limits of community and concern: although other passengers in the crowded streetcar are understandably discomfited by the incident, they immediately suspect him of being drunk; even those who help him do so only to the extent of solving the immediate problem. Left in the rain, he can be read as an image of urban alienation. Yet the poem records his name, Patrick Connolly, and quotes from the legal transcript that he had been travelling "'without the slightest impropriety of behavior,'" thus affording him dignity even in his abject distress, left "between the car tracks and the gutter." Whilst resisting any overtly emotive diction, the poem presents a powerful scene of human vulnerability in the industrial age when the man's convulsions cause his legs to intersect with the rails.

In the final pages of the book, Reznikoff returns to the motif of the ejected traveler. In "A young black sixteen years of age," the protagonist boards a waiting train to buy tobacco from the vendor located in the African American carriage. As the train is preparing to set off, he moves towards the exit, but is grabbed by the porter and conductor and pushed off the moving vehicle. He strikes his head on the ground near the cross-ties and dies instantly. The poem foregrounds its testimonial project, first by quoting the callously racist words of the conductor, "'That damned nigger won't mind hitting the cross-ties,'" and then in the final verse by recording the response of a white witness:

> One of the passengers in the car for whites
> saw what had happened,
> but was advised by his friends
> that the less he had to say about the matter
> the better.[54]

By incorporating the presence of the initial witness and his surrender to social pressure, the poem offers itself as a supplement, a corrective to the earlier repression of evidence. In doing so, the text juxtaposes what is perhaps the primary obligation of the witness, to tell the truth, with the dominant community ethos, that of solidarity among whites and a complaisant acceptance of violence towards Blacks. Reznikoff distills the mores of "the South" through the friends' vaguely threatening tone and generalized appeal to consequences. To adopt Ravit Reichman's terminology, they are "undiverted" by the knowledge of this wrong, unaffected by the sight of his body.[55] Meanwhile, as the poem ends in silence, the dead body of a respectful and sociable youth who had been attempting to alight from the train is left behind where he landed, an icon of ethical failure.

One of the regular categories in every part of *Testimony* is "Children," suggesting Reznikoff's awareness that they were particularly vulnerable during the "industrial accident crisis" and that they are exemplary of the "tiny, fragile human body" that is the focus of his analysis.[56] His poems address such topics as neglect and cruelty by parents and authorities, violence by strangers or neighbors, the effects of dangerous environments (whether natural or urban), and industrial accidents. Part Four is unique in including a separate section titled "Children at Work," but workplace injuries suffered by children are located beside those of adults as a recurrent feature of "The Machine Age" in every part. In Part Two: The North, six of the eleven poems grouped under "The Machine Age" tell stories of children injured in factories, saw-mills, and other industrial sites. The first of the group, "A boy of fourteen was one of several helpers in the spinning room," narrates how the boy, whose usual role was to "sweep the floor,/pick up waste, change bobbins," was asked to help mend a belt hanging from the shaft. The shaft was fifteen feet high and the boy had to stand high on a ladder, holding the belt away from the spinning shaft. "There was nothing by which the boy could steady himself/but the ladder," and when first in position, he became "frightened" and climbed down. His supervisor swore at him and gave him an ultimatum: go back up or be sacked. The poem ends: "And so the boy went up the ladder again—/to be caught by the belt and drawn over the shaft,/his arm wrapped around it."[57] The use of the infinitive injects a hint of inevitability into the result. The poem is structured around oppositions—descent and re-ascent of the ladder; the child's fearful foresight and the superior's harsh dismissal—which intensify the reader's sense of a failure of due care by the supervisor. Reznikoff withholds the outcome in favor of ending the poem at the moment of contact, leaving readers to imagine the horrific consequences, and the boy's terror as he is lifted up towards the shaft. The truncation of narrative points to the ethical losses involved when a life is violently cut short and as human concern is sacrificed to serve the interests of the machine.

The fifth poem in this group, "No longer a boy, in fact almost eighteen," highlights the issue of responsibility, as the seventeen-year-old protagonist whose role was to feed logs to the sawyers finds himself "given a chance to work at the saw." Reznikoff gives the viewpoint from the young man's previous role: "Sawing a stick of wood was simple." The alliteration here, which picks up the two consonants in the word "saw," retards the ease with which the words can be spoken, and hints at a gap between appearance and reality. As the next verse reveals, the saw was defective, with two broken teeth. The protagonist is warned to go more slowly and carefully by an older man who is now handing the logs in, but he continues in his own way:

> Just as he was sawing the last piece
> and shoving it hard against the saw because it was dull,
> when the saw came to where the two teeth were out,
> it jumped,
> and three fingers of his left hand were cut off.[58]

Through expert use of line breaks, Reznikoff recreates the young man's action in sawing, and the abrupt effect of the missing teeth, concluding with the catastrophic revelation of the injury. This stark image, combined with Reznikoff's use of demotic and physical language ("shoving it hard"), brings the event before readers with great immediacy, piercing our consciousness.

One of the effects of reading a group of poems rather than a single text is to see how Reznikoff highlights the uniqueness of each situation and the individuality of each character. The older worker knows that the defects in the saw make it a dangerous implement, even for those who are familiar with it, and in contrast to the previous example he is concerned enough to give a general warning to the novice. Instead of heeding the older man's advice, the youth carries on, confident in his new-found strength. Without specific information about the flaw in the equipment, he simply does what he has seen others do. In a legal context, this scenario may well have raised questions about whether the young worker voluntarily assumed the risks of handling a power-saw. In the current literary context, Reznikoff's comparison between the role of readers and that of a jury and his sustained neutrality of voice could well invite similar questions from readers. Ricœur argues that "poetry does not proceed conceptually [...]

[it] is not a teaching in the most didactic sense of the word, but more closely resembl[es] a conversion of the manner of looking."[59] Reznikoff's poems usually effect such transformations of perception through their imagery, and in particular through images that "pierce" readers. This text's culminating image of the industrial injury is an example of this phenomenon. It can be read as challenging ideologically dominant inferences about voluntary assumption of risk, and equally importantly does so whilst acknowledging the effort of the fellow-worker to warn the injured young man. As against the highly adversarial nature of legal proceedings, the poem models a concise but multi-perspectival understanding of the event and its causation.

In a well-known passage from *Time and Narrative*, Ricœur argues that "There are crimes that must not be forgotten, victims whose suffering cries less for vengeance than for narration."[60] Reznikoff's testimonial poetics appears to proceed from a similar conviction, except that like many modernist writers his narratives are incomplete, and his text has a collage-like, serial form that resists the unifying explanatory drive of traditional narration. Its open, fragmentary narratives and its composite structure emphasize the many-sidedness of reality and the ethical uncertainties of modernity. Equally attentive to the presence of ethical impulses as to systemic repressions of concern for the other, *Testimony* represents a significant reflection on ethics and law in twentieth-century poetry.

Embedded within the law reports, Reznikoff found phrases or passages that evoked the period from which the cases emerged. His poetic distillations of these cases provide insight into customs and practices of late nineteenth- and early twentieth-century America, a history that is informed by his own historical location both as a Jewish child in New York before World War I and as a writer working in the ideologically charged America of the Depression era, the 1940s, and the Cold War. The readings presented here show that despite the removal of affective and normative discourse, the poems consistently represent evil or negligent actions and their consequences for victims, an implicitly ethical and political orientation that parallels the legal and policy shifts towards workers' rights, racial equality, and social welfare that emerged in these decades.

Reznikoff's historicity is matched by that of his readers. As Michael argues, the ethical potentiality of a poem is realized in the response of readers for whom it contains a *punctum*.[61] When *Testimony* was first published in the 1960s, it found an audience responsive both to its representation of violence and to poetic experimentation, providing Reznikoff with long-delayed recognition. When the one-volume edition of *Testimony* was published by Black Sparrow Press in 2015, with an editorial introduction and textual notes, it appeared in a very different America, one in which neoliberalism and globalization had eroded many of the economic reforms and social values of the previous century. In this context, Reznikoff's text remains a vital source of ethical reflection, and a warning against complacency in our narratives of legal and social history.

CHAPTER EIGHT

What's Love Got to Do With It? Law and Literature in 1920s British Somaliland

Katherine Isobel Baxter

In the mid-twentieth century, Margery Perham was one of the most influential voices in Britain on matters of African colonial administration. As a research lecturer and later a Reader in Colonial Administration at the University of Oxford she trained a generation of colonial officers and became a prolific scholar. Her first publication, however, was not a scholarly publication but a novel, *Major Dane's Garden* (1925). The novel pitches two modes of colonial rule against each other: the first represented by a thrusting military careerist, Cavell; the second represented by Major Dane, a maverick administrator, loved by those over whom he rules. The novel is focalized through Cavell's wife Rhona, who embarks on a chaste yet erotically charged affair with Dane.

Major Dane's Garden has received scant critical interest. It sits apart from Perham's voluminous body of non-fiction writing on colonial administration and has been passed by in scholarship on interwar colonial fiction. Even when the novel was published, reviews were generally limited to small notices in the press. Yet the novel provides an important insight into how fiction that sits outside the modernist canon shaped the ethics of colonial ideology in the interwar period. In this chapter, therefore, I explore Perham's experimentation with popular genre, notably the vogues for district commissioner fiction and for desert romance. My argument is that Perham draws on these genres to develop an ethics of paternalist care for the colonies that is grounded in an affective relationship which oscillates between eroticism and restraint.

Perham was an extraordinary woman. The world of colonial administration was an emphatically male one, and before World War II, in the non-settler colonies in Africa, European women were a relative rarity. Yet Perham became, for a time, one of the best-informed and most knowledgeable people on British colonial administration in Africa. As early as 1926, as a tutorial fellow at St. Hugh's College, Oxford, Perham was devoting her teaching and research to colonial administration. Over the following decade she examined administrative practice from the vantage of archives in the UK and through a demanding program of global travel, with extended periods on the African continent and beyond. During these travels she interviewed governors and district commissioners alike and pored through their local administrative archives with extraordinary care. At the same time she lectured on the Tropical African (later Colonial Administrative) Service course, offered by Oxford and Cambridge on behalf of the Colonial Service for probationers, and established a regular summer school on colonial administration, while also writing for the press.[1] By the outbreak of World War II, Perham was not only extremely knowledgeable, she was also extraordinarily well-connected, both with those in the Colonial and Foreign Offices and with administrators in the colonies. It was to her that the government turned for a book when they wanted to shore up support for colonial administration among their colonial subjects in 1941. The resulting publication, *Africans and British Rule*, exemplifies Perham's paternalist outlook, at once defending her African audience from biologically racist prejudice yet patronizing them at every turn.

Perham's passion for Africa was borne of an adventurous trip that she made to British Somaliland in 1921. Perham's sister Ethel had emigrated to teach in Mombasa before World War I and within about a year she was married to a New Zealander, Harry Rayne, who was serving there in the British East Africa Police. At the end of the war, and four children later, Harry Rayne, now a major, was redeployed as a district commissioner in British Somaliland. Perham accompanied Ethel and the four children (who had been visiting the UK on leave) out to Rayne's posting in Hargeisa, close to British Somaliland's border with Ethiopia, then Abyssinia. Here it was she first began to learn about the practicalities of colonial administration, and it was also here that she experienced the privilege of adventure, riding out with Major Rayne and the Camel Corps patrolling the Abyssinian border.

As Roland Oliver notes, it was the "dominion of romance" that caught Perham's imagination as much as "the romance of dominion."[2] Indeed, using the very term "romance," in her introduction to *Major Dane's Garden*, she describes trekking along this "Ethiopian frontier, armed with a map which carried to me, at that period, the exhilarating inscription 'unexplored.'"[3] The map's label and Perham's claim that, until she and her sister reached Hargeisa, "no white woman had been able to enter the frontier region" are fictions that enhance this sense of romance in the novel's introduction. In fact, her map's label reflects primarily that the region had not been formally mapped topographically—the border with Abyssinia was not demarcated until 1936, following a three-year land survey.[4] Nonetheless, it had been repeatedly "explored" by European game hunters at the end of the nineteenth century, whose publications frequently included maps that straddled the frontier region.[5] Moreover, one such pair of hunters were the intrepid cousins Agnes Herbert and Cecily Baird, whose explorations in 1906 took them through British and Italian Somaliland as well as Abyssinia.[6] Such independent explorations had been curtailed during the war. Nonetheless, Perham's own brother-in-law attests to the presence of a white woman in Hargeisa, before the arrival of Perham and her sister, in his 1921 memoir, *Sun, Sand and Somals*.[7] The fictions of Perham's introduction, then, signal her own predisposition for romance, and how frequently fiction might shape the facts, even of well-respected authorities such as Perham.

British Somaliland

Britain had established the British Somaliland Protectorate in 1887. The protectorate was used to monitor trade routes through East Africa and the Gulf of Aden into the Red Sea. It also supplied the British Indian outpost of Aden with meat (Aden did not become a separate colony until 1937). Its largest export commodity was hides, and Somali goatskins were prized for their quality on the American market where they were sold for kid glove manufacture. Nevertheless, the cost of administering the protectorate regularly outstripped revenues, primarily accrued through various forms of taxation.[8] Its value to the British was thus primarily strategic rather than economic. Not only were the Gulf of Aden and the Red Sea Europe's primary trade route to the east since the opening of the Suez Canal in 1869, Aden itself was essential to this route as a coaling port. The ascendency of steam over sail in the second half of the nineteenth century, which was not unrelated to the opening of the Suez Canal, meant that secure refueling ports were necessary to safeguard trade. Aden provided that security to Britain but its geopolitical position, on the tip of the Arabian Peninsula, brought with it vulnerabilities. British occupation of the other side of the Gulf gave additional security to Aden and thereby Britain's trading routes south and east.

The British were not the only European power to seek a strategic toehold on the Horn of Africa, not least since Britain had a monopoly on fuel supplies for steam shipping to and from the east while Aden was the primary coaling port in the region. In 1888, a year after Britain established its protectorate through a series of treaties with several of the major Somali clans, Italy followed suit in the Somali region to the south of the British protectorate to form Italian Somaliland. The French were also a keen rival to the British for control of the Gulf, and in the same period the French also drew up treaties on the north-west border of British Somaliland around the city of Djibouti to create French Somaliland, foiling a Russian attempt to negotiate a settlement in the same region in the process.[9] The various clans with whom the French, Italians, and British negotiated, however, were not settled, nor did they necessarily get on with each other. Indeed, in the French instance, early treaties were drawn up on the basis that rival clans would be expelled from the French protectorate. Many clans extended across the borders of these various protectorates and also into Abyssinia to the west. Moreover, as noted above, as late as the 1920s these borders remained theoretical, drawn on political maps but not surveyed topographically. Even when boundaries began to be demarcated topographically, treaties were negotiated to permit movement either side of the borders in recognition of the grazing and watering needs of the graziers in these border zones.[10] Consequently, the question of what and whom the British Protectorate comprised was a matter of debate and at times of dispute.[11]

This nineteenth-century European incursion soon met with resistance and one reason that British Somaliland remained relatively uncharted through to the end of World War I was that occupation was resisted violently over two decades by a religious and anti-colonial movement led by Sayid Muhammed Abdullah Hassan. Hassan was both critical of the Qadiriyya Islamic order then dominant in Somali society and resistant to rule by the encroaching Christian nations, including Abyssinia. Hassan's revivalist religious movement, Salihiyya, thus fought for both religious reform and geopolitical autonomy. The ensuing war, which continued on and off from 1899 through to Hassan's final defeat in 1920, saw Hassan and the British mobilize rival clans in a series of outright battles and guerrilla warfare.[12] By the start of World War I, Britain had been forced, by and large, to retreat to the coast, and its attentions turned elsewhere between 1914 and 1918 as the Allies sought to contain German offensives in East Africa.

Hassan's final defeat came after the armistice, against the backdrop of the peace negotiations in Paris and London. Faced with a hugely expensive ground operation whose prospects of success were no better than earlier offensives, Lord Milner, then Colonial Secretary, turned to the RAF. In late December 1919, twelve aircraft were shipped from Egypt to the British Somaliland coast for assembly and on January 21, 1920, the first air offensive was conducted. Hassan's forces were driven back to Taleh, close to the Italian border, and were eventually defeated in early February. Hassan escaped into the Ogaden region which spread across the Italian, British, and Abyssinian borders but he never revived his resistance movement and died at the end of that year. This was the first time that the RAF had been used in combat since World War I and the success and cost efficiency of the offensive were celebrated immediately by the government and the press.[13] It was into this recently "pacified" country that Perham ventured with her sister in 1921.

Romance and *Major Dane's Garden*

Despite her emphatic disavowal in the foreword to the first edition, Perham's novel draws heavily on her experiences in British Somaliland. Even her eponymous hero's name is a near homonym of her brother-in-law, Major

Harry Rayne. Like Perham and her sister, the novel's heroine, Rhona, must wait on the coast for some weeks before finally being allowed to join her husband in Hargeisa. Her husband, Captain Cavell, is hyper-masculine, handsome, domineering, and manipulative—the last we learn from occasional moments of free indirect discourse where Cavell congratulates himself on his ability to control his pretty wife. Uninterested in the history, culture, or politics of the local populations, he is bent on a policy of disarmament in order to retain military supremacy in the region. Cavell is thus made to represent the view that the protectorate is essentially a military outpost, and his policy of disarmament reflects a concern to protect British security interests in the region rather than to instigate any development for the benefit of the Protectorate's colonial subjects. He is opposed by Major Dane, who, like Perham's brother-in-law Rayne, has given up his military career to devote himself to colonial administration. In contrast to Cavell, Dane studies the local population, speaks their languages, and works to understand the political pressures at play between the various communities. He believes that disarming the locals will lead to exploitation by militant factions beyond the border who, Dane argues, will rearm the newly resentful (because disarmed) locals, exacerbating the danger of rebellion. The determining metaphor of the novel is Dane's personal project to transform the desert of Hargeisa into a productive "garden" through a complex system of water containment and irrigation. The metaphor operates to characterize Dane in the benevolent role of gardener, cultivating his subjects until they blossom into civilization. Importantly, it also naturalizes the presumed waywardness of the indigenous population, suggesting barrenness of culture as their natural state rather than the product of twenty years of violent warfare conducted between Hassan and the British army. The novel thus pits two opposing approaches to colonial governance against each other in a debate that reflects contemporaneous debates about the purpose of colonial administration.

What intrigues me about this book is why Perham chose to present this debate about modes of colonial governance using the romantic novel genre. Memoir and travel writing were the more common genres to which colonialists of the period turned in order to explore the function, and to evaluate the success, of British administration overseas. Indeed, Perham's brother-in-law had published his own account of his time in

British Somaliland as District Commissioner in Zeila in his memoir *Sun, Sand and Somals* in 1921. What then did the romantic novel offer Perham? Patricia Pugh suggests that Perham was inspired to write fiction by her grandmother, J. H. Needell, who had published some twelve novels herself.[14] Rather leaden melodramas of love and life, Needell's works included *Lucia, Hugh and Another* (1884), a novel whose plot finds echoes in *Major Dane's Garden*. Whatever Needell's influence might have been, Perham had herself written poetry, stories, and plays from a young age and so the move to full-length fiction may have felt more natural than embarking on a form of life-writing. Furthermore, fiction may also have allowed her to side-step her own romantic entanglements in British Somaliland—Perham's biographers suggest that she fell in love with Rayne.[15] More than this, though, Perham's choice of genre enables her to draw repeatedly on the colorful tropes of adventure fiction and desert romance even as she disavows their glamor in favor of ethical restraint in the novel's denouement.

In his tribute to Perham at her memorial service on May 1, 1982, Roland Oliver notes that her holiday reading in British Somaliland was *King Solomon's Mines*, Rider Haggard's runaway success, published in 1885 (a year after *Lucia, Hugh and Another*). The fact that this was Perham's "favorite book" (in Oliver's words) reflects the ubiquity of colonial romance in the first decades of the twentieth century.[16] Indeed, these years saw a boom in what we might call District Commissioner fiction—novels and stories that revolved around the heroized figure of the colonial administrator, invariably "alone" and miles from "civilization," single-handedly "keeping the peace" among local populations who are characterized as childish, devious, truculent, and savage.[17] Edgar Wallace's *Sanders of the River* series, published between 1911 and 1928, epitomized this subgenre and the influence of his stories is signaled by the fact that Wallace is often referred to as the favorite reading of colonial characters in other novels, such as Joyce Cary's *Mr. Johnson* and Graham Greene's *The Heart of the Matter*.[18]

We can see the influence of this vogue for District Commissioner fiction in Perham's novel. Dane, like Edgar Wallace's Sanders before him, is a caring maverick administrator, loved by those over whom he rules. He is rugged, "altogether a weather beaten but reflective person" for whom "lonely and difficult work had seemed to become his by a natural law."[19] Adding a touch of the exotic, he also keeps a pet cheetah. Indeed, Major Dane's unique capacity for colonial rule ("you can do what no other man can do," exclaims Rhona)[20] was, ironically, already the stock-in-trade of his literary precursors, and his quiet magnetic charisma, which Perham presents as distinctive, was in fact a trait shared with many other fictional commissioners of the period. In *Play Up and Play the Game*, Patrick Howarth delineates the archetypical hero of the late Victorian adventure novels out of which District Commissioner fiction heroes such as Sanders and Dane emerge:

> Imbued with a strong sense of institutional loyalty, upper middle-class background, conformist in belief, dedicated to a concept, not simply of "my country right or wrong," but of a national enjoying a natural moral prerogative, accepting ungrudgingly the demands of service and duty, inclined to treat women either as companions or as unmentionable.[21]

As this definition suggests, colonial adventure fiction dramatized the exploits of white male protagonists for whom women are invariably a distraction at best and trouble more often than not. But, at the end of World War I, a hitherto unknown author, E. M. Hull, made a dramatic entrance into the field of colonial adventure fiction with her novel, *The Sheik*. Published in 1919, *The Sheik* tells the story of a strong-willed young woman, Diana Mayo, who sets off into the Algerian desert on an adventure, only to be captured by a mysterious and violent Bedouin leader, the sheik of the novel's title. The sheik rapes her repeatedly and Diana is at first cowed by her imprisonment. Gradually, though, she comes to love him, but fears she must hide her love in case, sensing her love for him, he becomes disinterested. As if this were not testing the reader's credulity enough, Diana eventually discovers that the sheik is not a Bedouin at all but has an English father and Spanish mother and that he is, in fact, in love with Diana. Pacy, vivid, and fanciful, the novel was an instant success and was rapidly optioned by Famous Players-Lasky, whose 1921 film was a box office smash, propelling Rudolf Valentino into superstardom with his performance as the titular sheik.

Much has been said, both at the time of publication and in scholarship since, about the novel's questionable approach to rape and race. What scholars like Hsu-Ming Teo have also observed in retrospect is how the novel opened up a space for colonial adventure romances with female protagonists at their center. Indeed, as Teo has demonstrated, the desert romance genre, whose popularity *The Sheik* catalyzed, has persisted through into the twenty-first century.[22] One author who was quick to occupy this space was Rosita Forbes, whose novels *Sirocco* (1927) and *Account Rendered, and King's Mate* (1928) borrow Hull's breathless narrative style for stories of hot-headed wealthy young women adventuring in Orientalized North African landscapes, often with sheiks on hand. Another such author, I would argue, is Margery Perham.

Thus, as much as *Major Dane's Garden* deploys the standard features of District Commissioner fiction in its characterization of Dane, the romantic drama of the novel borrows heavily from *The Sheik*. Clothing, for example, matters. Like Diana, Rhona loves to wear riding trousers, and, like Diana, men are attracted to her "boyish" good looks when she wears them. At the same time, like Diana, Rhona enjoys dressing up.[23] Both women slip into beguiling dresses at the end of the day, raising the pulses of the men around them. Perham repeatedly draws our attention to Rhona's pleasure when she feels her silk clothing against her skin, lending a physical sensuousness to the narrative and one clearly intended to contrast with the rough sensations of men's hands, the rocky landscape, and the heat of the sun.

Nor does Perham shy away from the domestic and sexual violence of *The Sheik*. Cavell and Dane both come close to but resist forcing themselves on Rhona on several occasions, enabling Perham to evoke the danger of rape without deploying Hull's levels of gratuity. Perham does, however, include a scene in which Cavell beats Rhona when he realizes she has crossed him and (in his words) "fallen in love with Somaliland."[24] This scene, replete with a love letter torn from Rhona's breast and the inevitable ripped dress, is a set piece of women's romance and positions the novel squarely in the burgeoning desert romance craze of the period.

So, what is going on here when Perham draws on these two genres in a novel that nonetheless seems to want to be more than simply an enjoyable page turner? In his 2001 essay, "What is a Romantic Novel?" Robert Miles examines the critical sidelining of romance as a genre in the Romantic period, and in doing so comes to a definition of romance that contrasts it with the emergence of the novel. According to Miles, in the late eighteenth and early nineteenth centuries, romance engages with the public sphere as opposed to the domestic and private interests of the novel. Romance is also self-conscious in its interest in ideology, Miles argues, defining "ideology," in line with John Schwarzmantel, as "a congeries of values an individual consciously adopts as part of his or her political self-definition, in opposition to other definitions."[25]

Miles is not thinking of what we recognize as popular romance, but his paradigm is useful here because it helps us to decode some of the awkwardness of *Major Dane's Garden* by demonstrating what is inherited from earlier traditions of romance, even while Perham's book maintains other typical tropes of the nineteenth-century novel. One such novelistic trope which Miles identifies is the invitation to "intense identification with [the novel's heroine] while undermining the reader's ability to do so through the irony inherent in free indirect speech."[26] Told in the third person, *Major Dane's Garden* is nonetheless focalized by Rhona. When the narrative moves to other protagonists, their thoughts and actions invariably have implications for Rhona, even when those protagonists may be many miles away. What these moments of changed perspective also create is exactly that irony we find in a novelist like Jane Austen (but not in Hull and Forbes), which flatters the reader by allowing them to see more, and to see more clearly than Rhona, the world which she inhabits. For example, Perham encourages the reader to sympathize with Dane many pages before that realization strikes Rhona. Nonetheless, Rhona is presented as a proxy for the reader, and her initial loyalty to Cavell's position provides Perham with an opportunity to stage the arguments by which Rhona and the reader must be educated into a full appreciation for the superiority of Dane's approach. The prize of Rhona's (and the reader's) judgment and affections provides a productive plot device on which to hang the ideological and ethical debates of the novel. Rhona must "consciously" choose her "values" in the development of her own "political self-definition."[27]

This is where desert romance becomes useful to Perham. For, while the choices that her plot prompts are clearly between ideologies in and of the public realm (in keeping with Miles's definition of romance), Rhona's decision-making process is nonetheless repeatedly dramatized in scenes of intimacy and physical frisson that are lifted straight from the desert romance playbook. For example, following a long falling out after Cavell destroys Dane's irrigation system, Rhona makes up with her husband in their bedroom dressed only in her negligee, suggesting to him that he can play with her hair. Cavell sweeps Rhona up, crushing her with the strength of his embrace as much as his political perspective, in an obliteration that Rhona relishes.[28] A similarly charged scene with Dane takes place in the open but is lent privacy and intimacy by evening darkness lit only by a new moon. When Dane offers to show her the horrors of the drought besetting Hargeisa, which are the immediate motivating force for his irrigation system, "Rhona had a strange sensation. It was as though she was an organ suddenly touched by a master-hand [...] So handled, of what glorious music might she not be capable of in the future," she wonders.[29] The eroticism of these scenes throws a particular glamor over the choices that Rhona must make—it can be sexy, the novel implies, to make a considered decision about the best modes of administration in the African colonies; moreover, that pleasure is available not only to the men of the administration but to women who choose to take an interest too.

If such scenes seduce the reader into a romantically charged consideration of administrative practice, the novel's ending reminds its reader that the work of colonial administration and its concomitant policy debates are ongoing. For whilst Perham's sympathies (and, as the novel progresses, Rhona's too) are clearly with Dane, the novel fails to give him a romantic victory, requiring of both Rhona and Dane an ethical restraint. Rhona finally chooses Dane's mode of colonial governance, but her romantic choices are circumscribed. Rhona refuses to run away with Dane because she recognizes it will ruin his reputation in the administration. At the same time, Cavell refuses to divorce her, explaining "I love you and I hate Dane."[30] Rhona returns to Britain unhappy, leaving both men to continue their work of colonial rule. Unlike the passionate consummation of *The Sheik*, in Perham's novel duty trumps all despite its failure to reward in the here and now. In their final moments together, Rhona challenges Dane: "Has happiness ever been enough for you? [...] [I]t is not I who am imposing this terrible thing upon us [...] it is this merciless self-sacrificing spirit of yours."[31] Thus, by the end of the novel, Rhona and Dane learn the reality and the naturalness of their mutual passion yet choose to forego it in service to the larger public institutions of marriage and colonial administration.

Perham underscores the ethical restraint of Rhona and Dane through a secondary plotline in the novel. A young man named Blaker is sent to be District Commissioner in Zeila (the district where Rayne had been posted before Perham's visit and which forms the basis of his memoir *Sun, Sand and Somals*). Here, miles from "civilization," Blaker sleeps with the beautiful betrothed of a local warrior, Ibrahim. Ibrahim kills him in vengeance. Blaker's sexual relationship with the Somali woman is a standard trope of colonial romance, signaling his moral weakness and unfitness for colonial rule. This weakness is made to contrast with Dane's strength of will in keeping his relationship with Rhona chaste. Dane thus comes to represent the perfection of the loving lawgiver. His relationship with Rhona is made to reflect his relationship with his colonial subjects. Dane is patronizing but fascinated, desires both to learn from and to educate, and he sacrifices himself to her and to them out of a spiritual and fanatical devotion. This allegory of love and legal practice thus eroticizes his embodiment of the law, presenting colonial administration as a mutually passionate yet platonic congress of the lawgiver and his subject.

"An Image of Africa"

I noted at the start that *Major Dane's Garden* received little notice on its publication. One more-detailed review did appear in the *New York Times*, however. Invoking Ecclesiastes 12:12, the reviewer comments:

> The problems which arise for England among her Indian and African dependencies seem to go on forever, and of the making of books dealing with some angle of the subject there is no end. In "Major Dane's Garden" […] we have a novel of life in Somaliland, where native problems make up less an end in themselves than a means for motivating the plot. Primarily the book is a love story, a triangle of no great originality.[32]

This review returns us to the issue of genre. In choosing the models of colonial and desert romance, popularized by Wallace and Hull, Perham banishes "native problems" from view. The novel's unoriginal triangulation is between its English protagonists Rhona, Cavell, and Dane. Even as their romantic affiliations are entangled in debates between competing modes of administration, these debates remain concerned with the ethical stance of each as white colonials.

The *New York Times* reviewer's criticism finds a telling echo in Chinua Achebe's criticism of *Heart of Darkness* fifty years later in "An Image of Africa."[33] In his essay, Achebe suggests that, for Conrad, "Africa [is a] setting and backdrop which eliminates the African as human factor. Africa [is] a metaphysical battlefield devoid of all recognizable humanity, into which the wandering European enters at his peril."[34] Achebe's summation might equally be applied to Perham's approach to Africa in *Major Dane's Garden*. If Somaliland is a setting for a European love story, as the *New York Times* reviewer suggests, it can also be read as a "metaphysical battlefield," on which Perham imagines an ethical victory for a benign form of colonialism, one that can justify the presence of Harry Rayne and others in the administrative service.

As a consequence, what Perham's novel fails to attempt is to enter imaginatively into the lives of the Somalis for whose benefit Dane claims to govern. That imaginative limitation has consequences. Missing, for example, are the non-British residents, sojourners, and businesses in British Somaliland, such as the Dinshaw (Adenwalla) family, who not only offered private banking services in the absence of a formal bank but also operated major shipping services between Aden and ports along the horn of Africa, including Berbera.[35] Although the protectorate's primary importance to the British was strategic security, it meant other things to these other international residents such as its Jewish, Parsi, Arab, and Chinese communities. These communities hover at the edges of Rayne's *Sun, Sand and Somals*, but are rendered invisible in Perham's novel.

Furthermore, in all but "eliminating the African as human factor," the practical complexities and challenges of living in the region under colonial rule are reduced to problems that can only be solved by the British administration finding the right solution. This approach is exemplified by the novel's titular garden. Dane's plan to transform Hargeisa through a system of water collection and irrigation is represented as a necessary response to famines brought on by drought. As I noted earlier, this trope naturalizes famine, making it a consequence of environmental factors that the local population is too inept to overcome. On the one hand, this obscures the potential political causes of famine, such as the twenty-year war with Hassan, about which the novel says nothing. On the other, it also obscures the fact that the Somalis were perfectly capable of devising water management systems for themselves without European intervention. In his memoir, Rayne recalls Captain Cross's account of Medishe, where Cross had routed Hassan. As well as "excellent buildings and [. . .] general[ly] sanitary arrangements," Cross reported that "[a] dam had been built across the stream, and an excellent garden had been laid out. There was no doubt about it, he stated, that the Mullah was a thoroughly capable man."[36] Perham's erasure of Somali water management systems from view reserves the care of the protectorate for the British administration alone.

This is not to argue that Perham's novel or her larger vision for British colonial administration are lacking an ethics. Both are steeped in an ethics of paternalist care. But this ethics is predicated on the erasure of agency in the very people who are the subject of that care. Moreover, the paradigm for that erasure can be traced directly back into popular colonial fiction. For, while the comparison with *Heart of Darkness* makes clear that such erasure is not simply a matter of genre, Perham's use of desert romance and District Commissioner fiction contributes to its effects. These genres rely upon narratives of white exceptionalism and assert the primacy of the white protagonists' emotions and innate sensibility in the resolution of their plots. As I noted at the start, these traits of exceptionalism are legible in Perham's account of her own trip to British Somaliland in the introduction she wrote for the 1970 reprint of *Major Dane's Garden*. Their presence in the introduction signals a blurring between fiction and reality through the application of genre tropes to historical events. Her exaggeration of the uncharted nature of the border and her false claim that no woman had been allowed to the region previously make her travels in British Somaliland exceptional and, in her own words, "romantic." Despite her qualification of that term ("as I saw it then"),[37] by retrospectively casting her experience in British Somaliland as romantic Perham elides that experience with Rhona's. After a long career devoted to study of colonial administration and ten years after British Somaliland's independence in 1960, Perham still chose to frame her novel in these romantic terms despite their evident limitations. The implication of this elision is that as much as the fictional inhabitants of British Somaliland disappear from view in the novel, the actual inhabitants of the colonies are likewise reduced to conceptual figures drawn more from fiction than reality.

The ethical risk of this reduction is evident in an article published by the Royal Geographical Society on "The Water-Supply of British Somaliland" in 1943.[38] Despite a brief description of a complex of "galleries" developed by the local population in Aden, which "draw off about 1,000,000 gallons a day [...] [for the irrigation of] plantations of tobacco, grains, dates, fruits and vegetables," the article erases from view Somali systems of water containment and management.[39] Instead, it represents the colonial administration as the benefactor of otherwise helpless subjects, in terms that emphasize the situation as exceptional and the colonial response as disposed with loving care: "Notwithstanding the *extreme difficulty* of developing sub-soil water supplies in Somaliland, much has been done to alleviate the trying conditions *suffered* by the indigenous population as well as by those civil and military officers *called upon* to administer and *protect* the colony."[40] We see here the same narrative structure applied to colonial administration that we find in *Major Dane's Garden*. The connection between increased international trade in Somali livestock products and overgrazing, for example, is never made and instead overpopulation is naturalized as a consequence of climate and geography.[41] At the same time, Somalis themselves are generalized into a single "population, *largely* nomadic, of *about* three hundred and fifty thousand [...] *mainly* pastoral."[42]

By comparing the shared tropes and narrative structures that we find in both *Major Dane's Garden* and the Royal Geographical Society's article, we start to see how the markers of popular colonial genre fiction were assimilated into practical colonial discourse. This assimilation shaped a justificatory ethical narrative for colonial rule that heroized its administrators as loving lawgivers, governed by a devotion to service. This narrative of colonial rule was also Perham's, a narrative that she expounded and expanded upon in her journalism, scholarship, and the training she ran for colonial officers. Although she never returned to fiction as a mode for promulgating her ethics of administration, *Major Dane's Garden* makes visible how popular romance shaped that ethics in the ensuing decades.

CHAPTER NINE

Modern Tort Law and Anthony Powell's *A Dance to the Music of Time*

Mimi Lu

The Industrial Revolution, which inaugurated "a whole new arena of suffering,"[1] was the crucible of modern tort jurisprudence, the civil law that offers remedies for parties who have been injured by negligent, reckless, or intentional acts, or by unsafe or defective products. In modernizing cities, torts caused personal injuries that were often permanently disabling or traumatizing. They occurred, moreover, with increasing frequency, especially in unsafe working environments and on the streets in the wake of mass private ownership of automobiles. Situated at the law and literature intersection, this essay argues that Anthony Powell's *roman-fleuve*, *A Dance to the Music of Time* (1951–75), offers rich insights into how twentieth-century literary writers responded critically and creatively to their risk-ridden and accident-prone modernity. Along with many of his contemporaries, Powell sought to articulate and reflect upon the fraught moral dynamics of interpersonal relations and obligations that are at the heart of tort jurisprudence. My close readings reveal how these literary emplotments of torts constituted an important part of a collective cultural project to interrogate the ethics of the law, including judicial and policy-driven delimitations of liability and the types of narratives and interests that the law tended to privilege and protect to the detriment of others. The modern novel, I argue, thus contributed to a significant (counter-)discourse that sounded out the coherences, frictions, and fault-lines between law and morality and elucidated the limitations of legal doctrines and judicial processes.

Narrativizing Modern Tort Law

The starting point for this essay is Ravit Reichman's eloquently argued view that legal and literary modernisms are yoked in

> a contingent relationship, in which the parameters and stakes of ethical life are set out in literature and reified—ever imperfectly—in law. These imperfections, in turn, reenter literature, bodying forth narratives that console, lament, and imagine possibilities that remain inexpressible in legal terms.[2]

As Maria Aristodemou similarly posits, with echoes of Shelley's tribute to the poet-as-legislator, fiction-writing can be "another form of lawmaking," which is "often quicker and more likely than other forms of legislation to challenge existing laws and dominant values."[3] Modern(ist) novels' interest in tort law has largely slipped the scholarly radar, which has tended to focus on the aesthetic and problematic depictions of violence in the contexts of war or crime.[4] But tort law served as a significant fulcrum in many literary works for exploring the oft-misaligned interests of the individual and the "common" good, diversely defined. From Kenneth Grahame's children's classic, *The Wind in the Willows* (1908), to the "high" modernist novels of Virginia Woolf, twentieth-century literary works emanate a growing unease about the harms for which tort law could offer monetary recompense, although usually not full reparation or restitution in the moral sense of these terms. As Costas Douzinas observes, "Legal rules and their mentality are strangely amoral; they promise to replace ethical responsibility with the mechanical application of predetermined and morally neutral rules, and justice with the administration of justice."[5] A significant number of literary works looked askance at the "amorality" of the law and called for higher standards of mutual responsibility and for more compassionate dispensations of justice.

Although he has received less scholarly treatment than some of his contemporaries, Anthony Powell was held in the highest esteem by fellow novelists. Evelyn Waugh quipped that he was "the only novelist who seems really worth watching."[6] Kingsley Amis declared *A Dance to the Music of Time* to be "[t]he most important effort in fiction since the war."[7] Published between 1951 and 1975, with a narrative span of almost six decades, from 1914 to 1971, Powell's novel sequence offers a macrocosmic chronicle of English social history. Broader cultural attitudes and moral values of the time are filtered through the ever-evolving consciousness of its narrator–protagonist, Nicholas Jenkins. Powell seems to share the Bakhtinian position that the writer's and reader's incomplete identification with the protagonist, "far from being an ethical flaw, is an ethical necessity."[8] As Desmond Manderson explains, "narrative is ethical not because we see what the hero sees but because we see what the hero, within the spatial and temporal limits of his own consciousness, cannot."[9] Powell appropriated and repurposed the *roman-fleuve* because its elongated spatiotemporal range enabled him to produce an ethical narrative that could offer readers multi-perspectival insights into a complex legal landscape and the wide-ranging spectrum of societal attitudes towards the law in this period.

Tort law was radically changed during Powell's lifetime as a result of statutory reforms and key judicial decisions. The year 1932 was the *annus mirabilis* in the history of negligence, which has become the predominant action in tort jurisprudence. In this year, Lord Atkin, in *Donoghue v. Stevenson*, articulated the seminal common law test for establishing liability:

> You must take reasonable care to avoid acts or omissions which you can reasonably foresee would be likely to injure your neighbour. Who, then, in law is my neighbour? The answer seems to be—persons who are so closely affected by my act that I ought reasonably to have them in contemplation as being so affected when I am directing my mind to the acts or omissions which are called in question.[10]

Lord Atkin's principle that every individual is duty-bound to honor his neighbor's right of property and person has become enshrined in English law.[11] In the mid-twentieth century, tort law played an increasingly vital role in vindicating the interests of injured individuals against more powerful entities, such as corporations and managers of public infrastructure.[12] Determinations of the content of duties of care became more principled and aligned with the tenets of corrective justice. The rules of privity, which had led to unjust rulings, were steadily eroded, immunities that had privileged certain tortfeasors were abolished, and the doctrines of product liability emerged. The injured and aggrieved could rely upon the neutral forums of civil law courts for the procedural mechanisms that would reinforce the values of individual responsibility and mutual accountability. Judges could vindicate basic rights relating to their bodily integrity, property interests, and reputation. By 1965, Professor Thomas F. Lambert would describe tort law as "the jurisprudence of hope." It had become, in his view, the most humanistic branch of law, as it placed a supreme value on the dignity and welfare of every citizen, especially the most vulnerable members of society.[13] Contemporary scholars like Manderson echo Lambert when opining that "If the law has a soul [...] it is to be found in the law of tort."[14] More intimately than other branches of private law, tort law is concerned with some of the fundamental ethical questions of human (co-)existence: What does it mean to be "responsible" and to act as would a "reasonable person"? Is the omission to act in certain circumstances as morally blameworthy as taking positive action?

However, for its critics, the protections offered by tort law fell short of an ethical ideal. As in other areas of law, there seemed to be a growing schism between what morality demanded and what the letter of the law stipulated. Historically, in tort jurisprudence, English courts were influenced by liberal economic principles and hesitated to hinder rapid industrial development by insisting upon improved safety protocols and practices. The major paradigm shift from the focus on "harm" in the traditional model of strict liability to that of "fault" in negligence marked a transition from a paternalistic to a *laissez-faire* model of legal "insurance."[15] Negligence law ultimately proceeds from the pragmatic concession that some risks are inevitable, even necessary, in modern societies. Moreover, tort law entrenched certain systemic and intersectional inequalities. David Hollingshead identifies it as "a crucial site for illuminating the state's sanctioned distribution of harms to particular segments of its population."[16] Those engaged in risky manual occupations bore a disproportionate personal cost for the rampant advances of industrialization and capitalist entrepreneurialism.[17] In her illuminating study of tort law in the nineteenth-century novel, Jan-Melissa Schramm notes that Victorian literature furnished very open-ended answers to the question "Who *is* my neighbor?" and intimated that "our relations—and thus perhaps our duties and obligations—were potentially limitless."[18] As this was the very antithesis of the delimiting impulse of twentieth-century tort jurisprudence, works of fiction like *The Music of Time* had to navigate disparate ethical inheritances from both the literary and legal discursive traditions.

Powell's *roman-fleuve* has often been categorized as a comedy. In Anthony Burgess's opinion, for example, it is "the finest long comic novel that England has produced this century."[19] However, the comedy often flags or falls flat. As Hilary Spurling notes in passing, "not the least disconcerting thing about *The Music of Time* is precisely its humorous tone."[20] An auxiliary aim of this essay is to reconsider the characterization of Powell as a comic writer by shifting the critical focus onto his narrativizations of torts. The younger Jenkins had mused that the interactions of "everyday life" are often "brought down to the level of farce even when the theme is serious enough."[21] However, when recalling a particular incident, such as the various persecutions of Kenneth Widmerpool (which will be discussed at greater length below), Jenkins often takes a less insouciant view, as the gravity of these occurrences has registered over time. Torts constitute vexed sites throughout the sequence, marking the moments when the euphonious flow of the narrative and its light-hearted tone are checked. Halfway through the sequence, Jenkins would retrospectively claim that he had "felt" since early childhood "that the precariousness of life was infinite."[22] This hyperconsciousness of the myriad dangers attendant upon daily life casts an ominous shadow across even the comic episodes. A tortious injury, as Reichman observes, "becomes, in many instances, the experience of unspeakable trauma."[23] Powell's novels hint at the ongoing psychological repercussions of torts, which generate a *tragi*comic narrative, as well as its broader critiques of socio-legal realities and injustices.

To a large extent, Powell shared Martin Amis's oft-cited view that "style *is* morality,"[24] a maxim that is traceable to one of modernism's projects: to suture ethical commitment and aesthetic experimentation. Jenkins's prose style, like his character, is urbane, polished, learned, and lyrical. But, crucially, it is also marked by hesitancy, vacillation, and (self-)

doubt, which take the form of equivocations (introduced by phrases like "for some reason," "perhaps") and modulations ("in its way," "not altogether," "more or less"). As Perry Anderson points out, Jenkins is "scarcely a cipher. Bemused, elated, ashamed; jealous, embarrassed, lonely; desiring, priggish, maladroit; furious, in despair; in tears, in love: at one point or another he is all of these."[25] These vehement emotions are triggered by his encounters with or observations of a four hundred-strong cast of characters, drawn from many spheres of society: business, finance, politics, publishing, academia, the civil service, as well as the misfits who drift between categories. Jenkins advances his narrative in a peripatetic manner, by way of surmise and hypothesis, and conscientiously avoids the oversimplifying binary of "cause" and "effect." As Namwali Serpell demonstrates, by the mid-twentieth century, uncertainty was "being declared as the very source of literature's ethical value."[26] Powell grasps the ethical import of cultivating an aesthetics of uncertainty. Isabelle Joyau astutely observes the novels' "indecisive tug-of-war between unrelenting fault-finding and compulsive criticalness, on the one hand, and a genial or lymphatic abdication of judgment, on the other."[27] Such vacillations, I would argue, are motivated by Powell's entwined ethical and aesthetical aims. They also reflect Powell's navigation of the tension between the literary tradition's flexible and expansive conceptualization of moral duty and the law's relatively mechanical and rigorous adherence to its precedents and due processes. Not unlike a man of law, Jenkins collates and evaluates hearsay and testimonial statements from eyewitnesses and *re*-presents incidents and characters through the bifocalized lens of his younger and more mature perspectives. But, as a literary character, he also models alternative ways of passing judgment—and of suspending it—when sympathy or moral duty demands it.

The remainder of this essay considers four specific issues within tort jurisprudence that Powell engages with in *The Music of Time*: the legal fiction of the reasonable man, occupiers' liability, negligence, and trespass to the person. The aim is to explore in greater depth how Powell's novels responded—through their content and form, as well as their style—to the fraught ethics of interpersonal duties and responsibilities and to the question of the adequacy of existing tort law as a form of protection against the careless and reckless behaviors that seemed endemic to modern society.

Fictionalizing the Reasonable Man

A noteworthy correspondence between twentieth-century tort law and modern(ist) literature is their heightened interest in psychology—in what Woolf famously dubbed every individual's "wedge-shaped core of darkness."[28] Historically, strict liability had been "strikingly indifferent to questions of interiority: what matters is not what one intends or how one feels, but what effects one engenders in the world."[29] Sandra Macpherson similarly highlights its "depersonalizing and instrumentalizing logic."[30] The emergence of the doctrine of negligence offered some redress for the marginality of the individual. Courts started comparing a defendant's conduct to what a fictitious "reasonable man" might have done in the same or similar situation. One of the overarching aims of *The Music of Time*, in Powell's own account, is an "investigation of human character."[31] In his analysis of "canons of behavior,"[32] Jenkins engages with contemporaneous discourses concerning the legal fiction of the "reasonable man."

If the criminal emblematized the violence of modernity,[33] the tortfeasor was a more ambivalent figure. The "wrongs" with which tort law is concerned do not ensue from malicious premeditation or even unambiguously antisocial tendencies. Instead, the causes are often moments of absent-mindedness, carelessness, or recklessness—states of mind that elude linguistic capture and moral censure. Near the beginning of *The Music of Time*, Jenkins muses upon the ethics of applying a benchmark of behavior at all, while preemptively exculpating his own failures to evaluate his acquaintances fairly:

> It is not easy—perhaps not even desirable—to judge other people by a consistent standard. Conduct obnoxious, even unbearable, in one person may be readily tolerated in another; apparently indispensable principles of behavior are in practice relaxed—not always with impunity—in the interests of those whose nature seems to demand an exceptional measure. That is one of the difficulties of committing human actions to paper [...] because some characters and some deeds [...] may be thought of only in terms appropriate to themselves, irrespective of their consequence.[34]

Jenkins's characteristic self-qualifications—interjectory or clarificatory phrases like "perhaps not ... ," "even unbearable," and "not always ... "—convey an inner struggle with his own double standards. He is vague as to why certain actions (and actors) are so exceptional in his subjective view that they are to be exempted from judgment altogether. He frequently circles back to this moral conundrum. In the second volume, he reaffirms "the difficulties involved in judging other people's behavior by a consistent standard," but adds the afterthought: "—for after all, one must judge them."[35] The mandatory modal "must" countermands the earlier "may" and infers his recognition of a positive moral duty to make such adjudications. Another striking pronouncement in the third volume, *The Acceptance World*, reveals a linchpin in his ethics: "All human beings [...] are at close range equally extraordinary."[36] The oxymoronic collocation, "equally extraordinary," suggests a deeply humanistic belief that every individual is singular and worthy of not only narrative attention but also, when appropriate, forbearance.

Nevertheless, over the course of the sequence, certain types of conduct consistently provoke narratorial rebuke for being "unreasonable," and thus the narrative's moral values materialize in a piecemeal fashion. Jenkins reprimands careless characters like Buster, who has a "consciously reckless manner of facing the world."[37] His old school friend, Charles Stringham, who is "obviously prepared to live dangerously,"[38] suffers a protracted fall from grace. The meting out of poetic justice offers a pyrrhic consolation for those who had fallen victim to his reckless behavior. Similarly, Jenkins disowns the flagrantly cavalier "Uncle" Giles, who displays an "unhesitating contempt for all human conduct but his own."[39]

Equally, the limitations of Jenkins's moral imagination are also underscored by Powell. For an illustrative example, we only have to turn to the sequence's opening scene, which evokes the then undeveloped subfield of law governing workplace safety and employers' duties of care: "The men at work at the corner of the street had made a kind of camp for themselves, where, marked out by tripods hung with red hurricane-lamps, an abyss in the road led down to a network of subterranean drain-pipes."[40] There are distinct echoes here of the social realist tradition of Charles Dickens, Elizabeth Gaskell, and D. H. Lawrence, who decried the high-risk, often subterranean, conditions to which manual laborers, those largely unacknowledged cogs of mass industrialization, were regularly consigned. The perilousness of the employment is conveyed by the makeshift nature of the camp and weakness of the lighting, which barely penetrates the pitch blackness of the "abyss." Instead of following the men down into this inferno, the yet unnamed narrator seeks to elevate their laboring bodies to the level of myth, equating them to "classical projections" that are "breaking into seemingly meaningless gyrations."[41] The narrator's use of orotund metaphors and mythopoeic allusions partially glosses the grim reality of these punishing midwinter conditions. The "bare life'" of those at the bottom of the social ladder is symbolized obliquely by the meagre remains of their sustenance, "the remains of two kippers." Powell is issuing an early caveat about the narrator–protagonist of *The Music of Time*, who, despite his ecumenist interest in humanity, is saddled with the biases and blind spots of his background and habitual social milieu, namely that of the English upper-middle class. One's upbringing, Powell suggests, becomes a problem when one is called upon to make moral determinations on what constitutes "reasonable" behavior.

The young Jenkins naively intimates that in the process of telling (and retelling) his life, he will discover organizing patterns and those titular "secret harmonies" that will illuminate an inherent sense of order within his frenetic modern society. "[F]orces hitherto unfamiliar," he adumbrates at the start of the first book, "become [...] uncompromisingly clear."[42] However, this promise of absolute clarity is never fulfilled. Nicholas Birns's view that "the twelfth book conveys the triumph of time, the way time, merely by its rolling, mute[s] persistence, will overcome inequity and bring right to light" warrants challenging.[43] Many narrative threads—and inequities—remain ultimately unresolved. Jenkins himself is compelled to repeatedly concede "the inevitability of circumstances,"[44] that modern society is at the mercy of "the drift of circumstance,"[45] and that "often inexplicable things must simply be accepted as matters of fact."[46] The unnamed "forces" and "inexplicable things" that he gestures vaguely towards include the actions, behaviors, and habits that culminate in torts—with consequences that are variously comic, poignant, and ultimately deeply troubling. At the end of the sequence, Jenkins burns "an untidy pile of miscellaneous debris,"[47] which can be read as a wry final meta-fictional acknowledgment of the "imperfections" and "possibilities" that his narrative has failed to imagine, let alone express.

Occupier's Liability

The second volume, *A Buyer's Market* (1952), presents a more concrete example of Powell's concern with the limitations of tort law as it then stood in the late 1920s, the time of the narrative. It culminates upon "the fatal accident" involving Edgar Deacon, an artist and old family friend of Jenkins's.[48] Deacon had been celebrating his birthday at a "shady" nightclub, where "soon after his arrival there, Mr. Deacon fell down the stairs."[49] He had been on his way "to lodge a complaint with the management regarding the club's existing sanitary arrangements: universally agreed to be deplorable enough."[50] Jenkins learns of the mishap from Barnby, who speculates, "He must have sustained some internal injury, for he died within the week."[51] It is darkly ironic that Deacon dies as a result of the club's negligent upkeep, while in the very act of protesting this very issue. To Barnby's mind, the chain of causation is clear: "Mr. Deacon had died *as the result* of an accident."[52] However, Jenkins has a more nuanced take on the incident. After collecting testimonies from other attendees, he rewrites it as follows:

> it was agreed by everyone present that the fall had been in no way attributable to anything more than a rickety staircase and his own habitual impetuosity. The truth was that, as a man no longer young, he would have been wiser in this, and no doubt in other matters too, to have shown less frenzied haste in attempting to bring about the righting of so many of life's glaring wrongs.[53]

Proceeding much like a tort lawyer, Jenkins divvies up the fault between club owner and customer. The owner had been remiss in his duty of care to maintain safe premises, but the latter's contributory negligence ("habitual impetuosity," compounded by mild inebriation) was also a relevant factor. Jenkins also forensically analyses Deacon's fall: it had been "not exactly dramatic," "not [...] commonplace," and "not [...] violent."[54] Nor was it "a bourgeois death," as it "partook [...] of that spirit of carelessness and informality."[55] He is only able to define the incident negatively, by eliminating what it was *not*, because the inchoate state of this area of tort law meant that there is little ready-made terminology to help him articulate, let alone legally vindicate, the wrong (which he can only refer to as an "undignified mishap"[56]) on behalf of his friend.[57] Jenkins's careful distribution of moral fault reflects his sense of disquiet that Deacon—or rather, his estate—was unable to obtain any formal vindication for the harm suffered. It would only be five years after the publication and thirty years after the 1928 setting of *A Buyer's Market* that the Occupier's Liability Act 1957 codified in statute the common law duty of care owed by occupiers to their visitors. In the absence of a legal remedy, and anxious to impose some kind of moral order in his narrative, Jenkins tacitly concurs with Barnby that it was "hard to think of Edgar without being overwhelmed with moralisings of a somewhat banal kind."[58] Thus "overwhelmed," he renders Deacon's fate into a sort of parable. His friend's "habitual impetuosity," "spirit of carelessness," and "frenzied haste," which are also the typical traits and behaviors of tortfeasors, had warranted, by the logic of "poetic justice," that he be taken out of action by the "rickety staircase" before he had the occasion to cause injury to others.

Negligence

This "spirit of carelessness," which rears up regularly in *The Music of Time*, usually provokes some degree of moral indignation on the part of Jenkins. The negligent driver—usually a member of either the genteel or "bourgeois" classes—is a recurring trope in the twentieth-century novel.[59] The most common form of negligence in Powell's fictions involves automobiles.[60] The high volume of car collisions in Powell's *roman-fleuve* is symptomatic of the prevalence of reckless behaviors in modern society. Jenkins acknowledges his own complicity with and contribution to this economy of pain: he remembers an occasion in 1934 when they "drove precariously [...], the car emitting a series of frightening crepitations and an evil fume."[61] In particular, Powell shows how it is the well-to-do social elite, much like the Gatsbys on the other side of the Atlantic, who careen about with reckless abandon and a flagrant disregard for fellow users of the roads.

A Question of Upbringing concludes with a scene where Jenkins's old schoolmate, Peter Templer, picks up a group of their mutual friends from Oxford in a run-down Vauxhall:

> Peter was not driving specially fast, but the road, which was slippery from rain fallen earlier in the evening, took two hairpin bends; and, as we reached the second of these, some kind of upheaval took place within the car. No one afterwards could explain exactly what happened [...]. Whatever the root of the trouble, the memorable consequence was that Peter—in order to avoid a large elm tree—drove into the ditch: where the car stopped abruptly, making a really horrible sound like a dying monster; remaining stuck at an angle of forty-five degrees to the road.[62]

The legal inclination of Jenkins's mind first reveals itself here, as he weighs up the relative blameworthiness of the parties involved. He notes Peter's moderate speed and enumerates other potential contributing factors to the accident: the weather conditions ("slippery from rain"), the road infrastructure ("two hairpin bends"), and, possibly, a disturbance caused by the passengers. The vagueness of the language—"some kind of," "No one afterwards could explain exactly," "whatever"—underlines how any forensic reconstruction of an accident soon becomes a matter of "supposition" and "theories." Five volumes and more than fifteen years later, Jenkins has a chance reencounter with Bob Duport, a fellow passenger, which unleashes a maelstrom of half-buried emotions: "A whole sequence of memories and sensations, luxuriant, tender, painful, ludicrous, wearisome, rolled up, enveloping like a fog."[63] This is typical of how torts or near-torts (as here) haunt Jenkins with a tenacity that is particularly striking when juxtaposed, say, to his relative insouciance when recalling his military service during World War II. One explanation for his fixation is that he sees these incidents as a symptom of a deeper social evil, namely, just how rampant unethical behaviors had become in the modern world. After all, the reason that tort laws had come into being at all was because there was a need for institutional enforcement of moral precepts that had been all but abandoned in a highly individualistic society.

As the "highly romantic view" of the young Jenkins is gradually attenuated,[64] such unethical behaviors lose some of their ability to disturb him. Towards the end of the sequence, Louis Glober, one of the American "temporary kings" is killed offstage in a motor accident. His compatriot, Professor Russell Gwinnett, relates the incident to Jenkins:

> The accident (on the Moyenne Corniche) had been one of those reflecting no marked blame on anyone, except that the car had been travelling at an unusually high speed. A friend of Glober's, a well-known French racing-driver, had been at the wheel. The story received very thorough press coverage. It was the sort of end Glober himself would have approved.[65]

Jenkins does not register any surprise or indignation at the "unusually high speed," or dispute Gwinnett's flippant quip that Glober would have been pleased with the manner of his death. In the final volume, the deaths of two of his military acquaintances are announced with similar casualness: "Bobrowski had been knocked down by a taxi, and killed. Oddly enough, Philidor, too, had died in a car accident." The world-weary Jenkins merely shrugs, "Perhaps such deaths were appropriate to men of action, better than a slow decline."[66] He has evidently become desensitized to the human tragedies that are caused daily by the thoughtlessness and carelessness of others. That Glober's death generated such "thorough press coverage" alone hints that Jenkins's jaded view is not universally shared and that vehicular torts are still capable of generating some public consternation— or, at least, interest.

Trespass to the Person

The tort of trespass to the person has historically played an important role in protecting the individual against direct or intentional interferences with their bodily integrity or liberty. It is necessary to question why it is Kenneth Widmerpool who falls victim to these offenses most frequently in *The Music of Time*. Jenkins struggles to apply his "consistent standard" when appraising this arch-nemesis and pseudo-doppelganger of his. Significantly, he draws upon tort legalese to try and articulate his relationship with Widmerpool, whom he deems is "neither [...] an intimate friend, nor yet sufficiently remote."[67] But even though he "felt his defence a duty,"[68] Jenkins never fully overcomes his innate revulsion to Widmerpool's "innate oddness; one might almost say his monstrosity."[69] Widmerpool is first introduced as an "uneasy, irrelevant figure," who is "too grotesque to take seriously."[70] He is certainly more sinned against than sinning, as schoolyard horseplay escalates into more serious torts, such as battery and assault.

Jenkins frequently recollects the incidents when Widmerpool had been victimized, and the unjustness of this collective persecution seems to haunt him. Jenkins's sense of moral outrage on behalf of Widmerpool is one of the rare instances when he abandons his habitual position of ambivalence. Moreover, with each retelling, his version of events changes ever so slightly. Powell thus draws attention to the ethics of testimony itself by showing how Jenkins, as "witness," either inadvertently or deliberately revises his "evidence" in the process of trying to comprehend the opaque motivations and emotions of the parties involved. The first instance of battery—when their school's cricket captain pelted Widmerpool with a piece of overripe banana—had been purely accidental. The latter's acceptance of the apology is gracious: "I don't mind at all, Budd. It doesn't matter in the least," he insists, as he cleans off the splattered fruit "with a great show of good cheer."[71] He reacts with a similar degree of equanimity and dignity after a later incident, when Barbara Goring infamously upends the contents of an entire sugar bowl over him at the Huntercombes Ball. At first, Jenkins suggests that Barbara's battery had been provoked: "I watched Widmerpool seize hold of Barbara in this way—by force—without at the precisely operative moment experiencing that amazement with which his conduct on this occasion afterwards, on reconsideration, finally struck me."[72] "Struck," dramatically delayed by tautological phrasing, underscores Jenkins's retrospective surprise at Widmerpool's uncharacteristically "vigorous and instantaneous assertion of the will."[73] On its second telling, in the next paragraph, Widmerpool's conduct is less aggressive: he had only "*snatch*[ed] at her with those blunt, gnarled fingers," which is a milder verb than "seize," and "[t]he grabbing movement had, indeed, taken *only a fraction of a second*."[74] Jenkins adds that it would have been reasonable for Widmerpool to have "turned white with shock."[75] But instead he displays both "dignity and good temper," and although "he glanced reproachfully toward Barbara," this was, Jenkins emphasizes, "only for a flash."[76] All these subsequent embellishments underscore his restraint, particularly laudable in light of his private admission to Jenkins that "I was upset—very upset" and thought it "a cruel thing to do."[77] The guests who witness the fiasco respond initially with "a great deal of laughter."[78] However, perhaps because they are shamed by Widmerpool's stoical reaction, the joviality is soon superseded by "a general public dejection" and a "frightful despondency."[79] Jenkins stresses that his own verdict is "final": his romantic attraction to Barbara has been irrevocably voided. Her thoughtless actions are exacerbated by her refusal to take responsibility for them. Jenkins indignantly recollects how she makes "no serious effort to repair, morally or physically, any of the damage she had caused." In fact, she even brazenly demurs, "It really wasn't my fault." Jenkins tersely decrees, "I felt quite certain that Barbara, if capable of an act of this sort, was not—and had never been—for me."[80]

The final battery of Widmerpool, during a "scuffle" at a ceremonial occasion in the "newish" university where he presides as chancellor, is televised to the entire nation.[81] Jenkins paints a gruesome scene: "At first sight, so ghastly seemed Widmerpool's condition that it was a wonder he was alive [...]. He had evidently been the victim of an atrocious assault."[82] This gory vignette soon subsides into bathos, when Jenkins realizes that the "inconceivable mess" is merely red paint that the Quiggin twins had thrown at him. A potential crime is demoted to a tort, specifically a trespass to the person. Widmerpool again exhibits what Jenkins refers to neologistically—and with grudging admiration—as his "unsnubbableness."[83] "Not the smallest resentment," he insists, and Jenkins observes that "he had now learned to convert such occasions [...] to good purpose where other ends were concerned."[84] To achieve one such end, Widmerpool arrives at the Magnus-Donners literary prize dinner to deliver an "unplanned oration," during which he converts this public humiliation into a clarion call for social reform. He exhorts his audience, who listen in a "somewhat horrified [...] silence," to join him in striving for "the catalysis of social, physical and spiritual revolution [...] in the name of contemporary counterculture." Jenkins is somewhat stirred by the speech and even senses that Widmerpool would be "coming on to something that might be worth hearing."[85] His peroration builds up to an anarchic denouncement of "the wrongness of the way we live, the wrongness of marriage, the wrongness of money, the wrongness of education, the wrongness of government, the wrongness of the manner we treat kids like these."[86] The anaphora evokes the etymological roots of tort itself, which is derived from the old French for "wrong." Through this subtle wordplay, Widmerpool clinches a thesis that Jenkins has been discursively exploring over the twelve volumes: the sheer prevalence of morally and legally wrongful conduct has been a manifestation of these broader systemic failings within their society.

As Lindsay Bagshaw, a literary editor in the sequence, had earlier opined, Widmerpool is "a man in a life-and-death grapple with the decadent society round him. Either he wins or it does."[87] The *roman-fleuve* ultimately leaves open-ended the question of whether it is Widmerpool or the society that strove to batter down his astronomic, anarchic ascent through its ranks that emerges triumphant from their agonistic contest. Jenkins's own antagonism towards Widmerpool, shared by others in his social set, is rooted in the classism that they seem reluctant to confront. After all, as an arriviste who rises from his father's liquid manure business to insinuate himself within the echelons of English society, Widmerpool is a harbinger of a new meritocratic order. It is worth noting that he never launches civil proceedings against any of his tortfeasors. This may be attributed to some magnanimity in his character or read as an oblique commentary on the limitations of the justice system itself. Perhaps Widmerpool perceived the judiciary as a mere extension of the British Establishment that had always held potential claimants like himself in contempt.

Wai Chee Dimock, a distinguished law-and-literature scholar, argues that it is the "messiness of representation" of a literary work that enriches our understanding of the law. Fictional universes, which simulate the real world, constitute vital testing grounds for legal rules and dicta.[88] For Powell, the perambulatory, synchronous, and capacious nature of the *roman-fleuve,* the loosest and baggiest of novelistic monsters, offered the optimal formal medium for accommodating what has been described as his "colossal cultural omnivorousness" and "encyclopaedic interests," including his lifelong fascination with contemporary legal developments.[89] The compositional and narrative timelines of *A Dance to the Music of*

Time eventually dovetail with a "Golden Age" of humanistic tort law, those mid-century decades when its pro-plaintiff principles had been formalized—before they came under assault from Thatcherite neoliberalism. In interweaving the principles of a modernizing tort jurisprudence into his narratives, Powell's oeuvre is as artistically ambitious as it is morally engaged, and one which continues to raise as many ethical questions as it attempted to answer.

IV

Intersectional Ethics

CHAPTER TEN

"Criteria of Negro Art"
Ethical Negotiations in the Harlem Renaissance

Laura Ryan

It is now widely acknowledged that the phenomenon best known as the Harlem Renaissance was not the isolated, geographically specific movement that this name suggests. Nor was it, strictly speaking, a "renaissance"—a "rebirth"—because nothing of its scale or significance had ever before occurred within African American art and culture. The term describes a flourishing of Black art that spread across the United States and into Europe and was at its height in the 1920s.[1] The artists associated with the New Negro movement, as it was then known, were intent upon countering racist stereotypes long propounded by white America. Largely prevented from gaining political power or economic advantage, they turned to art, music, and literature to create and celebrate a new, specific Black identity and aesthetic. Like their white modernist counterparts, then, Harlem Renaissance writers sought to break from the values and forms of the past to establish new ways of thinking and living. Yet young Black modernists were often not afforded the artistic autonomy enjoyed by white modernists; they were (to some extent at least) beholden to standards and expectations set by an older generation of leaders and intellectuals. The group W. E. B. Du Bois dubbed his "Talented Tenth" were—he preached—morally, intellectually, and politically responsible for the "racial uplift" of all African Americans.[2] The question—posed prominently in Alain Locke's landmark anthology *The New Negro* (1925)—of how "the Negro" should be portrayed in art was the subject of fierce debate; matters of aesthetics and ethics were thoroughly intertwined.

Yet while Locke lauded the "new psychology" and "new spirit" alive in the younger generation and a "renewed self-respect and self-dependence" in "the life of the Negro community," many New Negro writers and artists were financially supported (and often creatively restricted) by white patrons.[3] Meanwhile—even in Harlem—top entertainment venues hosting Black talent barred African American patrons entirely. Distinct difficulties arise in approaching ethical issues in the context of a profoundly unethical society: one that preaches Christian values, proclaiming itself a land of freedom, opportunity, and equality while enforcing discriminatory legislation that treated millions of its inhabitants as second-class citizens.

This chapter interrogates some of the ethical quandaries and pressures faced by Harlem Renaissance writers, how they negotiated them, and how these negotiations shaped their work and responses to it. With reference to key figures including Du Bois, Locke, Jean Toomer, Langston Hughes, and Zora Neale Hurston, the chapter deals with the ethics of responsibility to one's race, and particularly the ethical implications of racial passing, the involvement of white patrons, and individualism. There are no straightforward responses to these issues; this essay does not suggest any, nor does it debate—as many critics have—the "success" or "failure" of the Harlem Renaissance.[4] Rather, this chapter argues that the Harlem Renaissance must be understood as a phenomenon arising from a myriad of ethical binds, competing ideologies, and moral compromises. I am concerned here also with the ethics of criticism, and with the ethical issues that surface in our readings of these texts and contexts today. Later generations of African American writers and thinkers repudiated the Harlem Renaissance on grounds of both ethics and aesthetics. For the proponents of the Black Arts Movement, New Negro artists failed not only to create social and political change, but also to produce a truly Black aesthetic independent of white cultural standards and influence. Yet, a century on, the Harlem Renaissance is routinely evoked in relation to political struggles faced by marginalized peoples today. The subjects discussed here are by no means novel to those familiar with New Negro texts and contexts, but in considering these complex—and in some instances still controversial—cases together, we can better understand the art produced and the writers who worked within this contested arena. In light of present-day issues and social movements, a reading of the Harlem Renaissance that centers its ethical predicaments and debates highlights the extent to which Black art and artists today continue to bear the weight of communal responsibility.

Art or Propaganda? Du Bois, Locke, and the Function of Black Art

The New Negro movement had grand aspirations and lofty ideals; it aimed to reform the image of African Americans (in the minds of Black and white Americans alike) through artistic expression and the creation of a specifically Black aesthetic. In doing so, it looked to generate political change and improve economic opportunities for African Americans. The movement was, however, plagued from its outset by deep division and intense debate among the intellectuals at its forefront. Surely the fiercest, most public debate was between Locke and Du Bois, whose ideas on how best to achieve the movement's aims were often in stark opposition. This battle played out over many years, notably in the competition between *The Crisis* and *Opportunity* journals (and continued long after the dwindling of the Harlem Renaissance). Du Bois believed passionately that Black artists had a responsibility to portray African American life in ways that would "uplift" the race; he famously declared his indifference to "any art that is not used for propaganda."[5] Locke, conversely, argued that art should express the individual and speak to universal human themes and experiences; "In our spiritual growth," he averred, "genius and talent must more and more choose the role of group expression, or even at times the role of free individualistic expression,—in a word must choose art and put aside propaganda."[6] For Leonard Harris, this was "a conflict [...] predicated on what each understood as the nature of the beautiful and its role as an agent for social change."[7] Yet Locke and Du Bois were both grappling with the social function of art; both wanted to alter the lot of a socially disenfranchised population suffering under dehumanizing, humiliating laws. For both, art was not only about beauty; "the struggle to create an image of the black population as beautiful" was thus "simultaneously a struggle to create an image of the black population as possessing, or capable of possessing, character and moral virtues."[8]

For Du Bois, as for many of his generation, the purpose of Black art was to present positive images of Black life. This attitude was in many ways a continuation of the ways in which Black literature in the United States had historically been considered necessarily political. For early African American writers—those who wrote the first slave narratives and poetry collections—their very humanity was at issue, their freedom potentially at stake.[9] However, as Saidiya V. Hartman argues, in the postbellum period, "the recognition of humanity and individuality" often "acted to tether, bind, and oppress"; notions of "freedom" and "individuality" were mobilized in order to subject former slaves to a new kind of subjugation.[10] In dialogue with Hartman, Fred Moten posits the power of Black performance as Black radicalism, observing that "the emergence from political, economic, and sexual objection of the radical materiality and syntax that animates Black performances indicates a freedom drive that is expressed always and everywhere throughout their graphic (re)production."[11] By the 1920s, the extent to which Black art should be overtly propagandistic was subject to debate; writing in 1921, Eric Walrond warned that a tendency to propaganda would make it "very difficult for the American Negro poet to create a lasting work of art," opining that "[h]e must first purge himself of the feelings and sufferings and emotions of an outraged being."[12] Walrond's statement raises a number of questions for a consideration of art and ethics in this context. If art was not a viable means by which the artist might "purge himself" of "feelings and sufferings and emotions," then what was?

Locke's *The New Negro* registered and communicated a newly individuated and unfettered view of Black art in direct contrast to the "Old Negro" image that was, Locke observed, "more of a formula than a human being."[13] Such was the pervasive power and influence of the "Old Negro" stereotype, that African Americans themselves came to identify with it, to "see [themselves] in the distorted perspective of a social problem"; naturally, Locke remarks, "Little true social or self-understanding has or could come from such a situation."[14] The "New Negro," by contrast, was a liberated figure, buoyed by a "renewed self-respect and self-dependence," "transplanted" and "transformed," capable of "group expression and self-determination"; Locke's anthology—infused with optimism for the future—showcased this.[15]

For Du Bois, however, *The New Negro* represented a worrying development. He recognized the quality of work in Locke's anthology, but Du Bois needed it to do something tangible: to perform a social and political function rather than merely an aesthetic one. "Mr. Locke," he observed, "has newly been seized with the idea that Beauty rather than Propaganda should be the object of Negro literature and art."[16] Yet, Du Bois averred, "[h]is book proves the falseness of this thesis"; *The New Negro* was, he thought, "bursting with propaganda."[17] Nevertheless, he worried that "if Mr. Locke's thesis is insisted on too much it is going to turn the Negro renaissance into decadence"; decadence, for Du Bois, was an unacceptable recourse for the Black artist.[18] He was referring—at least in part—to decadence as a byword for sexual profligacy and perversion; as Jeffrey C. Stewart notes, "A Negro art movement based on Beauty was a slippery slope to decadence and homosexuality, and Du Bois was having none of it."[19] But this reference to decadence also evokes wider debates around degeneration in the late nineteenth and early twentieth centuries; Max Nordau's *Degeneration* (1892–93) notably diagnosed the degeneracy of *fin de siècle* literature and culture, taking aim at Oscar Wilde, Richard Wagner, and Friedrich Nietzsche, among others. Like Nordau, Du Bois could not sanction art without moral or didactic purpose; aestheticism, he felt, eroded traditional moral values and could not aid the cause of racial liberation.

In "Criteria of Negro Art" (1926), Du Bois puts forward perhaps most powerfully his ideas on the social and political function of art. He casts himself as a prophetic figure: "one who tells the truth and exposes evil and seeks with Beauty and for Beauty to set the world right."[20] He can conceive "[t]hat somehow, somewhere eternal and perfect Beauty sits above Truth and Right […], but here and now and in the world in which I work they are for me unseparated and inseparable."[21] "Thus," he affirms,

> all Art is propaganda and ever must be, despite the wailing of the purists. I stand in utter shamelessness and say that whatever art I have for writing has been used always for propaganda for gaining the right of black folk to love and enjoy. I do not care a damn for any art that is not used for propaganda.[22]

In a more egalitarian world, "Beauty" might be permitted to exist outside the ethical framework of "Truth" and "Right," but in Jim Crow America, Du Bois suggests, Black artists cannot afford the luxury of art for art's sake.

In "Art or Propaganda" (1928), Locke addresses this idea that only propagandistic art can serve the aims of the New Negro movement. He suggests instead why propaganda is not the most propitious way forward:

> My chief objection to propaganda [...] is that it perpetuates the position of group inferiority even in crying out against it. For it leaves and speaks under the shadow of a dominant majority whom it harangues, cajoles, threatens or supplicates. [...] Art in the best sense is rooted in self-expression and whether naive or sophisticated is self-contained.[23]

For Locke, "propaganda art" is ineffective because it fails to break from the dominant cultural narrative that it seeks to challenge; "self-conviction," he affirms, "must supplant self-justification and in the dignity of this attitude a convinced minority must confront a condescending majority."[24] Locke's ideal was not merely "'art for art's sake,' or cultivation of the last decadences of the over-civilized," it was rather "a deep realization of the fundamental purpose of art and of its function as a tap root of vigorous, flourishing living."[25] While Du Bois was intent upon art "gaining the right for black folk to love and enjoy," Locke felt that African American art should convey and play an active part in the joy of Black life. Moreover, it should be "self-contained" and self-expressive, rather than a response to white oppression. This was the strained, contested atmosphere within which New Negro artists worked. Not only were they attempting to survive financially (a feat that almost inevitably meant appealing to white audiences and patrons), they were also contending with a fractured leadership delivering contradictory messages and then proceeding to make both ethical and aesthetic judgments upon the art they produced.

The Ethics of "Passing": Jean Toomer's "new type of man"

When Jean Toomer's *Cane* emerged in 1923—before the debate described above had fully developed—it seemed to exemplify what the new movement in Black art should be about, and the kind of work it should generate. Often heralded as the founding text of the Harlem Renaissance and deemed its most modernist work, *Cane* was largely inspired by Toomer's short stint as acting principal of an agricultural school in Sparta, Georgia in autumn 1921. It reflects the period in which its mixed-race author felt most connected to—and stimulated by—his African American roots. So important and influential was this unique work—in three parts and combining short stories, sketches, poetry, and a dramatic piece—*Cane* and Toomer quickly became synonymous with the New Negro. Toomer was hailed as "the very first artist of the race" and "a bright morning star of a new day of the race in literature," but he was quick to distance himself from such descriptions, and from the New Negro movement itself; he would not be pigeonholed as a "Negro" writer.[26] In a 1922 letter to *The Liberator*, he described his heritage as "French, Dutch, Welsh, Negro, German, Jewish, and Indian," but later professed his wish to be considered merely as an American.[27] Exasperated by his publisher's insistence that he be marketed as a Black writer (to capitalize upon the 1920s New Negro vogue), he maintained his right to define his own racial identity. He did not object, he told his editor, to the use of "whatever racial factors" might aid in the book's marketing, but he would not be compelled to emphasize his own Blackness: "My racial composition and my position in the world are realities which I alone may determine. [...] Whatever statements I give will inevitably come from a sympathetic human and art point of view; not from a racial one."[28]

Thus, when Locke published excerpts of *Cane* (alongside his portrait) in *The New Negro*, Toomer was livid. The New Negro movement he thought "a splendid thing," but "something that had no special meaning for [him]."[29] That the author of one of the most celebrated, innovative works portraying African American life did not wish to be identified as "Negro" was inevitably problematic. It has remained so—for some critics—into the current century.[30] Toomer has been cast as a writer who forsook his racial roots (and consequently produced no further art of note) and accused of racial passing. "[T]o 'pass,'" Sinéad Moynihan explains, "is to appear to belong to one or more social subgroups other than the one(s) to which one is normally assigned by prevailing legal, medical and/or socio-cultural discourses."[31] The term originates in the era of slavery, when light-skinned slaves forged written passes to escape their masters. Moynihan notes that "[p]assing is typically associated with a period stretching from post-Reconstruction to the Civil Rights Movement [...] or, even more specifically, yoked to the years of the Harlem Renaissance."[32]

It seems curious—even paradoxical—that a movement concerned with acclaiming a specifically Black identity should be simultaneously fascinated by the idea of Black and mixed-race individuals choosing to live as white. Yet, in many Harlem Renaissance works, passing is a running theme and recurring trope. James Weldon Johnson's *Autobiography of an Ex-Colored Man* (first published anonymously, in 1912, republished in 1927), Nella Larsen's *Quicksand* (1928) and *Passing* (1929), Jessie Fauset's *Plum Bun* (1929) and George Schuyler's *Black No More* (1931) all take passing as their subject. The idea that someone of African descent could be lurking undetected within white American society intrigued and titillated Black and white audiences alike. Several of these texts—subverting the earlier trope of the "tragic mulatto"—satirize the idea of racial passing. Yet passing is also portrayed—as in *Autobiography of an Ex-Colored Man*— as a hollow life and a betrayal of one's race and identity. At the book's end, the eponymous "ex-colored man" bewails that he has "sold [his] birthright for a mess of potage."[33] Hughes's short story "Passing" (1934) similarly foregrounds the loss and betrayal that racial passing entails; in this story, mixed-race Jack writes to his mother explaining why he could not acknowledge her on the street (he was with his white girlfriend, who is unaware that his mother is Black). Jack (naively, Hughes implies) believes that he has successfully escaped "the mire of color" by passing.[34]

Johnson and Hughes present passing as a cowardly and unethical (if partially understandable) undertaking. Rudolph P. Byrd and Henry Louis Gates, Jr. espouse an even harsher view in their introduction to the 2011 Norton Critical Edition of *Cane*. Here they reference the certificate of Toomer's 1931 marriage to Margery Latimer, where both bride and groom are listed as "white"—as well as several censuses also recording him as "white"—as proof that Toomer was "passing" and "endlessly deconstructing his Negro ancestry."[35] In a formulation that associates Toomer's perceived renunciation of his Blackness with emasculation and erasure, Gates elsewhere describes Toomer's racial self-identification as an act of "racial castration," which "transformed his deep black bass into a false soprano."[36] Such claims are problematic for several reasons. Not only does Gates's metaphor hark back to archaic stereotypes around race and sexuality, evoking, as George Hutchinson notes, "an old racialist tradition that held male 'mulattoes' to be more effeminate, less potent sexually, than either blacks or whites," it also dismisses the legitimacy of any racial identity outside the Black/white binary.[37]

Toomer would undoubtedly have found such accusations of passing quite ridiculous: "I heard of 'passing,'" he writes in "On Being an American" (1934): "I heard that the white world was the world of opportunity, that the colored world was narrow and closed in. I heard of lynchings [...] but it never occurred to me that they might have some bearing on my personal career."[38] It seems almost unbelievable that *Cane*'s author could, only a decade later, appear so indifferent to and so insulated from fundamental issues and threats facing African Americans. Yet Toomer had long been formulating an alternative, utopian vision of "a new type of man" who is "not European, not African, not Asiatic—but American": "And in this American I saw the divisions mended, the differences reconciled— saw that [...] we would in truth be a united people existing in the United States, [...] once again members of a united human race."[39] Toomer's idea was rooted in racial mixing; the Americans he envisaged were true products of America's melting pot. In "The Blue Meridian" (1936), he imagines a future in which a "blue" race, an amalgamation of the African, European, and native American races, has come into existence: "Black is black, white is white/[...] Is truth for the mind of contrasts;/But here the high way of the third,/The man of blue or purple."[40] He previously foregrounded these ideas in *Cane*, notably in the character of Kabnis, whose ancestors are both "Southern blue-bloods" and "black," although he argues that there "[a]in't much difference between blue and black."[41] Toomer's attitudes regarding racial mixing, of course, were at odds with prevailing cultural and scientific discourses around miscegenation. The infamous "one-drop rule" became dominant under Jim Crow, but its influence has been enduring; it determined that an individual with any known Black ancestry (with "one drop" of Black blood)—regardless of other heritage—would be categorized as "Negro."

Toomer's racial self-definition is perhaps difficult—and ethically unsound—for critics like Byrd and Gates because it circumvents the perceived responsibility of the "Black" writer to his community. Perhaps even more troubling, though, is the possibility—suggested by Matthew Pratt Guterl—that these critics are intent upon squeezing Toomer into a pre-approved category: that of the "passing figure."[42] As Guterl observes, "the stakes are very high: if Toomer isn't 'black' and if he isn't passing, then the object of African American studies has been changed."[43] In other words, if Toomer cannot be accommodated within a set of conventions and types established under the banner of African American studies, then there is a danger that he—and *Cane*, more importantly—could be lost to the African American literary canon.

Either way, it would seem that in 2011 little had changed since the 1920s and 1930s, when, Hughes recalls, Toomer's declaration of himself as neither white nor Black "put all the critics, white and colored, in a great dilemma. How should they class the author of *Cane* in their lists and summaries?"[44] Byrd and Gates's judgments upon Toomer—which disregard his own, well-documented, feelings about his racial identity—perpetuate essentialist ideas about race, including the insidious "one-drop rule." The example of Toomer and the accusations of passing leveled against him indeed speak to how these debates persist and critics continue to pass ethical judgments upon New Negro writers and works today.

Black and White(?): White Patrons, Power, and Primitivism

If *Cane* was a founding text of the Harlem Renaissance, then Hughes's 1926 essay, "The Racial Mountain and the Negro Artist," was its clarion call to a new generation of African American writers. In it, he scorned those young Black artists who proclaimed, "I want to be a poet—not a Negro poet," and declared his indifference to and independence from the opinions of both white and Black audiences:

> We younger Negro artists who create now intend to express our individual dark-skinned selves without fear or shame. If white people are pleased we are glad. If they are not, it doesn't matter. We know we are beautiful. And ugly too. The tom-tom cries and the tom-tom laughs. If colored people are pleased we are glad. If they are not, their displeasure doesn't matter either. We build our

temples for tomorrow, strong as we know how, and we stand on top of the mountain, free within ourselves.[45]

Reading this essay today, it seems almost unfathomable that Hughes would—only the following year—enter into a formal agreement with a wealthy white patron that restricted both his personal and artistic freedom. Charlotte Osgood Mason agreed to provide him with $150 per month; his work would remain his own, but she was to be consulted on all important aspects "of his creative flight."[46] A primitivist, Mason believed that Native American and African cultures possessed a vitality that might restore white moderns to a kind of lost elemental health. She was already a serious collector of African art when she heard Locke speak on the subject in February 1927; here began her fervent interest in the New Negro. Through Locke, Mason met Hurston, Claude McKay, Aaron Douglass, and Hall Johnson (amongst others). Hughes, though, was her "most precious child," and he was genuinely fond of his "Godmother."[47] Her patronage allowed Hughes to live a relatively privileged life, and Mason instilled in her young protégé that he must be a shining beacon for African American art. She insisted that her "Godchildren" lived in Harlem and celebrated folk culture and the "primitive" aspects of Black life in their work, while "eschew[ing] subjects she judged as didactic or smacking of social reform."[48]

Mason was just one of many white patrons who funded the Harlem Renaissance. White figures were intimately involved in the New Negro movement from its inception; they were not only patrons, but publishers, mentors, and friends. Several, Carla Kaplan notes, stayed firmly in the background, even engineering their own erasure.[49] Carl Van Vechten, the photographer, writer, and patron, took a different approach; he played a prominent role as promoter and friend to writers including Hughes, Hurston, and Wallace Thurman. His novel, *Nigger Heaven* (1926), capitalized upon the 1920s vogue for all things "Negro" and the white fascination with Harlem, but its title and portrayal of Black life and sexuality offended many New Negro artists and intellectuals. Consequently, Allen Dunn and George Hutchinson note, Van Vechten has "been characterized as a kind of vampire, the very quintessence of the white cultural colonialism that purportedly destroyed the Harlem Renaissance."[50]

The ethics of white involvement in a movement that centered Black self-definition seem clear-cut to us today. The dynamics of these relationships were naturally prone to become exploitative: Black artists were often treated in a tokenistic fashion, expected to perform certain roles and match certain ideals. Mason's expectations of Hughes finally proved unrealistic and damaging. As Robert Hemenway observes, "[s]he thought of him as Africa; eventually he replied that he could be only Cleveland and Kansas City."[51] Ultimately, Arnold Rampersad notes, "[t]he need to write, to perform for Mrs. Mason, began to tax Hughes [...] Godmother wanted Langston to put out, but her intensity often made him weak and tense."[52] In May 1930, they underwent a painful parting that left Hughes physically and mentally depleted. By 1932, however—during a trip to the Soviet Union—he began composing stories critiquing various aspects of the New Negro movement. This culminated in the 1934 collection, *The Ways of White Folks*, featuring stories dealing with overbearing white patrons, the hypocrisy of white Christian charity, and primitivism. The satirical "Rejuvenation Through Joy" mocks the white followers of Eugene Lesche's phoney "Colony of Joy," while "Slave on the Block" pillories those "who [go] in for Negroes" yet regard them merely as "primitive" art objects.[53] These stories suggest the inequity and insincerity of relations between Black artists and white patrons.

"The Blues I'm Playing" in particular reflects Hughes's views on the (in)efficacy of the New Negro movement and his relationship with Mason. It follows a talented Black pianist, Oceola Jones, and her domineering patron, Dora Ellsworth. Like Hughes's "Godmother," Ellsworth interferes in Oceola's artistic and personal life, sending her to Paris in the hopes of curtailing a romance her patron deems distracting to her artistic project. Oceola and Ellsworth disagree on many topics; the young musician despises pointless high-mindedness and vain disputes over art: "If you wanted to play the piano or paint pictures or write books, go ahead! But why talk about it so much?"[54] Oceola furthermore scorns the idea that art has the capacity to overcome racial prejudice; she finally chooses love over art, much to Ellsworth's chagrin. At the final meeting between patron and protégé, Oceola plays a stirring blues song that emphasizes the cultural chasm between the two women. She moves seamlessly from classical music to "an earth-throbbing rhythm that shook the lilies in the Persian vases of Mrs. Ellsworth's music room."[55] Liberated from her patron's control, she is free to express herself fully, to own her art and proclaim, "This is mine."[56]

The irony, of course, is that the ostensible purpose of patronage is to offer artistic freedom. When financial matters are settled, the artist—liberated to an extent from the concerns of the marketplace—should be left to produce their best, truest art. For the New Negro movement, however, a reliance upon white patrons, intellectuals, and audiences would prove one of its central predicaments. White involvement facilitated the production of Black art, but it did not permit the artistic or psychological freedom Hughes described in "The Racial Mountain and the Negro Artist." By the early 1930s, even Du Bois acknowledged that "the Renaissance of literature" had failed to take "real and lasting root [...] because it was a transplanted and exotic thing. It was literature written for the benefit of white people and at the behest of white readers and started out primarily from the white point of view."[57] White patronage, in many ways, confounded and undermined the ideals and goals put forward by both Locke and Du Bois; it precluded the production of any truly independent Black art *or* effective propagandistic art.

"Every tub must sit on its own bottom": Zora Neale Hurston, the Individual, and the Group

Hurston was also among Mason's "Godchildren." Indeed, Hurston's contract with her patron was less favorable than Hughes's, and her personal and professional relationship with Mason undoubtedly had a tremendous impact upon her career.[58] Yet Hurston's work, life, and thought raise a number of other intriguing ethical issues, even if today she is—Kaplan notes—"often [...] loved too simply."[59] Hurston openly rejected Du Boisian rhetoric of racial uplift and wanted no part in the "Talented Tenth." In her 1942 autobiography, *Dust Tracks on a Road*, she explains that she "cannot accept responsibility for thirteen million people," because "[e]very tub must sit on its own bottom regardless."[60] Hurston did not see why her talent should require her to be a responsible spokesperson for her race, accountable to the community. Yet she was also one of the few New Negro writers who saw herself as truly representing the working-class folk of the

South; her work celebrated the common man, the blues, the folktale, and the folkways of her childhood.

Hemenway acknowledges this fundamental tension in his seminal biography, asking: "How can Zora Hurston express herself as both one of the folk and someone special? [...] How can Hurston claim identity with the masses, yet affirm the supremacy of the individual?"[61] "From my earliest remembrance," Hurston recalls, "I heard the phrases, 'Race problem,' 'Race pride,' 'Race man or woman,' 'Race solidarity,' 'Race consciousness,' 'Race leader,' and the like."[62] But race pride and race prejudice are useless concepts to Hurston; they are "scourges of humanity" that permit "[t]he solace of easy generalization."[63] Upon abandoning these falsities, Hurston affirms, she "received the richer gift of individualism," explaining that "[w]hen I have been made to suffer or I have been made happy by others, I have known that individuals were responsible for that, and not races. All clumps of people turn out to be individuals on close inspection."[64]

This focus upon "individuals" over "races" would seem to discount entirely—or at least minimize—structural racism and oppression. But Hurston's own individualism was rooted in a rejection of what she called "the sobbing school of Negrohood." In "How It Feels to Be Colored Me" (1928), she declares "I AM NOT tragically colored. There is no great sorrow dammed up in my soul, nor lurking behind my eyes. [...] I do not belong to the sobbing school of Negrohood who hold that nature somehow has given them a lowdown dirty deal and whose feelings are all but about it."[65] Raised in the all-black town of Eatonville, Florida, young Hurston was somewhat sheltered from the racial discrimination and violence that characterized everyday life for many African Americans. Yet her staunch repudiation of what she deemed useless self-pity extended to what appears today a dismissive attitude toward the suffering of others. In *Dust Tracks*, although Hurston acknowledges (in muted terms) the horrors of the past, she stresses her determination to focus upon the present: "I see no reason to keep my eyes fixed on the dark years of slavery and the Reconstruction. I am three generations removed from it, and therefore have no experience of the thing. [...] I want to get on with the business in hand."[66]

This defiant attitude is mirrored in Janie, the protagonist of Hurston's second (and best-known) novel. *Their Eyes Were Watching God* (1937) registers Hurston's prizing of the individual over the group, while also celebrating southern folk culture. The novel's ethics are grounded in these potentially contradictory facets of Hurston's identity and belief system. *Their Eyes* sees Janie go from burgeoning adolescence to womanhood, from a girl defined by the will of her grandmother, and later that of her husbands, to a woman of independent mind and means. Whether by her own choice or not, Janie is a character largely separated from her community throughout the novel. During her marriage to Joe Starks, Janie is barred from the community's rites and rituals; as the mayor's wife she must remain above the "mess uh commonness."[67] Later, with her younger lover Tea Cake "on the muck" in Florida, she has the chance to integrate with a community, even laboring in the fields with her husband. Yet, finally, Janie confides only in her best friend Pheoby and is alone as she "pull[s] in her horizon like a great fish-net" at the novel's close.[68] At base, then, *Their Eyes* is the story of Janie's journey to the "horizon and back": her quest for self-definition.[69]

The prioritization of individuality over community in the novel raises ethical issues regarding the perceived role of a Black writer (perhaps especially a Black female writer). Jennifer Jordan sees this aspect of *Their Eyes* as playing into "[o]ne of the major issues in the redefinition of black womanhood": "the role of individualism in a minority literature that has from its inception emphasized group development and salvation."[70] For Jordan, Janie "fails to achieve a communal identification with the black women around her or with the black community as a whole"; by ultimately choosing "isolation and contemplation" over "solidarity and action," she eschews "group development and salvation."[71] This implied accountability to the group, of course, is exactly what Hurston rejected. Jordan's judgment upon Janie (and Hurston) is grounded in an enduring belief in Black women's responsibility to serve their community above themselves. It seems quite radical, then, that in the wake of a cultural phenomenon dominated by men, masculinist discourse, and Du Bois's "Talented Tenth," Hurston declares her indifference to the project of racial uplift in an individuated female character for whom race and group development are *not* paramount. For Hurston, evidently, all art need not be propaganda; Janie did not need to espouse racial causes or "uplift" her community to be a successful Black heroine. Yet accusations that *Their Eyes* is entirely uninterested in community matters can surely be countered by attending to its celebration of southern folk culture and vernacular.

An anthropologist as well as a writer by trade, Hurston sought in her writing to faithfully render the sounds and rhythms of southern Black speech. Gates calls *Their Eyes* "the first example in our tradition of 'the speakerly text', [...] a text whose rhetorical strategy is designed to represent an oral literary tradition."[72] Soaring lyrical prose sits alongside dialect; sensuous descriptions are interrupted with vernacular speech, as in the second chapter's opening: "Janie saw her life like a great tree in leaf with the things suffered, things enjoyed, things done and undone. Dawn and doom was in the branches. 'Ah know exactly what I got to tell yuh, but it's hard to know where to start at.'"[73] Through free indirect discourse, the tension between standard English and southern Black dialect (the two dominant voices here) is resolved. As Janie is protagonist and narrator simultaneously, both voices are hers. Hurston thus demonstrates that the inner lives of these characters who speak in vernacular are as complex and passionate as any others and, in doing so, showcases her own ability to play skillfully in different registers.

Many of Hurston's contemporaries, however, were unimpressed by her rendering of southern oral culture. *Their Eyes*, now a twentieth-century classic, struggled to find a significant or appreciative audience in its time (especially in African American literary circles).[74] Critics targeted the novel's form and style as well as its content, and their reactions reflect the context in which *Their Eyes* emerged. Although heavily associated with the Harlem Renaissance, it is arguably a post-Renaissance text. Contemporary reviews thus register the post-Depression realization—grasped by New Negro artists as well the new generation emerging—that the tools and methods employed during the Harlem Renaissance had proven ultimately ineffective.

Locke applauded certain aspects of the book, but felt that Hurston concentrated too much on folklore. In *Opportunity*, he called *Their Eyes* "folklore fiction at its best."[75] "But," he laments, in a comment that seems at odds with the stance that characterized the 1920s debates with Du Bois, "when will the Negro novelist of maturity, who knows how to tell a story convincingly [...] come to grips with motive fiction and social document fiction?"[76] Richard Wright, writing in the *New Masses*, was more hostile:

> Miss Hurston can write, but her prose is cloaked in that facile sensuality that has dogged Negro expression since the days of Phillis Wheatley. [...] Miss Hurston voluntarily continues in her novel the tradition which was forced upon the Negro in the theatre, that is, the minstrel technique that makes the "white folks" laugh.[77]

Wright's complaints of "facile sensuality that has dogged Negro expression" and of the "minstrel technique that makes the 'white folks' laugh" take direct aim at Hurston's use of southern vernacular. Wright saw literature as a weapon in the fight for racial liberation; in "Blueprint for Negro Writing" (1937), he blasts New Negro writing for constituting little more than "a sort of conspicuous ornamentation" and/or "the voice of an educated Negro pleading with white America for justice."[78] This, Wright complains, is what results from "a liaison between inferiority-complexed Negro 'geniuses' and burnt-out white Bohemians with money."[79]

Conclusion: The Harlem Renaissance Today

Wright was among the first of a new generation who renounced the Harlem Renaissance as a whitewashed, emasculated movement that failed to achieve its aims and pandered to white America. In "Blueprint for Negro Writing," Wright posits that "[t]oday the question is: Shall Negro writing be for the Negro masses, molding the lives and consciousness of those masses toward new goals, or shall it continue begging the question of the Negroes' humanity?"[80] In rejecting all that the New Negro stood for, Wright continues to evoke the Black writer's responsibility to the "masses"; the aims of Wright and his contemporaries were not dissimilar to those of Locke and Du Bois, but the means of achieving them had to be radically different.

Later, those associated with the Black Arts Movement of the 1960s and 1970s were eager to distance themselves from the Harlem Renaissance. For LeRoi Jones (later Amiri Baraka),

> The rising middle class-spawned intelligentsia invented the term New Negro and the idea of the Negro Renaissance to convey to

the white world that there had been a change of tactics as to how to climb onto the bandwagon of mainstream American life. The point here is that this was to be conveyed to white America; it was another conscious reaction to that white America and another adaptation of the middle-class Negro's self-conscious performance to his ever-appreciative white audience.[81]

In *The Crisis of the Negro Intellectual* (1967), Harold Cruse similarly cited white cultural paternalism as key to the "failure" of the New Negro movement, blaming figures like Van Vechten, who colonized the "'spiritual and aesthetic' materials" of Black writers "for their own self-glorification."[82]

The Harlem Renaissance witnessed not only an unprecedented explosion of African American art, literature, and music, it also saw a cultural movement encumbered by a weight of ethical and political responsibility. Between the pressure to produce marketable work and the responsibility to please leaders and patrons alike, writers like Toomer, Hughes, and Hurston were constantly treading precarious ethical lines. It is hardly surprising that the resulting work was perhaps overburdened at times, and that the movement—as is generally the consensus—did not fulfill all of its aims. Contemporary views, however, are generally sensitive to the competing pressures endured by Harlem Renaissance writers and appreciative of what they did achieve. In concluding, it is worth briefly considering the ethical implications involved in our present-day relation to New Negro writers and texts.

Following the murder of George Floyd in May 2020, an earnest CBS News reporter cut to footage of a young Black poet reciting a portion of Hughes's 1936 poem "Let America Be America Again." Set against a collage of images of Black Lives Matter demonstrations and memorials to Floyd alongside black and white photographs showing the scarred bodies of slaves, downtrodden immigrants, and Native American families, more than eight decades later, Hughes's words—the newscaster affirmed—still seemed extremely relevant. It has become commonplace to evoke New Negro figures and works today, especially during unsettling times.[83] These writers and texts have come—in a US context at least—to represent almost a national conscience on matters of race: an ethical barometer against which the present might be measured. They—and the Harlem

Renaissance itself—have taken on a hallowed status that often raises them above censure.

Indeed, the New Negro movement has recently undergone a (re-)renaissance of sorts, with texts including McKay's *Amiable With Big Teeth* (2017) and *Romance in Marseille* (2020), as well as Hurston's *Barracoon: The Story of the Last Slave* (2018) finally seeing publication. New editions of Fauset's *There is Confusion* (1924) and *Plum Bun* (1928) appeared in 2020 and 2022 respectively, while a Netflix adaptation of Larsen's *Passing* debuted in 2021. The apparent thirst for New Negro works feels encouraging and redemptive—especially in the case of female writers once neglected—but it also raises uncomfortable questions about the status of today's society. As K. Merinda Simmons and James A. Crank observe, the re-emergence of Black modernist texts should come as little surprise during a period in which the same delineations "that identify an 'us' and a 'them', an 'insider' and an 'outsider'" remain prevalent.[84] In reflecting upon the ethical binds facing Black writers a century ago, we must also ponder the ethical impetuses confronting Black artists today.

Claudia Rankine's 2019 play, *The White Card*, stages a number of these issues, suggesting means of challenging, redirecting, and transcending the weight of responsibility that Black art and Black artists bear today. Rankine's white liberal art collectors—Charles and Virginia Spencer and their art-dealer friend Eric—exhibit a fetishizing approach to Black art reminiscent of the New Negro's white patrons. Their dinner guest, Charlotte Cummings—a successful African American artist—is subjected to both the clueless, ignorantly odious remarks of her hosts and the cringe-inducing "woke" retorts of their son, Alex. At the end of dinner, Charles unveils his newest acquisition: a representation of Michael Brown's autopsy report.[85] At the play's close, set a year later, Charles pays a visit to Charlotte's studio, where he discovers that she has been covertly photographing him. By changing the subject—from Black death to white life—and by making visible Charles's usually invisible whiteness, Charlotte (and Rankine) reverse the direction of attention from the peculiar "sense of always looking at one's self through the eyes of others" that characterizes Du Boisian double-consciousness in a move that forces Charles—and the audience—to confront and center their own whiteness.[86]

CHAPTER ELEVEN

"And This Is How 'The Feminists' Are Made"
Ethical Collaboration Between Eleonora Duse and Gabriele D'Annunzio

Zsuzsanna Balázs

And this is how "the feminists" are made, those whom you refer to with a slight sarcastic smile: but the women who today are aspiring to raise their own awareness and their own mission in the family and in society, like many have done before through a myriad of challenges and hostility, and who demand that the loftiness of ideals, the nobility of work, the equity of rights be acknowledged for them too, are not "the feminists": they are the women, they are the true women, they are all the women.[1]

The above passage features in Michele De Benedetti's 1913 interview with Eleonora Duse titled "La Duse parla del femminismo" (Duse speaks about feminism) in which Duse addresses several ethical issues regarding women's place and role in Italian society. She criticizes the regressive normative society of her time for considering women suitable only for love, motherhood, marriage, housework, and reproduction, while in other areas women are kept in moral, sexual, and intellectual subjection. Duse was an influential feminist and queer New Woman[2] who was regarded as Sarah Bernhardt's worthy heir, influenced generations of women, and had intense romantic relationships with the Irish-American dancer Isadora Duncan, Bernhardt, and the cross-dressing Italian playwright Lina/Cordula Poletti, among others. Nonetheless, in scholarship and in biographies of the Italian playwright Gabriele D'Annunzio, Duse is still often reduced to the status of a passive muse figure and object of heterosexual desire in the life of D'Annunzio. Duse's reduction to a mere object of desire for male playwrights by Italian scholarship could in itself be the subject of a long study on the ethics of scholarship written by men about women's role in male artists' lives, which tends to ignore these women's active contribution to the form, content, and style of literary texts and scripts. This chapter challenges such reductive representations of Duse in scholarship by arguing that she played an active role in making D'Annunzio's drama feminist and that she opened his work to a wide range of gender and sexual possibilities. Moreover, Duse introduced significant homoerotic undertones in D'Annunzio's plays through her highly androgynous stage presence.

First, I discuss Duse's role as a prominent feminist and queer voice in early twentieth-century Italy, followed by novel queer dramaturgical readings of D'Annunzio's *The Dead City* (*La città morta*, 1896), which features significant yet thus far largely neglected lesbian intimacies and other desires labelled as immoral by normative society. I engage mostly with the works of Lucia Re—the only Italian scholar thus far who has stressed Duse's role as an active agent and equal partner in D'Annunzio's dramatic work.[3] Re explains that Duse's gestures raised D'Annunzio's interest in a new type of tragedy which was influenced by classical Greek tragedy but was modern in terms of psychology and politics.[4] In fact, Duse inspired D'Annunzio to start writing for the stage and D'Annunzio wrote three of his first plays for her: *The Dead City* (1896), *Francesca da Rimini* (1901), and *The Daughter of Iorio* (1903), which all feature same-sex intimacies and invite criticism of normativity and patriarchal society. This chapter thus reinterrogates the ethics of theatrical collaboration and Duse's influence. It demonstrates the ways in which the Duse–D'Annunzio collaboration worked to question the deeply entrenched, regressive moral principles of early twentieth-century Italy regarding women's place in society, same-sex intimacies, and sexuality.

Duse and D'Annunzio: An Ethical Collaboration

D'Annunzio's collaboration with Duse hugely impacted his drama, infusing his work with themes such as the vicissitudes of marginalized subjectivities and their fight against the regressive violence of normalcy. I contend that the presence of these themes makes his drama significant to contemporary queer and feminist critics in ways that are only now being recognized. This chapter thus goes against the grains of the established perception of D'Annunzio in Italian scholarship and the national imagination.

Although the focus of this study is not D'Annunzio's life, it is important to note briefly that his actions as the most influential cultural figure of his time, his involvement in politics, as well as his affiliations with fascism rightfully raise several ethical concerns for readers. Scholarship has written extensively on the fascist as well as the anti-fascist aspects of D'Annunzio's life, mostly regarding his ambiguous relationship with Benito Mussolini and his highly controversial occupation of the city of Fiume (today's Rijeka).[5] While scholars such as John Woodhouse and mostly Giordano Bruno Guerri have stressed the anti-fascist, libertarian, and even feminist aspects of the Fiume project, this conquest was undoubtedly problematic ethically. It was an authoritarian act that D'Annunzio invaded a city whose inhabitants might not have wanted foreign intervention after the chaos caused by World War I. In addition, when D'Annunzio was forced out of Fiume by the Italian Government and Mussolini, there were violent clashes between his legionaries and the Italian army, resulting in casualties in the civilian population at the end of December 1920 (Bloody Christmas). What complicates analyses of the Fiume project is that, besides soldiers, D'Annunzio's legionaries included writers, aristocrats, industrial workers, and feminists—one of the most prominent supporters of the Fiume project was, for instance, Sarah Bernhardt. Guerri observes that "[f]or some women, going to Fiume constituted an act of feminism."[6] In addition, this carefully calibrated political performance offered sexual freedom for its members and its main principle was equality. As Guerri explicates, D'Annunzio's proposed constitution (*Carta del Carnaro*) promised to recognize everyone regardless of sex, lineage, language, class, or religion. It also guaranteed the freedom of thought and freedom of the press, cults, reunion, and association.[7] But its most progressive aspect concerned women, as it would have granted women the right to vote and the right to be elected.[8] Although by 1919 D'Annunzio's collaborations and relationship with Duse were over, I contend that Duse's feminism infused even the most problematic actions of D'Annunzio's public and private life.

Other established notions of D'Annunzio include the idea that he was merely a fascist ideologue and a racist colonial writer. For instance, Rhiannon Noel Welch presents D'Annunzio's novels and his Fiuman oratory as representative of post-unification Italy's literary formulations of race, which are preoccupied with genealogy, progeny, and blood belonging.[9] In addition, D'Annunzio is often referred to as a "notorious hyper-masculine womanizer"[10] who promoted a virile form of masculinity and a normative approach to women throughout his life. Elisa Bizzotto explicates that D'Annunzio shared a *machista* form of masculinity in line with fascist visions of gender stereotypes which were exalted by fascists in anti-Wildean terms. At the same time, D'Annunzio was deeply embedded in a cult of intimate male friendships: he was a so-called "*camerata*," which was a code word for "homosexual" besides its original meaning of "militant fascist."[11] Moreover, Barbara Spackman has argued that D'Annunzio was preoccupied with maternity and women's procreative duties just like fascists.[12] This study does not wish to whitewash these ethically problematic aspects of D'Annunzio's life—rather, it adds another, rarely mentioned angle to nuance the above-mentioned ethical concerns about D'Annunzio for which his works are often dismissed. What scholarship rarely acknowledges is that D'Annunzio placed great value on equality and the freedom of the individual: he supported women's rights, sexual freedom, divorce, and promulgated a fluid approach to sexuality and gender.[13] Crucially, his plays demonstrate that, for D'Annunzio, power and strength meant women: his role models were always women, and he fashioned himself according to the style of the independent, queer New Women that surrounded him. He intentionally imitated the style of Duse and Bernhardt in his dandy self-fashioning, and he "literally abused the system of the diva"; in this regard D'Annunzio was very much like Oscar Wilde.[14]

Accordingly, D'Annunzio's plays portray the institution of marriage, normative society, and the traditional family as constructs that threaten the liberty of the individual which, for him, was sacred. Hence his dissident protagonists always fight against the representatives of such regressive institutions. The types of *Eros* that appear in his plays are almost exclusively desires that were considered outside of the law in his time and some of which can raise serious ethical concerns even in contemporary audiences: adultery, spiritual and carnal incest, homoerotic desires, and sadomasochistic attachments. In fact, as Luisetta Elia Chomel has emphasized, sexual desire in D'Annunzio's plays acts as a catalyst to bring repressed feelings to the surface.[15] Although some of the desires that feature in his plays raise moral concerns, these enactments also bear an ethical function, as they help counteract gender-based assumptions and heteronormative expectations. Moreover, Charlotte Ross has discerned that representations of failure, breakdown of social relations, emotional yearning for same-sex characters, immoral heterosexual liaisons, effeminacy, "too strong" female desire for men, and any kind of non-reproductive desires were deemed as obscenities in early twentieth-century Italy, as these offended the national sentiment according to Article 339 of the 1889 Zanardelli Code and later Article 112 of the 1926 laws of Public Security.[16] D'Annunzio's drama abounds in such "obscenities," which work as a form of resistance in the plays. This resistant element in D'Annunzio's drama, therefore, inevitably performs an ethical function by undercutting the national/fascist narratives characterized by regressive notions of gender and sexuality.

The implicit same-sex bonds of D'Annunzio's plays are often framed through the safe frameworks of brotherhood and sisterhood. These bonds reflect the contradictions of Italian biopolitics of the first half of the twentieth century. Even though fascism condemned homosexuality, the colonies generated contradictions in this area. Since the main purpose of the regime was to maintain racial purity, "same-sex sexual relations had the advantage of not furthering 'miscegenation' as long as they remained conveniently invisible, covert, and unmarked, as the Catholic Church wanted them to be."[17] At the same time, homosexual practice was seen as the exact product of miscegenation, "the result of inadequately controlled sexuality that in turn weakened the race further."[18] As Derek Duncan observes, "[t]heir crime was non-reproductive sex that contradicted the regime's express wish to increase Italy's population."[19] Italian race laws thus harbored ambivalence around homosexuality instead of following Nazi Germany's strict discriminatory legislation. Rather than addressing homosexuality as deviancy in the national discourse, Italian fascists opted for a policy of silence.[20] Even though reproductive fantasy was the regime's sustaining myth, the purity of the race was even more important, and fears of racial amalgamation "even led to the promotion of homosexuality."[21]

Before the rise of fascism, the late nineteenth and early twentieth centuries in Italian literature saw an increase in representations of lesbian relationships, including Alfredo Oriani's novel *Beyond* (1889), Enrico Butti's *The Robot* (1892), Fede's *Sappho's Legacy* (1908), Sibilla Aleramo's *A Woman* (1906) and *The Passage* (1919), and Maria Volpi Nannipieri's *Perfide* (1919). Also, there was a widely accepted and fairly visible lesbian subculture in nineteenth-century Italy, and female same-sex inversion was not a taboo topic at all in post-unification Italy after 1861.[22] The upsurge in homoerotic literary content was due to the fact that "sexual science and recognizably modern notions of sexual identity had begun to take hold."[23] From the 1890s, Italian sexologists created discourses about lesbian desire, which were further circulated in scientific and literary texts, albeit these discourses were either outright condemnations of female homoerotic desire or voyeuristic depictions of sexual intimacy between women.[24] Only in literary texts did lesbian desire appear in positive contexts, including D'Annunzio's scripts.[25]

Unlike most of the roles written for women around the turn of the century, D'Annunzio created extremely complex characters for his queer and feminist New Woman collaborators to meet their expectations. The presence of these famous New Women in the first productions of D'Annunzio's plays inevitably entailed that the plays engaged critically in contemporary debates about the sexually ambiguous New Woman who posed a threat to heterosexuality and the institution of marriage. The appearance of powerful New Women on the European stage coincided with the fights for women's emancipation and sexual liberation in France, England, and Italy. Re stresses that in this debate New Women had a seminal ethical role, as they embodied the potential of women to be independent, suggesting that women can have multiple roles besides and beyond the domestic one.[26] Therefore, working with these women, who were the only women referred to as geniuses at the time, was a very important political, ethical, and social statement in an age that only accepted male geniuses. New Women actors could influence masses of people, and thanks to their almost sacred position they could portray sexually ambiguous, transgressive, and anti-authoritarian characters without major consequences. Re explicates that they were also referred to as phallic women and were compared to Oscar Wilde, which made them more disturbing for normative society:

> The phallic woman, armed and cruel (or disguised) is in a certain sense *not* a woman; yet it is not possible to say for sure, if not with a paradox worthy of Wilde, that she is therefore a man. Rather, she exhibits a sexual ambiguity, a "dangerous" oscillation which Wilde could identify with.[27]

This association between Wilde and New Women highlights the extent to which New Women on the stage had the potential to introduce ciphers of *homoeros* into the performances at a time when any explicit or implicit reference to Wilde functioned as a euphemism for homosexual desire.

The first time Duse directly raised her voice against the unethical treatment of women in Italian society was in the 1913 interview with Michele De Benedetti quoted at the beginning of this chapter. In this interview, Duse calls for a new type of education for all women to help their emancipation. She also speaks up for women whom society stigmatizes because they do not want to or cannot marry:

> [S]ociety considers the woman who does not have family as a fallen woman, a woman whom even if due to simple vicissitude of fate, no one wanted. Because men [...] cannot admit that a woman can freely and happily live without a man, that she can refuse to choose a husband, and that between the prospect of an unhappy, dubious marriage and that of remaining a "spinster," she has preferred the second one.[28]

Duse concludes that women's anger is entirely justified, as the "more a woman turns out to be like a man or even superior to a man in terms of productivity, energy, intelligence and will-power—or in what she thinks and does—the more she will in fact be diminished in men's eyes, deemed and treated as even more inferior."[29] It is rarely acknowledged in scholarship that Duse's acting was a form of feminist and queer activism and ethical action for the rights and visibility of the most vulnerable groups in society. She felt an immense sympathy for the stories of the characters she embodied on the stage, as they were theatrical representations of historically marginalized subjectivities. As part of the BBC podcast series *Great Lives*, Fiona Shaw and Matthew Parris discuss this aspect of Duse's life. Fiona Shaw cites Duse's letter to Francesco D'Arcais, written in 1884, in which Duse explained her relationship with acting and the women she had played:

> Those poor women in my place who have so entered my heart and my head, that while I do my utmost to make them understood to those who listen to me, almost as if I wanted to comfort them, it is them who have solely wound up comforting me. How and why and when this tender and affectionate interchange, inexplicable and undeniable, started happening between these women and me, would be too long and also too difficult to explain exactly. [...] I stand on their side with them and for them, and I dig and scavenge, not because I crave suffering but because feminine compassion is greater, more concrete, and sweeter and more complete than the grief that men are used to allowing us.[30]

This empathy did not only come from Duse's identification with the characters she embodied on the stage, but also from her intimate relationships with women intellectuals of the time whom Duse tried to help in achieving professional success and independence. For instance, Matilde Serao, Sibilla Aleramo, Grazia Deledda, and Cordula/Lina Poletti, among many others, all drew from Duse's performances. Duse thus became a feminist icon in Italy before World War I, mostly due to her roles in Henrik Ibsen's plays as Nora, Hedda, and Ellida, which took her on a performance tour of Europe at the turn of the century.[31] Her role as a feminist icon was attributed "to her new, both empathic and critical approach to the predicaments of women and femininity under patriarchy."[32] Re further explains that Duse "highlighted and heightened the capacity of the theatre to represent identity and gender as inherently performative and constructed, thus dismantling the myth of an essential femininity or masculinity, or even of an essential, unified, individual self."[33] Moreover, her stage presence was perceived as queer, as her acting style was a spectacle of strangeness and disruption, and reminded audiences of the neurosis afflicting the modern woman. Yet, for women in the audience, she also represented the possibility of freedom from patriarchy. In her roles, she could raise desire in both men and women: "Duse's eroticism on the stage, like her acting in general, was always very subtle, made of small, intimate, and often surprising gestures that 'seduced' both men and women."[34]

Duse's engagement in the sexual and gender politics of her time is thus inseparable from her acting, which functioned as an ethical action. Her last role on the stage was that of Ellida in Ibsen's *The Lady from the Sea*, staged in May 1921. The character of Ellida represented for Duse a woman's needs and desires in a male-centered world. However, after Mussolini's seizure of power in 1922, Duse gave up her hope of renewing Italian theatre. Although Mussolini and theatre critic Silvio D'Amico wanted to include her in their project to create a state-supported theatre under fascism, Duse declined the offer and refused Mussolini's proposal for a pension.[35] Instead of collaborating with fascists, she went abroad and toured Ibsen's plays in the 1920s. By this time Duse was an internationally renowned artist and Italy's most influential and most visible woman thanks to her successful acting career and feminist activism. Mussolini's offer would have provided her with financial stability and safety in an increasingly authoritarian world, but she chose a more precarious and financially unpredictable life instead, which sent a clear ethical message: everyone has a choice when it comes to compromises with fascists. Hence her renunciation of Mussolini's offer and her decision to spend the rest of her life abroad performing Ibsen's complex female characters and expressing her support of the marginalized had a crucial ethical significance. This decision did justice to her long career, which she had dedicated to raising a new generation of independent women who would no longer allow men to control their behaviors, thoughts, and bodies.

Besides influencing audiences through her acting, Duse also had a lasting impact on the younger women who surrounded her and who admired her confidence and authority, acquiring a stronger sense of self through their bond with Duse. Given that these women were mostly queer too, Duse acted as an older, more authoritative, inspiring role model for younger Italian women who felt out of place in normative society. As Re articulates it:

Duse, through her work with the interpretations of women's stories on the stage and through her complex web of—often very intimate—friendships with other, and especially younger women, enabled the emergence and recognition of a female symbolic that contributed to foster a new sense of legitimacy for women's thought, women's writing, women's experiences, women's desires, women's gendered subjectivity.[36]

We see this "female symbolic" dramatized in D'Annunzio's *The Dead City*, which largely focuses on women's experiences. The script portrays tender, intimate bonds between women as a consolation amidst the anxiety, melancholia, and sense of displacement they have to live with.

Same-Sex Intimacies in D'Annunzio's *The Dead City* (1896)

The Dead City is D'Annunzio's first play, written originally for Duse and under Duse's influence between the autumn of 1895 and 1896. Although Duse wanted to play the lead character, Anna, in the first performance of the play, she could not assume the role until 1901. As a result, Anna's character was first played by Sarah Bernhardt in Paris on January 21, 1898, at the Théâtre de la Renaissance. The tragedy was translated by George Hérelle, but it eventually did not feature the translator's name so that the audience would assume that it was written in French by D'Annunzio himself.[37] Chomel implies that this might have had to do with the fact that in 1896 Sarah Bernhardt played Wilde's *Salomé* in Paris, which was written in French directly for Bernhardt, and D'Annunzio might have wished to create the impression that he had written the play in French for Bernhardt too.[38] Bernhardt-as-Anna was followed by Duse-as-Anna on March 20, 1901, in the Teatro Lirico di Milano, in the first Italian production of the play.

The Dead City seemingly revolves around the controversial theme of incestuous heterosexual desire, as in the play the blind Anna's husband Alessandro desires Anna's friend Bianca Maria, while Bianca Maria desires her brother Leonardo and vice versa. In D'Annunzio's time, both incest and same-sex desires were deemed as obscenities and could be reasons for state censorship. While in France Napoleon decriminalized incest in 1810, in Italy it was considered a crime, and thus a much more problematic thematic choice for the play.[39] The theme of incest equally raises ethical issues about the institution of the family. Foucault has observed, for instance, that in our Western society since the eighteenth century, incest occupies a central place exactly because it posits the family as the obligatory focus of affects and love.[40] This makes sexuality "'incestuous' from the start" for Foucault, and "it is constantly being solicited and refused; it is an object of obsession and attraction, a dreadful secret and an indispensable pivot."[41] Although the theme of incest would be an ideal focus for a study on ethics and theatre, a closer examination of the play reveals that, in fact, incest plays only a marginal role in the play and it remains purely spiritual.

I contend that incestuous *Eros* in *The Dead City* works to distract attention from the intense same-sex bonds between characters who are not related to each other: between Anna and Bianca Maria and between Alessandro and Leonardo. It is striking, however, that despite the prevalence of lesbian desires in the play, scholarship has neglected this theme. Chomel's feminist reading stresses the importance of closeted desires and the characters' wish for liberation,[42] but she does not allude to the unmissable homoerotic desires that equally contribute to the plot. This policy of silence on the part of scholarship regarding same-sex love is highly problematic since it seems to erase even the possibility of *homoeros* as one of the many desires that feature in D'Annunzio's rich dramatic *oeuvre*. The dramaturgical reading that follows acts as an ethical action that wishes to elevate same-sex desire into discussions about D'Annunzio's drama.

The opening scene portrays the lead female characters in the act of reading. The blind Anna is listening to her intimate friend Bianca Maria reading an excerpt from *Antigone* about *Eros*, portraying the two women in a relationship of intimacy and mutual dependency. Bianca Maria needs the emotional support of Anna, while Anna needs someone to read for her. As Anna phrases it, "You see what I cannot. And I see what you cannot."[43] The quotation that Bianca Maria reads out from *Antigone* is also a description of her own character and foreshadows her prohibited desire for her own brother Leonardo: "And I myself am already outside the laws."[44] Bianca Maria's anxiety becomes corporeal here, as she begins gasping and her hands are shaking. Although the play's main conflict arises from the incestuous desire between Bianca Maria and Leonardo, this scene is undeniably homoerotic. Bianca Maria keeps admiring Anna's beauty, which is accompanied by touching each other's hair and hands, kissing each other on the mouth, and placing their heads in each other's laps: "Your eyes are always beautiful and pure, Anna";[45] "How beautiful you are, Anna!"[46]—which Bianca Maria repeats several times, holding Anna's hands. Since this scene is embedded in an atmosphere of unexplained anxiety and sadness, it creates the impression that the play's underlying closeted desire is a lesbian one:

> I understand, Anna. The hour that passes, in the light, gives sometimes an unbearable anxiety. It seems we are awaiting something that never happens. Nothing happens for a long time.[47]

Anna's anxiety remains unexplained, as she admits to her nurse, "I don't know: something holds me tight, like a knot; and then … I don't know what kind of fear …"[48]

The posture of these women displays an almost constant physical intimacy in Act I, which I believe requires more scholarly attention, given the length of these scenes. It is not only Bianca Maria who initiates this intimacy: Anna also reaches out gently to touch Bianca Maria's face and weave her fingers in her hair—which has been identified as a frequent motif in lesbian representations. Contemporary queer cinema, for instance, abounds in moments of so-called "hairplay" between women, most famously in *Reaching for the Moon* (2013), *Carol* (2015), and the television series, *Orange is the New Black* (2013–19). Clare Croft has explained the importance of small caresses and gestures between people of the same sex that might be nonverbal expressions of desire: "The slide of a hand across a hipbone might be just as much an act of coming out as an announcement offered in words."[49] The question Croft poses is relevant in relation to the bond between Bianca Maria and Anna and the subtle same-sex intimacies in D'Annunzio's drama in general: "How does queerness exist in the realm of affect and touch, and what then might we find out about queerness through these pleasurable and complex bodily ways of knowing?"[50]

When Bianca Maria takes Anna's hands and kisses them, she asks: "Don't you feel my lips on your soul?"[51] Anna's response reads like a confession of love and the stage direction states that she exclaims this with a secret despair: "They are burning, Bianca Maria. And they weigh, as if all the richness of life were gathered in them. Ah, how tempting your lips must be! All the promises and all the persuasions must be in them."[52] Strikingly, such physical intimacy appears only between women and between the two male characters Leonardo (Bianca Maria's brother) and Alessandro (Anna's husband), never between members of the opposite sex. For instance, when Anna praises Bianca Maria to Alessandro, he replies that he has never dared to touch her hair. Bianca Maria acts like the center of all forms of sexual desire in this play, which Anna articulates too: "All of us are attracted to her as if to a well of life. [...] Only she can extinguish our thirst."[53] The constant reference to thirst equally implies the sexual desire between Anna and Bianca Maria, which needs to be satisfied. Thirst reads like a longing for the fulfillment of these repressed desires, and the same motif appears between Alessandro and Leonardo, too. As Rockney Jacobsen states, "Hunger, thirst, and sexual arousal are the three paradigmatic appetites,"[54] and, in the arts, the first two are often used as symbols of sexual desire. Bianca Maria always mitigates the thirst that the other characters complain about, which thus becomes a symbolic gesture of partly fulfilling their sexual desires for her. John Newman, for instance, has demonstrated the affinity between the eating/drinking domain and the emotional domain, interpreting hunger/thirst as a symbolic expression of desire for emotional stimulation.[55] For Bianca Maria, Anna represents this desire for emotional stimulation, and instead of longing for Leonardo, she keeps returning to Anna: "Anna, Anna, I don't want to leave you any more, I don't want to part from you ever again! I would like to escape with you, go far away with you, remaining always at your side."[56] Moreover, in Act IV, Anna tells Alessandro that she thought she was the source of Leonardo's anxiety, which implies that she assumes that Leonardo was anxious because of the intimate relationship between the two women which distracted Bianca Maria's attention from him.

The intimacy between Alessandro and Leonardo is framed as a relationship of brotherhood, yet only these same-sex relationships read as honest in the play, while all the other ones come across as exaggerated and overidealized. The reason for Leonardo's growing anxiety is ambiguous:

it could be due to the prohibited desire for his sister or because of the possibility of losing Alessandro if Alessandro loves Bianca Maria. When Anna tells Alessandro that Leonardo is very ill, Alessandro talks about him tenderly and expresses his concerns about his health, recalling their past intimacy: "How many nights he stayed awake with me, reading aloud those great verses which exhausted him like shouts, too disproportionate for our human breath."[57] When Leonardo enters, he is trembling. His anxiety prevents him from speaking at first and his initial gesture is to touch Alessandro's shoulder. Although Anna and Bianca Maria are present too, Leonardo speaks only to Alessandro. Leonardo then takes Alessandro's hand, and they prepare to leave together, both men ignoring Bianca Maria's affection. Even in Act II, when Alessandro is alone with Bianca Maria, he is looking for Leonardo:

> I am not less sad than you, Bianca Maria, for him. I was looking for him, hoping [...]. For some days, when he is with me, he seems to be chased by the anxiety of revealing a secret to me. I then let silence fall on us; and wait, not less anxious than him. [...] And I don't dare to ask him, fearing that I will tear with force a word from him which his soul is not yet ready to tell me. And we suffer together, obscurely.[58]

The secret concerns Leonardo's desire for Bianca Maria, whom Alessandro also seems to love. However, Alessandro's concern for Leonardo reads as if they were in a romantic relationship, and it is much more honest than his sudden confession of love for Bianca Maria that follows. Out of the blue, Alessandro invades her with his love, despite Bianca Maria's lack of consent. She exclaims several times "Hush! Hush! I'm suffocating..."[59] Yet Alessandro ignores her and continues his exaggerated expressions of love, praising her beauty and claiming that they cannot live without each other. The relentless and even aggressive outburst of emotions that Alessandro pours on Bianca Maria, disregarding her unease with the situation, reads like a performance of idealized, heteronormative notions of love, which objectify women. Bianca Maria is clearly ill at ease with this idealization; hence she implies that what Alessandro sees in her is only an idealized image that he created, and that in fact Alessandro is in love with this idealized image of love and not with her. This confession of love appears almost misplaced in the play, especially in a scene which includes Alessandro's expression of concern for Leonardo's predicament. In fact, in the late nineteenth and early twentieth centuries, it was very common to flatten the prevalence of same-sex desires with such scenes of normative heterosexual love scenes. Although this scene is rarely analyzed in depth, I believe that Alessandro's behavior here—his treatment of Bianca Maria as an idealized object of male desire along with the issue of consent—makes this scene one of the most crucial ones, from an ethical point of view.

Act II scene iv reinforces the dishonesty of this previous "love scene," as Leonardo and Alessandro are finally alone, and their diction and physical posture are highly ambiguous. As they are looking at the mountains from the balcony, Leonardo touches Alessandro's arm and a confidential dialogue follows in which Leonardo comes out to Alessandro about his prohibited desire. Initially, Leonardo is afraid of making this confession, which hurts Alessandro, and prompts him to ask:

> So, I am not your soul's brother any more? For how many days I have been waiting for you to speak, for you to confess your pain to me ... Don't you trust me any more? Am I not that one for you who understands everything, to whom you can tell anything?[60]

Leonardo's answer resembles a confession of love: "What had I been before I got to know you, before communicating with your soul? Who was I? I owe you everything: the revelation of life ... You made me live from your flame."[61] Alessandro wants him to confess his secret so much that he is standing close to him, holding his hands firmly, which perturbs Leonardo as if the secret was related to his feelings for Alessandro:

> Yes, I will speak, I will tell you ... But do not look at me from so closely, don't hold my hands ... Sit down there ... Wait ... wait until there is more shade ... I will tell you ... I need to tell you ... to you ... to you only ... Horrible thing.[62]

Here Leonardo already judges himself for his incestuous desire, and his anxiety derives from his assumption that everyone around him would judge him as immoral.

When Leonardo finally confesses the truth, Alessandro's sudden melancholia can be attributed both to his feelings for Bianca Maria and to his feelings for Leonardo. What is more, the fact that Leonardo feels ashamed in front of Alessandro assumes a relationship of love and desire between the two men. This scene resonates with affect theory interpretations and Sara Ahmed's explanation that shame is like an exposure before the other—but it "is only felt given that the subject is interested in the other; that is, that a prior love or desire for the other exists."[63] This means that shame is not exclusively a negative relation to the other: "shame is ambivalent."[64] In this case, Alessandro acts as the ideal other for Leonardo, whose opinion matters and whom Leonardo fears losing by revealing his secret: "In shame, I expose myself that I am a failure through the gaze of an ideal other,"[65] and "my shame confirms my love."[66]

The same ambiguity marks Leonardo's realization that Alessandro loves his sister. The way he phrases his anger suggests that the main source of pain lies in Alessandro's feelings for Bianca Maria: "He loves her, he loves her. Since when? How? What happened between them? [...] Ah, God, God, everything in me is infected; everything gets contaminated ... And this thirst that consumes me!"[67] Even when he confronts Bianca Maria, he wants to know whether Alessandro loves her and not vice versa: "And he ... he told you that he loves you? When? When did he tell you? Answer!"[68] It is also striking that the two men never show anger towards one another. Even when they are standing above Bianca Maria's corpse in Act V, the two men continue their physical intimacy, with Alessandro consoling the trembling Leonardo. Moreover, when Alessandro wants to leave him, he is consumed by an invisible terror and exclaims: "No, no, don't go, don't leave me ... Let's stay here, let's stay here for a while!"[69] Chomel notices this surprising intimacy that remains between the two men even after both of them lose their love: "the presumed superman is only a man in pain, trembling, terrified, and Alessandro's fraternal compassion confirms this interpretation."[70] Even though I agree with this idea, Leonardo should not be criticized because he is not masculine in the conventional sense and is therefore not able to meet the standards of the virile heroic superman. Failing to meet this ideal of masculinity draws attention to the pressure such notions put on men, forcing them to go against their nature and perform a heteronormative gender role. The male characters, however, should be criticized because of their unfair and unethical behavior towards women: they abuse Anna's and Bianca Maria's feelings and bodies, maintaining a patriarchal (even if deeply homoerotic) society that blames women for their own closeted desires.

The two men do not touch Bianca Maria's body in the final act, but when Anna arrives, she rushes to her corpse in despair, touches her face and gently caresses her hair, as if protecting her from male abuse, and cries out "Ah! … I can see! I can see!"[71] This moment of miracle signals the importance of Bianca Maria for Anna, who, even in her death, is able to heal her soul and body. It is remarkable that in the play Bianca Maria's body is only touched by Anna, never by the male characters whose approach she continuously refused. This final scene reveals that the most sincere and profound relationships of the play are, in fact, the same-sex bonds whose repression in favor of forced heteronormative ideals of romance push the plot towards physical violence against women.

Conclusion

The Dead City is an exceptionally rich play with an interesting production history, which offers a wide range of topics for ethical consideration and discussion. In this chapter, I could have focused on D'Annunzio's drama in the context of his controversial political actions or his even more problematic private life. I could have equally centered my study on the relationship between ethics and the literary representations of incest. However, my aim was to shift the focus from D'Annunzio to Eleonora Duse on the one hand, and from heteronormative interpretations to an emphasis on same-sex intimacies on the other. This study has flagged the pervasive impact of Duse's feminist activism and queer stage presence on D'Annunzio's thinking and dramatic imagination. I have argued that the incestuous heterosexual desire that seems to be the play's focal point, in fact, works only as a distraction from the theme of same-sex desire which has been unethically written out of scholarship as a potential topic. This chapter thus serves as an ethical action to acknowledge Duse as an active agent and equal partner in D'Annunzio's life and to counter the heteronormative bias of scholarship which has tended to whitewash *homoeros* from D'Annunzio's drama.

From an ethical point of view, it is also highly problematic that the play associates excessive, uncontrolled desire with a female character (Bianca Maria). What is more, at times it seems to suggest that her beauty causes the main conflicts of the play. It could thus be argued that the play reinforces the misogynistic stereotype about female desire as a destructive force. Yet Duse's influence and a closer examination of the play invite another interpretation according to which the real destructive force is the heteronormative patriarchal world which pushes so many people's lives into tragedy. What happens to Bianca Maria in *The Dead City* recalls John Champagne's queer reading of Giacomo Puccini's ambiguous yet subversive female characters who can be interpreted in two different ways: the "representation of the sexually tarnished woman is always in tension with an acknowledgement that forces beyond her control—forces directly linked to male power and prestige—are equally if not more responsible for her unhappy fate."[72] In a similar manner, D'Annunzio's play draws attention to the harm imposed on women and same-sex bonds by patriarchal power which uses shame to enforce heteronormativity. In Italian scholarship and education, queer and feminist readings of male canonical figures like D'Annunzio are still extremely limited, as queer interpretations of the texts of canonical writers are often misinterpreted as attempts to question the authors' heterosexuality. I believe that queering D'Annunzio's drama in the context of his queer/feminist collaborations is crucial in order to do justice to the New Women who shaped the content and form of his drama, to acknowledge the prevalence of queer desire in Italian culture, and, mostly, to challenge the heteronormative bias of Italian criticism to date.

CHAPTER TWELVE

Reading James Joyce in the Wake of the #MeToo Movement

Julie McCormick Weng

James Joyce's short story "The Sisters," first published in 1904 and later revised for his collection, *Dubliners* (1914), follows a boy's response to the death of his priest and mentor, Father Flynn, who probably died from the effects of syphilis.[1] Representation of the boy's psychological trauma, his nightmares and feelings of "freedom as if [he] had been freed from something by his death," point to the likelihood of his sexual abuse, which is also intimated in conversations between adults around him. Old Cotter claims he would not want his children near the priest; instead, "let a young lad run about and play with young lads of his own age and not be.... Am I right, Jack?"[2] According to Joseph Valente and Margot Gayle Backus, "An uneasy awareness of something awry emerges in their dinner conversation but remains frozen at the level of knowing non-assertion, marked by a series of ellipses." The adults recognize what their words and careful silences conceal, devising "a shadowy form of group consensus designed to exist under erasure" of the truth.[3] For readers, this conspiracy draws greater attention to what is unspoken, prompting them to decode the allusions to what occurred between the boy and priest and to use their imaginations to fill in the blanks.

By beginning *Dubliners* with "The Sisters," Joyce foregrounds the threat of sexual abuse in turn-of-the-twentieth-century Dublin, suggesting that the city is dangerous, even in the most trusted of spaces. Further, by leaving the boy unnamed and the abusive acts undescribed,

Joyce renders him a representative victim-survivor of child molestation in Ireland.[4] Themes of sexual misconduct are explored elsewhere in Joyce's works, from the green-eyed man's lascivious harassment of young boys in "An Encounter," to recurring rumors and schemes of sexual assault in *Finnegans Wake* (1939).[5] Even the hero of *Ulysses* (1922), Leopold Bloom, understands himself to be a "Peeping Tom" after masturbating on a beach to the sight of a young woman.[6] A similar claim might be made of the adolescent protagonist in "Araby," who peeps through windows at his crush before following her through Dublin's streets. His habit of spying on and trailing her, while romanticizing his actions, cues readers to consider when youthful admiration may become violation, but Joyce leaves that question unanswered. This suspension of judgment is not an erasure of truth, but Joyce's outline of an opening in the text—an aperture through which the reader can cast light to illuminate responses to the question: When do amorous actions become predatory?

Joyce's fictional accounts of sexual abuse, assault, and harassment in Ireland's past are uncomfortably similar to accounts in the present.[7] The #MeToo movement of recent years has spotlighted the pervasiveness of sexual misconduct in our own time. First used in 2006 by activist Tarana Burke, the phrase "Me Too" was revived in 2017 amid allegations of sexual assault and harassment by Hollywood producer Harvey Weinstein.[8] As public outcry grew, actress Alyssa Milano encouraged women to post the hashtag #MeToo to Twitter to acknowledge personal experiences of sexual assault and harassment.[9] Like Joyce's "The Sisters," the hashtag was meant to point toward the violation(s) without the expectation of vivid accounts. In Ireland, #MeToo influenced public support for victim-survivors of sexual assault seeking justice through the legal system.[10] The movement was also brought into conversation with the repealing of the anti-abortion amendment, known as the Eighth Amendment of the Constitution Act of 1983. Other Irish matters related to submovements of #MeToo as well.[11] By 2017, Ireland had already been reckoning with the Catholic Church's history of child sexual abuse and cover-up, with the launch of the Commission to Inquire into Child Abuse in 1999 and the release of its subsequent report, known as the Ryan Report, in 2009. But Ireland's ongoing investigations ran parallel to the international social media campaign #ChurchToo, which brought awareness to acts of sexual abuse by church authorities.

As contemporary historians strive to make sense of this diverse, global movement, they are recognizing the #MeToo movement as a wave of feminism that shares common ambitions, including a quest to cultivate new discourses of sexual assault and consent in order to effect change and prevent sexual violence. This chapter argues that reading the works of James Joyce in the wake of #MeToo offers a lens through which to reflect on and shape these evolving discourses. While change must be sought on a global scale, transformation requires attention to local cultures and intervention in individual communities. Burke notes that #MeToo must consider how sexual violence affects a community and requires "community action" to promote change and heal collectively.[12] By wholly focusing on the community in which he was raised, Joyce exposes a devastating normalization of sexual predation across strata of Irish society and at a time when such matters were often given a blind eye, as they are by the adults in "The Sisters." However, through the experiences of Stephen Dedalus, Leopold Bloom, and Molly Bloom, Joyce offers pathways for imagining nonviolent, uncoercive sexual intimacy. He presents an ethic of sexual intimacy that is bound up with an ethic of empathy—what Joyce calls an ability "to bow" the "mind"—first presented during Stephen's adolescent sexual development and later illustrated more maturely through Bloom and Molly's courtship and marriage.

A Portrait of Adolescent Sexual Development

In *A Portrait of the Artist as a Young Man* (1916), Joyce explores Stephen Dedalus's national, spiritual, and artistic development alongside his sexual development. Stephen's first sexual experience occurs with a sex worker when he is around fourteen years old.[13] Leading up to the encounter, he received no formal sex education, but absorbed ideas about manhood, womanhood, and intimate relations from schoolyard bullying and the bawdy chatter of drunk men, and from internalizing the Catholic Church's stance on adolescent sexual desire as a "wicked sin."[14] His most affirming introduction came from literature. He enjoyed Alexandre Dumas's *The Count of Monte Cristo* (1844) and began fantasizing about meeting his own Mercedes. Adopting religious rhetoric, he imagined his body transfigured through an encounter of "supreme tenderness." His first experience, however, is nothing like his fantasy. The sex worker calls him a "little rascal" and asks for a kiss. Twice, Joyce writes that Stephen's "lips would not bend to kiss her," until she takes matters into her own hands and places her lips on his.[15] Although he was paying for services, his first erotic kiss is taken forcibly in a moment when he was so overcome that he "all but burst into hysterical weeping."[16] Joyce contrasts this incident with two others in the book, including a scene in which Stephen contemplates stealing a kiss from a girl and a second scene in which he fantasizes about having sex with her. Through the contrast of these events, which span a decade of his youth, Joyce reveals Stephen's emergent yearning for sexual intimacy that is not taken by force but shared consensually.

The first incident occurs before Stephen's sexual initiation. Aged between nine and ten years old, he attends a children's party and shares a tram ride home with Emma Cleary.[17] As they stand in the tramcar, he perceives a voice from "within him"—not her voice—urging him to "take her gift," a kiss.[18] Yet in the moment he loses confidence and does not "take" the kiss. Feeling like a failure, he "gloomily" rips his tram ticket into "shreds." He channels his frustrated desires into an original poem dedicated to "E— C—." Unrecorded in the novel, the poem is described by Stephen as capturing romantic imagery of young lovers kissing farewell in the moonlight. While the kiss is first "withheld by one," it is eventually "given by both," offering a picture of shared affection and an alternative ending to the failed kiss on the tram.[19]

At no point in *Portrait* does Stephen consider his near act of "tak[ing]" a kiss to be a sexual assault and neither would the courts of law in colonial Ireland, even if he had been fourteen, the age of male accountability for sex crimes. In the decades preceding Stephen's fictional birth, English law underwent dramatic transformation in its recognition and management of sex crimes, and a series of legislation was enacted as a consequence of religious groups and social reformers expressing concerns about the sex trafficking and exploitation of girls and the proliferation of venereal disease.[20] This legislation included the Offences Against the Person acts of 1828, 1861, and 1875, and the Criminal Law Amendment Act of 1885. Outlining the terms of sexual assault, these laws emphasized acts of penetration and determined the age of consent for girls only.[21] Under the Offences Against the Person Act, "rape" was defined as "having carnal knowledge of a woman by force, against her will."[22] Whereas the 1828 Act set the age of consent at ten years old, the Criminal Law Amendment Act raised it to sixteen. Because the legislation construed sexual assault through "some degree of consummation," proof was often required for conviction, including physiological proof of penetration or evidence of ejaculation.[23] Roger Cox writes that this legislation was remarkable as much for its social and moral reforms as well as the way legal "definitions of childhood became closely related to sexuality," with the age of consent serving as a "symbolic definition of the end of childhood." Still, there remained debate about not just when childhood was but what it was. What traits and "discernable developmental landmarks" defined adolescence? The Victorians were not yet equipped with a psychosocial description and struggled to delineate a concept of "teenage sexuality" in the way that adolescent psychologists do today.[24]

Through free indirect discourse, however, Joyce's *Portrait* interrogates the bounds of childhood and the psychosocial landmarks of Stephen's heterosexual male development, including his first instinct to initiate physical intimacy with a girl.[25] His unquestioned drive to "take" rather than request a kiss speaks to the presence of misogynistic codes in Victorian Ireland that may consider a boy's forced kiss of a girl as a rite of passage. The focus of Stephen's disappointment provides further evidence of this point. His distress lies not in the possibility that the intimacy may be unwelcome to Emma, but in the fact of his own inaction, his belief that not "tak[ing]" the kiss is evidence of his unmanliness. That he never questions the legitimacy of his impulse further reveals that he does not recognize the danger of his desire to Emma, the threat his physical force would pose to her safety, sense of bodily autonomy, and emotional well-being.

But later in the text, Joyce features a contrasting landmark in Stephen's sexual development, presented through the form of an epiphany, a luminous moment of insight that brings him into a new perspective of sexual intimacy, its relationship to society, himself, and his artistry. This moment occurs ten years later, when he is around nineteen or twenty years old. Emma, too, is above the legal age of consent. Lying in his bedroom, he recalls seeing Emma from afar earlier in the day, and he turns to the memory of their encounter on the tram. Taking himself back in time, he relives and revises the memory, writing the impulse to steal a kiss out of his story.

At first, the scene appears verbatim to the previous one. But then, right before Stephen's urge to kiss Emma, he halts the memory and thinks, "Let be! Let be!," telling himself not to visualize what happened next. Instead, he imagines he gave Emma his poem. Perhaps she would have shared it with her family. Her brothers would have playfully teased her over breakfast, while her uncle would have been impressed with his "literary form." The quixotic fiction dares to imagine her family accepting his affections. But "no: that was folly," he concludes, because she "would not" share the poem with her family. He changes his word choice. No, she "could not" share the poem.[26] But why does Stephen conclude it to be impossible?

His conclusion stems not just from insecurities about her admiration of him but from the nature of his poem, which depicts an intimate kiss shared freely between young lovers. The suggestive content, as Stephen intuits, may be acceptable for Romantic poets but contrary to Catholic attitudes toward adolescent sexuality, which Mary Lowe-Evans argues ensured that "sexual instincts, even of the most innocent kind, would forever be considered sinful."[27] While as a preteen he had romanticized his desire to kiss Emma, as a teenager he is persuaded to view such desires as perverse. The priest Stephen confesses to warns him that teenage sexual experience "kills the body and it kills the soul. It is the cause of many crimes and misfortunes." Stephen summarizes his experiences as "shameful thoughts, shameful words, shameful acts," worse than "murder." By the time he is sixteen, he believes his erotic fantasies violated Emma, that his interior "brutelike lust had torn and trampled upon her innocence." "Was that boyish love?" he asked, "Was that chivalry? Was that poetry? The sordid details of his orgies stank under his very nostrils."[28] Stephen accepts that "boyish love" should not coincide with sexual desire, and his private struggle made him feel like an abomination. His conviction that erotic thoughts were unchivalrous evinces further his perception of proper manhood as heroic protection of a woman's virtue, protection his fantasies disqualified him from being able to give.

Stephen's views may have also been influenced by the legacy of public discourse surrounding the passing of the Offences Against the Person Act and Criminal Law Amendment Act. Deborah Gorham argues that these laws were propelled by efforts to protect but also control female sexuality. Because they applied only to girls, they ensured a woman's development was managed by a male guardian, typically a father and then husband. The laws sought to "deny to a girl the right to make decisions about her sexuality," even when married, as the Offences Against the Person Act dismissed the possibility of marital rape.[29] Although Victorian women were expected to be "passive and reserved" in regard to sex, their bodies must be ever available to their husbands.[30] The social import of these consent laws, as Katherine Mullin writes, were diffused in Ireland through influential Protestant chastity leagues.[31]

Whether unmarried or married, a woman was allowed no time and space in which her sexual development, and even her body, was left in her own charge. Stephen fully understands this fact, which leads him to conclude that his desire for Emma is both inappropriate and futile. He believes Emma fits into the approved mold of Irish Catholic girlhood, being innocent and free from desires of the flesh. Yet when Stephen thinks of her as "loveless and sinless," "a figure of the womanhood of her country," he criticizes her supposed conformity to Irish expectations.[32] Like his view of his mother, he sees Emma as an entrapped figure, an ill-fated byproduct of the culture in which she was raised, and he begrudges what he believes is her complicity with local mores because it leaves them with no recourse for intimacy. He resents, not just that society has pigeonholed her, but that she appears to have obediently complied.

Through Stephen, Joyce depicts adolescent sexuality in crisis. With teenage desires deemed amoral and the existence and appropriateness of women's desires questioned entirely, he cannot fathom a situation of consensual sex with Emma in the past, present, or future. Writing of *Stephen Hero*, Joyce's discarded precursor to *Portrait*, Richard Brown claims that "Stephen wants a situation where women's sexual desires are recognized as legitimate and can be gratified in a straightforward way," but he knows that any "sexual proposition" he offers Emma would be "condemned."[33] In his mind, the only way they could come together is if he complied with Catholic instruction and cleansed himself through confession. If freed from his "agony of shame," he could draw near to God, the Virgin Mary, and Emma. "Humbly and in tears," he could finally share with her their first kiss, bending down in supplication to peck "the elbow of her sleeve." Here, he describes not an erotic kiss but one of repentance. Only then could the Virgin place Stephen's and Emma's hands together, officiating a kind of holy wedding, one enabled through his confession, repentance, and freedom from sexual sin—all of which he apprehends may be temporarily achieved but impossible to sustain.[34]

But, as Stephen lies in his bedroom, he comes to a new revelation, discarding the memory on the tram, the fiction of sharing his poem with Emma's family, and his old acceptance of sexual shame. Stephen's epiphany begins to emerge with an important insight. He had, indeed, "wronged" Emma, but *not* because he had lustful thoughts about her:

> He began to feel that he had wronged her. A sense of her innocence moved him almost to pity her, an innocence he had never understood till he had come to the knowledge of it through sin, an innocence which she too had not understood while she was innocent or before the strange humiliation of her nature had first come upon her. Then first her soul had begun to live as his soul had when he had first sinned, and a tender compassion filled his heart as he remembered her frail pallor and her eyes, humbled and saddened by the dark shame of womanhood.[35]

Through a new gaze, Stephen releases his former perceptions, which rendered Emma not only *innocent* but *ignorant*. In the past, he thought she was pure, and he was sinful, but he starts to doubt that difference, beginning to "recognize her in her own context," according to Marian Eide.[36] He "wronged" Emma by denying her introduction to "sin," which he associates with the acquisition of "knowledge" acquired during puberty. He thought his own elevated consciousness came from "carnal knowledge." Without sexual knowledge, he assumed she was "sinless," and therefore ignorant. But now Stephen affirms her *sinfulness* and *knowledge* in a scene without sexual initiation. He associates her development with the "strange humiliation of her nature," a reference to her menarche, her first menstruation, which is a sign of puberty and transition into womanhood. Menstruation is also historically correlated with a readiness for sexual initiation and childbearing, but its onset does not necessitate the act of sex. In the passage, Stephen determines that

Emma's biological, rather than sexual, maturity gives her knowledge unique to and independent from his.

By reconsidering Emma's experience, Stephen restores to her humanity that which his own imagination had taken away. While in part patronizing, his thoughts also empower her. Not only does he recognize that she is sinful like he is, but he wonders if she might be capable of erotic desire. This new idea allows Stephen to accept his attraction to Emma and to forge a fantasy of consensual sex:

> A glow of desire kindled again his soul and fired and fulfilled all his body. Conscious of his desire she was waking from odorous sleep, the temptress of his villanelle. Her eyes, dark and with a look of languor, were opening to his eyes. Her nakedness yielded to him, radiant, warm, odorous and lavish-limbed, enfolded him like a shining cloud, enfolded him like water with a liquid life; and like a cloud of vapour or like waters circumfluent in space the liquid letters of speech, symbols of the element of mystery, flowed forth over his brain.[37]

In this fantasy, Stephen acknowledges Emma's bodily autonomy and reconceptualizes sex as an act based in consent and reciprocal desire. As she yields to him, he yields to her. She enfolds him within herself, and there is no domination between them. Alluding to his villanelle, a second poem he had written about her, he presents a contrast. In the poem, she arouses him, but in his fantasy, he too arouses her, as he imagines "her eyes" "opening to his eyes." Quite significantly, his vision of shared pleasure recalls the erotic fantasy of his boyhood, the one about making love to an Irish Mercedes, but it reflects a kind of sex he has yet to experience.

Stephen's burgeoning sexual ethics requires him working through and against elements of Irish culture that would oppose such a premarital union. Through this scene, Stephen's epiphany is threefold; first, that his assumption of Emma being "loveless and sinless" was inaccurate and disrespectful; second, that his sexual desire for her, in and of itself, was *not* a violation; and third, that his desire could be reciprocated. He envisions Emma as an embodied sexual being who can serve as an enthusiastic partner during intimacy. The fantasy is all the more erotic to

Stephen because of its picture of enthusiastic consent between partners.[38] His epiphany thus counters what some critics have claimed of women in Joyce's works, that they are "matter over mind," evidence that the "Cartesian dichotomy" only describes men.[39] It also opposes old arguments that these women are mere "biological symbols."[40] Stephen is preoccupied with the transformation of mind through matter, with Emma's intellect empowered through an erotic experience of her body, through intimate relations with him. They *both* acquire new sight, as their eyes open to each other and their bodies connect. What is radical here is that Stephen recognizes Emma's capacity to contradict cultural norms, to choose sin, knowledge, and desire for herself—a choice he never before entertained about her or any respectable Catholic woman. This epiphany allows him to forge a more ethical view of Emma that no longer reduces her to a caricature of Irish womanhood.

Stephen's epiphany is enabled through an exercise in empathy, an action often feminized and set against masculinity. Empathy toward women is an uncommon experience for him and relates to an observation he makes of Cranly—that his friend "bow[s] his mind" to women, attempting to inhabit their "sufferings."[41] Bowing the mind is not just a Joycean synonym for empathy, but a description of a purposeful pursuit of the perspective of the other. Vicki Mahaffey writes that while Stephen tends to waver between idealizing and dismissing women's feelings, "Cranly is capable of empathy for them."[42] As much as Stephen rightly distinguishes himself from his friend, who he fears shares reciprocated feelings with Emma, he too bows his mind, imaginatively submitting to her perspective. Stephen's willingness to open his mind to Emma's while lying alone in the quiet of his bedroom results in his reconstructed view of female sexuality and sex itself.

Figures at the forefront of #MeToo have underscored the importance of nurturing empathy between survivors of sexual violence but also as a strategy for cultivating a respectful sexual culture. Michelle Rodino-Colocino writes that "promoting empathy" can challenge "systems of power that underlie harassment, discrimination, and assault."[43] But not all empathies are equal. So what kind of empathy does Stephen offer? And what are its effects? We might conclude that his empathy resembles what Clare Hemmings defines as a "sentimental attachment to the other, rather than a genuine engagement with her concerns," particularly because his epiphany supports his own secret longings.[44] We might also lean toward labeling it a "passive empathy," which Megan Boler asserts "produces no action towards justice."[45] Rodino-Colcino adds that passive empathy allows "oppressors, and even oppressed people, to project feelings of commonality, understanding, as well as fear and guilt rather than do the work of being self-reflexive."[46] All of these descriptions may be fairly attributed to Stephen's expression of empathy, but they might too hastily reduce the significance of his experience in the context of Joyce's broader study of sexual development and consent.

While Stephen's mind-bowing is an imperfect practice that he never masters, Joyce reveals it as a meaningful, self-reflexive process—one in which Stephen does the transformative work himself rather than expect that work to be done by others, including Emma. What Joyce exposes through Stephen's train of thought is more akin to what Gayatri Chakravorty Spivak calls an "uncoercive rearrangement of desires." Spivak employs this phrase to describe the personal, voluntary transformation required to liberate the subaltern—those kept on the margins of society, excluded from hegemonic power.[47] As Spivak describes, an uncoercive rearrangement of desires is a subject's renewed inclination, one derived from a willingness to undo and reimagine the very instincts within that uphold structures of oppression. Spivak is discussing both the desires of subaltern subjects themselves, whom she wishes would refuse to accept subalternity, but also those individuals who sustain the oppression. Rearranging desires, then, requires individuals to "step out of" themselves, as Spivak writes of her own journey, or in Joyce's framework, to bow their minds.[48]

In *Portrait*, Joyce depicts Stephen's live-action, uncoerced rearrangement of desires. He stages a stream of consciousness through which the flow of thought reveals Stephen's process of transformation. Eide writes that in the past Stephen had applied a "form of colonization" to Emma, "equivalent to, though different in its effects from, national imperialism" by imagining her "only through the structures of his own experience to the exclusion of her particular context."[49] But once he bows his mind to hers, his old view shatters. Although he initially blamed her as complicit with Irish culture, Stephen realizes *he* was the complicit one in trusting and then mapping stereotypes onto her experience. He played a part in her subordination, assuming a posture that took power away from her. But Joyce shows Stephen accepting that Emma had always been more than he imagined and was perhaps even inclined to resist her gendered colonial condition. His epiphany is not a single thought but a voluntary critical process and conclusion that women are sexually embodied and, despite religious and cultural conventions, they can enthusiastically consent to sexual intimacy. Thus, through Stephen's mind-bowing, Joyce presents a story of adolescent sexual development that contrasts with his broader picture of predatory Dublin. Stephen's evolving notions of intimacy and bodily autonomy demonstrate a positive model of sexual development and a picture of a character pushing back against harmful gender stereotypes and sexual norms in Ireland.

Those are interior effects of Stephen's epiphany, but Joyce leaves readers with the suggestion of externalized outcomes, including the anticipation of socially conscious creative action. Over the course of the book, Joyce proves that Stephen's sexual development is an integral part of his budding artistry, with his poems exhibiting a "youthful priggishness" that he begins to distance himself from over time. Suzette Henke argues that Joyce treats Stephen's "misogyny" ironically as "one of the adolescent traits that he must outgrow on the path to artistic maturity."[50] On this path, his new perception of Emma comes to harmonize with his creative ambition, to capture the "uncreated conscience" of Irish people.[51] He wants to authentically represent his community, and this achievement requires stepping outside of himself, bowing his mind, and empathizing with diverse subject positions. It requires interweaving an active empathy with his artistry, developing an ethic of empathy that orients his art. If Stephen can create literature representative of his community, his empathy can take material form and become externalized action. But *Portrait* ends and Stephen's depiction in *Ulysses* is limited to one frustrated day in his young adulthood, a day in which his artistic future and even where he will sleep that night are uncertain. Joyce never shares the end of Stephen's story, so it is left up to the reader's imagination.

Consent in Courtship and Marriage

The sexual ethics Joyce develops in *Portrait* are tested in the lives of Leopold and Molly Bloom in *Ulysses*. In "Circe," Joyce stages his own #MeToo reckoning, with Bloom put on trial for sexual misconduct. Seeming to anticipate our historical moment, Joyce depicts women corroborating Bloom's wrongdoings, releasing successive cries of "Me too."[52] The reality-bending scene includes allegations that are perhaps "phantasmatic projections" of Bloom's "unconscious," but may nonetheless carry truth, particularly in the case of Mary Driscoll, a former scullery maid with whom Molly intimates his misbehavior. The trial, then, while part psychedelic fantasy, reminds readers to reconsider Bloom's past and to hold him accountable—to question, as Valente suggests, "how we are to regard" the "fabled protagonist."[53] As with the young boy in "Araby," Joyce's suspension of judgment places the final verdict of Bloom's character trial in the hands of readers.

While we may never fully untangle fact from fantasy in "Circe," Joyce emphasizes elsewhere in the text the importance of bowing the mind during sex in a courtship and marriage. Consensual sex, in fact, is consequential to the story of *Ulysses*. The Blooms have not had penetrative intercourse for eleven years. Molly, or Bloom, or perhaps both "could never like it again after" their infant son's death.[54] They understood this change in sexual enjoyment to be a retraction of consent, and both partners have upheld that boundary. Yet they have not revisited the matter since, and Molly has grown sexually frustrated.

Bloom's obliviousness juxtaposes Molly's recollections of her husband and what she felt was his expert knowing of her mind. In her famous soliloquy, which begins and ends with "yes"—the very word of consent—Molly relives a cherished memory, the first time she and Bloom made love during a picnic on Howth Hill. It was an instance when Bloom's empathy stood out to her:

> I asked him with my eyes to ask again yes and then he asked me would I yes to say yes my mountain flower and first I put my arms around him yes and drew him down to me so he could feel my breasts all perfume yes and his heart was going like mad and yes I said yes I will Yes.[55]

She speaks first through the language of her body and then through her words of affirmation. Bloom remembers it this way, emphasizing the reciprocity of the intimacy:

> her hand touched me, caressed: her eyes upon me did not turn away. Ravished over her I lay, full lips full open, kissed her mouth. Yum. Softly she gave me in my mouth the seedcake warm and chewed. Mawkish pulp her mouth had mumbled sweetsour of her spittle. Joy: I ate it: joy. Young life, her lips that gave me pouting. Soft warm sticky gumjelly lips. Flowers her eyes were, take me, willing eyes. [...] Wildly I lay on her, kissed her: eyes, her lips, her stretched neck beating, woman's breasts full in her blouse of nun's veiling, fat nipples upright. Hot I tongued her. She kissed me. I was kissed. All yielding she tossed my hair. Kissed, she kissed me.[56]

Both Bloom and Molly demonstrate an awareness of the ongoing process of consent during sex, the notion that consent occurs not only at the moment of initiating sex but is a shared passage of communication during the full act. Bloom continues to seek Molly's enthusiastic consent, bowing his mind, studying the responses of her body and her expressions of pleasure.

Her sexual enjoyment with Bloom contrasts with her assessment of the sex with her colleague Hugh "Blazes" Boylan. She is bothered that he begins undressing in her bedroom "without even asking permission." During sex, he bites her nipples so aggressively that his teeth marks linger long after their tryst. In the moment, she "had to scream out" in pain, and she wonders afterward while studying her blemished breasts why men are not "fearful" of hurting women. Although she is attracted to Boylan and orgasms during the act, she does not care for the way he treats her as a person. It bothers her that he slaps her bottom after—and perhaps during—sex, making her wonder if he equates her with livestock: "Im not a horse or an ass am I," she asks herself.[57] Although the sex with Boylan somewhat fulfills Molly's physical desires after years of celibacy, she recognizes that he dehumanizes her. He never empathizes with her, which is why he fails to notice the unwelcome pain he inflicts. The brutish sex was more in service of his pleasure than hers.

While the novel never suggests that rough sex cannot be consensual or pleasurable, Molly's memories point to the difference between Boylan's and Bloom's sexual ethics. Bloom is attuned to her ongoing issuance of "yes" in a way that Boylan is not. This contrast motivates Molly to vow at the end of the episode to seduce her husband in the morning. As she thinks about Bloom, she remembers that during their courtship she was attracted to his expressions of empathy and his pleasure in her consent. She says, "yes that was why I liked him because I saw he understood or felt what a woman is and I knew I could always get round him and I gave him all the pleasure I could leading him on till he asked me to say yes."[58] Molly is not just saucily saying that she can get her way with Bloom. She is suggesting that in a world where women's voices may be diminished or ignored, she knew he would ask for and respect her "yes" and "no." Of course, she recognizes that Bloom does not literally understand what a woman feels, but she praises his effort to do so.[59]

Molly describes what readers have already witnessed—that Bloom habitually practices bowing his mind, imagining experiences of the people around him, often seeing those experiences in light of social, cultural, and political injustice. For example, Bloom bows his mind to Mina Purefoy's, imagining what her life is like, with her demanding husband and constant state of pregnancy. He thinks about her family's poverty and her endless experience of sleep deprivation, having to nurse infants night after night, year after year. He is so concerned about her health that he visits her at the maternity hospital on day three of her latest labor. Bloom also bows his mind to a diseased sex worker's. Encountering her twice during the day, he is loath to catch her eye, fearful that she knows Molly and might report an old misdeed to her, but he wonders about her well-being. Although he is perplexed that any man would risk his health to have sex with her, he acknowledges her right to seek work, "to live like all the rest of us," and he ponders her position in a misogynistic society where "some man is ultimately responsible for her condition."[60]

When Bloom bows his mind, he often considers solutions to the sufferings of others. Mina Purefoy's "life with hard labour" prompts his suggestion that the medical field "ought to invent something to stop" the pain of childbirth. In response to the sex worker's disease and lack of legal protection, he tells Stephen, with perhaps a touch of moralism, that he is a "stalwart advocate" of seeing the sex industry regulated, with its establishments "licensed and medically inspected." He argues these changes would "confer a lasting boon on everybody concerned."[61] These are but two of many instances of Bloom's exercises in empathy and support of actions that would improve Irish lives. Through these examples, Joyce shows that Bloom's sexual ethics are a symptom of his broader humanism, one developed through a practice of stepping outside of himself. These acts of empathy orient his approach to sex with his wife as well as the welfare of his neighbors.

Conclusion

Reading the works of James Joyce in the wake of the #MeToo movement shows a continuity of concerns between the past and present. Burke emphasizes that the movement she founded is focused first on intersections of sexual violence with marginalized populations, particularly American women of color.[62] Joyce drew attention to vulnerable populations of his homeland, bringing to the forefront examples of an Irish culture that enabled sexual predation to persist, often in the shadows of society and outside the purview of the legal system. His texts shine light on those shadows and legal inadequacies, spotlighting the experiences of victim-survivors as well as the processes of ordinary people, such as a teenage boy and married couple, trying to negotiate and determine their sexual ethics. As a child, Stephen poses a question relevant to this discovery process. When boys at school tease him for kissing his mother, he wonders, "What did that mean, to kiss?"[63] He does not ask what a kiss *is* but what the action *means*. No one provides him with an answer. And the difficult truth is, we are still searching for an answer to Stephen's question today. The work and goals of #MeToo underscore that we are still seeking to account for the meanings and consequences of intimacies shared consensually, solicited coercively, or taken forcibly.

While approaches to sex crimes in Ireland have changed over time—for instance, now criminalizing abuse of boys, forms of non-penetrative sexual assault, and marital rape—social and cultural perceptions are ever-evolving, and they influence public policy. Literature does not often initiate legislative change (although the obscenity trials regarding *Ulysses* did just that in the United States), but it is a form of soft power that beckons readers to bow their minds, to empathize. This soft power plays a part in prompting ongoing social and cultural analysis that implicates readers. Writing of "The Sisters," Valente and Backus explain that Joyce's "fuzzy" rendering of the child's violation "enjoins upon the reader a like sense of complicity [...] Joyce refuses to portray the scandal of child sexual abuse as purely external to any imagined community his work might reach."[64] Readers must confront the realism and proximity of the abuse alongside their own arrangements of desire. Boler describes this process of reading as a "testimonial" approach to engaging literature, a "commitment to rethink [...] assumptions, and to confront the internal obstacles encountered as one's views are challenged."[65] Still, Joyce's study of sexual abuse, assault, and harassment results in no prescriptive solution but is representative of what Eide asserts of his ethics: that he rejects "any system that would take another as its victim," designs no "moral system" of his own, but issues instead through his works an "envoy," a kind of "love letter" that is always "in circulation, addressed to, responsive to, another."[66] His works, then, are still awaiting our reply.

Notes

Introduction Katherine Ebury, Bridget English, and Matthew Fogarty

1 Wyndham Lewis, *Blasting and Bombardiering* (Berkeley and Los Angeles: University of California Press, 1967), 289–92; Richard Ellmann, *James Joyce*, rev. ed. (New York: Oxford University Press, 1983), 103.
2 Elsa Högberg, *Virginia Woolf and the Ethics of Intimacy* (London: Bloomsbury, 2020), 3.
3 Högberg, *Virginia Woolf*, 4.
4 See, for example, Susan Stanford Friedman, "Religion's Configurations: Modernism, Empire, Comparison," in *The New Modernist Studies*, ed. Douglas Mao (Cambridge: Cambridge University Press, 2021), 92. Friedman describes the power of the "postsecular," a mode in which the lasting power of religion is acknowledged beyond the revolution of secularism. See also Suzanne Hobson, *Angels of Modernism* (Basingstoke: Palgrave Macmillan, 2012); Matthew Mutter, *Restless Secularism* (New Haven, CT: Yale University Press, 2017); Anthony Domestico, *Poetry and Theology in the Modernist Period* (Baltimore, MD: Johns Hopkins University Press, 2017); Joanna Rzepa, *Modernism and Theology* (Cham: Palgrave Macmillan, 2021).
5 See Ben Ware, "Introduction," *Modernism, Ethics and the Political Imagination* (Cham: Palgrave Macmillan, 2017), 1–6. Due to his emphasis on politics, Ware aims in this work to reactivate the social dimensions of the term "moral" and to use both ethics and morals flexibly (3–4); in keeping with the claims made above, our authors in this volume tend to prefer the former term, but, similarly, often use both.

6 Lee Oser, "Introduction," *The Ethics of Modernism* (Cambridge: Cambridge University Press, 2009), 7.
7 Maksymilian Del Mar, "The Confluence of Rhetoric and Emotion: How the History of Rhetoric Illuminates the Theoretical Importance of Emotion," *Law & Literature* (2022): 9.
8 James Joyce, "I.ii. Notebook with accounts, quotations, book lists, etc., 1903–1904," Dublin, National Library of Ireland, MS 36,639/2/A, p.13. https://catalogue.nli.ie/Record/vtls000356987 (accessed September 26, 2022). To see how these questions are transformed and ironized, see James Joyce, *A Portrait of the Artist as a Young Man* (London: Penguin, 2000), 232–33.
9 W. H. Auden, "Kairos and Logos" and "In Memory of W. B. Yeats," *Collected Poems*, ed. Edward Mendelson (New York: Vintage 1991), 305, 247.
10 Robert Archambeau, "Aesthetics as Ethics: One and a Half Theses on the New Criticism," *Rereading the New Criticism*, ed. Miranda B. Hickman and John D. McIntyre (Columbus: Ohio State University Press, 2012), 29–30.
11 Douglas Mao and Rebecca L. Walkowitz, "The New Modernist Studies," *PMLA* 123, no. 3 (2008): 737–48.
12 Joe Cleary, *Modernism, Empire, World Literature* (Cambridge: Cambridge University Press, 2021), 11.
13 Kwame Anthony Appiah, *The Ethics of Identity* (Princeton, NJ: Princeton University Press, 2005).
14 Marian Eide, *Ethical Joyce* (Cambridge: Cambridge University Press, 2002), 2.
15 G. W. F. Hegel, *The Phenomenology of Spirit*, trans. A. V. Miller (Oxford: Oxford University Press, 1977), 114.
16 Sam Slote, *Joyce's Nietzschean Ethics* (New York: Palgrave Macmillan, 2013), 2.
17 Jessica Berman, *Modernist Commitments: Ethics, Politics, and Transnational Modernism* (New York: Columbia University Press, 2011), 93.
18 Alain Badiou, *Being and Event*, trans. Oliver Feltham (London: Continuum, 2005), 29.
19 Alain Badiou, *On Beckett*, trans. Nina Power and Alberto Toscano (Cardiff: Cinnamon Press, 2003), 17.
20 Andrew Gibson, *Badiou and Beckett: The Pathos of Intermittency* (Oxford: Oxford University Press, 2006), 26.
21 Shane Weller, *Beckett, Literature, and the Ethics of Alterity* (Basingstoke: Palgrave Macmillan, 2006), 194–95.
22 Russell Smith, "Introduction: Beckett's Ethical Undoing," *Beckett and Ethics*, ed. Russell Smith (London: Bloomsbury Publishing, 2008), 3.

23 For a detailed re-evaluation of Beckett's literary ethics, see Matthew Fogarty, *Subjectivity and Nationhood in Yeats, Joyce, and Beckett: Nietzschean Constellations* (Liverpool: Liverpool University Press, 2023), 194–205.
24 Emmanuel Levinas, *Otherwise than Being or Beyond Essence*, trans. Alphonso Lingis (Dordrecht: Kluwer Academic Publishers, 1998), 121.
25 Levinas, *Otherwise than Being*, 127.
26 Högberg, *Virginia Woolf*, 5.
27 Högberg, *Virginia Woolf*, 9.
28 Högberg, *Virginia Woolf*, 15–16.
29 Foucault uses the term "medical gaze" to describe the ways that doctors exert power over patients by modifying their stories to fit a biomedical paradigm. Michel Foucault, *The Birth of the Clinic: An Archeology of Medical Perception*, trans. A. M. Sheridan (London: Tavistock Publications, 1973 [1963]).
30 Djuna Barnes, "How it Feels to Be Forcibly Fed," *New York World Magazine*, September 6, 1914, University of Maryland Libraries Digital Collections. https://hdl.handle.net/1903.1/14687 (accessed April 15, 2023).
31 Gayatri Chakravorty Spivak, *Death of a Discipline* (New York: Columbia University Press, 2003), chap. 3.
32 Susan Stanford Friedman, *Planetary Modernisms: Provocations on Modernity Across Time* (New York: Columbia University Press, 2015), 3, 78.
33 Virginia Woolf, *Mrs Dalloway* (London: Penguin, 2018), 6–7.
34 Virginia Woolf, *Between the Acts* (Oxford: Oxford World's Classics, 2008), 8.
35 Greta Olson, "De-Americanizing Law and Literature Narratives: Opening Up the Story," *Law & Literature* 22, no. 2 (2010): 344, 361.
36 See Greta Olson, "The Turn to Passion: Has Law and Literature become Law and Affect?" *Law & Literature* 28, no. 3 (2016): 335–53.
37 Anthony Powell, *A Question of Upbringing* (London: Heinemann, 1969), 1–2.
38 For an ethico-philosophical reading of this scene, and of Powell's work in general, see Marcia Muelder Eaton, "The Aesthetic Life," *Merit, Aesthetic and Ethical* (Oxford: Oxford University Press, 2001), 99–113. Muelder Eaton uses Powell's work as a case study for understanding the ethics of the aesthetic life.
39 Melba Cuddy-Keane, "Ethics," in *Modernism and Theory: A Critical Debate*, ed. Stephen Ross (London: Taylor & Francis, 2008), 210.
40 Kimberlé Crenshaw, *On Intersectionality: Essential Writings* (New York: New Press, 2017).
41 See Mark Wollaeger, "Scholarship's Turn: Origins and Effects of the New Modernist Studies," *The New Modernist Studies*, ed. Douglas Mao (Cambridge: Cambridge University Press, 2021), 41–64.

42 Sonita Sarker, "On Remaining Minor in Modernisms: The Future of Women's Literature," *Literature Compass* 10, no. 1 (2013): 8–14. The 2018 conference was led by early-career scholars (Séan Richardson, Rio Matchett, and Lloyd (Meadhbh) Houston), titled "Queer Modernism(s) II: Intersectional Identities," and featured keynotes by Jana Funke and Sandeep Parmar.

43 Ann Mattis, "Introducing New Womanhood and Intersectionality Through the Threshold Concept Approach," *Teaching Modernist Women's Writing in English*, ed. Janine Utell (New York: Modern Language Association of America, 2021), 256.

44 Zora Neale Hurston, *Their Eyes Were Watching God* (New York: Virago, 2007), 9–10.

Chapter One: *An Béal Bocht* and the Ethics of the Modernist Laughing Apocalypse Paul Fagan

1 In a non-exhaustive survey, we may think of Wells's "The Star," Forster's *The Machine Stops*, Chesterton's "Apocalypse" and "The Three Horsemen of the Apocalypse," Yeats's "The Second Coming," Eliot's *The Waste Land* and "The Hollow Men," H.D.'s *Trilogy*, Samuel Beckett's *Endgame*, Auden and The Apocalypse Poets, and so on.

2 Frank Kermode, *The Sense of an Ending: Studies in the Theory of Fiction* (Oxford: Oxford University Press, 2000 [1967]), 98; Roger Griffin, *Modernism and Fascism: The Sense of a Beginning under Mussolini and Hitler* (Basingstoke: Palgrave Macmillan, 2007), 2.

3 Erik Tonning, "Introduction," in *Modernism, Christianity and Apocalypse*, ed. Erik Tonning, Matthew Feldman, and David Addyman (Leiden: Brill, 2014), 1.

4 Ruben Borg, "Ethics of the Event: The Apocalyptic Turn in Modernism," *Partial Answers: Journal of Literature and the History of Ideas* 9, no. 1 (2011): 188.

5 Elana Gomel, "Everyday Apocalypse: J. G. Ballard and the Ethics and Aesthetics of the End of Time," *Partial Answers: Journal of Literature and the History of Ideas* 8, no. 1 (2010): 187, 185.

6 We may think here of the regenerative eugenicist program for cultural renewal and genetic revitalization laid out in Yeats's *On the Boiler* (1939), or how Pound's sense "that a truly apocalyptic sensibility was necessary to shake the world out of its decline" was manifested in *both* literary innovation *and* fascist collaboration. James P. Leveque, "Failure and the Phantastikon: Ezra Pound and Apocalypse," *SKEPSI* 6 (2014–15): 2.

7 For analyses of Kristevan abjection in O'Nolan's writing, see Yaeli Greenblatt, "'the tattered cloak of his perished skin': The Body as Costume in

'Two in One', *At Swim-Two-Birds* and *The Third Policeman*," in *Flann O'Brien: Gallows Humour*, ed. Ruben Borg and Paul Fagan (Cork: Cork University Press, 2020), 131–45; and Maebh Long, "Abject Bodies: Brian O'Nolan and Immunology," in *Gallows Humour*, 163–77.
8   Ruben Borg, *Fantasies of Self-Mourning: Modernism, the Posthuman and the Finite* (Leiden: Brill, 2019), 182.
9   Kermode, *Sense of an Ending*, 8. See also Jean-Michel Rabaté's discussion of the recurring modernist "figure of a ghostly writer who imagines himself posthumous" as a means to an atemporal vantage that "constantly projects, anticipates, and returns to mythical origins, but […] also teaches us more about the 'present' which it historicizes," *The Ghosts of Modernity* (Gainesville: University Press of Florida, 1996), 3.
10 Kermode, *Sense of an Ending*, 30.
11 Kermode, *Sense of an Ending*, 10.
12 Kermode, *Sense of an Ending*, 103. See also Gomel, "Everyday Apocalypse," 185–86. While it is manifested differently according to changing historical, political, material, and cultural circumstances, this danger is ever-present. Gomel notes that the "delirium" of an actively desired cataclysm "has motivated some of the most destructive religious and political events in history, from the Crusades and the expulsion of Jews from Spain to Nazism and Stalinism."
13 Annalisa Zox-Weaver, *Women Modernists and Fascism* (Cambridge: Cambridge University Press, 2011), front matter.
14 Griffin, *Modernism and Fascism*, 2. See also Mark Antliff, "Fascism, Modernism, and Modernity," *Art Bulletin* 84, no. 1 (2002): 148–69, and various discussions of reactionary modernism.
15 Tonning, "Introduction," 2.
16 Kermode, *Sense of an Ending*, 30 (emphasis added).
17 Kermode, *Sense of an Ending*, 10.
18 Kermode, *Sense of an Ending*, 43.
19 Kermode, *Sense of an Ending*, 96.
20 Kermode, *Sense of an Ending*, 96.
21 Kermode, *Sense of an Ending*, 104.
22 Kermode, *Sense of an Ending*, 98.
23 Kermode, *Sense of an Ending*, 114.
24 Kermode, *Sense of an Ending*, 114.
25 Kermode, *Sense of an Ending*, 114.
26 Borg, *Fantasies of Self-Mourning*, 76.
27 Borg, *Fantasies of Self-Mourning*, 76.
28 Borg, *Fantasies of Self-Mourning*, 76.
29 Borg, *Fantasies of Self-Mourning*, 76.
30 Borg, *Fantasies of Self-Mourning*, 79.
31 Borg, *Fantasies of Self-Mourning*, 78.

32 Flann O'Brien, *The Complete Novels* (New York: Everyman's Library, 2007), 105–7.
33 O'Brien, *The Complete Novels*, 5.
34 See Maebh Long, *Assembling Flann O'Brien* (London: Bloomsbury Publishing, 2014), 20.
35 Borg, *Fantasies of Self-Mourning*, 157.
36 Brian O'Nolan's own description of *The Dalkey Archive* in a letter to Timothy O'Keeffe, September 21, 1962, collected in Flann O'Brien, *The Collected Letters of Flann O'Brien*, ed. Maebh Long (Victoria, TX: Dalkey Archive Press, 2018), 324.
37 O'Brien, *The Complete Novels*, 672.
38 Jacques Derrida, "Of an Apocalyptic Tone Recently Adopted in Philosophy," *Oxford Literary Review* 6, no. 2 (1984): 29–30.
39 Julia Kristeva, *Powers of Horror: An Essay on Abjection* (New York: Columbia University Press, 1982), 205.
40 Kristeva, *Powers of Horror*, 205.
41 Kristeva, *Powers of Horror*, 208.
42 Julia Kristeva, *Nations without Nationalism* (New York: Columbia University Press, 1993), 29.
43 Kristeva, *Powers of Horror*, 206.
44 Kristeva, *Powers of Horror*, 205.
45 Mikhail Bakhtin, *Rabelais and His World*, trans. Hélène Iswolsky (Bloomington: Indiana University Press, 1984), 67, 90. Bakhtin clarifies: "The serious aspects of class culture are official and authoritarian; they are combined with violence, prohibitions, limitations and always contain an element of fear and of intimidation. […] It was the victory of laughter over fear that most impressed medieval man. It was not only a victory over mystic terror of God, but also […] over the oppression and guilt related to all that was consecrated and forbidden. It was the defeat of divine and human power, of authoritarian command." Bakhtin, *Rabelais and His World*, 90–91.
46 Kristeva, *Powers of Horror*, 138.
47 Kristeva, *Powers of Horror*, 133.
48 Kristeva, *Powers of Horror*, 138.
49 Kristeva, *Powers of Horror*, 206.
50 On Beckett, see Linda Ben-Zvi, "Beckett and Disgust: The Body as 'Laughing Matter,'" *Modernism/modernity* 18, no. 4 (2011): 695; Borg, *Fantasies of Self-Mourning*, 185–86. In broader terms, such a genealogy compels us to think of Deleuze's definition of great literature: "What springs from great books is schizo-laughter or revolutionary joy, not the anguish of our pathetic narcissism, not the terror of our guilt. […] There is always an indescribable joy that springs from great books, even when they speak of ugly, desperate, or terrifying things." Gilles Deleuze, *Desert*

Islands and Other Texts, 1953–1974, ed. David Lapoujade (New York: Semiotexte, 2004), 258.
51 See Maebh Long, *Assembling Flann O'Brien*, 149–90.
52 See Danielle Jacquin, "Flann O'Brien's Savage Mirth," in *Conjuring Complexities: Essays on Flann O'Brien*, ed. Anne Clune and Tess Hurson (Belfast: Institute of Irish Studies, 1997), 1–7.
53 Kristeva, *Powers of Horror*, 138.
54 Ruben Borg and Paul Fagan, "Editors' Introduction," *Gallows Humour*, 2.
55 O'Brien, *Complete Novels*, 413.
56 O'Brien, *Complete Novels*, 42, 434, 462, 464.
57 O'Brien, *Complete Novels*, 413.
58 O'Brien, *Complete Novels*, 466.
59 O'Brien, *Complete Novels*, 482.
60 O'Brien, *Complete Novels*, 484.
61 O'Brien, *Complete Novels*, 485.
62 Gregory Darwin, "'As ucht a bhochtanais Ghaeiligh': Parody, Poverty, and the Politics of Irish Folklore in *An Béal Bocht*," *The Parish Review: Journal of Flann O'Brien Studies* 4, no. 1 (2018): 30. https://doi.org/10.16995/pr.3227 (accessed April 15, 2023).
63 O'Brien, *Complete Novels*, 434.
64 O'Brien, *Complete Novels*, 434–35.
65 O'Brien, *Complete Novels*, 435.
66 Ian Ó Caoimh, "The Ideal and the Ironic: Incongruous Irelands in *An Béal Bocht, No Laughing Matter* and Ciarán Ó Nualláin's *Óige an Deartháir*," in *Problems with Authority*, ed. Ruben Borg, Paul Fagan, and John McCourt (Cork: Cork University Press, 2017), 168.
67 Borg and Fagan, "Editors' Introduction," 1.
68 Borg and Fagan, "Editors' Introduction," 1.
69 O'Brien, *Complete Novels*, 414.
70 Amy-Jill Levine, "Tobit," in *The New Oxford Annotated Apocrypha*, 3rd ed., ed. Michael David Coogan (New York: Oxford University Press, 2007), 12.
71 O'Brien, *Complete Novels*, 411.
72 O'Brien, *Complete Novels*, 411.
73 See Radvan Markus, "The Prison of Language: Brian O'Nolan, *An Béal Bocht*, and Language Determinism," *The Parish Review: Journal of Flann O'Brien Studies* 4, no. 1 (2018): 40–52. https://parishreview.openlibhums.org/article/id/3229/ (accessed April 15, 2023).
74 O'Brien, *Complete Novels*, 417.
75 O'Brien, *Complete Novels*, 472.
76 O'Brien, *Complete Novels*, 426.
77 O'Brien, *Complete Novels*, 428.
78 O'Brien, *Complete Novels*, 485.

79 O'Brien, *Complete Novels*, 471.
80 O'Brien, *Complete Novels*, 488.
81 O'Brien, *Complete Novels*, 426.
82 O'Brien, *Complete Novels*, 481.
83 Kristeva, *Powers of Horror*, 147.
84 O'Brien, *Complete Novels*, 420–21, 453, 479.
85 Borg, *Fantasies of Self-Mourning*, 152n19.
86 O'Brien, *Complete Novels*, 425.
87 Borg and Fagan, "Editors' Introduction," 1.
88 O'Brien, *Complete Novels*, 442–43.
89 Edwin Black, *IBM and the Holocaust: The Strategic Alliance Between Nazi Germany and America's Most Powerful Corporation* (New York: Three Rivers Press, 2002), 189.
90 Borg and Fagan, "Editors' Introduction," 2.
91 Kristeva, *Powers of Horror*, 206.
92 Kristeva, *Powers of Horror*, 147.
93 Darwin, "'As ucht a bhochtanais Ghaeiligh'," 33.
94 O'Brien, *Complete Novels*, 417.
95 O'Brien, *Complete Novels*, 470.
96 O'Brien, *Complete Novels*, 470.
97 O'Brien, *Complete Novels*, 470.
98 Kristeva, *Powers of Horror*, 138.
99 Sean Pryor, "Making Evil, with Flann O'Brien," in *Flann O'Brien & Modernism*, ed. Julian Murphet, Ronan McDonald, and Sascha Morrell (London: Bloomsbury, 2014), 12, 14.
100 Rónán McDonald, "'An astonishing parade of nullity': Nihilism in *The Third Policeman*," *Flann O'Brien & Modernism*, 136.
101 Kristeva, *Powers of Horror*, 204, 154.

Chapter Two: "Grey Figures Bent Like Hooks": The Ethics of Representing Older Age in Djuna Barnes's Early Journalism and Late Interviews   *Jade French*

1 Cynthia Port, "'Money, For the Night Is Coming': Jean Rhys and Gendered Economies of Ageing," *Women: A Cultural Review* 2 (2001): 216.
2 Wouter De Tavernier, Laura Naegele, and Moritz Hess, "A Critical Perspective on Ageism and Modernization Theory," *Social Inclusion* 7, no. 3 (2019): 54–57.
3 Haim Hazan, *Old Age: Constructions and Deconstructions* (Cambridge: Cambridge: University Press, 1994), 74.
4 Amelia DeFalco, *Imagining Care Responsibility, Dependency, and Canadian Literature* (Toronto: University of Toronto Press, 2016).
5 Hanne Laceulle and Jan Baars, "Self-Realization and Cultural Narratives About Later Life," *Journal of Aging Studies* 31 (2014): 39.

6 Laceulle and Baars, "Self-Realization," 39.
7 Diane Warren, *Djuna Barnes' Consuming Fictions* (Farnham: Ashgate Publishing, 2008), 23.
8 Alex Goody, "Djuna Barnes on the Page," in *Shattered Objects: Djuna Barnes's Modernism*, ed. Elizabeth Pender and Cathryn Setz (University Park: Penn State University Press, 2019), 37.
9 Nancy Levine, "'Bringing Milkshakes to Bulldogs': The Early Journalism of Djuna Barnes," in *Silence and Power: A Reevaluation of Djuna Barnes*, ed. Mary Lynn Broe (Carbondale: Southern Illinois University Press, 1991), 30.
10 Cheryl J. Plumb, *Fancy's Craft: Art and Identity in the Early Works of Djuna Barnes* (Selinsgrove, PA: Susquehanna University Press, 1986), 25.
11 Lydia Steptoe, "Against Nature: In Which Everything that is Young, Inadequate and Tiresome is Included in the Term Natural," *Vanity Fair*, August 18, 1922, 60.
12 Djuna Barnes, "Becoming Intimate with the Bohemians," *New York Morning Telegraph Sunday Magazine*, November 19, 1916, 72.
13 Djuna Barnes, "Crumpets and Tea," *New York Morning Telegraph Sunday Magazine*, June 24, 1917, 266.
14 Djuna Barnes, "The Confessions of Helen Westley," *New York Morning Telegraph*, September 23, 1917, 5.
15 Barnes, "Confessions," 5.
16 Djuna Barnes, "Yvette Guilbert," *New York Morning Telegraph Sunday Magazine*, November 18, 1917, 2.
17 Djuna Barnes, "I Could Never Be Lonely Without a Husband, Says Lillian Russell," in *Interviews by Djuna Barnes*, ed. Alyce Barry (Los Angeles, CA: Sun & Moon Press, 1985), 55.
18 Barnes, "I Could Never Be Lonely," 55.
19 Jan Baars, "Time in Late Modern Ageing," in *Routledge Handbook of Cultural Gerontology*, ed. Wendy Martin and Julia Twigg (London: Routledge, 2015), 397–403.
20 Djuna Barnes, "There are Beads and Beads, But Peter Bender Knows Them All," *Brooklyn Citizen*, July 4, 1920, 5.
21 Goody, "Djuna Barnes on the Page," 38.
22 Barnes, "There Are Beads," 5.
23 Roland Barthes, *Image Music Text* (London: Fontana Press, 1977), 25–26.
24 Goody, "Djuna Barnes on the Page," 40–41.
25 Djuna Barnes, "Veterans In Harness No. 1: Postman Joseph H. Dowling, Forty-Two Years In Service," *Brooklyn Daily Eagle*, October 12, 1913, 60–61; "Veterans In Harness No. 3: Waiter Patrick Dunne, 40 Years Carrying a Tray," *Brooklyn Daily Eagle*, October 29, 1913, 14; "Veterans In Harness No. 6: 'Uncle Tom' Baird, Engineer: 65 Years Running Machines," *Brooklyn Daily Eagle*, November 16, 1913, 15.

26 Baars, "Time in Late Modern Ageing."
27 Christopher Simon Wareham, "What is the Ethics of Ageing?" *Journal of Medical Ethics* 44 (2018): 129.
28 Djuna Barnes, "Veterans In Harness No. 2: Conductor Kid Connors, Forty Years Ringing Up Fares," *Brooklyn Daily Eagle*, October 19, 1913, 15.
29 Barnes, "Veterans In Harness No. 2," 15.
30 Barnes, "Veterans In Harness No. 2," 15.
31 Wareham, "Ethics of Ageing," 129.
32 Barnes, "Veterans in Harness No. 6," 15.
33 Barnes, "Veterans in Harness No. 6," 15.
34 "Thomas Baird, 92, Veteran Mason and Odd Fellow, Dies," *Brooklyn Daily Times*, January 17, 1917, 6.
35 Catherine Degnen, "Temporality, Narrative and the Ageing Self," *Cambridge Anthropology* 25, no. 2 (2005): 60.
36 Alex Goody, *Modernist Articulations: A Cultural Study of Djuna Barnes, Mina Loy, and Gertrude Stein* (New York: Palgrave Macmillan, 2007).
37 Jennifer Parks, Martha Holstein, and Mark Waymack, *Ethics, Aging, and Society: The Critical Turn* (New York: Springer, 2011), 12.
38 Djuna Barnes, "The Hem of Manhattan," *New York Morning Telegraph Sunday Magazine*, July 29, 1917, 2.
39 Barnes, "Hem of Manhattan," 2.
40 Barnes, "Hem of Manhattan," 2.
41 Barnes, "Hem of Manhattan," 2.
42 Barnes, "Hem of Manhattan," 2.
43 Barnes, "Hem of Manhattan," 2.
44 Amelia DeFalco, *Uncanny Subjects: Aging in Contemporary Narrative* (Columbus: Ohio State University Press, 2010), 2.
45 DeFalco, *Uncanny Subjects*, 2.
46 Chris Gilleard and Paul Higgs, "Ageing Abjection and Embodiment in the Fourth Age," *Journal of Aging Studies* 25 (2011): 137.
47 Bernice L. Neugarten, "Age Groups in American Society and the Rise of the Young-Old," *The ANNALS of the American Academy of Political and Social Science* 415 (1974): 187–98.
48 Phyllis Rose, "The Stature of an Eccentric," *New York Times*, June 26, 1983, 9.
49 Djuna Barnes to Natalie Barney, May 16, 1963, Djuna Barnes papers, University of Maryland Libraries Special Collections, 0021-LIT, Series II, Box 1, Folder 45.
50 Daniela Caselli, *Improper Modernism: Djuna Barnes's Bewildering Corpus* (Farnham: Ashgate Publishing, 2009), 10.
51 Margaret Morganroth Gullette, *Declining to Decline: Cultural Combat and the Politics of Midlife* (Charlottesville: University Press of Virginia, 1997), 19.

52   Gullette, *Declining to Decline*, 19.
53   Laceulle and Baars, "Self-Realization," 39.
54   Laceulle and Baars, "Self-Realization," 42.
55   Quoted by Thomas Bernhard and Siegfried Unseld, *Der Briefwechsel (The Correspondence)*, ed. Raimund Fellinger, Martin Huber, and Julia Ketterer (Frankfurt am Main: Suhrkamp, 2009), 141.
56   Djuna Barnes to Helga Mulhauser, August 28, 1973, Djuna Barnes papers, 0021-LIT, Series II, Box 12, Folder 27.
57   Margaret Cruikshank, *Learning to be Old: Gender, Culture, and Aging* (Lanham, MD: Rowman & Littlefield, 2003), 23.
58   Djuna Barnes letter to Samuel Beckett, January 14, 1971, Djuna Barnes papers, 0021-LIT, Series II, Box 1, Folder 50.
59   Barnes letter to Beckett.
60   Barnes letter to Beckett.
61   Barnes letter to Beckett.
62   Henry Raymont, "From the Avant-Garde of the Thirties, Djuna Barnes," *New York Times*, May 24, 1971, 24.
63   Djuna Barnes handwritten notes on "From the Avant-Garde," Djuna Barnes papers, 0021-LIT, Series I, Box 4, Folder 8.
64   Caselli, *Improper Modernism*, 10.

Chapter Three: The Solar Plexus and Animalistic Power in D. H. Lawrence and Isadora Duncan   Carrie Rohman

1   Scholars of modernist dance do reference Duncan's interest in the solar plexus, but a sustained study of this topic has not been undertaken. See, for instance, Elizabeth Anderson, "Dancing Modernism: Ritual, Ecstasy and the Female Body," *Literature and Theology* 22, no. 3 (2008): 354–67; see also footnote 4 for work by Carrie Preston.
2   For work in this subfield, see, for instance, Jane Bennett, *Vibrant Matter: A Political Ecology of Things* (Durham, NC: Duke University Press, 2010); Eugene Thacker, *After Life* (Chicago: University of Chicago Press, 2010); Timothy Morton, "Guest Column: Queer Ecology," *PMLA* 125, no. 2 (2010): 273–82; Diana Coole and Samantha Frost, eds., *New Materialisms: Ontology Agency, and Politics* (Durham, NC: Duke University Press, 2010).
3   Taney Roniger, "If We Are the Asteroid, We Are Also the Deflector: Ed Kerns and the New Sympoietic Consciousness," in *Ed Kerns: Interconnected* (Exhibition Catalog); guest curator Daniel Hill (Easton, PA: Lafayette College Art Galleries, 2022), 52.
4   See Carrie J. Preston, *Modernism's Mythic Pose: Gender, Genre, Solo Performance* (New York: Oxford University Press, 2011), esp. 172.
5   Isadora Duncan, *My Life* (New York: Liveright, 1927), 75.

6   See Preston, *Modernism's Mythic Pose*, 154.
7   See Preston, *Modernism's Mythic Pose*, 97–98.
8   Duncan, *My Life*, 75.
9   See Carrie Rohman, "Nude Vibrations: Isadora Duncan's Creatural Aesthetic," in *Choreographies of the Living: Bioaesthetics in Literature, Art, and Performance* (Oxford: Oxford University Press, 2018), chap. 1.
10 I took a master class in Duncan technique with Lori Belilove of the Isadora Duncan Dance Foundation (IDDF) at Franklin and Marshall College, February 26, 2014. Belilove is founder and Artistic Director of the Foundation and is considered a premier performer and teacher of Duncan's choreographies. She studied with Anna and Irma Duncan and with second-generation Duncan dancers such as Julia Levien.
11 The Institute was co-founded in 1977 by Maria-Theresa Duncan and Kay Bardsley.
12 Jeanne Bresciani, telephone interview with the author, January 26, 2014.
13 Elizabeth Grosz, *Becoming Undone: Darwinian Reflections on Life, Politics, and Art* (Durham, NC: Duke University Press, 2011), 27. Original emphasis.
14 D. H. Lawrence, *Apocalypse and the Writings on Revelation*, ed. Mara Kalnins (Cambridge: Cambridge University Press, 1980), 149.
15 D. H. Lawrence, *Psychoanalysis and the Unconscious*, in *Psychoanalysis and the Unconscious and Fantasia of the Unconscious*, ed. Bruce Steele (Cambridge: Cambridge University Press, 2004), 17.
16 Lawrence, *Psychoanalysis and the Unconscious*, 17.
17 D. H. Lawrence, *Fantasia of the Unconscious*, in Steele, *Psychoanalysis and the Unconscious*, 79.
18 Gerald Doherty helpfully explains that Lawrence draws from and also adapts the yogic psychologies traditionally associated with the chakra centers in some of his work. See Gerald Doherty, "Connie and the Chakras: Yogic Patterns in D. H. Lawrence's *Lady Chatterley's Lover*," *D. H. Lawrence Review* 3, no. 1 (*D. H. Lawrence: Myth and Occult*) (1980): 79–93. Tianying Zang carefully acknowledges Lawrence's somewhat minimal exposures to and admirations of Hinduism, alongside his general sentiment that while he hated the "west," he was ambivalent about the direct or wholesale co-opting of various eastern traditions. See the introduction in Tianying Zang, *D. H. Lawrence's Philosophy of Nature: An Eastern View* (Bloomington, IN: Trafford Publishing, 2011).
19 Craig Gordon, *Literary Modernism, Bioscience, and Community in Early 20th Century Britain* (New York: Palgrave Macmillan, 2007), 35.
20 Duncan, *My Life*, 75. Emphasis added.
21 Lawrence, *Psychoanalysis and the Unconscious*, 41–42.
22 Layla Salter, "D. H. Lawrence and Fictional Representations of Blood-Consciousness," Ph.D. thesis, University of Birmingham, 2013, 37.

23 Lawrence, *Fantasia of the Unconscious*, 106.
24 Jane Bennett, *Vibrant Matter: A Political Ecology of Things* (Durham, NC: Duke University Press, 2010), 57.
25 Isadora Duncan, "Youth and the Dance," in *Art of the Dance*, ed. Sheldon Cheney (New York: Theatre Arts, 1969), 97.
26 Lawrence, *Fantasia of the Unconscious*, 75.
27 Lawrence, *Fantasia of the Unconscious*, 75.
28 For Bergson, the *élan vital* is an unstable and unpredictable "natural" force, internal to life and matter, which directs the evolution of life and matter. For a helpful discussion of this complex concept in Bergson, see Bennett, *Vibrant Matter*, esp. chap. 5.
29 For my earlier ecological reading of this story, see Carrie Rohman, "Ecology and the Creaturely in D. H. Lawrence's 'Sun,'" *Journal of D. H. Lawrence Studies* 2, no. 2 (2010): 115–31.
30 D. H. Lawrence, "Sun" (1925 version), in *The Woman Who Rode Away and Other Stories*, ed. Dieter Mehl and Christa Jansohn, with an introduction and notes by N. H. Reeve (Harmondsworth: Penguin, 1996), 275.
31 See, for instance, Jeffrey Meyers, *D. H. Lawrence and the Experience of Italy* (Philadelphia: University of Pennsylvania Press, 1982), 154.
32 Lawrence, *Woman Who Rode Away*, 275.
33 Lawrence, *Woman Who Rode Away*, 276.
34 Lawrence, *Psychoanalysis and the Unconscious*, 29.
35 Lawrence, *Woman Who Rode Away*, 276.
36 Lawrence, *Psychoanalysis and the Unconscious*, 25.
37 Lawrence, *Psychoanalysis and the Unconscious*, 25.
38 Lawrence, *Woman Who Rode Away*, 277.
39 William E. Connolly, *The Fragility of Things* (Durham, NC: Duke University Press, 2013), 162–63.
40 Connolly, *Fragility of Thing*, 163.
41 Quoted by Connolly, *Fragility of Thing*, 163.
42 See Terrence W. Deacon, *Incomplete Nature: How Mind Emerged from Matter* (New York: W. W. Norton, 2013).
43 Lawrence, *Psychoanalysis and the Unconscious*, 19.
44 For a detailed discussion of Lawrence's familiarity with and bristling against psychoanalytical ideas, including the "mother-complex," see the introduction to *Psychoanalysis and the Unconscious*.
45 Lawrence, *Woman Who Rode Away*, 278.
46 Lawrence, *Woman Who Rode Away*, 278.
47 Lawrence, *Woman Who Rode Away*, 278. Emphasis added.
48 See Janice Hubbard Harris, *The Short Fiction of D. H. Lawrence* (New Brunswick, NJ: Rutgers University Press, 1984), 197–98.
49 Lawrence, *Woman Who Rode Away*, 278. Emphasis added.
50 Lawrence, *Woman Who Rode Away*, 278.

51 Lawrence, *Woman Who Rode Away*, 278.
52 Lawrence, *Fantasia of the Unconscious*, 79.
53 For useful early discussions in this area, see Melissa Gregg and Gregory J. Seigworth, eds., *The Affect Theory Reader* (Durham, NC: Duke University Press, 2010). The relation between the cognitive and affective has been highly contested in affect theory. See, for instance, Brian Massumi, *Parables for the Virtual* (Durham, NC: Duke University Press, 2002) and Ruth Leys, "The Turn to Affect: A Critique," *Critical Inquiry* 37, no. 3 (2011): 434–72. Also, for details about work in neuroscience suggesting the interconnectedness of cognition and emotion, see António Damasio, *Descartes' Error: Emotion, Reason, and the Human Brain* (New York: Putnam, 1994).
54 Lawrence, *Fantasia of the Unconscious*, 79.
55 Lawrence, *Woman Who Rode Away*, 283. Emphasis added.
56 Lawrence, *Woman Who Rode Away*, 282.
57 For a color reproduction of this watercolor, see Keith Sagar, *D. H. Lawrence's Paintings* (London: Chaucer Press, 2003), 111.
58 See also Rachel Murry on the way the insects in Lawrence appear "at once representative of the decay of modern civilization and of the creative force capable of counteracting" its decline. Rachel Murray, *The Modernist Exoskeleton: Insects, War, Literary Form* (Edinburgh: Edinburgh University Press, 2020), 72.
59 See Jeff Wallace's discussion of Lawrence's comments on Botticelli's *Mystic Nativity*, in Lawrence's *Study of Thomas Hardy*, where Lawrence describes the "outburst of movement from the source of motion. The Infant Christ is a centre, a radiating spark of movement." D. H. Lawrence, *Study of Thomas Hardy and Other Essays*, ed. Bruce Steele (Cambridge: Cambridge University Press, 1985), 66. See also Jeff Wallace, "Practitioner Criticism: Painting," in *The Edinburgh Companion to D. H. Lawrence and the Arts*, ed. Catherine Brown and Susan Reid (Edinburgh: Edinburgh University Press, 2020).
60 Gilles Deleuze and Félix Guattari, *A Thousand Plateaus: Capitalism and Schizophrenia*, trans. Brian Massumi (Minneapolis: University of Minnesota Press, 1987), 320.
61 Gilles Deleuze and Félix Guattari, *What is Philosophy?*, trans. Hugh Tomlinson and Graham Burchell (New York: Columbia University Press, 1994), 182.
62 Deleuze and Guattari, *What is Philosophy?*, 183.
63 Deleuze and Guattari, *What is Philosophy?*, 183.
64 See the July 16, 2019, discussion between Geoff Dyer and Frances Wilson: www.youtube.com/watch?v=N86DQ55E2Ps (accessed April 15, 2023).
65 See "About this Symposium." www.thinglyaffinities.org/p/about-this-symposium_25.html (accessed April 15, 2023).

66 The Abram lecture can be viewed at www.youtube.com/watch?v=xsfMz4tPFck (accessed April 15, 2023).
67 Lawrence, *Fantasia of the Unconscious*, 79.

Chapter Four: Reparative Ethics, or the Case of Anna D. Whyte
Marian Eide

1 Kwame Anthony Appiah, "What Should I Do With My Grandfather's Cringey Canvases?" *New York Times*, June 29, 2021. www.nytimes.com/2021/06/29/magazine/art-ethics-vaccination.html? (accessed June 29, 2021).
2 L. P. Hartley, *The Go-Between* (New York: Penguin, 2015), 17.
3 Kwame Appiah Anthony, "What Should I Do with My Portrait of a Slaveholding Ancestor?" *New York Times*, October 1, 2021. www.nytimes.com/2021/09/28/magazine/ethics-art-slavery.html (accessed October 1, 2021).
4 "The fact is," Levinas elaborates, "that for Celan the poem is situated precisely in that pre-syntactic and (as is surely *de rigueur* these days!) pre-logical level, but a level also pre-disclosing: at the moment of pure touching, pure contact, grasping, squeezing—which is, perhaps, a way of giving, right up to and including the hand that gives. A language of proximity for proximity's sake, older than that of 'the truth of being'—which it probably carries and sustains—the first of the languages, response preceding the question, responsibility for the neighbor, by its *for the other*, the whole marvel of giving." Emmanuel Levinas, *Proper Names*, trans. Michael B. Smith (Palo Alto, CA: Stanford University Press, 1996), 41.
5 Levinas, *Proper Names*, 8.
6 "It is of the essence of art to signify only between the lines—in the intervals of time, between times—like a footprint that would precede the step, or an echo preceding the sound of a voice. Only exegesis, after the fact, completes and repeats again, indefinitely, that step and that call. [...] In this there is no belittling of the literal meaning. The letters bordering the interlinear trace remain, in literature, a refined, suggestive language, through imagery and metaphors, from which no speaking is exempt." Levinas, *Proper Names*, 7–8.
7 See, for example, Adam Zachary Newton, *Narrative Ethics* (Cambridge, MA: Harvard University Press, 1997); Jill Robbins, *Altered Reading: Levinas and Literature* (Chicago: University of Chicago Press, 1999); Andrew Gibson, *Postmodernity, Ethics, and the Novel* (New York: Routledge, 1999); Jill Larson, *Ethics and Narrative in the English Novel, 1880–1914* (Cambridge: Cambridge University Press, 2001); Derek Attridge, *Reading and Responsibility* (Edinburgh: Edinburgh University

Press, 2010); and Xiaojing Zhou, *Ethics and Poetics of Alterity in Asian American Poetry* (Iowa City: University of Iowa Press, 2006) among many others. Levinas's principal philosophical works include *Existence and Existents* (1947); *Time and the Other* (1948); *Totality and Infinity: An Essay on Exteriority* (1961); and *Otherwise than Being, or Beyond Essence* (1974).

8   "In discourse I expose myself to the question of the Other, and this urgency of the response—acuteness of the present—engenders me for responsibility; as responsible I am brought to my final reality." Emmanuel Levinas, *Totality and Infinity: An Essay on Exteriority*, trans. Alphonso Lingis, 4th ed. (Dordrecht: Kluwer Academic Publishers, 1991), 178. Or, as Marianne Noble summarizes, "For Levinas, subjectivity is created in a face-to-face encounter with another, in which one discerns both the other's infinitude and one's responsibility to defend that infinitude. We do not first exist and then approach others; rather our very being is called into existence by the claims of others upon us. […] Selfhood is external in nature; relationships do not augment a self but constitute it." Marianne Noble, "The Reality of the Self in the Priority of the Other: Hawthorne, Levinas, and Winnicott," *Textual Practice* 33, no. 10 (2019): 4.

9   Levinas, *Totality and Infinity*, 114.

10 Emmanuel Levinas, *Otherwise than Being or Beyond Essence*, trans. Alphonso Lingis (Dordrecht: Kluwer Academic Publishers, 1998), 121.

11 Levinas, *Otherwise than Being*, 127.

12 "We are speaking here of something different from the reflexive undoing of representation, the confronting of an aporia that exposes the indeterminacy of representation. The undoing of thematization would have to be construed as an undoing of literature insofar as it belongs to the discourse of the whole, or being." Joseph G. Kronick, "Levinas and the Plot against Literature," *Philosophy and Literature* 40, no.1 (2016): 266.

13 Clinton Derricks, *Buy Golly: The History of Black Collectables* (London: New Cavendish Books, 2005). "Golliwogs were a popular children's toy in New Zealand as elsewhere in the first half of the twentieth century, but by the late twentieth century were increasingly seen as symbols of racial insensitivity. Upton's character was drawn as a caricature of a black-faced minstrel—which itself represented a demeaning image of Black people—and her books reinforced racist stereotypes. Later depictions of golliwogs often reflected negative and deeply offensive attitudes about people of African descent. Many New Zealanders fondly remember playing with golliwogs as children and some people still defend their right to make and sell them. However, while they were once considered acceptable many people now regard golliwogs as offensive because they perpetuate the sorts of stereotypes that underpin racism." https://collections.tepapa.govt.nz/object/1470631. Museum of New Zealand/Te Papa Tongarewa (accessed April 15, 2023).

14 "The 1895 publication of Florence K. Upton and Bertha Upton's *The Adventures of Two Dutch Dolls and a "Golliwog"* introduces an additional and subsequently pervasive characterization of the African person. [...] modeled on a minstrel doll Florence Upton acquired as a child from "an American Fair." "[T]he origins of Upton's golliwog are firmly grounded in American and British racist popular culture." Donna Varga and Rhoda Zuk, "Golliwogs and Teddy Bears: Embodied Racism in Children's Popular Culture," *Popular Culture* 46, no. 3 (2013): 653.
15 R. Macgregor, "The Appropriation of a Commercial Trademark: The Golliwog as a Cultural Marker," *Children's Folklore Review* 33 (2011), 51.
16 Derricks, *Buy Golly*, 16.
17 James Joyce, *Ulysses*, rev. ed. (New York: Random House, 1986 [1922]), 338.
18 For extended commentary on this encounter, see Casey Lawrence, "'The Link between Nations and Generations': Cissy Caffrey as Racialized and Sexualized Other in James Joyce's *Ulysses*," *Joyce Studies Annual* 2018: 108–21.
19 Homi Bhabha, "Of Mimicry and Man: The Ambivalence of Colonial Discourse," *October* 28 (1984): 125–33.
20 Paul Ricœur, *Freud and Philosophy: An Essay on Interpretation*, trans. Denis Savage (New Haven, CT: Yale University Press, 2008).
21 Eve Kosofsky Sedgwick first offered an alternative to the hermeneutics of suspicion in *Touching Feeling: Affect, Pedagogy, Performativity* (Durham, NC: Duke University Press, 2003). The discussion of the hermeneutics of suspicion and reparative reading gained a lot of traction following the publication of Sedgwick's book. Stephen Best and Sharon Marcus proposed the practice of "Surface Reading: An Introduction," *Representations* 108, no. 1 (2009): 1–21. Heather Love amplified Sedgwick's theory in "Truth and Consequences: On Paranoid Reading and Reparative Reading," *Criticism* 52, no. 2 (2010): 235–41. Rita Felski proposed a turn to postcritique in *The Limits of Critique* (Chicago: University of Chicago Press, 2015). Franco Moretti explored the alternative offered by digital interventions in *Distant Reading* (London: Verso, 2013). While Caroline Levine presented the crucial role of form in aesthetic politics, her theory is more reparative than suspicious in *Forms: Whole, Rhythm, Hierarchy, Network* (Princeton, NJ: Princeton University Press, 2015).
22 Sedgwick, *Touching Feeling*, 149–50.
23 Sedgwick, *Touching Feeling*, 150–51.
24 Ta-Nehisi Coates, "The Case for Reparations," *The Atlantic*, June 2014. www.theatlantic.com/magazine/archive/2014/06/the-case-for-reparations/361631/ (accessed April 15, 2023).
25 Gérard Genette, *Paratexts: Thresholds of Interpretation* (Cambridge: Cambridge University Press, 1997).

26 James Joyce explored the commonalities between literary interpretation and Talmudic conversation in the "Night Lessons" chapter of *Finnegans Wake*.

27 Fyodor Dostoyevsky, *The Brothers Karamazov*, trans. David McDuff (Harmondsworth: Penguin, 1993), 177.

28 Emmanuel Levinas, *Ethics and Infinity: Conversations with Philippe Nemo*, trans. Richard A. Cohen (Pittsburgh, PA: Duquesne University Press, 1985), 196. Levinas, *Otherwise than Being*, 146.

29 For example, when I am frustrated by someone's lack of gravitas, but reminding myself of their potential, I often think of W. H. Auden's description of W. B. Yeats, "you were silly like us." And I am comforted. As literary critics we will want to make certain not to distort the text even as we incorporate its language into our own consciousness. I am, for example, less accommodating of a decontextualized citation of another line from the same poem, "For poetry makes nothing happen," which is distorted without subsequent lines that claim poetry "survives,/A way of happening, a mouth." W. H. Auden, "In Memory of W. B. Yeats," *Collected Poems*, ed. Edward Mendelson (New York: Vintage 1991), 247.

30 Arthur Cools, "The Anarchy of Literature," in Michael Fagenblat and Arthur Cools, eds., *Levinas and Literature: New Directions* (Berlin: De Gruyter, 2021), 8. Here reduction as a principle draws on the Latin root of the word "to bring back" in which the scene brings back the narrative as a whole in its fundamental core rather than its distracting details. Given my own dedication to the formal complexity of textual instances, I find this scenic approach problematic while at the same time admitting that much of my own critical intervention is to reduce in this sense, to reveal an essential idea in the complexity of its textual manifestation. Cools provides two examples of this scenic method: "the drapes (representative of the power of institutions that guarantee the meaningful world) that are ablaze and that fall (their representative function and the power of institutions have collapsed)." Regarding *Macbeth* as it is referred to in *Existence and Existents*, Cools notes that "it is not the main character and his dispositions to act that attract Levinas's attention, but rather the experience of the spectacular presence of existence at the margins of world," "Anarchy of Literature," 9.

31 Cools, "Anarchy of Literature," 8.

32 Anna D. Whyte, *Change Your Sky* (London: Hogarth Press, 1935), 284. Perceiving the room as venomous recalls the prevalent use of poisons during the period. "The Medici reign over Tuscany began during a period of rampant poisonings of political figures, and amidst an expanding field of available poisons due to both global trade networks and the spread of alchemical experimentation." Sheila Barker, "Poisons and the Prince: Toxicology and Statecraft at the Medici Grand Ducal Court," in *Toxicology*

in the Middle Ages and Renaissance, ed. P. Wexler (London: Academic Press, 2017), 71.
33 Elvira Grifi, *Saunterings in Florence: A New Artistic and Practical Handbook for English and American Tourists* (London: Kessinger Publishing, 1899), 162.
34 Whyte, *Change Your Sky*, 289.

Chapter Five: Interrogating the Ethics of Cosmopolitanism in Stella Benson's Travel Writing *Shinjini Chattopadhyay*

1 Melissa Sullivan and Sophie Blanch, "Introduction: The Middlebrow—Within or Without Modernism," *Modernist Cultures* 6, no. 1 (2011), 2.
2 Virginia Woolf, "Middlebrow," in *The Death of the Moth and Other Essays* (London: Hogarth Press, 1947), 115.
3 Woolf, "Middlebrow," 115.
4 Woolf, "Middlebrow," 115.
5 Faye Hammill, *Women, Celebrity, and Literary Culture Between the Wars* (Austin: University of Texas Press, 2007), 12.
6 Hammill, *Women, Celebrity, and Literary Culture*, 6.
7 Sullivan and Blanch, "Introduction," 5.
8 Bruce Robbins and Paulo Lemos Horta, "Introduction," in *Cosmopolitanisms*, ed. Bruce Robbins and Paulo Lemos Horta (New York: New York University Press, 2017), 2. Emphasis added.
9 Janet Lyon, "Cosmopolitanism and Modernism," in *The Oxford Handbook of Global Modernisms*, ed. Mark Wollaeger and Matt Eatough (New York: Oxford University Press, 2012), 389.
10 Eddy Kent and Terri Tomsky, "Introduction," in *Negative Cosmopolitanism: Cultures and Politics of World Citizenship after Globalization*, ed. Eddy Kent and Terri Tomsky (Montreal: McGill-Queen's University Press, 2017), 10.
11 Jessica Berman, "Modernist Cosmopolitanism," in *A History of the Modernist Novel*, ed. Gregory Castle (New York: Cambridge University Press, 2015), 429.
12 Berman, "Modernist Cosmopolitanism," 429.
13 Alexandra Peat, *Travel and Modernist Literature: Sacred and Ethical Journeys* (New York: Routledge, 2011), 4.
14 Tim Youngs, "Travelling Modernists," in *The Oxford Handbook of Modernisms*, ed. Peter Brooker, Andrzej Gąsiorek, Deborah Longworth, and Andrew Thacker (New York: Oxford University Press, 2010), 270.
15 David Farley, "Modernist Travel Writing," in *The Routledge Companion to Travel Writing*, ed. Carl Thompson (New York: Routledge, 2019), 279.
16 Faye Hammill and Michelle Smith, *Magazines, Travel, and Middlebrow Culture: Canadian Periodicals in English and French, 1925–1960* (Liverpool: Liverpool University Press, 2015), 1.

17 Benson, quoted by Katrina Gulliver, "Stella Benson (1892–1933)," *Modern Women in China and Japan: Gender, Feminism and Global Modernity Between the Wars* (London: I.B. Tauris, 2012), 70.
18 Gulliver, "Stella Benson," 56–57.
19 Gulliver, "Stella Benson," 70.
20 Debra Rae Cohen, "The Secret World: Stella Benson Re-Genres the War Story," *Remapping the Home Front: Locating Citizenship in British Women's Great War Fiction* (Boston: Northeastern University Press, 2002), 48.
21 Klaudia Hiu Yen Lee, "'Wherefore Remember Pain?': Women and Transnational Crossing in Stella Benson's *I Pose* and *The Poor Man*," *English Studies* 101, no. 5 (2020): 570.
22 Walter D. Mignolo, "The Many Faces of Cosmo-polis: Border Thinking and Critical Cosmopolitanism," *Public Culture* 12, no. 3 (2000), 723.
23 Kwame Anthony Appiah, *Cosmopolitanism: Ethics in a World of Strangers* (New York: W. W. Norton, 2006), xv.
24 Nicola Humble, *The Feminine Middlebrow Novel, 1920s to 1950s: Class, Domesticity, and Bohemianism* (Oxford: Oxford University Press, 2001), 5.
25 Stella Benson, *The Little World* (London: Macmillan, 1925), 45.
26 Benson, *The Little World*, 46.
27 Martha Nussbaum, "Patriotism and Cosmopolitanism," *Boston Review* 19, no. 5 (1994): 4.
28 Susan Bassnett, "Travel Writing and Gender," in *The Cambridge Companion to Travel Writing*, ed. Peter Hulme and Tim Youngs (Cambridge: Cambridge University Press, 2002), 225.
29 Robert Aldrich, "Gender and Travel Writing," in *The Cambridge History of Travel Writing*, ed. Nandini Das and Tim Youngs (New York: Cambridge University Press, 2019), 522.
30 Benson, *The Little World*, 86.
31 Benson, *The Little World*, 32.
32 Benson, *The Little World*, 146.
33 Bassnett, "Travel Writing and Gender," 234.
34 Gulliver, "Stella Benson," 59.
35 Benson, *The Little World*, 32.
36 Benson, *The Little World*, 252.
37 Benson, *The Little World*, 101–2.
38 Berman, "Modernist Cosmopolitanism," 430.
39 Benson, *The Little World*, 23.
40 Benson, *The Little World*, 36.
41 Benson, *The Little World*, 105.
42 Benson, *The Little World*, 81.
43 Benson, *The Little World*, 84.
44 Benson, *The Little World*, 39.

45 Benson, *The Little World*, 60.
46 Benson, *The Little World*, 230.
47 Appiah, *Cosmopolitanism*, 98–99.
48 Benson, *The Little World*, 35.
49 Bassnett, "Travel Writing and Gender," 227.
50 Aldrich, "Gender and Travel Writing," 524.
51 Isabelle Bauche Massieu, *Népal et pays himalayens* (Paris: Librairie Félix Alcan, 1914), 1.
52 Benson, *The Little World*, 56–57.
53 Benson, *The Little World*, 107.
54 Benson, *The Little World*, 150.
55 Appiah, *Cosmopolitanism*, 113.
56 Benson, *The Little World*, 39–40.
57 Benson, *The Little World*, 41.
58 For a detailed history of the colonial occupation and conflicts in Macao, see Zhidong Hao, *Macau: History and Society* (Hong Kong: Hong Kong University Press, 2011).
59 Benson, *The Little World*, 267.
60 Benson, *The Little World*, 67.
61 Benson, *The Little World*, 305.
62 Thomas Bender, "The Cosmopolitan Experience and its Uses," in Robbins and Horta, *Cosmopolitanisms*, 121.

Chapter Six: Wittgenstein's Modernism: Apocalypse and Ethics
Ben Ware

1 Immanuel Kant, "The End of All Things," trans. Allen W. Wood, in *Religion and Rational Theology*, ed. Allen W. Wood and George di Giovanni (Cambridge: Cambridge University Press, 1996).
2 Ludwig Wittgenstein, *Tractatus Logico-Philosophicus*, trans. C. K. Ogden (London: Routledge, 2000), §6.54.
3 Terry Eagleton, "Introduction to Wittgenstein," in *Wittgenstein: The Terry Eagleton Script/The Derek Jarman Film* (London: BFI Publishing, 1993), 5.
4 Terry Eagleton, "My Wittgenstein," in *The Eagleton Reader* (Oxford: Blackwell, 1998), 336.
5 Marjorie Perloff, *Wittgenstein's Ladder: Poetic Language and the Strangeness of the Ordinary* (Chicago: University of Chicago Press, 1996), 15.
6 See Stanley Cavell, *The World Viewed: Reflections on the Ontology of Film* (Cambridge, MA: Harvard University Press, 1979), 14.
7 Letter, Ludwig Wittgenstein to Ludwig von Ficker (October 1919), cited in Ludwig Wittgenstein, *Prototractatus*, ed. B. F. McGuinness, T. Nyberg, and G. H. von Wright, trans. D. F. Pears and B. F. McGuinness (London: Routledge & Kegan Paul, 1971), 14n2.

8   Letter, Gottlob Frege to Ludwig Wittgenstein (September 16, 1919), in *Loneliness*, Boston University Studies in the Philosophy of Religion 19, ed. Leroy S. Rouner (Notre Dame, IN: University of Notre Dame Press, 1998), 91.
9   *Gilles Deleuze from A to Z*, directed by Pierre-André Boutang, trans Charles J. Stivale (Semiotext(e)/Foreign Agents, 2012). www.youtube.com/playlist?list=PLiR8NqajHNPbaX2rBoA2z6IPGpU0IPlS2 (accessed April 15, 2023). The program comprises a series of 26 interviews with Deleuze, in which each letter of the alphabet evokes a word: From A ("Animal") to "Zig Zag." The letter "W," for Deleuze evokes "Wittgenstein."
10 Gilles Deleuze, *Difference and Repetition*, trans. Paul Patton (New York: Columbia University Press, 1994), xvi; Gilles Deleuze and Félix Guattari, "Treatise on Nomadology—The War Machine," *A Thousand Plateaus: Capitalism and Schizophrenia*, trans. Brian Massumi (London: Athlone Press, 1988), 351–423.
11 Gilles Deleuze and Félix Guattari, *What is Philosophy?*, trans. Graham Burchell and Hugh Tomlinson (London: Verso, 1994), 67.
12 Theodor W. Adorno, *Hegel: Three Studies*, trans. Shierry Weber Nicholsen (Cambridge, MA: MIT Press, 1993), 7.
13 Adorno, *Hegel*, 101.
14 Herbert Marcuse, *One Dimensional Man: Studies in the Ideology of Advanced Industrial Society* (London: Routledge & Kegan Paul, 1991), 196.
15 Ludwig Wittgenstein, *Culture and Value*, trans. Peter Winch (Chicago: Chicago University Press, 1980), 24. Subsequent citations from *Culture and Value* refer also to a series of revised and updated editions.
16 M. O'C. Drury, "Some Notes on Conversations with Wittgenstein," in *Ludwig Wittgenstein: Personal Recollections*, ed. Rush Rhees (Oxford: Blackwell, 1981), 94.
17 Alain Badiou, *Wittgenstein's Antiphilosophy*, trans. Bruno Bosteels (London: Verso, 2011), 49, 67.
18 Badiou, *Wittgenstein's Antiphilosophy*, 156.
19 Badiou, *Wittgenstein's Antiphilosophy*, 80.
20 Badiou, *Wittgenstein's Antiphilosophy*, 80.
21 Ludwig Wittgenstein, *Culture and Value*, rev. 2nd ed. (Oxford: Blackwell, 1998), 3.
22 Walter Benjamin, "The Destructive Character," *Selected Writings*, trans. Rodney Livingstone et al. vol. 2, part 2, *1931–1934*, ed. Michael W. Jennings, Howard Eiland, and Gary Smith (Cambridge, MA: Belknap Press, 2005), 541–42.
23 Ludwig Wittgenstein, *Philosophical Investigations*, trans, G. E. M. Anscombe (Oxford: Blackwell, 2001), §118.
24 Wittgenstein, *Tractatus*, §6.54.

25 Wittgenstein, *Culture and Value* (1980), 21.
26 Ludwig Wittgenstein, *Public and Private Occasions*, ed. James Klagge and Alfred Nordmann (Oxford: Rowman & Littlefield, 2003), 73.
27 Ludwig Wittgenstein, *The Big Typescript* (Oxford: Blackwell, 2005), 305, 362.
28 Wittgenstein, *Culture and Value* (1998), 55–56.
29 Gertrude Stein, "Reflections on the Atomic Bomb" (1946), *Yale Poetry Review* (1947). www.writing.upenn.edu/~afilreis/88/stein-atom-bomb.html (accessed April 4, 2020).
30 Wittgenstein, *Culture and Value* (1998), 64.
31 Wittgenstein, *Culture and Value*, 2nd ed. (Chicago: Chicago University Press, 1984), 63; and Wittgenstein, *Investigations*, x.
32 Theodor Adorno and Max Horkheimer, *Dialectic of Enlightenment*, trans. John Cumming (London: Verso, 1997), 3.
33 For a reading of Wittgenstein's later work in relation to politics and the transformation of existing forms of life, see Ben Ware, "Right in Front of Our Eyes: Aspect-Perception, Ethics and the Utopian Imagination in Wittgenstein's *Philosophical Investigations*," *Modernism, Ethics and the Political Imagination: Living Wrong Life Rightly* (London: Palgrave Macmillan, 2017), 7–36.
34 Günther Anders, "Theses for the Atomic Age," *Massachusetts Review* 3, no. 2 (1962): 496. On Anders's use of the universalizing pronoun "we": we might argue that it serves (or attempts to serve) the purpose of an emancipatory interpellation.
35 Anders, "Theses for the Atomic Age."
36 Günther Anders, "Reflections on the H Bomb," *Dissent* 3, no. 2 (1956): 146.
37 Ibid. Emphasis added.
38 Anders, "Theses for the Atomic Age," 493.
39 Anders, "Theses for the Atomic Age," 498.
40 The phrase is from Jean-Pierre Dupuy, one of Anders's most sophisticated readers. See, for example, Jean-Pierre Dupuy, "The Precautionary Principle and Enlightened Doomsaying: Rational Choice Before the Apocalypse," *Occasion: Interdisciplinary Studies in the Humanities* 1, no. 1 (October 15, 2009): 1–13.
41 Cited in Jean-Pierre Dupuy, *The Mark of the Sacred*, trans. M. B. Debevoise (Stanford, CA: Stanford University Press, 2013), 203.
42 Anders, "Theses for the Atomic Age," 494.
43 Wittgenstein, *Culture and Value* (1998), 72.
44 The phrase is from Ludwig Wittgenstein, *Remarks on the Foundations of Mathematics*, trans. G. E. M. Anscombe, ed. G. H. von Wright, Rush Rhees, and G. E. M. Anscombe (Oxford: Blackwell, 1978), 132.
45 Anders, "Theses for the Atomic Age," 505.

46 Rush Rhees, ed., *Recollections of Wittgenstein* (Oxford: Oxford University Press, 1984), 201–2.
47 Wittgenstein, *Investigations*, §§193, 466, 420.
48 Wittgenstein, *Investigations*, §§107, 98, 91.
49 Ludwig Wittgenstein, *The Blue and Brown Books* (Oxford: Blackwell, 1969), 18.
50 Wittgenstein, *Investigations*, §103.
51 Wittgenstein, *Investigations*, §129.
52 Fredric Jameson, "Utopia as Replication," in *Valences of the Dialectic* (London: Verso, 2009), 434.

Chapter Seven: Charles Reznikoff's *Testimony*: Ethics and the Reader   Kieran Dolin

1 Charles Reznikoff, *Testimony: The United States (1885–1915): Recitative*, 2 vols. (paginated continuously) (Boston: Black Sparrow, 2015).
2 David Perkins, *A History of Modern Poetry*, vol. 2, *Modernism and After* (Cambridge, MA: Belknap Press, 1987), 326.
3 Geneviève Cohen-Cheminet, "Charles Reznikoff: New World Poetics," in *Strategies of Difference in Modern Poetry: Case Studies in Poetic Composition*, ed. Pierre Lagayette (Madison, NJ: Fairleigh-Dickinson University Press, 1998), 127, 130, 132.
4 Benjamin Watson, "Reznikoff's *Testimony*," *Legal Studies Forum* 29, no. 1 (2005): 74.
5 Ranen Omer-Sherman, "Charles Reznikoff," *Encyclopedia of American Poetry: The Twentieth Century*, ed. Eric L. Harelson (London: Taylor & Francis, 2001), 603, 604.
6 Ravit Reichman, *The Affective Life of Law: Legal Modernism and the Literary Imagination* (Stanford, CA: Stanford University Press, 2009), 1.
7 Reichman, *Affective Life of Law*, 6.
8 Quoted by Kenneth Burke, "Introduction" to the 1934 prose edition of *Testimony* (New York: Objectivist Press, 1934), reprinted in *Testimony: The United States (1885–1915)*, 534.
9 Reznikoff, *Testimony: The United States (1885–1915)*, 389. The poem is from Part Four: The North, Machine Age, section III, number viii.
10 Burke, "Introduction," *Testimony* (1934), 535.
11 Burke, "Introduction," *Testimony* (1934), 536.
12 Reproduced by Watson, "Reznikoff's *Testimony*," 76.
13 See Alan Golding, "Macro, Micro, Material: Rachel Blau DuPlessis' *Drafts* and the Post-Objectivist Serial Poem," *Blackbox Manifold* 16 (2016): 1–16.
14 Watson, "Reznikoff's *Testimony*," 76.
15 Cohen-Cheminet, "Charles Reznikoff: New World Poetics," 130.

16 Charles Reznikoff, *Testimony: The United States 1885–1890: Recitative* (New York: New Directions, 1965); *Testimony: The United States 1891–1900: Recitative* (New York: Charles Reznikoff, 1968).
17 Watson, "Reznikoff's Testimony," 76.
18 Quoted by Watson, "Reznikoff's Testimony," 76.
19 Reznikoff, *Testimony: The United States (1885–1915)*, xv.
20 My thanks to Richard Read and Matthew Bulfer, whose questions helped sharpen my awareness of this issue.
21 Michael Eskin, "Introduction: The 'Double Turn' to Ethics and Literature," *Poetics Today* 25, no. 1 (2004): 559.
22 G. Matthew Jenkins, *Poetic Obligation: Ethics in Experimental American Poetry After 1945* (Iowa City: University of Iowa Press, 2008), 3.
23 Jil Larson, *Ethics and Narrative in the English Novel, 1880–1914* (Cambridge: Cambridge University Press, 2001); Melba Cuddy-Keane, "Ethics," in *Modernism and Theory: A Critical Debate*, ed. Stephen Ross (London: Taylor & Francis, 2008).
24 Cuddy-Keane, "Ethics," 210.
25 Cuddy-Keane, "Ethics," 217.
26 Jenkins, *Poetic Obligation*, 4, citing Rachel Blau DuPlessis and Peter Quartermain, eds., *The Objectivist Nexus* (Tuscaloosa: University of Alabama Press, 1999).
27 George Oppen, letter to Serge Fauchereau, quoted by Jerome J. McGann, *The Point is to Change It* (Tuscaloosa: University of Alabama Press, 2007), 67, from Serge Fauchereau, "Three Oppen Letters," *Ironwood* 5 (1975): 78–87.
28 William Carlos Williams, quoted by McGann, *The Point*, 222n2.
29 DuPlessis and Quartermain, *Objectivist Nexus*, 3.
30 Rachel Blau DuPlessis, *The Selected Letters of George Oppen* (Durham, NC: Duke University Press, 1990), quoted by Monique Claire Vescia, *Depression Glass: Documentary Photography and the Medium of the Camera-Eye in Charles Reznikoff, George Oppen and William Carlos Williams* (London: Routledge, 2006), xix.
31 L. S. Dembo and Charles Reznikoff, "Charles Reznikoff," *Contemporary Literature* 10, no. 2 (1969): 194–95.
32 Dembo and Reznikoff, "Reznikoff," 193.
33 Reznikoff, *Testimony: The United States (1885–1915)*, 5. The poem is from Part One: The South, I.
34 Reznikoff, *Testimony: The United States (1885–1915)*, 49. The poem is from Part One: The South, section V, "Boys and Girls."
35 For a discussion of parataxis in Reznikoff, see Charles Bernstein, "Reznikoff's Nearness," in *My Way: Speeches and Poems* (Chicago: University of Chicago Press, 1999), 197–228.
36 Derek Attridge, *The Singularity of Literature* (London: Routledge, 2004), 126–27.

37 Paul Ricœur, *Oneself as Another*, trans. Kathleen Blamey (Chicago: University of Chicago Press, 1992), 170. Ricœur notes that this usage is a conventional one.
38 In formulating this argument, I have drawn on Reznikoff's interview with L. S. Dembo, note 31, above, and on John Michael's argument in "Lyric History: Temporality, Rhetoric and the Ethics of Poetry," *New Literary History* 48 (2017): 265–84, that the ethical and political effect of poetry depends on a future engagement of a reader.
39 John Fabian Witt, *The Accidental Republic: Crippled Workingmen, Destitute Widows, and the Remaking of American Law* (Cambridge, MA: Harvard University Press, 2004), 21.
40 Witt, *Accidental Republic*, 25.
41 See Witt, *Accidental Republic*, 37n88, and 131n18, on the inclusion of Hine's photographs in Crystal Eastman's 1910 treatise, *Work-Accidents and the Law*.
42 Monique Claire Vescia, *Depression Glass*, 11.
43 Vescia, *Depression Glass*, 39.
44 Bernstein, "Reznikoff's Nearness," 221, 217, 223.
45 Bernstein, "Reznikoff's Nearness," 216, 224, 225.
46 Cohen-Cheminet, "New World Poetics," 138. The concept of "second-degree witness" is derived from Jewish philosophy and the work of Shoshana Felman and Dori Laub. For another reading of Reznikoff's *Testimony* in terms of Jewish intellectual history, see Daniel Listoe, "'With all malice': The Testimonial Objectives of Charles Reznikoff," *American Literary History* 26 (2014): 110–31.
47 Bernstein, "Reznikoff's Nearness," 220.
48 Roland Barthes, *Camera Lucida: Reflections on Photography*, trans. Richard Howard (London: Fontana, 1984), 26, 45, 49.
49 Michael, "Lyric History," 275.
50 Bernstein, "Reznikoff's Nearness," 204, quoted by Vescia, *Depression Glass*, 48.
51 For Reznikoff's aims, see n. 8, above. On accumulation, see Vescia, *Depression Glass*, 50.
52 Bernstein, "Reznikoff's Nearness," 207.
53 Reznikoff, *Testimony: The United States (1885–1915)*, 5–6. The poem is from Part One: The South, II.
54 Reznikoff, *Testimony: The United States (1885–1915)*, 501–2. The poem is from Part Five: The South, number IV.
55 Reichman, *Affective Life of Law*, 4, 165.
56 Walter Benjamin, "The Storyteller," quoted by Reichman, *Affective Life of Law*, 4.
57 Reznikoff, *Testimony: The United States (1885–1915)*, 230. The poem is from Part Two: The North.

58 Reznikoff, *Testimony: The United States (1885–1915)*, 233.
59 Ricœur, *Oneself as Another*, 245.
60 Paul Ricœur, *Time and Narrative*, vol. 3, trans. Kathleen Blamey and David Pellauer (Chicago: University of Chicago Press, 1988), 188.
61 Michael, "Lyric History," 271–73.

Chapter Eight: What's Love Got To Do With It? Law and Literature in 1920s British Somaliland *Katherine Isobel Baxter*

1 See Anthony Kirk-Greene, "Forging a Relationship with the Colonial Administrative Service, 1921–1939," in *Margery Perham and British Rule in Africa*, ed. Mary Bull (London: Frank Cass, 1991), 73.
2 Roland Oliver, "Margery Perham," *African Affairs* 81, no. 324 (1982): 409.
3 Margery Perham, *Major Dane's Garden* (London: Rex Collings, 1920), unpag.
4 See *British Somaliland and Sokotra*, ed. G. W. Prothero (London: H. M. Stationery Office, 1920), 1; "Geographical Record," *Geographical Review* 26, no. 3 (1936): 504.
5 See, for example, C. V. A. Peel, *Somaliland: Being an Account of Two Expeditions into the Far Interior* (London: F. E. Robinson, 1900).
6 See Agnes Herbert, *Two Dianas in Somaliland: The Record of a Shooting Trip* (London: John Lane, 1908).
7 Major H. Rayne, *Sun, Sand and Somals: Leaves from the Notebook of a District Commissioner in British Somaliland* (London: H. F. & G. Witherby, 1921), 199.
8 Between 1905 and 1920, the Colonial Office were obliged to subsidize the protectorate with over a million pounds of imperial grants-in-aid. See *Colonial Reports—Annual. No. 1051, Somaliland, Report for the Year 1919–20* (London: H. M. Stationery Office, 1920), 3.
9 For a more detailed account of the nineteenth-century European scramble for the Horn of Africa, see Patrick K. Kakwenzire, "Colonial Rule in the British Somaliland Protectorate, 1905–1939," Ph.D. thesis, University of London, 1976, 32–58.
10 See, for example, the Royal Geographical Society's report on the 1898 Abyssinian treaty which notes that "tribes owning grazing-grounds on both sides of the boundary [...] are not to be interfered with in their migrations," "Treaty with Abyssinia," *Geographical Journal* 11, no. 3 (1898): 294.
11 For an illuminating examination of such border disputes and their racialization, see Daniel K. Thompson, "Border Crimes, Extraterritorial Jurisdiction, and the Racialization of Sovereignty in the Ethiopia–British Somaliland Borderlands During the 1920s," *Africa* 90, no. 4 (2020): 746–73.

12 Kakwenzire's thesis provides a detailed account of this period in British Somaliland history.
13 While Douglas Jardine's *The Mad Mullah of Somaliland* became the best known immediate narrative of the war, the first book to provide an account was, coincidentally, by Perham's brother-in-law, Major Rayne, whose memoir ends with a twenty-eight-page chapter, "The Breaking of the Mad Mullah." See Douglas Jardine, *The Mad Mullah of Somaliland* (London: Herbert Jenkins, 1923).
14 Patricia Pugh, "Margery Freda Perham, 1895–1982," in *Proceedings of the British Academy* 111 (2001): 617.
15 See, for example, Pugh, "Margery Freda Perham," 620.
16 Oliver, "Margery Perham," 409.
17 For a fuller discussion of District Commissioner fiction, see Katherine Isobel Baxter, *Imagined States: Law and Literature in Nigeria 1900–1966* (Edinburgh: Edinburgh University Press, 2019).
18 Protagonists who enjoy popular colonial and adventure fiction appear repeatedly across a range of higher-brow and modernist literature at the turn of the century and through the interwar period. Ostensibly, such reading is used to suggest a weakness in the protagonist (e.g., Jim's "course of light holiday literature," which inspires his "vocation for the sea" in *Lord Jim*). Nonetheless, such references are also deployed to signal a flattering intellectual distinction between the literary work in the reader's hand and the adventure fiction that the protagonist enjoys. Joseph Conrad, *Lord Jim: A Tale* (Edinburgh: William Blackwood & Sons, 1900), 4.
19 Perham, *Major Dane's Garden*, 61, 65.
20 Perham, *Major Dane's Garden*, 359.
21 Patrick Howarth, *Play Up and Play the Game: The Heroes of Popular Fiction* (London: Eyre Methuen, 1973), 13–14.
22 See Hsu-Ming Teo, *Desert Passions: Orientalism and Romance Novels* (Austin: University of Texas Press, 2012).
23 See Perham, *Major Dane's Garden*, 285: "She was wearing khaki trousers, and one boyish leg was twisted under the other. Her slender waist was buckled by a stout leather belt. He felt a rush of tenderness for the child in her which so loved these man's trappings and wore them so bravely."
24 Perham, *Major Dane's Garden*, 207, 209–10.
25 Robert Miles, "What is a Romantic Novel?" *NOVEL: A Forum on Fiction* 34, no. 2 (2001): 186. John Schwarzmantel, *The Age of Ideology: Political Ideologies from the American Revolution to Postmodern Times* (Basingstoke: Macmillan, 1998), 63. Miles's definition of the romantic sits at odds with high modernists like T. E. Hulme, but it chimes in interesting ways with the negotiations of genre that we find in novelists of the period like Conrad and Ford, whose works repeatedly explore the ethical fault

lines of political and personal ideology. T. E. Hulme, "Romanticism and Classicism," *Speculations: Essays on Humanism and the Philosophy of Art* (London: Kegan Paul, Trench, Trubner & Co., 1936), 111–40.

26 Miles, "What is a Romantic Novel?" 196.
27 Miles, "What is a Romantic Novel?" 186.
28 Perham, *Major Dane's Garden*, 176.
29 Perham, *Major Dane's Garden*, 147.
30 Perham, *Major Dane's Garden*, 343.
31 Perham, *Major Dane's Garden*, 360.
32 "In Somaliland," *New York Times Book Review*, June 6, 1926, 9.
33 Chinua Achebe, "An Image of Africa," *Research in African Literatures* 9, no. 1 (1978): 1–15.
34 Achebe, "Image of Africa," 9.
35 See *Somaliland, Report for the Year 1919–20*, 4.
36 Rayne, *Sun, Sand and Somals*, 215. Earlier in his memoir, Rayne also notes the "native gardens" at Tokusha, which are "irrigated from the wells" there (135).
37 Perham, *Major Dane's Garden*, unpag.
38 A. Beeby Thompson, "The Water-Supply of British Somaliland," *Geographical Journal* 101, no. 4 (1943): 154–60.
39 Thompson, "Water-Supply of British Somaliland," 160.
40 Thompson, "Water-Supply of British Somaliland," 160. Emphases added.
41 Thompson, "Water-Supply of British Somaliland," 154.
42 Thompson, "Water-Supply of British Somaliland," 154. Emphases added.

Chapter Nine: Modern Tort Law and Anthony Powell's *A Dance to the Music of Time* Mimi Lu

1 Wai Chee Dimock, *Residues of Justice: Literature, Law, Philosophy* (Berkeley: University of California Press, 1996), 151.
2 Ravit Reichman, *The Affective Life of Law: Legal Modernism and the Literary Imagination* (Stanford, CA: Stanford University Press, 2009), 2.
3 Maria Aristodemou, *Law and Literature: Journeys from Her to Eternity* (Oxford: Oxford University Press, 2000), 9. Original emphasis.
4 See, e.g., Marina MacKay, *Modernism, War, and Violence* (London: Bloomsbury Academic, 2017); Jonathan P. Eburne, *Surrealism and the Art of Crime* (Ithaca, NY: Cornell University Press, 2008); Paul Sheehan, *Modernism and the Aesthetics of Violence* (New York: Cambridge University Press, 2013); Sarah Cole, *At the Violet Hour: Modernism and Violence in England and Ireland* (Oxford: Oxford University Press, 2012); Matthew Levay, *Violent Minds: Modernism and the Criminal* (Cambridge: Cambridge University Press, 2019).

5 Costas Douzinas, "Law and Justice in Postmodernity," in *The Cambridge Companion to Postmodernism*, ed. Steven Connor (Cambridge: Cambridge University Press, 2004), 213.
6 Cited in Zachary Leader, "Friendship, Social Class, and Art in Powell and Amis," *Essays in Criticism* 63, no. 1 (2013): 30.
7 Cited in Isabelle Joyau, *Investigating Powell's* A Dance to the Music of Time (New York: St Martin's Press, 1994), x.
8 Desmond Manderson, *Kangaroo Courts and the Rule of Law—The Legacy of Modernism* (London: Routledge, 2012), 13.
9 Manderson, *Kangaroo Courts and the Rule of Law*, 13.
10 *Donoghue v. Stevenson* [1932] AC 562, at 580.
11 It is worth noting the close alignment of Lord Atkin's principle with both Kantian deontology and biblical precept.
12 The Employer's Liability Act 1880 and the Workmen's Compensation Acts 1897, 1906 reflected parliamentarians' attempts to extend greater protections to employees engaged in risky occupations. Statutory regulation of employer liability and workplace safety in the mid-twentieth century offered additional protection for workers. The Law Reform (Personal Injuries) Act 1948 abolished the doctrine of common employment and the Law Reform (Contributory Negligence) Act 1945 introduced partial remedies in cases where there was contributory negligence from employees.
13 Thomas F. Lambert, Jr., *The Jurisprudence of Hope*, 31 ATLA L.J. 29 (1965).
14 Desmond Manderson, *Proximity, Levinas, and the Soul of Law* (Montreal: McGill-Queen's University Press, 2006), 4.
15 David Hollingshead, "Nonhuman Liability: Charles Chesnutt, Oliver Wendell Holmes, Jr., and the Racial Discourses of Tort Law," *American Literary Realism* 50, no. 2 (2018): 105.
16 Hollingshead, "Nonhuman Liability," 97. Original emphasis.
17 See, e.g., Jason Robert Puskar, *Accident Society: Fiction, Collectivity, and the Production of Chance* (Stanford, CA: Stanford University Press, 2012), 1. In America, for example, the incidence of industrial accidents peaked during the first decade of the twentieth century. In 1908 alone, the Bureau of Labor Statistics estimated around 25,000 worker fatalities. Even though work safety reform efforts were redoubled to address the crisis, in 1913, there were still the same number of industrial casualties, with 36,140 injured or killed on the railroads.
18 Jan-Melissa Schramm, "Wrongs: Negligence, Neighbourliness, and the Duty of Care in Nineteenth-Century Narrative," in *The Cultural History of Law in the Age of Reform*, ed. Ian Ward (Oxford: Hart Publishing 2018), 136.
19 Cited in Joyau, *Investigating Powell's* A Dance to the Music of Time, x.

20 Hilary Spurling and Anthony Powell, *Handbook to Anthony Powell's Music of Time* (London: Heinemann, 1977), xv.
21 Anthony Powell, *A Question of Upbringing: A Novel* (London: Heinemann, 1969), 52.
22 Anthony Powell, *The Kindly Ones* (London: Heinemann, 1962), 2.
23 Reichman, *Affective Life of Law*, 17.
24 Martin Amis, "The American Eagle" (1995), in *The War Against Cliché: Essays and Reviews 1971–2000* (London: Vintage, 2002), 467. Emphasis added.
25 Perry Anderson, "Different Speeds, Same Furies." Review of *Anthony Powell: Dancing to the Music of Time*, by Hilary Spurling, *London Review of Books* 40, no. 14, July 19, 2018.
26 Carla Namwali Serpell, *Seven Modes of Uncertainty* (Cambridge, MA: Harvard University Press, 2014), 11.
27 Joyau, *Investigating Powell's* A Dance to the Music of Time, 143.
28 Virginia Woolf, *To the Lighthouse* (New York: Harcourt, 1981), 63.
29 Hollingshead, "Nonhuman Liability," 99.
30 Sandra Macpherson, *Harm's Way: Tragic Responsibility and the Novel Form* (Baltimore, MD: Johns Hopkins University Press, 2009), 14.
31 D. M. Davis, "An Interview with Anthony Powell," *College English* 24 (1963), 533, cited in Joyau, *Investigating Powell's* A Dance to the Music of Time, 74.
32 Powell, *A Question of Upbringing*, 53.
33 Matthew Levay, *Violent Minds: Modernism and the Criminal* (Cambridge: Cambridge University Press, 2019).
34 Powell, *A Question of Upbringing*, 52.
35 Anthony Powell, *A Buyer's Market* (London: Heinemann, 1967), 207–8.
36 Anthony Powell, *The Acceptance World* (London: Heinemann, 1955), 85.
37 Powell, *A Question of Upbringing*, 77.
38 Powell, *A Question of Upbringing*, 129
39 Powell, *A Buyer's Market*, 96.
40 Powell, *A Question of Upbringing*, 1
41 Powell, *A Question of Upbringing*, 2.
42 Powell, *A Question of Upbringing*, 3.
43 Nicholas Birns, *Understanding Anthony Powell* (Columbia, SC: University of South Carolina Press, 2011), 246.
44 Powell, *A Question of Upbringing*, 229.
45 Powell, *A Buyer's Market*, 152.
46 Powell, *The Acceptance World*, 43.
47 Anthony Powell, *Hearing Secret Harmonies* (London: Heinemann, 1975), 243.
48 Powell, *A Buyer's Market*, 228.
49 Powell, *A Buyer's Market*, 229.

50 Powell, *A Buyer's Market*, 229.
51 Powell, *A Buyer's Market*, 231.
52 Powell, *A Buyer's Market*, 227. Emphasis added.
53 Powell, *A Buyer's Market*, 230.
54 Powell, *A Buyer's Market*, 229.
55 Powell, *A Buyer's Market*, 227.
56 Powell, *A Buyer's Market*, 229.
57 It should be noted that limited public understanding of the law means that Jenkins fails to recognize the possibility that some form of medical negligence during the week that Deacon was in the hospital broke the chain of causation running from the staircase to the fatality altogether.
58 Powell, *A Buyer's Market*, 231.
59 The trope of the hurtling car in post-1930s literature is partly a reaction to the Road Traffic Act 1930. While the statute legislated against offenses of dangerous, reckless, and careless driving, and driving whilst being unfit and under the influence of drink or drugs, it also controversially removed all speed limits on British roads.
60 In fact, in his memoirs, Powell reveals that the genesis of the title, *A Question of Upbringing*, was a personal narrow escape from a collision in the mid-1930s. Anthony Powell, *To Keep the Ball Rolling: The Memoirs of Anthony Powell*, vol. 3, *Faces in My Time* (London: Heinemann, 1980), 38.
61 Anthony Powell, *At Lady Molly's* (London: Heinemann, 1957), 19–20.
62 Powell, *A Question of Upbringing*, 195–96.
63 Powell, *The Kindly Ones*, 163.
64 Powell, *A Buyer's Market*, 22.
65 Anthony Powell, *Temporary Kings* (London: Heinemann, 1973), 252.
66 Anthony Powell, *Hearing Secret Harmonies* (London: Heinemann, 1975), 19–20.
67 Powell, *A Buyer's Market*, 82. "Remoteness" is a key component of the legal test of causation which is used to determine the types of loss caused by a breach of duty. The courts ask whether the kind of damage suffered was reasonably foreseeable by the defendant at the time of the breach.
68 Powell, *A Buyer's Market*, 59.
69 Powell, *The Acceptance World*, 178.
70 Powell, *A Buyer's Market*, 69, 262.
71 Powell, *A Question of Upbringing*, 11.
72 Powell, *A Buyer's Market*, 69.
73 Powell, *A Buyer's Market*, 69.
74 Powell, *A Buyer's Market*, 69–70. Emphasis added.
75 Powell, *A Buyer's Market*, 71.
76 Powell, *A Buyer's Market*, 72.
77 Powell, *A Buyer's Market*, 79.
78 Powell, *A Buyer's Market*, 71.

79 Powell, *A Buyer's Market*, 73.
80 Powell, *A Buyer's Market*, 73.
81 Powell, *Hearing Secret Harmonies*, 43.
82 Powell, *Hearing Secret Harmonies*, 45.
83 Powell, *Hearing Secret Harmonies*, 230.
84 Powell, *Hearing Secret Harmonies*, 46–47.
85 Powell, *Hearing Secret Harmonies*, 109–10.
86 Powell, *Hearing Secret Harmonies*, 111.
87 Powell, *Temporary Kings*, 16.
88 Dimock, *Residues of Justice*, 10.
89 Joyau, *Investigating Powell's* A Dance to the Music of Time, 75.

Chapter Ten: "Criteria of Negro Art": Ethical Negotiations in the Harlem Renaissance Laura Ryan

1 Chicago and Detroit were among the American cities also swept up in this "renaissance"; in Europe, Paris became a significant center of Black culture, attracting writers, musicians, and artists from the United States and the Caribbean in particular. On the importance of Paris, see, for example, Brent Hayes Edwards, *The Practice of Diaspora: Literature, Translation, and the Rise of Black Internationalism* (Cambridge, MA: Harvard University Press, 2003).
2 W. E. B. Du Bois, "The Talented Tenth," in *The Negro Problem: A Series of Articles by Representative American Negroes of Today* (New York: James Pott & Company, 1903). The term "Talented Tenth" was first used by white Northern liberal philanthropists in the final years of the nineteenth century, but it was first brought to wide public attention by Du Bois; it described the prospect that one in ten African Americans—if offered a proper (classical) education—might become race leaders and public intellectuals capable of "inspiring the masses" (63).
3 Alain Locke, ed., "The New Negro," in *The New Negro: Voices of the Harlem Renaissance* (New York: Simon & Schuster, 1997), 3–4.
4 See, for example, Nathan Irvin Huggins, *Harlem Renaissance* (New York: Oxford University Press, 1973) and Houston A. Baker, Jr., *Modernism and the Harlem Renaissance* (Chicago: University of Chicago Press, 1987). Huggins's seminal study argues that the Harlem Renaissance failed both to produce an authentically new or exclusively Black identity or art or to achieve its social and political goals. Baker, conversely, repudiates any approach in which the question "Why did the Harlem Renaissance fail?" is the starting point. For Baker, the strength of the New Negro movement lay in its ability to offer an alternative to mainstream (white) modernism.
5 Du Bois, "Criteria of Negro Art," *The Crisis* 32 (October 1926): 296.
6 Alain Locke, "Art or Propaganda?" *Harlem* 1, no. 1 (November 1928): 12.

7   Leonard Harris, "The Great Debate: W. E. B. Du Bois vs. Alain Locke on the Aesthetic," *Philosophia Africana* 7, no. 1 (2004): 16.
8   Harris, "The Great Debate," 15.
9   Phyllis Wheatley's *Poems on Various Subjects, Religious and Moral* (1773) is credited as the first published book by an African American. Important and popular slave narratives include Frederick Douglass's *Narrative of the Life of Frederick Douglass, an American Slave* (1845); William Wells Brown's *Narrative of William Wells Brown, a Fugitive Slave* (1847); and Harriet Jacobs's *Incidents in the Life of a Slave Girl* (1861).
10 Saidya V. Hartman, *Scenes of Subjection: Terror, Slavery, and Self-Making in Nineteenth-Century America* (New York: Oxford University Press, 1997), 5.
11 Fred Moten, *In the Break: The Aesthetics of the Black Radical Tradition* (Minneapolis: University of Minnesota Press, 2003), 7.
12 Eric Walrond, "Art and Propaganda," in Henry Louis Gates, Jr. and Gene Andrew Jarrett, eds., *The New Negro: Readings on Race, Representation, and African American Culture, 1892–1938* (Princeton, NJ: Princeton University Press, 2007), 255.
13 Locke, "The New Negro," 3–4.
14 Locke, "The New Negro," 4.
15 Locke, "The New Negro," 4, 6, 7. Locke, of course, did not coin the term "New Negro," which had been in use since the late nineteenth century among writers and intellectuals. Booker T. Washington's 1900 *A New Negro for a New Century* is a notable example of its early usage.
16 Du Bois, "Review," *The Crisis* 31 (January 1926): 140–41.
17 Du Bois, "Review," 141.
18 Du Bois, "Review," 141.
19 Jeffrey C. Stewart, *The New Negro: The Life of Alain Locke* (New York: Oxford University Press, 2018), 523.
20 Du Bois, "Criteria," 292.
21 Du Bois, "Criteria," 292. This statement suggests an evolution in Du Bois's thought since his seminal 1903 work, *The Souls of Black Folk*. In that book, he seems to suggest literature as an area in which one can rise above the "color line": "Across the color line I move arm in arm with Balzac and Dumas, where smiling men and welcoming women glide in gilded halls." W. E. B. Du Bois, *The Souls of Black Folk* (New York: Dover, 2012), 67.
22 Du Bois, "Criteria," 296.
23 Locke, "Art or Propaganda?" 12–13.
24 Locke, "Art or Propaganda?" 13.
25 Locke, "Art or Propaganda?" 13.
26 William Stanley Braithwaite, "The Negro in American Literature," in Alain Locke, *The New Negro: An Interpretation* (New York: Albert and Charles Boni, 1925), 44.

27 Toomer, quoted by Frederik L. Rusch, in *A Jean Toomer Reader: Selected Unpublished Writings*, ed. Rusch (New York: Oxford University Press, 1993), 15.
28 Toomer, quoted by Rusch, *Toomer Reader*, 94.
29 Toomer, quoted by Cynthia Earl Kerman and Richard Eldridge, *The Lives of Jean Toomer: A Hunger for Wholeness* (Baton Rouge: Louisiana State University Press, 1987), 112.
30 Alice Walker, reacting to Darwin T. Turner's *The Wayward and the Seeking: A Collection of Writings by Jean Toomer* (Washington, DC: Howard University Press, 1980), later labelled Toomer a "racial opportunist" and expressed her disappointment that "the man who wrote so piercingly of 'Negro' life in 'Cane' chose to live his own life as a white man, while Hughes, Hurston, Du Bois, and other black writers were celebrating the blackness in themselves." See Alice Walker, "The Divided Life of Jean Toomer," *New York Times Book Review*, July 13, 1980, 16, 11. More recently, much discussion of Toomer's supposed passing was generated by the 2011 publication of a new Norton Critical Edition of *Cane*, edited by Rudolph P. Byrd and Henry Louis Gates, Jr. In an interview preceding the edition's publication, Gates opined that Toomer "was running away from a cultural identity that he had inherited," attributing his lack of literary success after *Cane* to the fact that "he spent so much time running away from his identity." Quoted by Felicia R. Lee, "Scholars Say Chronicler of Black Life Passed for White," *New York Times*, December 26, 2010.
31 Sinéad Moynihan, *Passing Into the Present: Contemporary American Fiction of Racial and Gender Passing* (Manchester: Manchester University Press, 2010), 8.
32 Moynihan, *Passing Into the Present*, 2.
33 James Weldon Johnson, *The Autobiography of an Ex-Colored Man* (New York: Dover, 1995), 100.
34 Hughes, *The Ways of White Folks* (New York: Vintage, 1990), 54.
35 Rudolph P. Byrd and Henry Louis Gates, Jr., eds., "Introduction" to *Cane* (New York: W. W. Norton, 2011), lxvii–lxviii. That Toomer's mother's maiden name is recorded incorrectly on the 1931 marriage certificate indicates that he may not have provided the information himself; Byrd and Gates do not consider that the registrar may have assumed a light-skinned man marrying a white woman to be white.
36 Henry Louis Gates, Jr., *Figures in Black: Words, Signs, and the "Racial" Self* (New York: Oxford University Press, 1989), 208.
37 George Hutchinson, "Jean Toomer and American Racial Discourse," *Texas Studies in Literature and Language* 35, no. 2 (1993): 229.
38 Jean Toomer, "On Being an American," Jean Toomer Papers, Beinecke Rare Book and Manuscript Library, Yale University, Box 20, Folder 513, 20–21.

39. Jean Toomer, "On Being an American," in Turner, *The Wayward and the Seeking*, 121.
40. Toomer, "The Blue Meridian," in Turner, *The Wayward and the Seeking*, 232.
41. Toomer, *Cane* (Norton Critical Edition), 106.
42. Matthew Pratt Guterl, "Jean Toomer and the History of Passing," *Reviews in American History* 41, no. 1 (2013): 119.
43. Guterl, "Jean Toomer and the History of Passing," 119.
44. Hughes, *The Big Sea* (Columbia: University of Missouri Press, 2002), 188.
45. Hughes, "The Negro Artist and the Racial Mountain," in *The Collected Works of Langston Hughes*, vol. 9, *Essays on Art, Race, Politics, and World Affairs*, ed. Christopher C. De Santis (Columbia: University of Missouri Press, 2002), 31.
46. Arnold Rampersad, *The Life of Langston Hughes*, vol. 1, *1902–1941, I, Too, Sing America* (New York: Oxford University Press, 2002), 156. Mason's arrangement with Hurston, by contrast, meant that she *did* own much of Hurston's anthropological work.
47. Charlotte Osgood Mason, quoted by David Levering Lewis, *When Harlem Was in Vogue* (New York: Penguin, 1997), 153.
48. Bruce Kellner, "'Refined Racism': White Patronage in the Harlem Renaissance," in Harold Bloom, ed., *The Harlem Renaissance* (New York: Chelsea House, 2004), 57.
49. Carla Kaplan, *Miss Anne in Harlem: The White Women of the Black Renaissance* (New York: HarperCollins, 2013), xx.
50. Allen Dunn and George Hutchinson, "The Future of the Harlem Renaissance," *Soundings: An Interdisciplinary Journal* 80, no. 4 (1997): 451.
51. Robert Hemenway, *Zora Neale Hurston: A Literary Biography* (Urbana: University of Illinois Press, 1977), 107.
52. Rampersad, *Life of Langston Hughes*, 1.167.
53. Hughes, *Ways of White Folks*, 19.
54. Hughes, *Ways of White Folks*, 112–13.
55. Hughes, *Ways of White Folks*, 122.
56. Hughes, *Ways of White Folks*, 122.
57. Du Bois, "The Field and Function of the American Negro College," in Herbert Aptheker, ed., *The Education of Black People: Ten Critiques, 1906–1960* (New York: Monthly Review Press, 2001), 125.
58. Hurston's contract stated, for example, that Mason was the legal owner of the folk materials she collected during her trips to the southern states. Much of this would later form *Mules and Men* (1935).
59. Carla Kaplan, ed., *Zora Neale Hurston: A Life in Letters* (New York: Doubleday, 2002), 30.
60. Zora Neale Hurston, *Dust Tracks on a Road* (New York: Harper Perennial, 2006), 249.
61. Hemenway, *Zora Neale Hurston: A Literary Biography*, 283.

62 Hurston, *Dust Tracks*, 248.
63 Hurston, *Dust Tracks*, 248.
64 Hurston, *Dust Tracks*, 248.
65 Hurston, "How It Feels to Be Colored Me," in Alice Walker, ed., *I Love Myself When I Am Laughing ... and Then Again When I Am Looking Mean and Impressive: A Zora Neale Hurston Reader* (New York: Feminist Press at CUNY, 1979), 153.
66 Hurston, *Dust Tracks*, 254.
67 Zora Neale Hurston, *Their Eyes Were Watching God* (London: Virago, 2007), 80.
68 Hurston, *Their Eyes*, 259.
69 Hurston, *Their Eyes*, 257.
70 Jennifer Jordan, "Feminist Fantasies: Zora Neale Hurston's *Their Eyes Were Watching God*," *Tulsa Studies in Women's Literature* 7, no. 1 (1988): 107.
71 Jordan, "Feminist Fantasies," 107, 108.
72 Henry Louis Gates Jr., *The Signifying Monkey: A Theory of African-American Literary Criticism* (New York: Oxford University Press, 2014), 195.
73 Hurston, *Their Eyes*, 11.
74 White reviewers were kinder: they "liked the story, but usually for the wrong reasons." Hemenway, *Hurston: A Literary Biography*, 240–41.
75 Locke, "Jingo, Counter-Jingo, and Us," *The New Negro Aesthetic: Selected Writings*, ed. Jeffrey C. Stewart (New York: Penguin, 2022), 309.
76 Locke, "Jingo," 309. Hurston was wholly uninterested in producing "social document fiction": as she informed one critic, she wanted to write "a novel and not a treatise on sociology," quoted by Hemenway, *Hurston: A Literary Biography*, 42.
77 Richard Wright, "Between Laughter and Tears," *New Masses*, October 5, 1937, 25–26. Hurston replied to Wright's criticism in a review of his 1938 collection of novellas, *Uncle Tom's Children*, calling it "a book about hatreds" and commenting that "[Wright's] stories are so grim that the Dismal Swamp of race hatred must be where they live." See Hurston, "Stories of Conflict: Review of *Uncle Tom's Children*," in Cheryl A. Wall, ed., *Zora Neale Hurston: Folklore, Memoirs, and Other Writings* (New York: Library of America, 1995), 912.
78 Richard Wright, "Blueprint for Negro Writing," in Angelyn Mitchell, ed., *Within the Circle: An Anthology of African American Literary Criticism from the Harlem Renaissance to the Present* (Durham, NC: Duke University Press, 1994), 97–98.
79 Wright, "Blueprint," 97.
80 Wright, "Blueprint," 99.
81 LeRoi Jones, *Blues People* (New York: William Morrow & Company, 1967), 134.

82 Harold Cruse, *The Crisis of the Negro Intellectual* (New York: New York Review Books, 2005), 35.
83 Following the fatal September 2016 shooting of Keith Lamont Scott in Charlotte, North Carolina, the *New York Times* dedicated a whole page to Hughes's 1926 poem "I, Too."
84 K. Merinda Simmons and James A. Crank, *Race and New Modernisms* (London: Bloomsbury, 2019), 186.
85 Brown, an eighteen-year-old Black man, was shot dead by a police officer in Ferguson, Missouri, in August 2014.
86 Du Bois, *The Souls of Black Folk*, 2.

Chapter Eleven: "And This Is How 'The Feminists' Are Made": Ethical Collaboration Between Eleonora Duse and Gabriele D'Annunzio Zsuzsanna Balázs

1 Eleonora Duse, "La Duse parla del femminismo," quoted by Anna Laura Mariani, "Sibilla Aleramo. Significato di tre incontri col teatro: il personaggio di Nora, Giacinta Pezzana, Eleonora Duse," *Teatro e Storia: orientamenti per una rifondazione degli studi teatrali* 2, no. 1 (1987): 132-33. The quotations from Italian primary and secondary sources are provided in my own translations. The original Italian texts are not included in this short chapter due to limitations of word count. Should any questions arise regarding the translations, please do not hesitate to contact me.
2 The "New Woman" was a feminist ideal which appeared at the end of the nineteenth century across Europe. New Women threatened conventional notions about the ideal Victorian womanhood by being free-spirited, independent, highly educated, and uninterested in the institution of marriage, motherhood, and domestic duties traditionally assigned to women.
3 Lucia Re, "D'Annunzio, Duse, Wilde, Bernhardt: il rapporto autore/attrice fra decadentismo e modernità," *MLN* 117, no. 1 (2002), 118.
4 Re, "D'Annunzio, Duse, Wilde, Bernhardt," 119.
5 On September 12, 1919, D'Annunzio conquered the city of Fiume with two thousand rebel soldiers. He managed to keep the city for sixteen months, opposing both conservative and liberal political powers.
6 Giordano Bruno Guerri, *Disobbedisco: Cinquecento giorni di rivoluzione. Fiume 1919-1920* (Milan: Mondadori, 2019), 177.
7 Guerri, *Disobbedisco*, 318.
8 Guerri, *Disobbedisco*, 318.
9 Rhiannon Noel Welch, *Vital Subjects: Race and Biopolitics in Italy, 1860-1920* (Liverpool: Liverpool University Press, 2016), 204.

10 Elisa Bizzotto, "'Children of Pleasure': Oscar Wilde and Italian Decadence," in *The Reception of Oscar Wilde in Europe*, ed. Stefano Evangelista (New York: Continuum, 2010), 135.
11 Bizzotto, "'Children of Pleasure,'" 135.
12 Barbara Spackman, *Fascist Virilities: Rhetoric, Ideology, and Social Fantasy in Italy* (Minneapolis: University of Minnesota Press, 1996), 17.
13 For a detailed analysis of D'Annunzio's progressive views of women's rights and sexuality associated with his Fiume project, see Guerri's recent book *Disobbedisco* (2019), quoted above.
14 Re, "D'Annunzio, Duse, Wilde, Bernhardt," 125.
15 Luisetta Elia Chomel, *D'Annunzio: un teatro al femminile* (Ravenna: Longo Editore, 1997), 153.
16 Ross, "'La carezza incompiuta,'" 404–7.
17 Sandra Ponzanesi, "Queering European Sexualities Through Italy's Fascist Past: Colonialism, Homosexuality, and Masculinities," in *What's Queer About Europe? Productive Encounters and Re-Enchanting Paradigms*, ed. M. Rosello and S. Dasgupta (New York: Fordham University Press, 2014), 85.
18 Ponzanesi, "Queering European Sexualities," 85.
19 Derek Duncan, "Secret Wounds: The Bodies of Fascism in Giorgio Bassani's *Dietro la porta*," in *Queer Italia: Same-Sex Desire in Italian Literature and Film*, ed. Gary P. Cestaro (New York: Palgrave Macmillan, 2004), 191.
20 Ponzanesi, "Queering European Sexualities," 86.
21 Duncan, "Secret Wounds," 192.
22 Charlotte Ross, "Italian Medical and Literary Discourses Around Female Same-Sex Desire, 1877–1906," in *Italian Sexualities Uncovered, 1789–1914*, ed. Valeria Babini, Chiara Beccalossi, and Lucy Riall (London: Palgrave Macmillan, 2015), 228.
23 Gary P. Cestaro, "Introduction: Queer Italia: Same-Sex Desire in Italian Literature and Film," *Queer Italia*, 8.
24 Ross, "Italian Medical and Literary Discourses," 228.
25 See also Chiara Beccalossi, *Female Sexual Inversion: Same-Sex Desires in Italian and British Sexology, c.1870–1920* (London: Palgrave Macmillan, 2012).
26 Re, "D'Annunzio, Duse, Wilde, Bernhardt," 116.
27 Re, "D'Annunzio, Duse, Wilde, Bernhardt," 129.
28 Duse, quoted by Mariani, "Sibilla Aleramo," 132.
29 Duse, quoted by Mariani, "Sibilla Aleramo," 131.
30 Matthew Parris, host, "Fiona Shaw Nominates Actress Eleonora Duse," *Great Lives*, series 49 (BBC Radio 4 podcast), September 10, 2019. https://podcasts.apple.com/ca/podcast/fiona-shaw-nominates-actress-eleonora-duse/id261779765?i=1000449541014 (accessed February 9, 2022).

31 Lucia Re, "Eleonora Duse and Women: Performing Desire, Power and Knowledge." *Italian Studies* 70, no. 3 (2015): 349.
32 Re, "Eleonora Duse," 349.
33 Re, "Eleonora Duse," 349.
34 Re, "Eleonora Duse," 350.
35 Re, "Eleonora Duse," 352–53.
36 Re, "Eleonora Duse," 353.
37 Chomel, *D'Annunzio*, 53.
38 See Chomel, *D'Annunzio*, 53.
39 Sergio Benvenuto, *What are Perversions? Sexuality, Ethics, Psychoanalysis* (London: Routledge, 2016), xvi.
40 Michel Foucault, *The History of Sexuality*, vol. 1, *An Introduction* (New York: Pantheon Books, 1978), 108.
41 Foucault, *History of Sexuality*, 1.109.
42 Chomel, *D'Annunzio*, 54.
43 Gabriele D'Annunzio, *Tutto il teatro di Gabriele D'Annunzio* (Verona: Mondadori, 1950), 64.
44 D'Annunzio, *Tutto il teatro*, 56.
45 D'Annunzio, *Tutto il teatro*, 56.
46 D'Annunzio, *Tutto il teatro*, 57.
47 D'Annunzio, *Tutto il teatro*, 57.
48 D'Annunzio, *Tutto il teatro*, 60.
49 Clare Croft, "Introduction," in *Queer Dance: Meanings and Makings*, ed. Clare Croft (New York: Oxford University Press, 2017), 14.
50 Croft, "Introduction," 14.
51 D'Annunzio, *Tutto il teatro*, 63.
52 D'Annunzio, *Tutto il teatro*, 63.
53 D'Annunzio, *Tutto il teatro*, 91.
54 Rockney Jacobsen, "Arousal and the Ends of Desire," *Philosophy and Phenomenological Research* 53, no. 3 (1993): 624.
55 John Newman, "Eating and Drinking as Sources of Metaphor in English," *Cuadernos de Filología Inglesa* 6, no. 2 (1997): 218–19.
56 D'Annunzio, *Tutto il teatro*, 97.
57 D'Annunzio, *Tutto il teatro*, 67.
58 D'Annunzio, *Tutto il teatro*, 74.
59 D'Annunzio, *Tutto il teatro*, 78.
60 D'Annunzio, *Tutto il teatro*, 85.
61 D'Annunzio, *Tutto il teatro*, 85.
62 D'Annunzio, *Tutto il teatro*, 86.
63 Sara Ahmed, *The Cultural Politics of Emotion* (New York: Routledge, 2004), 105.
64 Ahmed, *Cultural Politics*, 105.
65 Ahmed, *Cultural Politics*, 106.

66 Ahmed, *Cultural Politics*, 106.
67 D'Annunzio, *Tutto il teatro*, 103.
68 D'Annunzio, *Tutto il teatro*, 104–5.
69 D'Annunzio, *Tutto il teatro*, 114.
70 Chomel, *D'Annunzio*, 64.
71 D'Annunzio, *Tutto il teatro*, 114.
72 John Champagne, *Italian Masculinity as Queer Melodrama: Caravaggio, Puccini, Contemporary Cinema* (New York: Palgrave Macmillan, 2015), 88.

Chapter Twelve: Reading James Joyce in the Wake of the #MeToo Movement *Julie McCormick Weng*

1 Burton A. Waisbren and Florence L. Walzl, "Paresis and the Priest: James Joyce's Symbolic Use of Syphilis in 'The Sisters,'" *Annals of Internal Medicine* 80, no. 6 (1974): 758–62.
2 James Joyce, "The Sisters," in *Dubliners*, ed. Margot Norris (New York: W. W. Norton, 2006), 3–11.
3 Joseph Valente and Margot Gayle Backus, *The Child Sex Scandal and Modern Irish Literature: Writing the Unspeakable* (Bloomington: Indiana University Press, 2020), 44, 54, 53.
4 For more on the term "victim-survivor," see "Survivor, Victim, Victim-Survivor," *force: upsetting rape culture*. https://upsettingrapeculture.com/survivor-victim/ (accessed August 1, 2021).
5 Stanislaus Joyce claimed the sexual predator in "An Encounter" was based on a man he and Joyce met while playing truant from Belvedere. See Richard Ellman, *James Joyce* (New York: Oxford University Press, 1983), 47. I have written about a curate's scheme to sexually assault a woman in *Finnegans Wake* in "Her 'Bisexycle,' Her Body, and Her Self-Propulsion in *Finnegans Wake*," *Journal of Modern Literature* 39, no. 4 (2016): 49–66. See also Finn Fordham, *Lots of Fun at* Finnegans Wake: *Unravelling Universals* (New York: Oxford University Press, 2007), 68.
6 James Joyce, *Ulysses* (New York: Vintage, 1986), 13.794.
7 Scholars Sarah L. Cook, Lilia M. Cortina, and Mary P. Koss discuss legal definitions of sexual abuse, assault, and harassment as they are construed today in many national jurisdictions: "What's the Difference between Sexual Abuse, Sexual Assault, Sexual Harassment and Rape?" *The Conversation*, September 20, 2018. https://theconversation.com/whats-the-difference-between-sexual-abuse-sexual-assault-sexual-harassment-and-rape-88218 (accessed April 15, 2021).
8 Burke first posted "me too" to MySpace as a way of building up victim-survivors' "sense of self-worth" and to establish a community of "survivors supporting survivors." Chris Snyder, "Tarana Burke on

Why She Created the #MeToo Movement—and Where It's Headed," *Business Insider*, December 13, 2017. www.businessinsider.com/how-the-metoo-movement-started-where-its-headed-tarana-burke-time-person-of-year-women-2017-12 (accessed April 15, 2021).

9. Alyssa Milano, "If You've Been Sexually Harassed or Assaulted Write 'Me Too' as a Reply to This Tweet." *Twitter*, October 15, 2017. https://twitter.com/Alyssa_Milano/status/919659438700670976 (accessed April 15, 2021).
10. For example, the hashtag #IBelieveHer was deployed to advocate for a victim-survivor of rape during a trial in Belfast.
11. See Lisa Fitzpatrick, "Contemporary Feminist Protest in Ireland: #MeToo in Irish Theatre," *Irish University Review* 50, no. 1 (2020): 82–93.
12. Snyder, "Tarana Burke."
13. Stephen's first sexual experience likely occurs around the same time as the author's in 1896. See Ellman, *James Joyce*, 47–48.
14. James Joyce, *A Portrait of the Artist as a Young Man* (New York: W. W. Norton, 2007), 126.
15. *Portrait of the Artist*, 56, 88.
16. *Portrait of the Artist*, 88.
17. The party occurs after the family's move to Dublin but before Stephen begins school at Belvedere. In Joyce's biography, these events occurred between 1891 and 1893. If born in 1882, Stephen would be around nine or ten years old.
18. *Portrait of the Artist*, 60. Emma's voice and awareness of Stephen's desires are absent from the scene. See Suzette Henke, "Stephen Dedalus and Women: A Portrait of the Artist as a Young Misogynist," in *Women in Joyce*, ed. Elaine Unkeless and Suzette Henke (Urbana: University of Illinois Press, 1982), 88. Henke writes that Emma "probably feels confused by the excitations of a budding sexuality. Her gestures of affection are limited to the subtle patterns of courtship available in nineteenth-century Ireland to a young girl who wants to attract a suitor but to remain pure, chaste, and respectable."
19. *Portrait of the Artist*, 61, 62.
20. The birth of this legislation also coincided with changing theories of childhood. See Deborah Gorham, "The 'Maiden Tribute of Modern Babylon' Re-examined: Child Prostitution and the Idea of Childhood in Late Victorian England," *Victorian Studies* 21, no. 3 (1978): 363. Gorham notes that the Victorians innovated the idea that "children were beings apart from adults" and required protection against exploitative labor and juvenile delinquency. They also concluded that children deserved the right to an education.

21 Gorham, "The 'Maiden Tribute of Modern Babylon' Re-examined," 363. She writes that some reformers lobbied without success to "extend age of consent legislation to cover boys."
22 John Wade, *The Cabinet Lawyer, Or, Popular Digest of the Laws of England* (London: W. Simpkin and R. Marshall, 1828), 372.
23 Wade, *The Cabinet Lawyer*, 373.
24 Roger Cox, "The Child of the Victorians: Gender and Sexuality in Childhood," *Shaping Childhood: Themes of Uncertainty in the History of Adult–Child Relationships* (London: Routledge, 1996), 150, 152.
25 Sam Slote argues that Joyce's approach to style, including his use of free indirect discourse and stream of consciousness, are informed by Nietzsche's belief that "stylistic variety projects an ethical stance in that it conveys a manner of living." Sam Slote, *Joyce's Nietzschean Ethics* (New York: Palgrave Macmillan, 2013), 2. In a similar vein, I am suggesting that Joyce's free indirect discourse bolsters his study of the psychological evolution of Stephen's sexual ethics.
26 *Portrait of the Artist*, 196.
27 Mary Lowe-Evans, "Sex and Confession in the Joyce Canon: Some Historical Parallels," *Journal of Modern Literature* 16, no. 4 (1990): 568.
28 *Portrait of the Artist*, 126, 101.
29 Gorham, "The 'Maiden Tribute of Modern Babylon' Re-examined," 365.
30 Joseph Valente, *The Myth of Manliness in Irish National Culture, 1880–1922* (Urbana: University of Illinois Press, 2011), 6; Wade, *The Cabinet Lawyer*, 374.
31 Katherine Mullin, *James Joyce, Sexuality and Social Purity* (Cambridge: Cambridge University Press, 2003), 21.
32 *Portrait of the Artist*, 194.
33 Richard Brown, *James Joyce and Sexuality* (Cambridge: Cambridge University Press, 1990), 116.
34 *Portrait of the Artist*, 102.
35 *Portrait of the Artist*, 196.
36 Marian Eide, *Ethical Joyce* (Cambridge: Cambridge University Press, 2002), 60.
37 *Portrait of the Artist*, 196.
38 "What Consent Looks Like," RAINN (Rape, Abuse & Incest National Network). www.rainn.org/articles/what-is-consent (accessed August 1, 2021).
39 Sandra Gilbert and Susan Gubar, "Sexual Linguistics: Gender, Language, Sexuality," *New Literary History* 16, no. 3 (1985): 518.
40 S. L. Goldberg, *The Classical Temper: A Study of James Joyce's* Ulysses (New York: Barnes & Noble, 1961), 159.
41 *Portrait of the Artist*, 216.

42 Vicki Mahaffey, "Framing, Being Framed, and the Janus Faces of Authority," in *James Joyce's* A Portrait of the Artist as a Young Man: *A Casebook*, ed. Mark A. Wollaeger (New York: Oxford University Press, 2003), 235.

43 Michelle Rodino-Colocino, "Me Too, #MeToo: Countering Cruelty with Empathy," *Communication and Critical-Cultural Studies* 15, no. 1 (2018): 96.

44 Clare Hemmings, "Affective Solidarity: Feminist Reflexivity and Political Transformation," *Feminist Theory* 13, no. 2 (2012): 152.

45 Megan Boler, "The Risks of Empathy: Interrogating Multiculturalism's Gaze," *Cultural Studies* 11, no. 2 (1997): 259.

46 Rodino-Colocino, "Me Too, #MeToo," 96.

47 Spivak proposes an "ungeneralizable subaltern," and she acknowledges the "asymmetries" through which subjugation occurs, opening her ideas for testing across times, cultures, and national contexts. See Spivak's "How Do We Write, Now?" *PMLA* 133, no. 1 (2018): 169 and *Death of A Discipline* (New York: Columbia University Press, 2003), 70. A range of scholars have written about Ireland and theories of the subaltern, including in Joyce's works. See Enda Duffy, *The Subaltern Ulysses* (Minneapolis: University of Minnesota Press, 1994).

48 Gayatri Chakravorty Spivak, "In Response," in *Reflections on the History of an Idea: Can the Subaltern Speak?*, ed. Rosalind C. Morris (New York: Columbia University Press, 2010), 230, 235.

49 Eide, *Ethical Joyce*, 60.

50 Henke, "Stephen Dedalus and Women," 102.

51 *Portrait of the Artist*, 224.

52 *Ulysses*, 15.1074–77.

53 Joseph Valente, "Et Tu, Bloom: or, #MeToo, Male Masochism, and Sexual Ethics in *Ulysses*," *Joyce Studies Annual* 2021: 11. For more on the Mary Driscoll incident, see Kimberly J. Devlin, *Wandering and Return in* Finnegans Wake: *An Integrative Approach to Joyce's Fictions* (Princeton, NJ: Princeton University Press, 1991), 150–51; Margot Norris, *Virgin and Veteran Readings of* Ulysses (New York: Palgrave Macmillan, 2011), 172–73; Peter Kuch, *Irish Divorce/Joyce's* Ulysses (New York: Palgrave Macmillan, 2017), 68–69, 171–72; Casey Lawrence, "#Me Too Is Nothing New," *Medium*, March 5, 2019. https://clawrenc.medium.com/metoo-is-nothing-new-d429b2c1784c (accessed April 15, 2021).

54 *Ulysses*, 8.610. The interpretation of this line is debated. For example, Harry Blamires argues that Molly is the partner who cannot enjoy sex after Rudy's death, while Margot Norris claims it is Bloom. The indeterminate subject of the sentence can support multiple readings. See Blamires, *The New Bloomsday Book: A Guide Through Joyce's* Ulysses (London: Routledge, 1988), 56, and Norris, *Virgin and Veteran Readings of* Ulysses, 221.

55 *Ulysses*, 18.1604–8.
56 *Ulysses*, 8.905–916.
57 *Ulysses*, 18.1373, 18.569–70, 18.1369, 18.123–24.
58 *Ulysses*, 18.1578–81.
59 Although in "Circe" Bloom transforms for a moment into "the new womanly man," giving birth to octuplets who have disappeared by the episode's end; *Ulysses*, 15.1798–99.
60 *Ulysses*, 8.1116, 8.1145, 11.1260, 16.732.
61 *Ulysses*, 8.377–78, 16.739–47.
62 Elizabeth Adetiba, "Tarana Burke Says #MeToo Should Center Marginalized Communities," *The Nation*, November 17, 2017. www.thenation.com/article/archive/tarana-burke-says-metoo-isnt-just-for-white-people/ (accessed April 15, 2021).
63 *Portrait of the Artist*, 12.
64 Valente and Backus, *Child Sex Scandal and Modern Irish Literature*, 54.
65 Boler, "Risks of Empathy," 261–62.
66 Eide, *Ethical Joyce*, 144–46.

Index

abjection 32–33, 38–41, 46–48, 155–56, 256n7
Abram, David 84, 267n66
Abyssinia 162–65
Achebe, Chinua 173
acting 26, 68, 223–25
activism 3, 26, 223, 225, 233
Aden 163–64, 173, 175
Adkins, Peter 17
Adorno, Theodor 19, 126, 129, 136
affect 16, 20, 21, 22, 79, 81, 146, 228, 232
ageing studies 14–15, 52, 62
    see also ethics and ageing
Ahmed, Sara 232
Aldrich, Robert 112
ambiguity 223, 232
Amis, Kingsley 179
Amis, Martin 182
"Am I the Asshole?" Subreddit 1–2
Anand, Mulk Raj 9, 107
Anders, Günther 19, 126, 137–39
animals 48, 70, 73, 79
    suffering of 21
    see also creatural/animality
anti-philosophy 132
apocalypse 16, 19, 31–33, 34, 35, 37, 42, 44–46
    laughing apocalypse 14, 32–33, 38–41, 47–48, 49

modernist apocalypse 14, 31–32, 33, 36, 38, 49
naïve apocalypse 34–35
Appiah, Kwame Anthony 7–8, 10, 18, 87–89, 91, 93, 94, 96, 99, 110–11, 117–18, 119, 120, 121, 124
Archambeau, Robert 5
Arendt, Hannah 9, 137
Aristodemou, Maria 178
Aristotle 3–4, 10
Artaud, Antonin 40
Atkin, Lord 179
atom bomb 19, 126, 134–37
Attridge, Derek 152, 267n7
Aub, Max 10
Auden, W. H. 5, 108, 256n1, 270n29
Austen, Jane 170

Baars, Jan 54–55, 57, 261n19
    see also Laceulle, Hanne
Backus, Margot Gayle 235, 251
Badiou, Alain 10–11, 100, 130–31
Bahbha, Homi 94
Baird, Cecily 163
Bakhtin, Mikhail 39, 179
Barnes, Djuna 6, 13–14, 17
    "Against Nature: In Which Everything that is Young, Inadequate

299

and Tiresome is Included in the Term Natural" 54
"Becoming Intimate with the Bohemians" 54
The Book of Repulsive Women 40
The Confessions of Helen Westley 54
"Hem of Manhattan" 14, 60–61
"How it Feels to Be Forcibly Fed" 13
interviews 52, 57–60
journalism 51–52, 53–57, 60–61
late-life creativity 61–65
New York 14–15, 51–52, 59, 60–62, 64
Nightwood 40, 64
Steptoe, Lydia (pseud.) 53, 54
"Veterans in Harness" 14, 52, 57–60
Barthes, Roland 56, 154–55
Bassnett, Susan 112, 113, 119
beauty 4, 54, 55, 95, 98, 199, 201–2, 206, 228, 230, 234
Beckett, Samuel 3, 6, 10–11, 40, 63, 256n1
Begam, Richard 16
Bell, Gertrude 112
Bender, Thomas 124
Benjamin, Walter 124, 132, 134
Bennett, Jane 75, 84
Benson, Stella 6, 16, 19, 109–10, 111–17, 119–24
 I Pose 108, 109
 The Little World 18, 106, 107, 108–9, 118–19
 Living Alone 108
 The Poor Man 108, 109
 This is the End 108
Bergson, Henri 70, 76–77
Berman, Jessica 107, 115, 9–10, 11
Bernhardt, Sarah 26, 217–18, 219, 220, 226
Bernstein, Charles 154, 155
bioaesthetics 76, 82
Bizzotto, Elisa 220
Black Arts Movement 198, 213
Black Sun Press 82
Blanch, Sophie 106

bodies 12–13, 38, 102, 150–51, 185, 214, 225, 233, 241, 244
 abject 32, 40–41, 46
 embodiment 12, 33, 80, 82, 84, 172
 material 14, 32, 40
 suffering 13, 14, 21, 33
Boler, Megan 245, 251
Bookman 109
The Book of Revelation 47
The Book of Tobit 43
Borg, Ruben 31, 32, 36, 37, 47
Boyd White, James 4
Brecht, Bertolt 137
British Somaliland Protectorate 163
Brooklyn Daily Eagle 53, 57, 59
brotherhood 221, 229
Burgess, Anthony 181
Burke, Kenneth 100, 147
Burke, Tarana 236–37, 250
Butler, Judith 11

carnivalesque 14, 32–33, 37, 39, 40–41, 46, 48–49
Cary, Joyce 167
Caselli, Daniela 62, 65
Catholic Church 43, 78, 221, 236, 237, 240, 241, 244
Cavell, Stanley 127
Céline, Louis-Ferdinand 40, 47, 49
Champagne, John 234
Chomel, Luisetta Elia 221, 226, 227, 232
#ChurchToo movement 236
civil law 177, 180
Cleary, Joe 6–7
Coates, Ta-Nehisi 96
Cohen, Debra Rae 109
Cohen-Cheminet, Geneviève 145, 148, 154
Colangelo, Jeremy 12
Cold War 7, 16, 126, 159
collaboration 23, 26, 218–19, 220, 234
colonialism 2, 6, 109–10, 111, 122, 124, 173, 207
 see also modernity, and coloniality

INDEX 301

Connolly, Patrick 156
Connolly, William 78–79, 265n39
Conrad, Joseph 16, 173, 280n18, 280n25
  Heart of Darkness 173, 174
consciousness 1, 3, 7, 12, 68, 73, 75, 79,
  81–83, 84, 102, 155, 158, 179
  American consciousness 96
  birth of consciousness 79–80
  blood consciousness 76–77
  creatural consciousness 74
  double consciousness 215
  dynamic consciousness 15, 73, 74,
    76, 84
  embodied consciousness 67–69, 73
  hyperconsciousness 181
  infantile consciousness 77
  primal consciousness 73, 74, 79, 81,
    84
  race consciousness 210, 213
  self-consciousness 80
  stream of consciousness 8, 245
consent 2, 23, 26–27, 230, 231, 237,
  238–39, 241, 243–44, 245, 246,
  247–49
Cools, Arthur 100, 270n30
Corpus Juris 146, 148
cosmopolitanism 7, 9, 18–19, 106–7,
  108, 109–12, 113, 114, 115, 116, 117,
  120, 121, 123–25
Country Life 109
creatural/animality 47, 48, 81, 83
Crenshaw, Kimberlé 23
Criminal Law Amendment Act 238–39,
  240
Cruikshank, Margaret 63
Cruse, Harold 214
Cuddy-Keane, Melba 21, 149
Cummings, E. E. 61, 64, 108

Dada 35, 44
dance 21, 46–47, 68–70, 72, 74, 76, 81,
  82, 118–19, 218
D'Annunzio, Gabriele 23
  The Dead City 26, 218, 226–34
  fascism 26, 219–20, 221

homosexuality 26, 218, 220, 221–22
  obscenity 221, 226
David-Néel, Alexandra 119
Davidson, Michael 12
Davis, Thomas S. 16
Deacon, Edgar 186–87, 284n57
Deacon, Terrance 79
De Benedetti, Michele 217, 223
DeFalco, Amelia 52, 60
degeneration 201
Degnen, Catherine 59, 262n35
Deleuze, Gilles 70–71, 83, 128–29,
  258n50
Del Mar, Maksymilian 4
deontology 149, 153, 282n11
Depression era 159
Derrida, Jacques 38
desert romance 161, 167, 169, 170–71,
  172, 174
Dickens, Charles 184
Dimock, Wai Chee 192
disability studies 12
District Commissioner fiction 161,
  167–68, 169, 174
Dos Passos, John 108
Douglass, Aaron 207
Douzinas, Costas 178
Du Bois, W. E. B. 6, 25, 197, 198,
  199–202, 209, 211, 212, 213, 215
Dumas, Alexandre 237, 286n21
Duncan, Isadora 6, 13, 15, 67–76, 79, 81,
  82–83, 84, 218, 264n10
DuPlessis, Rachel Blau 149, 150, 277n26
Duse, Eleonora 26, 218–19
  on education for women 223
  feminist icon 217–18, 220, 224–26,
    233
  rejection of collaboration with
    fascists 225
duty of care 186–87

Eagleton, Terry 127, 130,
Ebury, Katherine 20
Ecclesiastes 172
Eide, Marian 7, 8, 242, 245, 251

Einstein, Albert 135
Eliot, T. S. 2, 3, 35, 256n1
empathy 26, 224, 237, 244–45, 246, 247, 249, 250
epiphany 239, 242, 243–44, 245, 246
Eskin, Michael 149
ethics
    and aesthetics 4–5, 25, 197–98
    and ageing 14, 52, 58, 61, 62, 63
    and apocalypse 33–34, 46, 48
    and colonialism 161–62, 174–75
    and cosmopolitanism 18, 22, 110–11
    and journalistic gaze 53
    and law 19, 159, 177, 182, 190
    and middlebrow 111, 124
    morality distinction 3, 152–53
    and race 198, 208
    responsibility for industrial actions 69
    and sexuality 26–27, 243, 247, 249, 250
    solar 68–69
    and temporality 36–37
    and theatre 218, 227
    and transnationalism 106, 108, 109–11
    witnessing through poetry 21
    see also deontology
Eurocentrism 6, 107

Farley, David 108
fascism 16, 34, 49, 123, 219, 221–22, 225
Fauset, Jessie 204, 215
feminism/feminist analysis 13–14, 23, 27, 69, 77–78, 217–18, 219–20, 222–25, 227, 233–34, 237
Ferguson, Rex 20
Fifield, Peter 12
Fiume 219, 291n13
Floyd, George 214
Forbes, Rosita 169, 170
Frege, Gottlob 127–28
French-Sheldon, May 119
French Somaliland 164
Friedman, Susan Stanford 3, 16, 19
Fussell, Paul 108

Gaedtke, Andrew 12
Gaskell, Elizabeth 184
Gates, Henry Louis 204–5, 212, 287n30
gender 3, 7, 9, 10, 23, 26, 38, 40, 80, 111–12, 114–15, 118, 124, 218, 220–21, 224–25, 233, 246
Genette, Gérard 97
gerontology 54–55
Gibson, Andrew 10–11
Gilleard, Chris and Paul Higgs 61
Gomel, Elena 32
Goody, Alex 17, 53, 55, 56, 59
Gorham, Deborah 240, 294n20
Grahame, Kenneth 178
Greene, Graham 108, 167
Griffin, Roger 31, 34
Grifi, Elvira 101
Grosz, Elizabeth 70, 83
Guattari, Félix 83, 129
Guerri, Giordano Bruno 219
Gullette, Margaret 62
Gulliver, Katrina 109

Haggard, Rider 167
Hammill, Faye 106
Harlem Renaissance 197–99, 203–4, 206, 207, 212–14
Harris, Leonard 199
Hartley, L. P. 88
Hartman, Saidiya V. 200
Hassan, Sayid Muhammed Abdulla 165–66, 174
Hazan, Haim 51
Hegel, G. W. F. 8, 129
Hegglund, Jon 17
Hemenway, Robert 208, 210
Hemmings, Clare 244
Henke, Suzette 246, 294n18
Hensley, Nathan K. 16
Herbert, Agnes 163
hermeneutics of suspicion 94, 97, 98
heroism 112–13
heterosexuality 80, 218, 221, 222, 226, 231, 233–34, 239
Hine, Lewis 153–54

Hirschfeld's Institut für Sexualwissenschaft 38
Högberg, Elsa 2, 11, 25
Hollingshead, David 180
Holstein, Martha 56–60
homoeros 223, 227, 234
homosexuality 201, 220, 221–22, 223
Horkheimer, Max 136
Howarth, Patrick 168
Hughes, Langston 25, 198, 204, 206–9, 214
    "Passing" 204
    "The Blues I'm Playing" 208
    "The Racial Mountain and the Negro Artist" 206, 209
Hull, E. M. 168, 169, 170, 172
    The Sheik 168–69, 171
Humble, Nicola 111
Hurston, Zora Neale 24–25, 198, 207, 209–13, 214, 215
    Dust Tracks on a Road 209
    "How It Feels To Be Colored Me" 210
    Their Eyes Were Watching God 24, 210
Hussain, Iqbalunnisia 9

Imagism 145, 150
imperialism 6, 107, 108, 109–11, 117, 122–24, 245
incest 221, 226–27, 228, 232, 233
Industrial Revolution 177
intersectionality 23, 25, 26, 112, 180
Ishvani, G. 9
Italian Somaliland 163, 164

Jacobsen, Rockney 229
James, Henry 107
Jameson, Fredric 141
Jenkins, G. Matthew 149
Johnson, Hall 207
Johnson, James Weldon 204, 205
Jordan, Jennifer 211
Joyce, James
    Dubliners 8, 235–36
    A Portrait of the Artist as a Young Man 237–46

Ulysses 8–9, 93, 236, 247–51
Finnegans Wake 40, 236

Kafka, Franz 40
Kant, Immanuel 125
Kaplan, Carla 207
Kermode, Frank 31, 33–36
    see also apocalypse, naïve apocalypse
Kierkegaard, Søren 129, 130
Kingsley, Mary 112
Kristeva, Julia 11, 32–33, 38–41, 46, 47, 48
    see also apocalypse, laughing apocalypse

Lacan, Jacques 130
Laceulle, Hanne and Jan Barrs 52, 62, 64–65
Lambert, Thomas F. 180
Larsen, Nella 204, 215
Larson, Jil 2, 149, 152
Law & Literature (journal) 19
law and literature 4, 19–20, 172, 175, 177, 192
Lawrence, D. H. 15, 67–68, 71–75, 77–82, 108, 184
Lee, Klaudia Hiu Yen 109
Lemos Horta, Paulo 106
LeRoi Jones (Amiri Baraka) 213–14
Levay, Matthew 20
Levinas, Emmanuel 8, 9–11, 17, 89–91, 97–100, 103, 149
Levine, Amy-Jill 43
Levine, Nancy 53
Lewis, Wyndham 2, 108
Linnett, Maren Tova 12
Locke, Alain 197
Lowe-Evans, Mary 240

McCracken, Saskia 17
McIntyre, John 17
McKay, Claude 207
MacNeice, Louis 108
Mahaffey, Vicki 244
Mallarmé, Stéphane 130

Manderson, Desmond 179, 180
Mansfield, Katherine 108
Mao, Douglas 6, 106
Marcuse, Herbert 129–30, 137
Mason, Charlotte Osgood 207
Massieu, Isabelle 119
maternal 44, 68, 75–77, 81–82
Mattis, Ann 23
medical humanities 12
Medici family 270n32, 92, 100–2
#MeToo movement 236–37, 244, 250
Michael, John 155
Michelangelo (Michelangelo di Lodovico Buonarroti Simon) 101
middlebrow 105–6, 108, 110–11, 124
Mignolo, Walter 109
Milano, Alyssa 236
Miles, Robert 169–70, 280–81n25
mimicry 94, 98
modernism
 and cosmopolitanism 7, 18, 106–11, 115, 117, 124
 legal 145–46
 new modernist studies 1, 19, 23, 27, 106
 transnational 6, 9, 106–11
 see also philosophical modernism
Modernism/modernity (journal) 16, 19
modernity 6, 21, 40, 64, 109, 136–37, 146, 183
 and coloniality 117–24
Mombasa 162
morality 3, 33, 39, 42, 48, 149, 152, 153, 178, 180, 181
Morton, Timothy 83
Moses, Michael Valdez 16
Moten, Fred 200
Moynihan, Sinéad 203–4
Mullin, Katherine 241
multicultural/multiculturalism 106–7, 115, 116, 121
Mussolini, Benito 219, 225

nationalism 11, 107
Nation and Athenaeum 109

Needell, J. H. 167
negligence 146, 150, 153, 179–80, 183, 186, 187–89, 282n12, 284n57
Nestroy, Johann 140
new criticism 5
new materialism 67, 75, 82
new modernist studies *see* modernism
New Negro 197–98, 200, 202, 203, 207, 208, 209, 212, 213–15
New Statesman 105
New Woman 217, 222–23, 226, 234, 290n2
New York Morning Telegraph 53, 60
New York Times 61, 63, 87–89, 172–73
Nietzsche, Friedrich 79, 129–30, 201
Noel, Rhiannon 220
Nordau, Max 201
normativity 111, 218
Nussbaum, Martha 112

Objectivism/Objectivist 145, 149–50, 153
occupier's liability 186–87
O'Conner Drury, Maurice 130
Offences Against the Person acts 238–41
Old Testament 138
Oliver, Roland 163, 167
Olson, Greta 20
Omer-Sherman, Ranen 145
O'Nolan, Brian
 An Béal Bocht 41–46, 48
 At Swim-Two-Birds 33, 37
 The Dalkey Archive 33, 37
 Flann O'Brien (pseud.) 33
 Myles na gCopaleen (pseud.) 33, 43
 The Third Policeman 33, 37, 47
Oppen, George 149–50
Orientalism 87–88, 118, 120, 124, 169
Outka, Elizabeth 12

paratexts 43, 89, 97–99, 101, 103
Parks, Jennifer 56–60
Parnet, Claire 128
parochialism 106–7
passing 198, 202–6, 287n30

patriarchy 224–25
patronage 207, 209
Peat, Alexandra 107
Perham, Margery 162–63
　Africans and British Rule 162
　Major Dane's Garden 161, 169, 170, 172, 174–75
Perkins, David 145
Perloff, Marjorie 127, 130
personal injury 153, 177, 282n12
philosophical modernism 126, 132–33
Picasso, Pablo 127
Pinthus, Kurt 149
"planetarity" 15–17
Plumb, Cheryl 53, 261n10
Poetry (magazine) 149
Poletti, Linda/Cordula 218, 224
postmodernism 36, 49
Pound, Ezra 2
Powell, Anthony 178,179, 181–82
　A Dance to the Music of Time 20, 183–85, 188–89, 193
Preston, Carrie 69, 263n4, 264n6 and n7
primitivism 35, 109, 208
propaganda 10, 199–202, 211
Pugh, Patricia 167
punctum 155, 160

Quartermain, Peter 149
queer theory 23, 40, 83, 219, 228, 234

racism/racist 87, 89, 91, 154, 156, 162, 197, 210, 220
　"golliwog" 92–94, 98, 100–1
　Jim Crow 202, 205
　"one-drop rule" 205
Rampersad, Arnold 208
Rankine, Claudia
　The White Card 215
Raymont, Henry 63–64
Rayne, Major Harry 162, 166
　Sun, Sand and Somals: Leaves from the Notebook of a District Commissioner in British Somaliland 163
Re, Lucia 218

reasonableness 179, 180, 182–83, 185
recklessness 183, 184, 187
Reichman, Ravit 20, 146–47, 156, 178, 181
reparations 18, 88, 96
reparative reading 18, 23, 91–96, 97–99
responsibility 3, 17, 81, 88–91, 95, 98–99, 151–53, 157, 178, 180, 181, 198–99, 209, 214–15, 267n4, 268n8
Reznikoff, Charles 148, 153, 159
　Testimony 145, 147, 149, 150, 153, 154, 155, 159
Rhees, Rush 139
Rhys, Jean 107
Richards, I. A. 5
Ricœur, Paul 18, 94, 152, 158, 159
Riordan, Kevin 16
Robbins, Bruce 106
Rodino-Colocino, Michelle 244
romance 163, 167, 169–71, 208, 233
roman-fleuve 179, 181, 192
Roniger, Taney 68, 84, 263n3
Rose, Phyllis 61, 262n48
Ross, Charlotte 221
Royal Geographical Society 175, 279n10
Rundquist, Eric 12
Russell, Bertrand 125, 127

Saint-Amour, Paul K. 20
Salter, Layla 75, 76–77
Sarker, Sonita 23
Sartre, Jean-Paul 127
Sathianadhan, Kamala 9
Schoenberg, Arnold 127
Schuyler, George 204
Schwarzmantel, John 170
Sedgwick, Eve Kosofsky 95, 269n21
sexual development/adolescent sexual development 237, 239, 241, 245–46
sexuality 201, 205, 220–22, 227, 239, 240–41
sexual misconduct/assault/harassment/abuse 236–39, 247, 250, 293n7
sex work 237–38, 249
Shelley, Percy Bysshe 178
sisterhood 221

Slote, Sam 8, 295n25
Snaith, Anna 16
solar plexus 15, 67–83
Somaliland 162, 164–67, 172–75
Sorabji, Cornelia 9
South China Morning Post 109
Spectator 108
spirituality 69, 74, 96–97, 107, 199
Spivak, Gayatri Chakravorty 16, 245, 296n47
Spoo, Robert 20
Spurling, Hilary 181
Stark, Dame Freya 112
Stein, Gertrude 126, 135
Steinbeck, John 108
Sternburg, Janet 148
Stewart, Jeffrey C. 201
Stoicism 106–7
Suez Canal 164
Sullivan, Melissa 106

Tagore, Rabindranath 107
"Talented Tenth" 25, 197, 209, 211, 285n2
temporality 32, 36, 45, 48
Teo, Hsu-Ming 169
Thailand 109
theology 3
Thurman, Wallace 207
Tonning, Erik 31, 34
Toomer, Jean 202–6
    Cane 202–3, 205, 287n30
tort law 179–81, 183, 186
    Donoghue v. Stevenson 179–80
    Occupier's Liability Act 1957 186–87
    trespass to the person 182, 189, 191
transnationalism 6, 9, 106–11
travel writing 18–19, 107, 166
Trigoni, Thalia 12

Upton, Florence K. 92, 98, 268n13, 269n14

Valente, Joseph 235, 247, 251
Van Vechten, Carl 207, 214

Vescia, Monique Claire 154–55
violence 33, 34, 46–48, 151, 154–57, 169, 178, 183, 210, 219, 233, 237, 244, 250
vitalism 67, 70, 77

Wagner, Richard 201
Walkowitz, Rebecca 6
Wallace, Edgar
    Sanders of the River 167
Walrond, Eric 200
Warren, Diane 53, 261n7
Watson, Benjamin 145, 148
Waugh, Evelyn 108, 179
Wareham, Christopher 58, 262n27, n31
Waymack, Mark 56–60
Weller, Shane 11
West, Rebecca 108
Westminster Gazette 108
Wharton, Edith 108
Wheatley, Phillis 213, 286n9
Whitehead, Alfred North 78, 79
Whyte, Anna D. 91–93
    Change Your Sky 18, 91–93, 100–3, 270n32
Wilde, Oscar 5, 201, 220, 223, 226
Williams, William Carlos 149
Witt, John Fabian 153
Wittgenstein, Ludwig, 19, 126–40, 125–31
    Philosophical Investigations 19, 126–40
    Tractatus Logico-Philosophicus 125–31
Woman's Leader 109
Woodhouse, John 219
Woolf, Virginia 2, 3, 9, 11, 16, 17, 105, 183
World War I 123, 125, 149, 162, 165, 168, 219
World War II 5, 44, 126, 162, 188
Wright, Richard 212–13, 289n77

Yeats, William Butler 2, 3, 35, 256n1, n6
Youngs, Tim 108

Ziegler, Alan 148

Printed in the USA
CPSIA information can be obtained
at www.ICGtesting.com
CBHW032243140524
8586CB00001B/4

9 781638 040750